LEGAL REASONING AND LEGAL WRITING

How to use your Connected Casebook

Step 1: Go to **www.CasebookConnect.com** and redeem your access code to get started.

Access Code:

Step 2: Go to your **BOOKSHELF** and select your Connected Casebook to start reading, highlighting, and taking notes in the margins of your e-book.

Step 3: Select the **STUDY** tab in your toolbar to access a variety of practice materials designed to help you master the course material. These materials may include explanations, videos, multiple-choice questions, flashcards, short answer, essays, and issue spotting.

Step 4: Select the **OUTLINE** tab in your toolbar to access chapter outlines that automatically incorporate your highlights and annotations from the e-book. Use the My Notes area for copying, pasting, and editing your book notes or creating new notes.

Step 5: If your professor has enrolled your class, you can select the **CLASS INSIGHTS** tab and compare your own study center results against the average of your classmates.

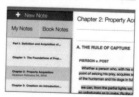

ASPEN COURSEBOOK SERIES

LEGAL REASONING AND LEGAL WRITING

EIGHTH EDITION

Richard K. Neumann, Jr.
Professor of Law
Maurice A. Deane School of Law
   at Hofstra University

Ellie Margolis
Professor of Law
Temple University Beasley School
   of Law

Kathryn M. Stanchi
Jack E. Feinberg '57 Professor
   of Litigation
Temple University Beasley School
   of Law

 Wolters Kluwer

Library of Congress Cataloging-in-Publication Data

Names: Neumann, Richard K., 1947- author. | Margolis, Ellie, author. |
  Stanchi, Kathryn M., author.
Title: Legal reasoning and legal writing / Richard K. Neumann, Jr. (Professor
  of Law, Maurice A. Deane School of Law at Hofstra University), Ellie
  Margolis (Professor of Law, Temple University Beasley School of Law),
  Kathryn M. Stanchi (Jack E. Feinberg '57 Professor of Litigation, Temple
  University Beasley School of Law).
Description: Eighth edition. | New York : Wolters Kluwer, [2017] | Series:
  Aspen coursebook series | Includes index.
Identifiers: LCCN 2017000191 | ISBN 9781454886525
Subjects: LCSH: Legal composition. | Trial practice — United States. |
  Practice of law — United States. | Law — United States — Language.
Classification: LCC KF250 .N48 2017 | DDC 808.06/634 — dc23
LC record available at https://lccn.loc.gov/2017000191

About Wolters Kluwer Legal & Regulatory U.S.

Wolters Kluwer Legal & Regulatory U.S. delivers expert content and solutions in the areas of law, corporate compliance, health compliance, reimbursement, and legal education. Its practical solutions help customers successfully navigate the demands of a changing environment to drive their daily activities, enhance decision quality and inspire confident outcomes.

Serving customers worldwide, its legal and regulatory portfolio includes products under the Aspen Publishers, CCH Incorporated, Kluwer Law International, ftwilliam.com and MediRegs names. They are regarded as exceptional and trusted resources for general legal and practice-specific knowledge, compliance and risk management, dynamic workflow solutions, and expert commentary.

For

Marjorie Batter Neumann
and in memory of Richard K. Neumann Sr.

—RKN Jr.

Adam, Isaac, and Naomi Guth

—EM

Jeanette M. Stanchi and
in memory of Edward J. Stanchi, Jr.

—KMS

The power of clear statement is the great power at the bar.

—Daniel Webster
(also attributed to
Rufus Choate,
Judah P. Benjamin,
and perhaps others)

Summary
of Contents

Contents

II
INTRODUCTION TO LEGAL WRITING

10.   Working with Facts   **105**

IV
ORGANIZING PROOF OF A CONCLUSION OF LAW   **113**

11.   A Paradigm for Organizing Proof of a Conclusion of Law   **115**

12.   Varying the Depth of Rule Proof and Rule Application   **125**

18. Oral Presentations to Your Supervising Lawyer   **177**

19. Client Advice Letters   **183**

VI
GENERAL WRITING SKILLS   189

20. Paragraphing   **191**

Preface

We created this book to help students learn how to make professional writing decisions — to think simultaneously as lawyers and writers. As we say on page 1, a lawyer's life is a writer's life.

Richard K. Neumann, Jr.
Ellie Margolis
Kathryn M. Stanchi

January 2017

Acknowledgments

We're grateful to many people who generously contributed their thoughts to various editions of this book, among them Burt Agata, Lisa Aisner, Jamie Abrams, Aaron Balasny, Kathleen Beckett, Sara Bennett, Barbara Blumenfeld, Sonya Bonneau, Ben Bratman, Ralph Brill, Susan Brody, Susan Bryant, Juli Campagna, Kenneth Chestek, J. Scott Colesanti, Leona Cunningham, Deborah Ezbitski, Neal Feigenson, Judith Fischer, Eric Freedman, Ian Gallacher, William Ginsburg, Marc Grinker, Donna Hill, Sam Jacobson, Derek Kiernan-Johnson, Lawrence Kessler, Martha Krisel, Eric Lane, Jan Levine, Noah Messing, Karin Mika, Alex Neumann, Lillianna Neumann, Stuart Rabinowitz, Terry Seligman, Amy Rima Sirota, Sloan, Judith Stinson, Amy Stein, Mary Rose Strubbe, David Thomson, Grace Tonner, Marshall Tracht, Ursula Weigold, Grace Wigal, Mark Wojcik, Cliff Zimmerman, and particularly Lyn Entrikin and Little, Brown and Aspen's anonymous reviewers.

And we're grateful for research assistance by Elizabeth L. Driscoll, Stevie Tran, Heather Canning, Samantha Hynes, Vicky Ku, Fusae Nara, Karen Nielsen, Rachael Ringer, and Carolyn Weissbach.

We'd like to recognize the lawyers at the American Civil Liberties Union and the Richmond law firm of Harman, Claytor, Corrigan & Wellman. Excerpts of their briefs appear in Appendices G and H.

Richard Heuser, Carol McGeehan, Dana Wilson, Richard Audet, Nick Niemeyer, Cate Rickard, Lisa Wehrle, and their colleagues at Aspen and earlier at Little, Brown have had much insight into the qualities that make a text useful. Their perceptiveness and skill caused this book to become a different and far better text than it otherwise would have been.

Copyright Acknowledgment

Permission to reprint copyrighted excerpts from the following is gratefully acknowledged: Ramage, John D. & Bean, John C., *Writing Arguments: A Rhetoric with Readings,* 4th ed., pp. 10-11, © 1998. Reprinted by permission of Pearson Education, Inc., New York, New York.

LEGAL REASONING
AND LEGAL WRITING

INTRODUCTION
TO LAW

Legal Writing and Law

§1.1 Legal Writing Is Decisional Writing

Before law school, you probably wrote primarily to communicate information that would satisfy the reader's curiosity. Lawyers write for a different reason — to guide decision-making.

A junior lawyer in a law firm might write an office memorandum to a senior lawyer explaining how the law affects a decision the senior lawyer must make. The memorandum's purpose is to help the senior lawyer make that decision. This is called *objective* or *predictive* writing. *[handwritten: objective/ predictive]*

In a courthouse, a lawyer might submit a motion memorandum or an appellate brief to persuade a judge or several judges to decide in favor of the lawyer's client. The document's purpose is to persuade each judge that the client's position is the legally preferable one. This is called *persuasive* writing. *[handwritten: persuasive]*

A lawyer's job is to get good results for clients. A lawyer does that by making the right decisions herself and by helping or persuading other people to make the right decisions. In legal writing, your reader — your audience — reads for the purpose of *deciding*. *[handwritten: end goal → reader makes favorable decision]*

§1.2 Writing Skills Can Profoundly Affect a Lawyer's Career

A lawyer's life is a writer's life.

To a lawyer, words are professional tools. Everything depends on how well the lawyer uses words — speaking them, interpreting them, and writing them.

Law is "one of the principal literary professions" because "the average lawyer in the course of a lifetime does more writing than a novelist."[1]

Good writing skills are essential to a young lawyer looking for a job. Employers will use your writing sample to confirm that you have those skills. A person who supervised 400 lawyers at a major corporation put it this way: "You are more likely to get good grades in law school if you write well. You are more likely to become a partner in your law firm, or receive comparable promotions in your law department or government law office."[2] It really is true that "good writing pays well and bad writing pays badly."[3] Now is the time to learn how to write professionally.

§1.3   Where Law Comes From

Law is primarily rules, which Chapters 2 and 3 explain in detail. Asking where law comes from is the same as asking who makes the rules.

Sources of law can be divided into two categories: one is statutes and statute-like provisions; the other is judge-made law.

Statutes and statute-like materials.   Legislatures create rules by enacting statutes. When we say, "There ought to be a law punishing people who text-message while driving," we vaguely imagine telling our state representative about the dangers of distraction behind the wheel and suggesting that she introduce a bill along these lines and persuade her colleagues in the legislature to enact it into law. If the legislature does that, and if the governor approves, the result is a statute. At the federal level, statutes are enacted by Congress with presidential approval. In the first-year of law school, the most statutory courses are Criminal Law (the Model Penal Code) and Contracts (the Uniform Commercial Code).

Statute-like provisions include constitutions, administrative regulations, and court rules. They are not enacted by legislatures, but in some — though not all — ways they are drafted like statutes. In your course on Constitutional Law, you will study the federal constitution. And in your course on Civil Procedure, you will study court rules called the Federal Rules of Civil Procedure.

Judge-made law.   Courts record their decisions in judicial opinions, which establish precedents. Under the doctrine of *stare decisis*, those precedents can bind other courts in circumstances explained in Chapter 7. Lawyers

---

1. William L. Prosser, *English as She Is Wrote*, 7 J. Leg. Educ. 155, 156 (1954).
2. Richard S. Lombard (formerly general counsel at Exxon), remarks reprinted in *Lost Words: The Economical, Ethical and Professional Effects of Bad Legal Writing*, Occasional Paper 7 of the ABA Section of Legal Educ. Admissions to the Bar, at 54 (1993).
3. Donald N. McCloskey, *The Writing of Economics* 2 (1987).

use the words *cases*, *decisions*, and *opinions* interchangeably to refer to those precedents. Finding them is called *researching the case law.*

Courts make law in two ways. One is by interpreting statutes and statute-like provisions, which can be vague or ambiguous. Often we don't know what a statute means until the courts tell us through the judicial decisions that enforce it. When a court *interprets* the statute, it essentially finishes legislature's job. The other method is by creating and changing the *common law*, which is entirely judge-made, for reasons explained in the next section of this chapter.

§1.4   The Common Law

The past is never dead. It's not even past.

— *William Faulkner*

Courts originally created the common law through precedent, and they have the power to change it through precedent. Before you arrived in law school, you may not have realized that courts are able to create their own body of law, separate from the law made in legislatures. The idea of law created without legislatures seems so counter-intuitive that it needs explanation.

The common law exists because of events that happened over 900 years ago, with consequences for law-making and legal vocabulary that lawyers still encounter daily. In the autumn of 1066, a French duke named William of Normandy got together an army, crossed the English Channel in boats, invaded England, defeated an English army in the Battle of Hastings, terrorized the rest of the country, and had himself crowned king in London. He then expropriated nearly all the land in England and parceled it out among his Norman followers, who became a new aristocracy. And he set about systematically making English institutions, including law, subservient to his will.

Before the Norman Conquest, English law had differed from one place to another based on local custom. In a village, law had been whatever rules people had followed there for generations. In another village, law might be somewhat different because people there had been following somewhat different rules. Law amounted to traditions reflecting community views on what was right and wrong.

For two reasons, William's royal descendants would not allow this to continue. The political reason was that to complete the Conquest, the monarchy centralized power in itself and eventually created national courts with judges under royal control. The practical reason was that a judge of a national court cannot be expected to know the customary law of each locality. Law had to become uniform everywhere. It had to become *common* to the entire country. This common law could not come from a legislature. The modern concept of a legislature — one that could enact law — did not yet exist.

How was the common law created? The somewhat oversimplified answer is that the judges figured it out for themselves. They started with the few rules that plainly could not be missing from medieval society, and over centuries — faced with new conditions and reasoning by analogy — they discovered other rules of common law, as though each rule had been there from the beginning, but hidden.

Centuries later, British colonists in North America were being governed according to that common law. Their rebellion was not against common law, which they accepted as fair. Their quarrel was instead with the British government and its officeholders. During and after the Revolution, as each colony became a state, it adopted common law as state law. Today, state courts continue to evolve the common law. In your Torts and Contracts courses, you will see examples of this process at work.

Law-passing legislatures — the English Parliament, the U.S. Congress, and state legislatures — were all created centuries *after* the common law began. Today, however, legislatures have the superior law-making power. Common law is still judge-made law. But if a legislature enacts a statute that directly contradicts a common law rule, the statute prevails, and the common law rule ceases to exist. Common law reasoning, however, permeates the practice and study of law.

§1.5   Law's Vocabulary

To a lawyer, words are professional tools, and the law is full of specialized vocabulary, which you will learn to use. Many of law's technical terms aren't from the English language; they're from Latin or from an old dialect called Norman Law French — or just Law French.

Before the Norman Conquest, people in England all spoke a language called Old English. Almost everyone was illiterate. The few people who could read and write tended to do so in Latin because it was a uniform language not broken up into regional dialects. Law had been conducted partly in English but mostly in Latin, and many technical terms in our law are still in Latin. *Stare decisis*, for example, is Latin for "let stand that which has been decided" — in other words, follow earlier decisions, which are precedent.

After the Conquest, government was conducted in Norman French, and law was conducted both in Latin and in Norman Law French, which could still be heard in courtrooms many centuries later. Even today the bailiff's cry that still opens many American court sessions — "Oyez, oyez, oyez!" — is the Norman French equivalent of "Be quiet and listen."

Law is filled with terms of art that express technical and specialized meanings, and a large proportion of these terms survive from Norman Law French. Some of the more familiar examples include *allegation, appeal, arrest, assault, attorney, contract, counsel, court, crime, damages, defendant, evidence, felony, judge, jury, misdemeanor, plaintiff, slander, suit, tenant, tort,* and *verdict.* In the next few months, you'll also encounter *battery, damages, demurrer, devise, easement, estoppel, indictment, lien, livery of seisin,* and *replevin.*

Some words entered the English language directly from the events of the Conquest itself. In the course on Property, you'll soon become familiar with various types of *fees: fee simple absolute, fee simple conditional, fee simple defeasible, fee tail.* These aren't money paid for services. They're forms of property rights, and they're descended directly from the feudal enfeoffments that William introduced into England in order to distribute the country's land among his followers. Even today, these terms appear in the French word order (noun first, modifiers afterward).

Law has a huge vocabulary of technical terms. It is derived from three languages: English, French, and Latin. And law is impossible without its specialized use of words. Medicine is applied biology, and engineering is physics and math. But in law the exact meaning of a word can make the difference between winning a case and losing it.

Use a legal dictionary—either a small book you can carry around with other books or an online legal dictionary if you'd rather work from your laptop. Look up every word that seems like lawyer-talk. But don't stop there. Look up every word or phrase that seems to be used in an unusual way. Some words or phrases obviously have a special meaning to lawyers, such as *parol evidence, habeas corpus,* and *res ipsa loquitur.* But others are deceptive. They might look like words you've seen many times before, but they mean something different in the law. Examples are *consideration, performance,* and *remedy.* Look up in a legal dictionary *every word or phrase that seems to be used in an unusual way.*

Rule-Based Reasoning

§2.1 The Inner Structure of a Rule

At this moment the King, who had for some time been busily writing in his notebook, called out "Silence!" and read from his book, "Rule Forty-two. *All persons more than a mile high to leave the court.*"
Everyone looked at Alice.
"*I'm* not a mile high," said Alice.
"You are," said the King.
"Nearly *two* miles high," added the Queen.

> — *Lewis Carroll,*
> Alice in Wonderland

Law is made up of rules. A rule is a formula for making a decision.

Every rule has three components: (1) a set of *elements*, collectively called a test; (2) a result that occurs when all the elements are present (and the test is thus satisfied); and (3) a causal term that determines whether the result is mandatory, prohibitory, discretionary, or declaratory. (As you'll see in a moment, the result and the causal term are usually integrated into the same phrase or clause.) Additionally, many rules have (4) one or more exceptions that, if present, would defeat the result, even if all the elements are present. *exceptions involved*

Alice was confronted with a test of two elements. The first was the status of being a person, which mattered because at that moment she was in the company of a lot of animals — all of whom seem to have been exempt from any requirement to leave. The second element went to height — specifically a height of more than a mile. The result would have been a duty to leave the court, because the causal term was mandatory ("*All* persons . . . *to* leave . . .."). No exceptions were provided for.

Alice has denied the second element (her height), impliedly conceding the first (her personhood). The Queen has offered to prove a height of two miles. What would happen if the Queen were not able to make good on her promise and instead produced evidence showing only a height of 1.241 miles? (Read the rule.) What if the Queen were to produce no evidence and if Alice were to prove that her height was only 0.984 miles? (Read the rule.)

A causal term can be *mandatory, prohibitory, discretionary,* or *declaratory.* Because the causal term is the heart of the rule, if the causal term is, for example, mandatory, then the whole rule is, too.

A mandatory rule requires someone to act and is expressed in words like "shall" or "must" in the causal term. "Shall" means "has a legal duty to do something." "The court shall grant the motion" means the court has a legal duty to grant it.

A prohibitory rule is the opposite. It forbids someone to act and is expressed by "shall not," "may not," or "must not" in the causal term. "Shall not" means the person has a legal duty *not* to act.

A discretionary rule gives someone the power or authority to do something. That person has discretion to act but is not required to do so. It's expressed by words like "may" or "has the authority to" in the causal term.

A declaratory rule simply states (declares) that something is true. That might not seem like much of a rule, but you're already familiar with declaratory rules and their consequences. For example: "A person who drives faster than the posted speed limit is guilty of speeding." Because of that declaration, a police officer can give you a ticket if you speed, a court can sentence you to a fine, and your state's motor vehicle department can impose points on your driver's license. A declaratory rule places a label on a set of facts (the elements). Often the declaration is expressed by the word "is" in the causal term. But other words could be used there instead. And some rules with "is" in the causal term aren't declaratory. You have to look at what the rule *does.* If it simply states that something is true, it's declaratory. If it does more than that, it's something else.

Below are examples of all these types of rules. The examples come from the Federal Rules of Civil Procedure, and you'll study them later in the course on Civil Procedure. (Rules of law are found not just in places like the Federal Rules. In law, they are everywhere—in statutes, constitutions, regulations, and judicial precedents.)

If the rules below seem hard to understand at first, don't be discouraged. In a moment, you'll learn a method for taking rules like these apart to find their meaning. For now, just read them to get a sense of how the four kinds of rules differ from each other. The key words in the causal terms have been italicized to highlight the differences.

mandatory: If a defendant located within the United States fails, without good cause, to sign and return a waiver requested by a plaintiff located within the United States, the court *must* impose on the defendant (A) the expenses later incurred in making service and (B) the reasonable expenses, including attorney's fees, of any motion required to collect those service expenses.[1]

prohibitory: The court *must not* require a bond, obligation, or other security from the appellant when granting a stay on an appeal by the United States, its officers, or its agencies, or on an appeal directed by a department of the federal government.[2]

discretionary: The court *may* assert jurisdiction over property if authorized by a federal statute.[3]

declaratory: A civil action *is* commenced by filing a complaint with the court.[4]

Here's a three-step method of figuring out what a rule means:

Step 1: Break the rule down into its parts. List and number the elements in the test. (An element in a test is something that must be present for the rule to operate.) Identify the causal term and the result. If there's an exception, identify it. If the exception has more than one element, list and number them as well. (Exceptions can have elements, too; an exception's element is something that must be present for the exception to operate.) In Step 1, *you don't care what the words mean.* You only want to know the *structure* of the rule. You're breaking the rule down into parts small enough to understand. Let's take the mandatory rule above and run it through Step 1. Here's the rule diagrammed:

---

1. Rule 4(d)(2) of the Federal Rules of Civil Procedure.
2. Rule 62(e) of the Federal Rules of Civil Procedure.
3. Rule 4(n)(1) of the Federal Rules of Civil Procedure.
4. Rule 3 of the Federal Rules of Civil Procedure.

> **elements in the test:**
>
> If
> 1. a defendant
> 2. located within the United States
> 3. fails to sign and return a waiver
> 4. requested by a plaintiff
> 5. located within the United States,

> **causal term:**
>
> the court must

> **result:**
>
> impose on the defendant (A) the expenses later incurred in making service and (B) the reasonable expenses, including attorney's fees, of any motion required to collect those service expenses

> **exception:**
>
> unless the defendant has good cause for the failure.

You don't need to lay out the rule exactly this way — and you certainly don't need to use boxes. You can use any method of diagramming that breaks up the rule so you can understand it. The point is to break the rule up visually so that it's no longer a blur of words and so you can *see separately* the elements in the test, the causal term, the result, and any exception. When can you combine the causal term and the result? You can do it whenever doing so does not confuse you. If you can understand what's in the box below, you can combine, at least with this rule:

> **causal term and result:**
>
> the court must impose on the defendant (A) the expenses later incurred in making service and (B) the reasonable expenses, including attorney's fees, of any motion required to collect those service expenses

Step 2: Look at each of those small parts separately. Figure out the *meaning* of each element, the causal term, the result, and any exception. Look up the words in a legal dictionary, and read other material your teacher has assigned until you know what each word means. You already know what a plaintiff and a defendant are. Find the word *service* in a legal dictionary and read the definition carefully. Do it now. After reading the definition, look again at the "result" box above. What does the phrase "the expenses later incurred in making service" mean there?

If you read other material surrounding this rule in Civil Procedure, you'll learn that a request for a waiver is a plaintiff's request that the defendant accept service by mail and *waive* (give up the right to) service by someone who personally brings the papers to the defendant. The surrounding materials also tell you that the expenses of service are whatever the plaintiff has to pay to have someone hired for the purpose of delivering the papers personally to the defendant.

Step 3: Put the rule back together in a way that helps you *use* it. Sometimes that means rearranging the rule so that it's easier to understand. If when you first read the rule, an exception came at the beginning and the elements came last, rearrange the rule so the elements come first and the exception last. It will be easier to understand that way. For many rules — though not all of them — the rule's inner logic works like this:

What events or circumstances set the rule into operation?
(*These are the test's elements.*)

When all the elements are present, what happens?
(*The causal term and the result tell us.*)

Even if all the elements are present, could anything prevent the result?
(*An exception, if the rule has any.*)

Usually, you can put the rule back together by creating a flowchart and trying out the rule on some hypothetical facts to see how the rule works. A flowchart is essentially a list of questions. You'll be able to make a flowchart because of the diagramming you did earlier in Step 1. Diagramming the rule not only breaks it down so that it can be understood, but it also permits putting the rule back together so that it's easier to apply. The flowchart below comes straight out of the diagram in Step 1 above. (When you gain more experience at this, it will go so quickly and seamlessly that Steps 1, 2, and 3 *will seem to merge into a single step.*) Assume that Keisha wants Raymond to pay the costs of service.

elements:

1. Is Raymond a defendant?
2. Is Raymond located within the United States?
3. Did Raymond fail to comply with a request for waiver?
4. Is Keisha a plaintiff who made that request?
5. Is Keisha located within the United States?

If the answers to all these questions are yes, the court must impose the costs subsequently incurred in effecting service on Raymond—but only if the answer to the question below is no.

exception:

Does Raymond have good cause for his failure to comply?

Step 3 helps you add everything up to see what happens when the rule is applied to a given set of facts. If all the elements are present in the facts, the court must order the defendant to reimburse the plaintiff for whatever the plaintiff had to pay to have someone hired for the purpose of delivering the papers personally to the defendant—unless good cause is shown.

The elements don't have to come first. If you have a simple causal term and result, a long list of elements, and no exceptions, you can list the elements last. For example:

Common law burglary is committed by breaking and entering the dwelling of another in the nighttime with intent to commit a felony inside.[5]

How do you determine how many elements are in a rule? Think of each element as an integral fact, the absence of which would prevent the rule's operation. Then explore the logic behind the rule's words. If you can think of a reasonably predictable scenario in which part of what you believe to be one element could be true but part not true, then you have inadvertently combined

---

5. This was the crime at common law. It does a good job of illustrating several different things about rule structure. But the definition of burglary in a modern criminal code will differ.

two or more elements. For example, is "the dwelling of another" one element or two? A person might be guilty of some other crime, but he is not guilty of common law burglary when he breaks and enters the *restaurant of another*, even in the nighttime and with intent to commit a felony inside. The same is true when he breaks and enters *his own* dwelling. In each instance, part of the element is present and part missing. "The dwelling of another" thus includes two factual integers — the nature of the building and the identity of its resident — and therefore two elements.

Often you cannot know the number of elements in a rule until you have consulted the precedents interpreting it. Is "breaking and entering" one element or two? The precedents define "breaking" in this sense as the creation of a gap in a building's protective enclosure, such as by opening a door, even where the door was left unlocked and the building is thus not damaged. The cases further define "entering" for this purpose as placing inside the dwelling any part of oneself or any object under one's control, such as a crowbar.

Can a person "break" without "entering"? A would-be burglar would seem to have done so where she has opened a window by pushing it up from the outside, and where, before proceeding further, she has been apprehended by an alert police officer — a moment before she can "enter." "Breaking" and "entering" are therefore two elements, but you could not know for sure without discovering precisely how the courts have defined the terms used.

Where the elements are complex or ambiguous, enumeration may add clarity to the list:

> Common law burglary is committed by (1) breaking and (2) entering (3) the dwelling (4) of another (5) in the nighttime (6) with intent to commit a felony inside.

Instead of elements, some rules have *factors*, which operate as criteria or guidelines. These tend to be rules empowering a court or other authority to make discretionary decisions, and the factors define the scope of the decision-maker's discretion. The criteria might be few ("a court may extend the time to answer for good cause shown"), or they might be many (like the following, from a typical statute providing for a court to terminate a parent's legal relationship with a child).

> In a hearing on a petition for termination of parental rights, the court shall consider the manifest best interests of the child. . . . For the purpose of determining the manifest best interests of the child, the court shall consider and evaluate all relevant factors, including, but not limited to:
>
> (1) Any suitable permanent custody arrangement with a relative of the child. . . .

(2) The ability and disposition of the parent or parents to provide the child with food, clothing, medical care or other remedial care recognized and permitted under state law instead of medical care, and other material needs of the child.

(3) The capacity of the parent or parents to care for the child to the extent that the child's safety, well-being, and physical, mental, and emotional health will not be endangered upon the child's return home.

(4) The present mental and physical health needs of the child and such future needs of the child to the extent that such future needs can be ascertained based on the present condition of the child.

(5) The love, affection, and other emotional ties existing between the child and the child's parent or parents, siblings, and other relatives, and the degree of harm to the child that would arise from the termination of parental rights and duties.

(6) The likelihood of an older child remaining in long-term foster care upon termination of parental rights, due to emotional or behavioral problems or any special needs of the child.

(7) The child's ability to form a significant relationship with a parental substitute and the likelihood that the child will enter into a more stable and permanent family relationship as a result of permanent termination of parental rights and duties.

(8) The length of time that the child has lived in a stable, satisfactory environment and the desirability of maintaining continuity.

(9) The depth of the relationship existing between the child and the present custodian.

(10) The reasonable preferences and wishes of the child, if the court deems the child to be of sufficient intelligence, understanding, and experience to express a preference.

(11) The recommendations for the child provided by the child's guardian ad litem or legal representative.[6]

Only seldom would all of these factors tip in the same direction. With a rule like this, a judge does something of a balancing test, deciding according to the tilt of the factors as a whole, together with the angle of the tilt.

Factors rules are a relatively new development in the law and grow out of a recent tendency to define more precisely the discretion of judges and other officials. But the more common rule structure is still that of a set of elements, the presence of which leads to a particular result in the absence of an exception.

---

6. Fla. Stat. § 39.810 (2006).

§2.2 Organizing the Application of a Rule

Welty and Lutz are students who have rented apartments on the same floor of the same building. At midnight, Welty is studying, while Lutz is listening to a Black Keys album with his new four-foot concert speakers. Welty has put up with this for two or three hours, and finally she pounds on Lutz's door. Lutz opens the door about six inches, and, when he realizes that he cannot hear what Welty is saying, he steps back into the room a few feet to turn the volume down, without opening the door further. Continuing to express outrage, Welty pushes the door completely open and strides into the room. Lutz turns on Welty and orders her to leave. Welty finds this to be too much and punches Lutz so hard that he suffers substantial injury. In this jurisdiction, the punch is a felonious assault. Is Welty also guilty of common law burglary?

You probably said "no," and your reasoning probably went something like this: "That's not burglary. Burglary happens when somebody gets into the house when you're not around and steals all the valuables. Maybe this will turn out to be some kind of trespass." But in law school a satisfactory answer is never merely "yes" or "no." An answer necessarily includes a sound *reason*, and, regardless of whether Welty is guilty of burglary, this answer is wrong because the reasoning is wrong. The answer can be determined only by applying a rule like the definition of common law burglary found earlier in this chapter. *Anything else is a guess.*

Where do you start? Remember that a rule is a structured idea: The presence of all the elements causes the result, and the absence of any of them causes the rule not to operate. Assume that in our jurisdiction the elements of burglary are what they were at common law:

1. a breaking
2. and an entry
3. of the dwelling
4. of another
5. in the nighttime
6. with intent to commit a felony inside

To discover whether each element is present in the facts, simply annotate the list:

1. *a breaking:* If a breaking can be the enlarging of an opening between the door and the jam without permission, and if Lutz's actions do not imply permission, there was a breaking.
2. *and an entry:* Welty "entered," for the purposes of the rule on burglary, by walking into the room, unless Lutz's actions implied permission to enter.
3. *of the dwelling:* Lutz's apartment is a dwelling.

4. *of another:* And it is not Welty's dwelling; she lives down the hall.
5. *in the nighttime:* Midnight is in the nighttime.
6. *with intent to commit a felony inside:* Did Welty intend to assault Lutz when she strode through the door? If not, this element is missing.

Now it's clear how much the first answer ("it doesn't sound like burglary") was a guess. By examining each element separately, you find that elements 3, 4, and 5 are present, but that you're not sure about the others without some hard thinking about the facts and without consulting the precedents in this jurisdiction that have interpreted elements 1, 2, and 6.

The case law might turn up a variety of results. Suppose that, although local precedent defines Welty's actions as a breaking and an entry, the cases on the sixth element strictly require corroborative evidence that a defendant had a fully formed felonious intent when entering the dwelling. That kind of evidence might be present, for example, where an accused was in possession of safecracking tools when he broke and entered, or where, before breaking and entering, the accused had told someone that he intended to murder the occupant. Against that background, the answer here might be something like the following: "Welty is not guilty of burglary because, although she broke and entered the dwelling of another in the nighttime, there's no evidence that she had a felonious intent when entering the dwelling."

Suppose, on the other hand, that under local case law Welty's actions again are a breaking and an entry; that the local cases don't require corroborative evidence of a felonious intent; and that local precedent defines a felonious intent for the purposes of burglary to be one that the defendant could have been forming—even if not yet consciously—when entering the dwelling. Under those sub-rules, if you believe that Welty had the requisite felonious intent, your answer would be something like this: "Welty is guilty of burglary because she broke and entered the dwelling of another in the nighttime with intent to commit a felony inside, thus meeting all the elements of common law burglary."

These are real answers to the question of whether Welty is guilty of burglary. They state not only the result, but also the reason why.

§2.3   Some Things to Be Careful About with Rules

A rule might be expressed in any of a number of ways. Where law is made through precedent—as much of our law is—different judges, writing in varying circumstances, may enunciate what seems like the same rule in a variety of distinct phrasings. At times, it can be hard to tell whether the judges have spoken of the same rule in different voices or instead have spoken of slightly different rules. In either situation, it can be harder still to discover — because of the variety — exactly what the rule is or what the rules are.

Ambiguity and vagueness can obscure meaning unless the person stating the rule is particularly careful with language. The classic example asks whether a person riding a bicycle or a skateboard through a park violates a rule prohibiting the use there of "vehicles." What had the rule-maker intended? How could the intention have been made more clear?

A rule usually doesn't express its purpose — or, as lawyers say, the policy underlying the rule. A rule's policy or purpose is the key to unravelling ambiguities. Is a self-propelled lawn mower a prohibited "vehicle"? Try to imagine what the rule-makers were trying to accomplish. Why did they create this rule? What harm were they trying to prevent, or what good were they trying to promote?

Not only is it difficult to frame a rule so that it controls all that the rule-maker wishes to control, but once a rule has been framed, situations will inevitably crop up that the rule-maker didn't contemplate or couldn't have been expected to contemplate. Would a baby carriage powered by solar batteries be a "vehicle"?

Finally, the parts of a rule may be so complex that it may be hard to pin down exactly what the rule is and how it works. And this is compounded by interaction between and among rules. A word or phrase in one rule may be defined, for example, by another rule. Or the application of one rule may be governed by yet another rule — or even a whole body of rules.

Two skills will help you become agile in the lawyerly use of rules. The first is language mastery, including an "ability to spot ambiguities, to recognize vagueness, to identify the emotive pull of a word . . . and to analyze and elucidate class words and abstractions."[7]

The second is the capacity to *think structurally*. A rule is a structured idea, and the rule's structure is more like an algebraic formula than a value judgment. You need to be able to figure out an idea's structure and apply it to facts.

§2.4 Causes of Action and Affirmative Defenses

The law cannot remedy every wrong. Many problems are more effectively resolved through other means, such as the political process, mediation, bargaining, and economic and social pressure. Unless the legal system focuses its resources on resolving those problems it handles best, it would collapse under the weight of an unmanageable workload and would thus be prevented from attempting even the problem-solving it does well.

---

7. William L. Twining & David Miers, *How to Do Things with Rules* 120 (1976).

A harm the law will remedy is called a *cause of action* (or, in some courts, a *claim*). If a plaintiff proves a cause of action, a court will order a remedy unless the defendant proves an *affirmative defense.* If the defendant proves an affirmative defense, the plaintiff will get no remedy, even if that plaintiff has proved a cause of action. Causes of action and affirmative defenses (like other legal rules) are formulated as tests with elements and the other components, as explained in §2.1.

For example, where a plaintiff proves that a defendant intentionally confined him and that the defendant was not a law enforcement officer acting within the scope of an authority to arrest, the plaintiff has proved a cause of action called *false imprisonment.* The test is expressed as a list of elements: "False imprisonment consists of (1) a confinement (2) of the plaintiff (3) by the defendant (4) intentionally (5) where the defendant is not a sworn law enforcement officer acting within that authority." Proof of false imprisonment would customarily result in a court's awarding a remedy called *damages,* which obliges the defendant to compensate the plaintiff in money for the latter's injuries.

But that isn't always so: If the defendant can prove that she caught the plaintiff shoplifting in her store and restrained him only until the police arrived, she might have an affirmative defense that is sometimes called a *shopkeeper's privilege.* Where a defendant proves a shopkeeper's privilege, a court will not award the plaintiff damages, even if he has proved false imprisonment. The affirmative defense has its list of elements: "A shop-keeper's privilege exists where (1) a shopkeeper or shopkeeper's employee (2) has reasonable cause to believe that (3) the plaintiff (4) has shoplifted (5) in the shopkeeper's place of business and (6) the confinement occurs in a reasonable manner, for a reasonable time, and no more than needed to detain the plaintiff for law enforcement purposes."

Notice that some elements encompass physical activity ("a confinement"), while others specify *states of mind* ("intentionally") or address status or condition ("a shopkeeper or shopkeeper's employee") or require *abstract qualities* ("in a reasonable manner, for a reasonable time, and no more than needed to detain the plaintiff for law enforcement purposes"). State-of-mind and abstract-quality elements will probably puzzle you more than others will.

How will the plaintiff be able to prove that the defendant acted "intentionally," and how will the defendant be able to show that she confined the plaintiff "in a reasonable manner, for a reasonable time, and no more than needed to detain the plaintiff for law enforcement purposes"? Because thoughts and abstractions cannot be seen, heard, or felt, the law must judge an abstraction or a party's state of mind from the actions and other events surrounding it. If, for example, the plaintiff can prove that the defendant took him by the arm, pulled him into a room, and then locked the door herself, he may be able — through inference — to carry his burden of showing that she acted "intentionally." And through other inferences, the defendant may be able to carry her burden of proving the confinement to have been reasonably carried out if she can show that when she took the defendant by the arm, he had been trying to run from the store; that she called the police immediately; and that she turned the defendant over to the police as soon as they arrived.

Exercise
Rule 11 of the Federal Rules of
Civil Procedure

Provisions from Rule 11 appear below. For each provision, decide whether it is mandatory, prohibitory, discretionary, or declaratory. Then diagram it. Finally, create a flowchart showing the questions that would need to be answered to determine when a court must strike a paper.

Provision A The court <u>must</u> strike an unsigned paper unless the omission is promptly corrected after being called to the attorney's or party's attention. *mandatory*

Provision B If, after notice and a reasonable opportunity to respond, the court determines that Rule 11(b) has been violated, the court may impose an appropriate sanction on any attorney, law firm, or party that violated the rule or is responsible for the violation. *discretionary*

Provision C Absent exceptional circumstances, a law firm must be held jointly responsible for a violation committed by its partner, associate, or employee. *mandatory*

Provision D This rule does not apply to disclosures and discovery requests, responses, objections, and motions under Rules 26 through 37. *declaratory*

3 Issues, Facts, Precedents, and Statutes

§3.1 A Precedents' Anatomy

An opinion announcing a court's decision — also called a *precedent* or, most commonly, a *case* — can include up to nine ingredients:

1. a description of procedural events (what lawyers and judges did before the decision was made)
2. a narrative of pleaded or evidentiary events (what the witnesses saw and the parties did *before* the lawsuit began)
3. a statement of the issue or issues to be decided by the court
4. a summary of the arguments made by each side
5. the court's holding on each issue
6. the rule or rules of law the court enforces through each holding
7. the court's reasoning
8. dicta
9. a statement of the relief granted or denied

doesn't necessarily include all

Most opinions don't include all these things, although a typical opinion probably has most of them. Let's look at each.

Opinions often begin with (1) a recitation of *procedural events* during the litigation that have raised the issue decided by the court. Examples are motions, hearings, trial, judgment, and appeal. Although the court's description of these events may — because of unfamiliar terminology — seem at first confusing, you must be able to understand them because the manner in which an issue is raised determines the method a court will use to decide it. A court decides a motion for a directed verdict, for example, very differently from the way it rules on a request for a jury instruction, even though both might require the court to consider the same point of law. The procedural events add up to the case's *procedural posture* at the time the decision was made.

Frequently, the court will next describe (2) the *pleaded events* or the *evidentiary events* on which the ruling is based. In litigation, parties allege facts in a pleading and then prove them with evidence. The court has no other way of knowing what transpired between the parties before the lawsuit began. A party's pleadings and evidence tell a story that favors that party. The other party's pleadings and evidence tell a different and contrary story.

As you read the court's description of the pleadings and evidence, you can often tell, even before reading the rest of the opinion, which party's story persuaded the court. Stories persuade. Usually the court tells you, the reader, the same story that the winning lawyer told the court. An effective lawyer can tell an effective story and tell it well through pleadings or evidence or both.

A court might also set out (3) a statement of the *issue or issues* before the court for decision and (4) a *summary of the arguments* made by each side, although either or both are often only implied. A court will further state, or at least imply, (5) the *holding* on each of the issues and (6) the *rule or rules of law* the court enforces in making each holding, together with (7) the *reasoning behind* — often called the *rationale for* — its decision. Somewhere in the opinion, the court might place some (8) *dicta.* You'll learn more about dicta in the next few months, but for the moment think of it as discussion unnecessary to support a holding and therefore not mandatory precedential authority.

An opinion usually ends with (9) a *statement of the relief granted or denied.* If the opinion is the decision of an appellate court, the relief may be an affirmance, a reversal, or a reversal combined with a direction to the trial court to proceed in a specified manner. If the opinion is from a trial court, the relief is most commonly the granting or denial of a motion.

An opinion announcing a court's decision is called *the court's opinion* or *the majority opinion.* If one or more of the judges involved in the decision don't agree with some aspect of the decision, the opinion might be accompanied by one or more *concurrences* or *dissents.* A concurring judge agrees with the result the majority reached but would have used different reasoning to justify that result. A dissenting judge disagrees with both the result and the reasoning.

Concurrences and dissents are themselves opinions, but they represent the views only of the judges who are concurring or dissenting. Because concurrences and dissents are opinions, they contain some of the elements of a court's opinion. A concurring or dissenting judge might, for example, describe procedural events, narrate pleaded or evidentiary events, state issues, summarize arguments, and explain reasoning.

Be an active and engaged reader. Most people read passively most of the time — breezing through paragraphs, understanding some or most of what's on the page and guessing about the rest. Lawyers don't read cases and statutes that way. You cannot succeed in law school by reading passively.

Active and engaged reading includes pulling apart, in your mind, what's on the page and wringing meaning out of it. Consciously or unconsciously, active readers have silent dialogs with themselves about what they're reading. They ask themselves questions, which they try to answer while reading. For example:

"Why is the judge emphasizing this fact?"
(This is active reading. A passive reader isn't curious.)

"What does that phrase mean? How can I find out?"
(A passive reader will skim over the phrase without trying to understand it.)

"What's preventing me from understanding that paragraph?"
(A passive reader will give up and ignore the paragraph.)

Who's in charge — the reader or the page? For a passive reader, the page is in charge because the passive reader lets words hide their meaning. An active reader won't allow words to do that. An active reader silently interrogates until the words surrender and confess what they mean.

Exercise I
Dissecting the Text of *Roberson v. Rochester Folding Box Co.*

Read *Roberson v. Rochester Folding Box Co.* below and determine where (if anywhere) each ingredient occurs. Mark up the text generously and be prepared to discuss your analysis in class. Look up in a legal dictionary every unfamiliar word as well as every familiar word that is used in an unfamiliar way.

The majority opinion in *Roberson* discusses — and disagrees with — one of the most influential articles ever published in an American law review: Samuel Warren & Louis Brandeis, *The Right to Privacy*, 4 Harv. L. Rev. 193 (1890). Law reviews are periodicals that publish articles analyzing legal questions in scholarly depth. Almost every law review is sponsored by a law school and edited by students.

Like the cases reprinted in your casebooks for other courses, the version of Roberson printed here has been edited extensively to make it more readable. In casebooks and in other legal writing, certain customs are observed when quoted material is edited. Where words have been deleted, you'll see ellipses (strings of three or four periods). Where words have been added, usually to substitute for deleted words, the new words will be in brackets (squared-off parentheses).

ROBERSON v. ROCHESTER FOLDING BOX CO.
64 N.E. 442 (N.Y. 1902)

PARKER, Ch. J. [The defendant demurred] to the complaint . . . upon the ground that the complaint does not state facts sufficient to constitute a cause of action. [The courts below overruled the demurrer.]

[We must decide] whether the complaint . . . can be said to show any right to relief either in law or in equity. [We hold that it does not show any right to relief.]

The complaint alleges that the Franklin Mills Co., one of the defendants, was engaged . . . in the manufacture and sale of flour; that before the commencement of the action, without the knowledge or consent of plaintiff, defendants, knowing that they had no right or authority so to do, had obtained, made, printed, sold and circulated about 25,000 lithographic prints, photographs and likenesses of plaintiff . . . ; that upon the paper upon which the likenesses were printed and above the portrait there were printed, in large, plain letters, the words, "Flour of the Family," and below the portrait in large capital letters, "Franklin Mills Flour," and in the lower right-hand corner in smaller capital letters, "Rochester Folding Box Co., Rochester, N.Y."; that upon the same sheet were other advertisements of the flour of the Franklin Mills Co.; that those 25,000 likenesses of the plaintiff thus ornamented have been conspicuously posted and displayed in stores, warehouses, saloons and other public places; that they have been recognized by friends of the plaintiff and other people with the result that plaintiff has been greatly humiliated by the scoffs and jeers of persons who have recognized her face and picture on this advertisement and her good name has been attacked, causing her great distress and suffering both in body and mind. . . .

[The] portrait . . . is said to be a very good one, and one that her friends and acquaintances were able to recognize; indeed, her grievance is that a good portrait of her, and, therefore, one easily recognized, has been used to attract attention toward the paper upon which defendant mill company's advertisements appear. Such publicity, which some find agreeable, is to plaintiff very distasteful, and thus, because of defendants' impertinence in using her picture without her consent for their own business purposes, she has been caused to suffer mental distress where others would have appreciated the compliment . . . implied in the selection of the picture for such purposes; but as it is distasteful to her, she seeks the aid of the courts to enjoin a further circulation of the lithographic prints containing her portrait made as alleged in the complaint, and as an incident thereto, to reimburse her for the damages to her feelings, which the complaint fixes at the sum of $15,000.

There is no precedent for such an action to be found in the decisions of this court. . . . Nevertheless, [the court below] reached the conclusion that plaintiff had a good cause of action against defendants, in that defendants had invaded what is called a "right of privacy"—in other words, the right to be let alone. Mention of such a right is not to be found in Blackstone, Kent or any other of the great commentators upon the law, nor so far as the learning of counsel or the courts in this case have been able to discover, does its existence seem to have been asserted prior to about the year 1890, when it was [theorized] in the Harvard Law Review . . . in an article entitled, "The Right of Privacy."

right of privacy

The so-called right of privacy is, as the phrase suggests, founded upon the claim that a man has the right to pass through this world, if he wills, without having his picture published, his business enterprises discussed, his successful experiments written up for the benefit of others, or his eccentricities commented upon either in handbills, circulars, catalogues, periodicals or newspapers, and, necessarily, that the things which may not be written and published of him must not be spoken of him by his neighbors, whether the comment be favorable or otherwise. . . .

If such a principle be incorporated into the body of the law through the [process of judicial precedent], the attempts to logically apply the principle will necessarily result, not only in a vast amount of litigation, but in litigation bordering upon the absurd, for the right of privacy, once established [through judicial precedent], cannot be confined to the restraint of the publication of a likeness but must necessarily embrace as well the publication of a word-picture, a comment upon one's looks, conduct, domestic relations or habits. [Thus, a] vast field of litigation . . . would necessarily be opened up should this court hold that privacy exists as a legal right enforceable in equity by injunction, and by damages where they seem necessary to give complete relief. *would make it:*

absurdity of litigation

issues?

The legislative body could very well interfere and arbitrarily provide that no one should be permitted for his own selfish purpose to use the picture or the name of another for advertising purposes without his consent. In such event, no embarrassment would result to the general body of the law, for the rule would be applicable only to cases provided for by the statute. The courts, however, being without authority to legislate, are . . . necessarily [constrained] by precedents. . . .   *constrained by precedent*

So in a case like the one before us, which is concededly new to this court, it is important that the court should have in mind the effect upon future litigation and upon the development of the law which would necessarily result from a step so far outside of the beaten paths of both common law and equity [because] the right of privacy as a legal doctrine enforceable in equity has not, down to this time, been established by decisions.

The history of the phrase "right of privacy" in this country seems to have begun in 1890 in a clever article in the Harvard Law Review — already referred to — in which a number of English cases were analyzed, and, reasoning by analogy, the conclusion was reached that — notwithstanding the unanimity of the courts in resting their decisions upon property rights in cases where publication is prevented by injunction — in reality such prevention was due to the necessity of affording protection to . . . an inviolate personality, not that of private property. . . .

. . . Those authorities are now to be examined in order that we may see whether they were intended to and did mark a departure from the established rule which had been enforced for generations; or, on the other hand, are entirely consistent with it.

The first case is *Prince Albert v. Strange* (1 Macn. & G. 25; 2 De G. & S. 652). The queen and the prince, having made etchings and drawings for their own amusement, decided to have copies struck off from the etched plates for presentation to friends and for their own use. The workman employed, however, printed some copies on his own account, which afterwards came into the hands of Strange, who purposed exhibiting them, and published a descriptive catalogue. Prince Albert applied for an injunction as to both

case history / procedural posture

distinction w/ rights of property

exhibition and catalogue, and the vice-chancellor granted it, restraining defendant from publishing . . . a description of the etchings. [The] vice-chancellor . . . found two reasons for granting the injunction, namely, that the property rights of Prince Albert had been infringed, and that there was a breach of trust by the workman in retaining some impressions for himself. The opinion contained no hint whatever of a right of privacy separate and distinct from the right of property. . . .

[In similar ways, the other English cases cited in the Harvard article do not actually support a common law cause of action for invasion of privacy.] In not one of [them] was it the basis of the decision that the defendant could be restrained from performing the act he was doing or threatening to do on the ground that the feelings of the plaintiff would be thereby injured; but, on the contrary, each decision was rested either upon the ground of breach of trust or that plaintiff had a property right in the subject of litigation which the court could protect. . . .

[Of the American cases offered in support of a common law right to privacy, none actually does so when the decisions are examined in detail.] An examination of the authorities [thus] leads us to the conclusion that the so-called "right of privacy" has not as yet found an abiding place in our jurisprudence, and, as we view it, the doctrine cannot now be incorporated without doing violence to settled principles of law by which the profession and the public have long been guided. [Thus, there is no common law right of privacy in New York.]

The judgment of the Appellate Division and of the Special Term [is] reversed. . . .

revert the judgment

GRAY, J. (dissenting). . . . These defendants stand before the court, admitting that they have made, published and circulated, without the knowledge or the authority of the plaintiff, 25,000 lithographic portraits of her, for the purpose of profit and gain to themselves; that these portraits have been conspicuously posted in stores, warehouses and saloons, in the vicinity of the plaintiff's residence and throughout the United States, as advertisements of their goods; that the effect has been to humiliate her . . . and, yet, claiming that she makes out no cause of action . . . .

Our consideration of the question thus presented has not been fore-closed by the decision in *Schuyler v. Curtis,* (147 N.Y. 434). In that case, it appeared that the defendants were intending to make, and to exhibit, at the Columbian Exposition of 1893, a statue of Mrs. Schuyler, . . . conspicuous in her lifetime for her philanthropic work, to typify "Woman as the Philanthropist" and, as a companion piece, a statue of Miss Susan B. Anthony, to typify the "Representative Reformer." The plaintiff, in behalf of himself, as the nephew of Mrs. Schuyler, and of other immediate relatives, sought by the action to restrain them from carrying out their intentions as to the statue of Mrs. Schuyler; upon the grounds, in substance, that they were proceeding without his consent, . . . or that of the other immediate members of the family; that their proceeding was disagreeable to him, because it would have been disagreeable and obnoxious to his aunt, if living, and that it was annoying to have Mrs. Schuyler's memory associated with principles, which Miss Susan B. Anthony typified and of which Mrs. Schuyler did not approve. His right to maintain the action was denied and the denial was expressly placed upon the ground that he, as a relative, did not represent any right of privacy which Mrs. Schuyler possessed in her lifetime and that, whatever her right had been, in that respect, it died with her. The existence of the individual's right to be protected against the invasion of his privacy, if not actually affirmed in the opinion, was, very certainly, far from being denied. "It may be admitted," Judge Peckham observed, when delivering the opinion of the court, "that courts have power, in some cases, to enjoin the doing of an act, where the nature, or character, of the act itself is well calculated to wound the sensibilities of an individual, and where the doing of the act is wholly unjustifiable, and is, in legal contemplation, a wrong, *even though the existence of no property,* as that term is usually used, *is involved in the subject.*" . . .

[The majority misinterprets both the English and the American precedents.] Security of person is as necessary as the security of property; and for that complete personal security, which will result in the peaceful and wholesome enjoyment of one's privileges as a member of society, there should be afforded protection, not only against the scandalous portraiture and display of one's features and person, but against the display and use thereof for another's commercial purposes or gain. The proposition is, to me, an inconceivable one that these defendants may, unauthorizedly, use the likeness of this young woman upon their advertisement, as a method of attracting widespread public attention to their wares, and that she must submit to the mortifying notoriety, without right to invoke the exercise of the preventive power of a court of equity.

Such a view, as it seems to me, must have been unduly influenced by a failure to find precedents in analogous cases . . . ; without taking into consideration that, in the existing state of society, new conditions affecting the relations of persons demand the broader extension of . . . legal principles. . . . I think that such a view is unduly restricted, too, by a search for some property, which has been invaded by the defendants' acts. Property is not, necessarily, the thing itself, which is owned; it is the right of the owner in relation to it. . . . It seems to me that the principle, which is applicable, is analogous to that upon which courts of equity have interfered to protect the right of privacy, in cases of private writings, or of other unpublished products of the mind. The writer, or the lecturer, has been protected in his right to a literary property in a letter, or a lecture, against its unauthorized publication; because it is property, to which the right of privacy attaches. . . . I think that this plaintiff has the same property in the right to be protected against the use of her face for defendant's commercial purposes, as she would have, if they were publishing her literary compositions. The right would be conceded, if she had sat for her photograph; but if her face, or her portraiture, has a value, the value is hers exclusively; until the use be granted away to the public. . . .

O'Brien, Cullen and Werner, JJ., concur with Parker, Ch. J.; Bartlett and Haight, JJ., concur with Gray, J.   *plaintiff didn't have cause for action*

A decision's *citation* is made up of the case's name, references to the reporter or reporters in which the decision was printed, the name of the court where the decision was made, and the year of the decision. For *Roberson,* all this information appears in the heading on page 26.

The case name is composed by separating the last names of the parties with a "v." If the opinion was written by a trial court, the name of the plaintiff appears first. In some appellate courts, the name of the appellant comes first, but in others the parties are listed as they were in the trial court. In a case with multiple plaintiffs or defendants, the name of only the first listed per side appears in the case name. That's why the *Roberson* opinion mentions two defendants, but only one appears in the case name.

In Torts casebooks, *Roberson* is often used as an example of how the law makes false starts as it grows. The 1890 Harvard Law Review article to which Judge Parker refers is probably the most famous law review article in history.[1] It was written by Louis Brandeis, who was later appointed to the U.S. Supreme Court, and Samuel Warren, who was Brandeis's law partner at the time the article was published. Brandeis and Warren argued that the common law should recognize a new cause of action for tortious invasion of privacy. In *Roberson*, the New York Court of Appeals refused to do so. But eventually courts in other states — virtually all of them after *Roberson* — did adopt Brandeis and Warren's cause of action.

Facts typically make the case, and the *Roberson* facts illustrate why Brandeis and Warren were right. A large company used an 18-year-old girl's photograph in advertising without her permission and without offering to compensate her with the kind of fee that models are paid today. She was a private person who didn't want that kind of publicity. She felt used — which she had been. Even if the Court of Appeals wasn't moved by her story, the public certainly was, and the New York legislature enacted a statute specifically written to overrule the Court's decision.

Despite that statute, *Roberson* is some respects still the law in New York. The reasons are explained, with the statute, later in this chapter.

In 1904, two years after *Roberson,* Judge Alton Parker, author of the majority opinion, ran for president of the United States. He lost in a landslide to the incumbent, Theodore Roosevelt. During the campaign, Parker complained that newspaper photographers often took his picture while he was slouching or looking otherwise unpresidential, and that his family had lost their privacy because they were so frequently photographed. He demanded that photographers stop.

When Abigail Roberson learned of this, she wrote a letter to Parker sarcastically pointing out that "you have no such right as that which you assert. I have very high authority for my statement, being nothing less than a decision of the Court of Appeals of this State wherein you wrote the prevailing opinion [and] I was the plaintiff."[2] She was 21 years old when she wrote the letter, and it was printed on the front page of the *New York Times.*

---

1. Samuel Warren & Louis D. Brandeis, *The Right to Privacy,* 4 Harv. L. Rev. 193 (1890).
2. *Parker Taken to Task by Indignant Woman; If I Can Be Photographed, Why Not You Asks Miss Roberson; Quotes His Own Decision,* N.Y. Times, July 26, 1904.

§3.2   The Interdependence of Facts, Issues, and Rules

Many facts are in an opinion only to provide background, continuity, or what journalists call "human interest" to what would otherwise be a tedious and disjointed recitation. Of the remaining facts, some are merely related to the court's thinking, while others *caused* the court to come to its decision. This last group could be called the *determinative facts* or the *essential facts.* They are essential to the court's decision because they determined the outcome. If they had been different, the decision would have been different.

The determinative facts lead to the rule of the case — the rule of law for which the case stands as precedent. The most important goal of case analysis is discovering and understanding that rule. Where several issues are raised together in a case, the court must make several rulings and an opinion may thus stand for several rules.

Identify determinative facts by asking the following question: *If a particular fact had not happened, or if it had happened differently, would the court have made a different decision?* If so, that fact is one of the determinative facts. This can be illustrated through a nonjudicial decision of a sort with which you might recently have had some experience. Assume that a rental agent has just shown you an apartment and that the following facts are true:

A.   The apartment is located half a mile from the law school.

B.   It's a studio apartment (one room plus a kitchenette and bathroom).

C.   The building appears to be well maintained and safe.

D.   The apartment is on the third floor, away from the street, and the neighbors do not appear to be disagreeable.

E.   The rent is $500 per month, furnished.

F.   The landlord will require a year's lease, and if you don't stay in the apartment for the full year, subleasing it to someone else would be difficult.

G.   You have a widowed aunt, with whom you get along well and who lives alone in a house 45 minutes by bus from the law school, and she has offered to let you use the second floor of her house during the school year. The house and neighborhood are safe and quiet, and the living arrangements would be satisfactory to you.

H.   You have made a commitment to work next summer in El Paso.

I.   You neither own nor have access to a car.

J.   Reliable local people have told you that you probably won't find an apartment that is better, cheaper, or more convenient than the one you've just inspected.

Which facts are essential to your decision? If the apartment had been two miles from the law school (rather than a half-mile), would your decision be different? If the answer is no, the first listed fact couldn't be determinative. It might be part of the factual mosaic and might explain why you looked at the apartment in the first place, but you wouldn't base your decision on it. (Go through the listed facts and mark in the margin whether each would determine your decision.)

Facts recited specifically in an opinion can sometimes be reformulated generically. In the hypothetical above, for example, a generic restatement of fact *G* might be the following: "You have a rent-free alternative to the apartment, but the alternative would require 45 minutes of travel each way plus the expense of public transportation." This formulation is generic because it would cover other possibilities that would have the same effect. It could include, for example, the following, seemingly different, facts: "You're a member of the clergy in a religion that has given you a leave of absence to attend law school; you may continue to live rent-free in the satisfactory quarters your religion has provided, but to get to the law school, you will have to walk 15 minutes and then ride a subway for 30 minutes more, at the same cost as a bus."

A rule of law is a principle that governs how a particular type of decision is to be made — or, put another way, how certain types of facts are to be treated by the official (such as a judge) who must make a decision. Where a court ambiguously states a rule, you might arrive at an arguably supportable formulation of the rule by considering the determinative facts to have caused the result. There's room for interpretive maneuvering wherever you could reasonably interpret the determinative facts narrowly (specifically) or broadly (generically).

Notice how different formulations of a rule can be extracted from the apartment example. A narrow formulation might be the following:

> A law student who has a choice between renting an apartment and living in the second floor of an aunt's house should choose the aunt's house where the apartment's rent is $500 per month but the aunt's second floor is free except for bus fares; where the student must work in El Paso during the summer; and where it would be difficult to sublease the apartment during the summer.

Because this formulation is limited to the specific facts given in the hypothetical, it could directly govern only a tiny number of future decision-makers. It would not, for example, directly govern the member of the clergy described above, even if she will spend next summer doing relief work in Rwanda.

Although a decision-maker in a future situation might be able to reason by analogy from the narrow rule set out above, a broader, more widely applicable formulation, stated generically, would directly govern *both* situations:

> A student should not sign a year's lease where the student cannot live in the leased property during the summer and where a nearly free alternative is available.

The determinative facts, the issue, the holding, and the rule are all dependent on each other. In the apartment hypothetical, if the issue were different — say, "How shall I respond to an offer to join the American Automobile Association?" — the selection of determinative facts would also change. (In fact, the only determinative one would be fact I: "You neither own nor have access to a car.") You'll often find yourself using what the court tells you about the issue or the holding to fill in what the court hasn't told you about the determinative facts, and vice versa.

For example, if the court states the issue but doesn't identify the rule or specify which facts are determinative, you might discover the rule and the determinative facts by answering the following questions:

1. Who is suing whom over what series of events and to get what relief?
2. What issue does the court say it intends to decide?
3. How does the court decide that issue?
4. On what facts does the court rely in making that decision?
5. What rule does the court enforce?

In answering the fifth question, use the same kind of reasoning we applied to the apartment hypothetical: Develop several different phrasings of the rule (broad, narrow, middling) and identify the one the court is most likely to have had in mind.

Exercise II
Analyzing the Meaning of *Roberson v. Rochester Folding Box Co.*

What was the issue on appeal in *Roberson*? What rule did the appellate court enforce? What were the determinative facts?

§3.3   The Anatomy of a Statute

The *Roberson* decision was so unpopular that the following year the New York legislature enacted a statute providing exactly the relief that the *Roberson* court held was unavailable under the common law. The *Roberson* majority understood that that might happen. Recall the majority's words: "The legislative body could very well interfere and arbitrarily provide that no one should be permitted for his own selfish purpose to use the picture or the name of another for advertising purposes without his consent." The statute has been amended several times. Here is its current form:

New York Civil Rights Law §§ 50 – 51

§ 50.   Right of Privacy

A person, firm or corporation that uses for advertising purposes, or for the purposes of trade, the name, portrait or picture of any living person without having first obtained the written consent of such person . . . is guilty of a misdemeanor.

§ 51.   Action for Injunction and for Damages

Any person whose name, portrait, picture or voice is used within this state for advertising purposes or for the purposes of trade without the written consent first obtained as above provided [in § 50] may maintain an equitable action in the supreme court of this state against the person, firm or corporation so using his name, portrait, picture or voice, to prevent and restrain the use thereof; and may also sue and recover damages for any injuries sustained by reason of such use and if the defendant shall have knowingly used such person's name, portrait, picture or voice in such manner as is forbidden or declared to be unlawful by [§ 50], the jury, in its discretion, may award exemplary damages. . . .

A statute expresses rules the legislature has enacted. It does nothing else. Unlike judicial opinions, statutory text on its face contains no stories. Usually a statute does not explain the legislature's reasoning. Typically the explanations are in other documents, such as legislative committee reports. Most statutes are pure rules, structured as Chapter 2 describes. Sometimes those rules are straightforward, like the one in § 50 above. Sometimes they are convoluted like the one in § 51.

Exercise III
Analyzing the Meaning of §§ 50 and 51 of the New York Civil Rights Law

Reading §§ 50 and 51 together as a single statute, what do they prohibit or require? If a person subject to New York law were to violate this prohibition or requirement, what might be the consequences? In what ways did §§ 50 and 51 change the rule of *Roberson*?

§3.4   How Statutes and the Common Law Interact

The common law has grown to include four separate invasion of privacy torts, and many states recognize all four of them. *Intrusion upon seclusion* is invasion of a person's private space — for example, by opening his mail or by spying through his windows with binoculars. *Public disclosure of private facts* is the dissemination of facts that don't legitimately concern the public and that are sufficiently private that a reasonable person would consider their disclosure highly offensive. *False light* is the dissemination of facts that, even if true, create a misleading and highly offensive impression about a person. *Appropriation of name or likeness* is what happened to Abigail Roberson.

The Court of Appeals held in *Roberson* that no common law right to privacy of any kind existed in New York. Section 51 of the New York Civil Rights Law created a statutory cause of action for appropriation. But no legislation in New

York has created a statutory cause of action for intrusion, public disclosure of private facts, or false light.

Because the legislature created a statutory cause of action *only* for appropriation, *Roberson* is still the law in New York on the other three invasion of privacy torts. If a plaintiff sues in New York for intrusion, public disclosure of private facts, or false light, that plaintiff will lose. A court will hold that those common law torts don't exist in New York, citing *Roberson*, and that New York recognizes only appropriation.

A statute does only what its words express. Sections 50 and 51 are narrowly drafted, and they only create a misdemeanor and a cause of action for appropriation. The following case illustrates that.

COSTANZA v. SEINFELD
181 Misc. 2d 562, 693 N.Y.S.2d 897
(Sup. Ct., N.Y. County 1999)

HAROLD TOMKINS, J.

A person is seeking an enormous sum of money for claims that the New York State courts have rejected for decades. This could be the plot for an episode in a situation comedy. Instead, it is the case brought by plaintiff Michael Costanza who is suing the comedian, Jerry Seinfeld, Larry David (who was the cocreator of the television program "Seinfeld"), the National Broadcasting Company, Inc. and the production companies for $100 million. He is seeking relief for violation of New York's Civil Rights Law §§50 and 51. . . .

The substantive assertions of the complaint are that the defendants used the name and likeness of plaintiff Michael Costanza without his permission, that they invaded his privacy, [and] that he was portrayed in a negative, humiliating light. . . . Plaintiff Michael Costanza asserts that the fictional character of George Costanza in the television program "Seinfeld" is based upon him. In the show, George Costanza is a long-time friend of the lead character, Jerry Seinfeld. He is constantly having problems with poor employment situations, disastrous romantic relationships, conflicts with his parents and general self-absorption.

. . . Plaintiff Michael Costanza points to various similarities between himself and the character George Costanza to bolster his claim that his name and likeness are being appropriated. He claims that, like him, George Costanza is short, fat, bald, that he knew Jerry Seinfeld from college purportedly as the character George Costanza did and they both came from Queens. Plaintiff Michael Costanza asserts that the self-centered nature and unreliability of the character George Costanza are attributed to him and this humiliates him.

The issues in this case come before the court [through] a preanswer motion to dismiss. . . . [P]laintiff Michael Costanza's claims for being placed in a false light and invasion of privacy must be dismissed. They cannot stand because New York law does not and never has allowed a common-law claim for invasion of privacy, *Howell v. New York Post Co.*, 81 N.Y.2d 115 (1993);

Freihofer v. Hearst Corp., 65 N.Y.2d 135 (1985). As the New York Court of Appeals explained,

> While legal scholarship has been influential in the development of a tort for intentional infliction of emotional distress, it has had less success in the development of a right to privacy in this State. In a famous law review article written more than a century ago, Samuel Warren and Louis Brandeis advocated a tort for invasion of the right to privacy. . . . Relying in part on this article, Abigail Marie Roberson sued a flour company for using her picture, without consent, in the advertisement of its product (*Roberson v. Rochester Folding Box Co.*, 171 N.Y. 538). Finding a lack of support for the thesis of the Warren-Brandeis study, this Court, in a four to three decision, rejected plaintiff's claim.
>
> The *Roberson* decision was roundly criticized. . . . The Legislature responded by enacting the Nation's first statutory right to privacy (L. 1903, ch. 132), now codified as sections 50 and 51 of the Civil Rights Law. Section 50 prohibits the use of a living person's name, portrait or picture for "advertising" or "trade" purposes without prior written consent. . . . Section 50 provides criminal penalties and section 51 a private right of action for damages and injunctive relief.

Howell at 122-123. In New York State, there is [still] no common law right to privacy, *Freihofer v. Hearst Corp.* at 140, and any relief must be sought under the statute.

The court now turns to the assertion that plaintiff Michael Costanza's name and likeness are being appropriated without his written consent. This claim faces several separate obstacles. First, defendants assert that plaintiff Michael Costanza has waived any claim by [personally] appearing on the show. [This defense fails because the] statute clearly provides that written consent is necessary for use of a person's name or likeness, *Kane v. Orange County Publs.*, 232 A.D.2d 526 (2d Dept. 1996). However, defendants note the limited nature of the relief provided by Civil Rights Law §§ 50 and 51. It extends only to the use of a name or likeness for trade or advertising, *Freihofer v. Hearst Corp.*, at 140. The sort of commercial exploitation prohibited and compensable if violated is solicitation for patronage, *Delan v. CBS, Inc.*, 91 A.D.2d 255 (2d Dept. 1983). In a case similar to this lawsuit involving the play "Six Degrees of Separation," it was held that "works of fiction and satire do not fall within the narrow scope of the statutory phrases 'advertising' and 'trade,'" *Hampton v. Guare*, 195 A.D.2d 366 (1st Dept. 1993). The Seinfeld television program was a fictional comedic presentation. It does not fall within the scope of trade or advertising. . . .

Plaintiff Michael Costanza's claim for violation of Civil Rights Law §§ 50 and 51 must be dismissed. . . .

INTRODUCTION TO LEGAL WRITING

4 Predictive Writing

§4.1 How Predictive Writing Differs from Persuasive Writing

Predictive writing and persuasive writing are *decisional* — but in different ways. In predictive writing, you help your reader — a supervising lawyer or your client — make a decision. In persuasive writing, you try to convince a judge to decide a case in favor of your client.

Predictive writing: A newspaper might ask its lawyer whether an article it wants to publish would make the newspaper liable for defamation, which is the tort of communicating damaging falsehoods about a person. This article describes certain people in unflattering ways, and the newspaper worries about whether it has gone too far. The newspaper might ask, "Is the article defamatory?" That's the same as asking, "If we publish the article, will a court hold us liable for defamation?" Regardless of how the question is put, the only way a lawyer can answer is to predict what a court would do. The article is defamatory if a court would hold the newspaper liable for defamation. If a court would not do that, the article is not defamatory.

The newspaper asks the question so it can decide whether to publish the article. If the lawyer says the article is defamatory, the newspaper might ask a follow-up question: "How can the article be changed so that it isn't defamatory?" The lawyer might answer, "It won't be defamatory if you delete the fourth sentence." The lawyer predicts to help the client make a decision.

After the article is published, a person mentioned in it consults her lawyer and asks what her rights are. Regardless of how the client phrases the question, she is really asking, "If I sue the newspaper, will a court award me damages for defamation?" The lawyer's prediction will help her decide whether to sue.

Predictive writing is neutral and objective. If the client will lose in court, good predictive writing should say that even though the client will be disappointed. The best predictions are accurate ones.

Persuasive writing: Here a lawyer explains to a court why it should make rulings the lawyer's client wants. Persuasive writing is not neutral. It is advocacy. The court's decision will determine who wins and who loses. Good persuasive writing *influences* the court to decide in favor of the lawyer's client.

§4.2   The Documents Lawyers Write

Predictive writing is often done in office memoranda (which are explained in Chapter 16), professional emails (Chapter 17), and client letters (Chapter 18).

Persuasive writing is often done in trial court motion memoranda (Chapter 25) and in appellate briefs (Chapters 28–32). Chapters 23–24 and 26–27 explain how to make persuasive arguments and tell a client's story persuasively in writing.

Many skills are common to both predictive and persuasive writing. They include working with statutes, cases, and other authority (Chapters 7–9); working with facts (Chapter 10); organizing written analysis (Chapters 11–14); as well as paragraphing, style, and quoting (Chapters 20–22).

Lawyers write a wide range of other documents as well: contracts, wills, pleadings, motions, interrogatories, affidavits, stipulations, judicial opinions, orders, judgments, statutes, administrative regulations, and more. But those documents usually aren't covered in a first-year writing course. They're covered instead in second- or third-year drafting courses.

§4.3   How to Predict

> The prophecies of what the courts will do in fact, and nothing more pretentious, are what I mean by the law.
>
> — *Oliver Wendell Holmes*

Let's take up Welty's facts from Chapter 2. Here they are again:

Welty and Lutz are students who have rented apartments on the same floor of the same building. At midnight, Welty is studying, while Lutz is listening to a

Black Keys album with his new four-foot concert speakers. Welty has put up with this for two or three hours, and finally she pounds on Lutz's door. Lutz opens the door about six inches, and, when he realizes that he cannot hear what Welty is saying, he steps back into the room a few feet to turn the volume down, without opening the door further. Continuing to express outrage, Welty pushes the door completely open and strides into the room. Lutz turns on Welty and orders her to leave. Welty finds this to be too much and punches Lutz so hard that he suffers substantial injury. In this jurisdiction, the punch is a felonious assault. Is Welty also guilty of burglary?

(Before continuing here, you should review §2.2 in Chapter 2 on how legal rules are structured.)

Assume that in your state the crime of common law burglary has been codified and renamed burglary in the first degree:

> *Criminal Code § 102:* A person commits burglary in the first degree by breaking and entering the dwelling of another in the nighttime with intent to commit a felony inside.

Also assume that the elements of burglary in the first degree have been statutorily defined as follows:

> *Criminal Code § 101(c):* A "breaking" is the making of an opening, or the enlarging of an opening, so as to permit entry into a building, or a closed off portion of a building, if neither the owner nor the occupant has consented thereto.
>
> *Criminal Code § 101(d):* An "entering" or an "entry" is the placing, by a defendant, of any part of his body or anything under his control within a building, or a closed off portion of a building, if neither the owner nor the occupant has consented thereto.
>
> *Criminal Code § 101(e):* A "closed off portion" of a building is one divided from the remainder of the building by walls, partitions, or the like so that it can be secured against entry.
>
> *Criminal Code § 101(f):* A "dwelling" is any building, or any closed off portion thereof, in which one or more persons habitually sleep.
>
> *Criminal Code § 101(g):* A dwelling is "of another" if the defendant does not by right habitually sleep there.
>
> *Criminal Code § 101(h):* "Nighttime" is the period between sunset and sunrise.
>
> *Criminal Code § 101(k):* "Intent to commit a felony inside" is the intent to commit, while inside a building or closed off portion of a building, a crime classified in this Code as a felony, but only if the defendant had that intent at the moment the defendant broke and entered.

And assume that the legislature has also enacted the following:

> *Criminal Code § 11:* No person shall be convicted of a crime except on evidence proving guilt beyond a reasonable doubt.
> *Criminal Code § 403:* An assault causing substantial injury is a felony.

Finally, assume — for the sake of simplicity — that none of these sections has yet been interpreted by the courts, and that you are therefore limited to the statute itself. (That is an unusual situation. More often, you will also be working with judicial decisions that have interpreted the statute.)

If you were Welty's lawyer and must predict whether Welty will be convicted of first-degree burglary, you might think about it in the following way. (*What you say to yourself is shown in the box below.*)

First-degree burglary has six elements and no exceptions. Welty will be guilty if the prosecutor proves every element beyond a reasonable doubt. I'll make a list of the elements and annotate it by writing next to each element the relevant facts.

[You start making notes while continuing talking to yourself silently.]

It's an apartment. Lutz lives there. Welty doesn't.

[In your notes, you put a checkmark next to the "dwelling" element and another checkmark next to the "of another" element. The checkmarks mean that you believe the prosecutor can prove those elements.]

It was midnight.

[Next to the "nighttime" element, you write "midnight" and add a checkmark. The prosecutor can obviously prove that element.]

When Welty pushed the door back, she enlarged an opening. Neither Lutz nor the landlord (the owner) told her that she had permission.

[In your notes, you write three facts next to the "breaking" element:

Welty pushed door open
no permission from Lutz
no permission from owner/landlord

Then you put a checkmark next the breaking element because the prosecutor can prove it.]

She entered when she walked in. Neither Lutz nor the landlord (the owner) told her that she had permission to be inside.

[Next to the "entering" element you write that Welty walked in without permission. And you add a checkmark because the prosecutor can prove she entered.]

What she did next, punching Lutz, is a felony. But under § 101(k), the intent-to-commit-a-felony element isn't satisfied unless — at the moment she pushed the door open and walked in — she already had the intent to hit him. She was furious. But before the punch, Lutz had turned on her and ordered her to leave. She'll testify that she "found this to be too much." That creates reasonable doubt about whether, at the moment she opened the door and walked in, she already had the intent to strike him. She may have been angry when she pushed the door open and walked in. But anger doesn't necessarily include intent to assault somebody. Most of the anger that people feel in life isn't followed by violence.

[You look at your notes. Next to the intent-to-commit-a-felony element, you write these facts:

> *angry when came in*
> *Lutz ordered her out*
> *will testify that was "too much"*
> *only then did she punch him*

But you don't write a checkmark.]

The prosecutor can't prove the intent-to-commit-a-felony element beyond a reasonable doubt.

[You have a good argument for acquitting Welty of burglary.]

To *write* your prediction, you might produce something like the left column below. In the right column are our comments on the writing and how it is organized. Pay close attention to the organization, which matters a great deal in legal writing.

The prosecution cannot prove all the elements of first degree burglary in Welty's case.

Under § 102 of the Criminal Code, the elements of first degree burglary are (1) breaking and (2) entering (3) the dwelling (4) of another (5) in the nighttime (6) "with intent to commit a felony inside." Under § 11, a defendant can be convicted only "on evidence proving guilt beyond a reasonable doubt." Although Welty broke and entered Lutz's dwelling in the nighttime, and although the assault she committed there is classified as a felony by § 403, the evidence does not prove beyond a reasonable doubt that she had the intent to assault Lutz when she broke and entered.

Section 101(k) defines "intent to commit a felony inside" as "the intent to commit, while inside a building or closed off portion of a building, a crime classified in this Code as a felony, but only if the defendant had that intent at the moment the defendant broke and entered." When Lutz turned around and ordered her to leave, she had been complaining about his noise. She says that she found his ordering her out to be "too much" and punched him. A reasonable explanation is that she entered the apartment to complain and, after she was already in the room, decided to punch him. Section 101(k) requires that, when she walked through the door, she intended to punch him. The prosecution would have to prove that beyond a reasonable doubt. But no words or action on her part show that she when she walked through the door she intended to punch Lutz.

Welty's pushing open Lutz's apartment door was, however, a breaking, which § 101(c) defines as "the making of an opening, or the enlarging of an opening, so as to permit entry into a building, or a closed off portion of a building,

This is your bottom-line conclusion.

Section 102 is the basic rule governing the dispute.

Section 11 operates together with § 102.

This is a roadmap sentence telling the reader the route your analysis will follow.

The determinative issue is addressed before the other elements. Why consider at the beginning an element that the statute lists last? (Reread § 102.) The reason is that if one element is unprovable, that element becomes the most important one. Welty can be convicted only if all the elements are proved. If one element can't be proved, that element is the most important one because it makes her not guilty.

Why bother to consider the other elements at all? The reason is that you might be wrong about the element you think is dispositive, and the reader is entitled to a full accounting.

if neither the owner nor the occupant has consented thereto." Lutz's apartment is a "closed off portion" of a building, which is defined by § 101(e) as "one divided from the remainder of the building by walls, partitions, or the like so that it can be secured against entry." It is difficult to imagine an apartment that is not divided from the rest of the building in which it is located. Lutz opened his front door about six inches after Welty knocked on it to complain of noise, and, when she walked into his apartment, he immediately ordered her out. His opening the door by six inches would not have been enough to let Welty in, and Lutz's prompt order to leave shows that he had not consented to her opening the door farther. And nothing suggests that Welty had consent from the landlord who owns the apartment.

Welty's walking into Lutz's apartment was an entry, which § 101(g) defines as "the placing, by a defendant, of any part of his body or anything under his control within a building, or a closed off portion of a building, if neither the owner nor the occupant has consented thereto." Welty walked into Lutz's apartment, and the circumstances do not show consent to an entry for the same reasons that they do not show consent to a breaking.

The prosecution can also prove the other elements beyond a reasonable doubt. Lutz's apartment is a dwelling, which § 101(f) defines as "any building, or closed off portion thereof, in which one or more persons habitually sleep." Lutz will testify that he habitually sleeps in his apartment. To Welty, that apartment is the dwelling of another, as defined by § 101(n), because she does not habitually sleep there. Finally, these events happened at midnight and within § 101(m)'s definition of nighttime.

This paragraph begins with your conclusion on the breaking issue, followed by the rule defining a breaking, and an application of the rule to the facts. This is a natural sequence in legal writing. State your conclusion. Then state the rule. Then apply the rule to the facts. Later chapters in this book expand that sequence and explain how to make it work.

This paragraph is structured like the preceding one, except that for economy it incorporates by reference the parallel analysis set out earlier.

These elements are so straightforward that a reader will quickly agree that the prosecution can prove all of them. You must account for them. But they aren't dispositive, and the analysis can be compressed.

Exercises
Nansen and Byrd

Exercise A. With the aid of §§ 16 and 221(a) of the Criminal Code (below), break down the rule in § 220 into a list of elements and exceptions. Annotate the list by adding definitions for the elements (and for any exceptions you might come across). Under each element you list, leave lots of white space. When you do the second part of this exercise, you will need room to write more.

Criminal Code § 16: When a term describing a kind of intent or knowledge appears in a statute defining a crime, that term applies to every element of the crime unless the definition of the crime clearly indicates that the term is meant to apply only to certain elements and not to others.

Criminal Code § 220: A person is guilty of criminal sale of a controlled substance when he knowingly sells any quantity of a controlled substance.

Criminal Code § 221(a): As used in section 220 of this code, "sell" means to exchange for goods or money, to give, or to offer or agree to do the same, except where the seller is a licensed physician dispensing the controlled substance pursuant to a permit issued by the Drug Enforcement Commission or where the seller is a licensed pharmacist dispensing the controlled substance as directed by a prescription issued by a licensed physician pursuant to a permit issued by the Drug Enforcement Commission.

Exercise B. You've interviewed Nansen, who lives with Byrd. Neither is a licensed physician or a licensed pharmacist. At about noon on July 15, both were arrested and charged with criminal sale of a controlled substance. Nansen has told you the following:

Byrd keeps a supply of cocaine in our apartment. He had been out of town for a month, and I had used up his stash while he was gone. I knew that was going to bend Byrd completely out of shape, but I thought I was going to get away with it. I had replaced it all with plaster. When you grind plaster down real fine, it looks like coke. For other reasons, I had decided to go to Alaska on an afternoon flight on July 15 and not come back. Byrd was supposed to get back into town on July 16, and by the time he figured out what had happened, I'd be in the Tongass Forest.

But on the morning of the 15th, Byrd opened the door of the apartment and walked in, saying he had decided to come back a day early. I hadn't started packing yet — I wouldn't have much to pack anyway — but I didn't know how I was going to pack with Byrd standing around because of all the explaining I'd have to do. I also didn't want Byrd hanging around the apartment and working up an urge for some cocaine that wasn't there. So I said, "Let's go hang out on the street."

We had been on the sidewalk about ten or fifteen minutes when a guy came up to us and started talking. He was dressed a little too well to be a regular street person, but he looked kind of desperate. I figured he was looking to buy some drugs. Then I realized that that was the solution to at least some of my problem.

I took Byrd aside and said, "This guy looks like he's ready to buy big. What do you think he'd pay for your stash?" Byrd looked reluctant, so I turned to the guy and said, "We can sell you about three ounces of coke, but we have to have a thousand for it." When the guy said, "Yeah," Byrd said, "Wait here" and ran inside the apartment building. A thousand was far more than the stuff was worth.

Byrd walked out onto the stoop with the whole stash in his hand in the zip-lock bag he kept it in. While he was walking down the steps, about ten feet away from me and the guy who wanted to buy, two uniforms appeared out of nowhere and arrested Byrd and me.

The "guy" turned out to be Officer D'Asconni, an undercover policeman who will testify to the conversation Nansen has described. The police laboratory reports that the bag contained 2.8 ounces of plaster and 0.007 ounces of cocaine. When you told Nansen about the laboratory report, he said the following:

I didn't think there was any coke in that bag. What they found must have been residue. I had used up every last bit of Byrd's stuff. I clearly remember looking at that empty bag after I had used it all and wondering how much plaster to put in it so that it would at least look like the coke Byrd had left behind. I certainly didn't see any point in scrubbing the bag with cleanser before I put the plaster in it.

With the aid of Criminal Code § 221(b) (below), finish annotating your list of elements by writing, under each element, the facts that are relevant to that element.

Criminal Code § 221(b): As used in section 220, "controlled substance" includes any of the following: . . . cocaine . . . .

Exercise C. You've been asked to determine whether Nansen or Byrd is likely to be convicted of criminal sale of a controlled substance. The question isn't whether Nansen or Byrd criminally sold a controlled substance, but whether either of them is likely to be convicted of doing that. To make that prediction, take into account § 10(a) of the Criminal Code.

Criminal Code § 10(a): No person shall be convicted of a crime except on evidence proving guilt beyond a reasonable doubt.

Using your annotated outline of elements, decide whether each element can be proved beyond a reasonable doubt, and whether any exceptions are satisfied. Then make your prediction. Finally, decide the order in which the elements would best be explored in the Discussion section of an office memo.

5 Inside the Writing Process

§5.1 Product and Process

A writing course teaches both the *product* created through writing and the *process* of creating it.

Your product — the document you produce — might be an office memo, a motion memo for a trial court, a client letter, a professional email, or a brief filed in an appellate court. Every type of document has its own purposes and characteristics. Later chapters in this book explain what each type of document should look like and what it should accomplish.

Your writing process is how you go about creating a legal document — what goes through your mind as you write. Part of that is analyzing the law, perhaps by interpreting statutes and precedent, which involves several aspects of thinking like a lawyer. The other part is thinking like a writer: how you organize your thoughts and find the best words to express them, as well as how you manage the work and in general perform the act of creation. Later chapters explain legal analysis. This chapter and Chapter 6 explain some basics of how writers think and work.

Process is harder to learn than product. Product is tangible. It can be held in the hand. A sample office memo, like the one in Appendix C, can be discussed in class to learn what makes it effective or ineffective. Process is much harder to observe because it happens mostly in your mind when you're alone. And there are many different effective processes of writing. If you put 50 best-selling book authors in one room and ask them how they write, they'll probably give you 50 different answers. But most effective processes of writing share some basic traits, which this book explains.

A process that works for one writer won't necessarily work for another. Finding one that works best for you can happen only through experimentation in which you simultaneously do the writing *and* think about how you're doing it. Observe yourself writing. What did you do first? Second? Did you feel ready to write? How did you organize your materials? What did you do when you felt stuck?

Afterward ask yourself some more questions. Which aspects of your process seemed to work well? Which seemed inefficient or counterproductive? Some questions are much more important than you might think. What do *you like about yourself* as a writer, both in what you produced and in how you produced it? Is there anything about the work that you *enjoyed*? In §6.7, we'll explain why what you like and enjoy are important questions.

§5.2   Five Phases of Writing

Writing happens in five phases:

1. Researching authorities and analyzing what you find (§5.4)
2. Organizing your raw materials into an outline (§5.5)
3. Producing a first draft (§5.6)
4. Rewriting it through several more drafts (§5.7)
5. Polishing it (§5.8)

Writers tend not to go through these phases in strict order, finishing one phase before beginning the next. Rarely, if ever, do they start at the beginning, write until they get to the end, and then stop.

Instead, writers often circle back to reopen something already done and redo some aspect of it. For example, you'll continue to analyze while you organize, while you write the first draft, and while you rewrite it several times, although much of the analytical work comes at the beginning. While writing the first draft, you might decide to go back and rewrite something you wrote a few pages ago. While rewriting, you might reorganize.

Still, it helps to think about writing in the five phases listed above. Each phase is a different *kind* of work, requiring somewhat different skills.

§5.3   Planning the Work

Suppose your teacher distributes an assignment with a deadline three weeks later for submitting your work. On the day you receive the assignment, you have two options.

The first is to toss it aside when you get home so you can try not to think about it for at least two weeks, leaving only the last few days before the deadline to do the entire job. Many students did this in college and turned in their first draft as their final product. When they try that again in law school, the result is disappointment because legal writing requires much more preparation and many more drafts.

When you're learning professional skills, each new task will usually take longer to accomplish than you might think because the complexities of the task are not immediately apparent. Later, with experience, you'll get much better at predicting how long it will take to get things done.

The other, and better option is to use the full three weeks to get the job done. Very few students have good internal clocks that pace them through the work. Instead plan by creating a schedule:

1. Estimate how much time it will take you to do the research and analyze the results, to organize your raw materials, to produce a first draft, to rewrite it through several more drafts, and to polish it; and
2. budget time so that you can do each one of these tasks well.

When you first get the assignment, it can seem huge and intimidating. But once you break it down into a group of smaller tasks, it's not as big and seems much more doable. Anne Lamott, a writer by profession, remembers when her brother, who was not yet a teenager, had been assigned to write a school report on birds —

> and he was at the kitchen table close to tears, surrounded by binder paper and pencils and unopened books on birds, immobilized by the hugeness of the task ahead. Then my father [also a writer by profession] sat down, put his arm around my brother's shoulder, and said, "Bird by bird, buddy. Just take it bird by bird."[1]

Although you're not writing about birds, you can use the same approach. Divide the document into parts. Take it part by part. Write one part. Then write another. Keep going until you've written everything. The prospect of writing a big legal document can seem paralyzing. But it's manageable to write several shorter chunks that, added together, are the document. That's several smaller tasks, not one huge one.

§5.4 Researching and Analyzing

Begin by identifying the issues. What questions about law and facts need to be resolved? As you research, analyze, and write, you may change your

---

1. Anne Lamott, *Bird by Bird* 19 (1994).

mind about the precise definitions of these questions. And while working you may identify subissues not apparent at the outset. But start researching and analyzing.

Researching is finding relevant authority, such as statutes and cases. Your teacher has probably assigned a research textbook or other materials that explain how to research. Allot plenty of time for research. It may take more time than you realize.

Analysis is identifying the authorities on which you rely (Chapter 7), figuring out what they mean (Chapters 8 and 9) and how they govern the client's facts (Chapter 10). It helps to outline the rules of law (Chapter 2).

§5.5   Organizing Raw Materials into an Outline

Good organization is crucial in legal writing. Legal writing is a highly *structured* form of expression because rules of law are by nature structured ideas. The structure of a rule controls how you organize its application to facts—and thus controls the organization of a written discussion of the rule and its application. Good organization makes your analysis more easily understandable to the reader by leading the reader through the steps of your reasoning.

In college, most teachers criticize organization only infrequently. But the reader of legal writing is different from the reader for whom you might have written college essays. Legal writing is organized in ways that reflect the way lawyers and judges analyze legal issues. Good organization puts material exactly where the reader will need it. Unplanned writing is inefficient because it ignores the reader's needs and frustrates the reader's expectations. And a reader whose needs are ignored and whose expectations are frustrated quickly becomes an irritated reader.

Students are told to outline but often resist doing it. Outlining seems like an arbitrary and useless requirement. If you dislike outlining, the problem might be that you were taught an outlining method that is unnecessarily rigid. Rigid methods of outlining demand that you draw an outline tree with roman numerals, capital letters, arabic numerals, lowercase letters, and italic numerals. That represses creativity, and it isn't the way effective writers plan their writing in detail.

A fluid outlining method is simpler and *helps* you write. A fluid outline is a flexible collection of lists. Your raw materials (statutes, cases, facts, hypotheses, and so on) flow through it and into your first draft.

Several chapters in this book explain how to outline and how to organize. Chapter 11 sets out the most effective methods of organizing analytical legal writing. Chapters 12 and 13 explore those methods in further detail. And Chapter 14 explains how to make a fluid outline.

§5.6   Producing a First Draft

All good writers write [horrible first drafts]. This is how they end up with good second drafts and terrific third drafts. . . .

Start by getting something — anything — down on paper. A friend of mine says that the first draft is the down draft — you just get it down. The second draft is the up draft — you fix it up. . . . And the third draft is the dental draft, where you check every tooth . . . .

— *Anne Lamott*

Many students treat the first draft as the most important part of writing. But that's wrong. The first draft is often the *least* important part. Most of the other phases contribute more to an effective final product. And when writing on a computer, first-draft writing might not be separate from rewriting. That's because of the ease with which you can interrupt your first draft and go back to rewrite something you initially wrote only a few minutes ago.

The only purpose of a first draft is to get things down on the page so you can start rewriting. The first draft *has no other value*. A first draft accomplishes its entire purpose merely by existing. It can be full of errors. That's fine. It just needs to exist.

You don't need to write the first draft from beginning to end. You can start with any part of the document you feel ready to write — no matter where in the document it will finally be. You can write the middle before you write the beginning, for example. If your mind is mulling over a certain part of the document, start writing that part. Write the rest later.

Do your first draft as early as possible. The first draft may be the least important part of the writing process, but you can't start rewriting until you have a first draft. And if you leave little time for rewriting, the document you submit will disappoint both you and your reader.

§5.7   Rewriting

There is no such thing as good writing. There is only good rewriting.

— *Justice Louis Brandeis*

A clear sentence is no accident. Very few sentences come out right the first time, or the third.

— *William Zinsser*

A scrupulous writer, in every sentence that he writes, will ask . . . : What am I trying to say? What words will express it? What image or idiom will make it clearer? . . . Could I put it more shortly?

— *George Orwell*

A first draft is for the writer. You write to get your thoughts onto the page.

Later drafts are for the reader. In rewriting, you continue to develop your thinking, getting more thoughts onto the page while deleting weak ideas. But your focus shifts to the reader. How much will *this* reader need to be told? Will this reader understand what you say without having to read twice? Will this reader become convinced that you're right?

To answer these questions while you read your first and later drafts, pretend to be your reader — the one described in Chapter 4. Will this skeptical person see issues that you haven't addressed? Will this busy person become impatient at having to wade through material of marginal value that got into your first draft? Will this careful person be satisfied that you have written accurately and precisely?

You'll do a better job of impersonating the reader if, between drafts, you stop writing for a day or two, clear your mind by working on something else, and come back to do the next draft both "cold" and "fresh." Obviously, that can't happen if you put off starting the project and later have to do the whole thing frantically at the last minute. To make sure that you have time to rewrite, start on an assignment as soon as you get it, and then pace yourself, working at regular intervals within the time allotted.

Most of the writing lawyers do in the practice of law can be made effective in three to six drafts. Larger documents need more drafts than shorter ones. Beginning lawyers need to go through more drafts than experienced lawyers do. An experienced lawyer might be able to produce a client letter with three drafts. A first-year law student might need six or eight or even ten drafts to produce a high-quality appellate brief.

Focus on the big picture as well as individual sentences and paragraphs. Is your organization natural and effective? As you reread and rewrite, do you have doubts about your analysis? Don't limit yourself to "surface-level changes," but instead use rewriting as "an opportunity to re-see" the whole document.[2]

For many people, rewriting is the hardest phase in the writing process. Set aside a lot of time for it. Sometimes you'll get discouraged because the problems you thought you'd solved earlier really haven't been solved. At other times, when you piece things together well, you might experience relief (or even a little thrill because of what you've accomplished).

Rewriting is hard because much of it involves reimagining your first draft and reexamining the decisions you made there. Experienced writers say that they can enjoy rewriting because that's where they can turn barely adequate writing into top-quality material. "The pleasure of revision [another name for rewriting] often arises when you refine what you intend to say and *even discover that you have more to say, a new solution, a different path, a better*

---

2. Patricia Grande Montana, *Better Revision: Encouraging Students to See Through the Eyes of the Legal Reader*, 14 J. Legal Writing 291, 292 (2008).

presentation."[3] Empirical studies of the writing process have shown that experienced writers use rewriting for deep rethinking, and usually they reorganize the earlier draft.[4]

Don't be afraid to delete material from your first draft, even if it hurts to take it out. The fact that you've written something doesn't mean you have to keep it.

While rewriting, use the checklists on the inside front and back covers of this book to test your writing for good organization, paragraphing, style, and proper use of quotations.

To experience what the reader will experience, some writers read their drafts out loud. When they hear themselves speaking a draft's words, they are better able to imagine how the same words will strike the reader for whom they're writing. Other writers can get the same effect without speaking because they've developed the ability to "hear" a voice saying the words they read. Reading a draft aloud can also alert you to wording problems. Bad phrasing often sounds terrible when you say it.

Eventually while putting the writing through several drafts, you'll notice that after a certain point the problems you find are mostly typographical errors and small matters of grammar, style, and citation. When that happens, you've moved from rewriting into polishing (see the next section in this chapter), and the project is nearly finished.

Don't confuse rewriting with polishing. If all you do after the first draft is fix typographical errors, awkward wording, grammatical errors, and errors in citation form, you're polishing, and you've skipped rewriting completely.

§5.8   Polishing

This is the last phase. Allow a day or more to pass before coming back to the writing to polish it. If you're away from it for at least a day, you'll come back fresh and be able to see things you'd otherwise miss.

Read through the document differently from the way you've been seeing it on the screen as you wrote. Print it out. Readers and writers often see problems on a printed page that aren't obvious on a computer screen. Read it aloud. If it *sounds* awkward, it is awkward. If you work sitting down, read it standing up or lying down. Do something that puts you in a different frame of mind while you review your writing.

Take one last look for wording that doesn't say clearly and unambiguously what you mean. This is the biggest reason for waiting at least a day. When you wrote the words, they seemed clear because at that moment you knew what

---

3. Christopher M. Anzidei, *The Revision Process in Legal Writing: Seeing Better to Write Better,* 8 J. Legal Writing 23, 44 (2002) (italics added).
4. *Id.* at 40.

you were trying to say. But after some time has passed, you're no longer in that frame of mind. If you're not sure what the words mean or what you intended them to mean, fix them.

And take one last look for wording to be tightened up. Can you say it equally well in fewer words? If you can, do so.

Look for typographical errors, awkward wording, grammatical errors, and errors in citation form. Does the formatting make the document attractive to read? If not, choose a different font (but one that looks professional), add white space so the document doesn't seem crowded, or find other ways to make it look attractive. Use your word processor's spell-check function. Make sure the pages are numbered.

Now, you're finished.

6 More About Writing

§6.1   Writing and Thinking Are One Process

[T]here is no better way to master an idea than to write about it.

— *Robert H. Frank*

I write to discover what I think.

— *Daniel Boorstin*

Writing is thinking.

— *Deirdre McCloskey*

[L]earning to write as a lawyer is another way to learn to think as a lawyer.

— *Terrill Pollman*

Writing and thinking are one process. Writing enriches thought. You can't write without rethinking what you're trying to say. Writing and rewriting *help* you think.

Wherever you are in writing — the first draft, rewriting, or even polishing — don't be afraid to change your mind about your analysis of the law and the facts. Most writers have abandoned ideas that seemed fine when first thought about, sounded good when spoken, but proved faulty when — in the end — they "wouldn't write."

Most writers have experienced the reverse as well: sitting down to write with a single idea and finding that the act of writing draws the idea out, fertilizes it, causes it to sprout limbs and roots, and spread into a forest of ideas.

The amount of thought reflected in a final draft is many times the amount in the first draft because the writing process and the thinking process are inseparable, each stimulating and advancing the other.

§6.2 Your Readers

You are writing mostly for professionals, who have expectations that you might not be used to.

Decisional reading and decisional writing. Your documents will be read by judges and supervising lawyers who must make decisions based on what you have written. They don't read out of general curiosity. They are decisional readers and need you to be a decisional writer. Each reader will expect your document to explain everything she needs to know in order to make a wise decision.

Skepticism. Your readers are skeptical by nature and for good reason. Skepticism helps them make better decisions. Their job is look for weaknesses in your analysis. If they find any, your writing is not helpful to them, and they will react negatively to it. A supervising lawyer might be disappointed in you and tell you to do the work over again. A judge might reject your thinking and rule against your client. But if your readers can't find any weaknesses, they will rely on you, respect you as a professional, and be grateful for your guidance.

Time pressure. Your readers are busy people who work under great time pressure. Usually they have no time to read your document twice. They need your writing to be so concise and crystal clear that they can read it just once and, in that one reading, learn from you everything they need to know. You cannot afford to waste their time.

Credibility and details. Your readers expect your grammar to be perfect, your documents to have no typographical errors, and your citations to comply in every respect with citation format rules and to have no inaccurate volume or page numbers. This isn't because your readers are overly critical fussbudgets. They're just careful professionals who will draw inferences about your credibility. If you aren't careful with details, they will wonder whether you have been careful in your legal analysis.

§6.3 Voice

Voice is a personal quality in a person's writing, something that speaks from the page in a writer's own way. Most people have only a slight voice in their writing — and prefer not to write in a way that's unique. There's nothing wrong with that.

Some students enter law school with distinctive written voices of their own. In legal writing courses, they learn that their writing must conform to a number of professional standards. Does that mean that you can no longer write in a voice that is yours? No, but you might need to adapt it to a professional situation. The legal audience has a set of expectations for legal writing, and you'll need to conform to them.

Your voice in professional documents will grow into something different from what it was before law school. But it will still be yours and distinctive — although recognizably professional. Most people who enter law school with distinctive written voices say later, after they have developed a professional voice, that they are fond of the professional version.

§6.4 Overcoming Writer's Block

Suppose you sit down to write your first draft, and nothing happens. You stare at the computer screen, and it seems to stare right back at you. This does *not* mean you're an inadequate writer. Writer's block happens to everybody from time to time, even to the very best writers. What can you do to overcome it? Here are some strategies:

Do something unrelated for a while. Prepare for class, do the dishes, or jog. While you're doing that, your unconscious mind will continue to work on the first draft. After a while, ideas will pop unexpectedly into your conscious mind, and you can sit down and start writing again. But be careful. In law, you're usually writing against a deadline, and doing something else shouldn't go on for too long.

If writing the document's beginning is blocking you, start somewhere else. The reader starts at the beginning, but you don't have to. The beginning of a document is often the hardest part to write. And within each part of the document, the first paragraph is often the hardest to write. One of the reasons is that if you aren't sure exactly what you are going to say, you won't know how to introduce it. Sometimes beginnings turn out to be better in quality — as well as easier to write — if you write them later.

If you're not going to start writing at the beginning, where should you start? Look over your outline. Does something in the outline reach out to you because what you want to say about it is already forming in words in your mind? Even if it's a tiny part of your third issue, write it now. Later, you can go back and write the other issues. Some people write many small passages and then stitch them together to create the whole document.

If a beginning already exists in your mind and wants to be written, go ahead and write it. But if you're blocked, work on something else until the beginning comes to you.

Use writing to reduce your fear.   The most effective way to reduce anxiety is to start writing early — long before your deadline — and to keep working steadily until you're finished. If you start early, you'll lose less sleep and be a happier writer. Many students procrastinate because they worry about writing. But procrastination *increases* anxiety and puts you farther and farther behind. The only way to break this cycle is to start writing so you can bring the task under control.

Don't expect perfection in first drafts.   If you're chronically blocked when you try to do first drafts, it might be because you expect yourself to produce, in one draft, a polished final version. That's expecting too much. Even well-known novelists can't do it. Really bad first drafts are just fine. See §5.6, especially the Anne Lamott quote at the beginning of that section. Keep reminding yourself that the first draft is the *least* important part of writing. You can afford to write horribly in the first draft because you can fix everything during rewriting (§5.7).

Start writing while researching and analyzing.   While you're reading a case, some words of what you'd like to say might flash through your mind. Type them or write them down. As you do, sentences might start coming to you. You sat down to research and analyze, but now you're writing. When you run out of steam while writing, go back to researching and analyzing. Reading, thinking, and writing are all part of a single process. To read is to trigger thinking, which can trigger writing. It doesn't matter that you're writing without consulting your outline. You can figure out later where in the document what you're writing goes, or whether it goes in at all.

Separate yourself physically from distractions.   If you're distracted by roommates or by the temptation to watch television or play computer games, leave the distractions in one place while you work in another.

§6.5 Plagiarism

Plagiarism is using other people's words or ideas as though they are your own. You commit plagiarism if you lift words or an idea from *anywhere* else and put them into your own work without quotation marks (to avoid word plagiarism) and a citation (to avoid idea plagiarism or word plagiarism). Your law school or your teacher might have a policy or guidelines to help you avoid plagiarism, and all teachers punish plagiarism in one way or another.

You already know the ethical and moral reasons not to plagiarize. You heard them in college and earlier. Here are three more reasons:

First, you'll feel better about yourself if you don't steal words or ideas from someone else. You'll have professional self-respect and pride in your own work only if you did the work yourself. And pride in your own work is one of life's pleasures.

Second, a teacher can easily catch plagiarism. You should assume you'll be caught and punished. A teacher can take some of your words and search for them in any legal research database to find the case or article from which they were taken. Many teachers routinely do that. Teachers can also electronically search other students' papers for words like yours. A teacher who designed the assignment and grades the other students' papers knows where all the ideas came from. Even if you copy the detailed structure of your paper from another student, that can be plagiarism, and a teacher who grades both papers will notice it.

Third, legal writing gains value from appropriate citation to the sources of words and ideas. Much of what you write will have credibility only if you show exactly where words and ideas come from. Proper attribution of ideas will allow your reader to rely on your work and to give you credit for ideas that are truly yours.

§6.6 Professional Tone

A professional gets results for a client by acting on good judgment appropriate to the situation.

Degrees of formality. Writing tone is similar to speaking tone, with different levels of formality depending on the audience. Documents filed in a court, such as motion memos and briefs, are probably more formal than anything you wrote before law school. Client letters and emails to supervisors can be somewhat informal but not chatty. Office memoranda are somewhere in the middle, although the degree of formality can differ from firm to firm.

No contractions in formal documents. A choice related to tone is whether to use contractions (combining two words with an apostrophe). We use contractions in this book because our audience is you, and students tend to be comfortable with contractions. Clients, too, are comfortable with contractions, which you can use in a client letter. Few supervisors would object to contractions in professional email.

But never use a contraction in a document filed in court. Some firms will not allow contractions in office memos. Unless you are confident that contractions are considered acceptable by your audience, do not use them.

§6.7   For *All* Writers — Even the Famous Ones — Writing Is Very Hard Work

Writing is easy. You just sit at a typewriter until blood appears on your forehead.

— *Red Smith*

It's not *that* hard. But at times it can feel that way. If you know the sensation Smith described, it doesn't mean that you're a bad writer. Red Smith was the leading sports journalist of his time. Every day, millions of people opened their newspapers to read what he had written the night before. Obviously, he wasn't a bad writer — but still he knew that feeling. So has nearly everybody else whose writing you've ever enjoyed reading.

Learning a skill at a higher level of proficiency, with new requirements, can make you feel that the competency you thought you had before has been taken away from you. Most students feel at least some of that while learning to write at a professional level. Doubt is sharpest near the beginning. But gradually — very gradually — it's replaced with a feeling of *strength*. By the end of law school instruction in writing, many students feel like much stronger writers than before because they've *become* stronger.

For now, please remember this: If in the weeks ahead you fall into doubt about your writing abilities, it'll be because you're learning a lot very quickly. *It doesn't necessarily mean you're a bad writer.* You might be learning to be a good writer. Once you absorb what you're learning and start producing professional writing — and that will happen — your prior confidence will return and be stronger than before because you'll now be reaching for mastery.

Many law students and young lawyers report that while learning legal writing they felt discouraged but later experienced a first moment of validation. That moment might have come when a legal writing teacher told them that they had done something really well. Or it might have come in a summer or part-time job, when a supervising lawyer complimented them on a well-written memo. Or it might have come in court when a judge leaned over the bench and said, "It was a pleasure to read your brief, counselor." That first moment of validation was the beginning of the recognition of *mastery*. Mastery was not yet complete. That would take much longer. But it had begun.

Many students and young lawyers also say that they wish they had realized while they were working so hard in a legal writing course that a moment marking the beginning of mastery could eventually arrive. For most students, even for many who feel deeply discouraged along the way, that moment can come.

§6.8 Don't Imitate Older Judicial Writing, Even If You Find It in Casebooks

Avoid the temptation to imitate unquestioningly whatever you happen to find in judicial opinions that appear in your casebooks. Those opinions are in casebooks for what they tell you about the law — *not* for what they tell you about how to write.

In the last few decades, lawyers and judges have changed the way they look at writing. Verbosity, obscurity, arcaneness, and disorganization that were tolerated a generation ago are now viewed as unacceptable because they make the reader's job harder and sometimes impossible. Before you imitate something you've seen in an opinion, ask yourself whether you want to do it because it will actually accomplish your purpose or because you feel safer doing what a judge has done. The latter is not a sound basis for a professional decision.

To get an idea of how things have changed since many of the opinions in your casebooks were written, read the opening paragraphs below from two decisions interpreting the same statute — 18 U.S.C. § 1708, which penalizes stealing "from or out of any mail, post office, or station thereof, letter box, mail receptacle, or any mail route or other authorized depository for mail matter, or from a letter or mail carrier." One opinion is written in a style that was once common, while the other has the clarity and forthrightness that supervisors and judges will expect of you.

UNITED STATES v. ASKEY
108 F. Supp. 408 (S.D. Tex. 1952)

Counts 1 and 2 of the indictment charged defendant with violating 18 U.S.C. § 1708. Counts 3 and 4 charged violation of 18 U.S.C. § 495. The court sustained a motion to dismiss Count 2 and submitted the remaining counts to a jury which found defendant guilty as charged. The court had carried defendant's motion for judgment of acquittal on Count 1 along with the case. After receiving the verdict, the court announced that the verdict would be set aside as to Count 1.

. . . There is no allegation that the letter, from which defendant abstracted the Treasury check, was a mailed letter or one which

UNITED STATES v. PALMER
864 F.2d 524 (7th Cir. 1988)

About a month after settling into a house, Mildred Palmer found in her mailbox three envelopes addressed to Clifton Powell, Jr., the former occupant. Instead of returning the envelopes to the Postal Service, Palmer opened them. She found three checks (technically, warrants on Illinois's treasury) — no surprise, for the envelopes in which Illinois mails checks are distinctive. The district court described what happened next:

Richard Morrison was present when Palmer brought the mail into the house and knew she had

had been removed from some office, station, letter box, receptacle or authorized depository. The language . . . from the statute prohibits the abstracting or removing from "such letter," clearly referring back to the first part of the statute, dealing with letters in the mails, or taken from some post office, receptacle or depository. In other words, it would be no offense to remove the contents of a letter never deposited for mailing or transmitted through the mails. . . .

received the state warrants. Palmer and Morrison discussed negotiating the warrants and getting the proceeds. Someone endorsed Clifton Powell, Jr.'s name without his authority on the reverse side of each warrant. The warrants were then delivered by Morrison to a man named Lawrence Armour, Sr. Armour had something which neither Palmer nor Morrison had: a bank account. For a fee Armour negotiated the three state warrants through his bank account and returned the balance of the proceeds to Morrison who shared them with Palmer.

. . . We must decide whether converting the contents of an envelope violates § 1708 when the envelope was delivered to an outdated address . . .

Which opinion would you rather finish reading?

GENERAL
ANALYTICAL
SKILLS

7 Selecting Authority

§7.1 Why Authority Matters

You're in a courtroom, hoping to persuade a judge to dismiss criminal charges against your client. After the client was arrested, police held him in an interrogation room from 1:00 A.M. until 10:00 A.M. They refused to let him sleep or visit a restroom, and they refused to supply breakfast. Finally, after nine hours of this, he signed a confession. You want the confession thrown out as coerced, and you want the charges dismissed because the only evidence against him is the confession itself.

Standing before the judge, you say, "Depriving a person, for an extended period, of opportunities to fulfill necessary bodily functions is coercion, and any resulting confession is inadmissible evidence." That sounds like a rule of law with elements (Chapters 2 and 4).

The judge doesn't know for certain that what you said is law. And even if something like it is law, the judge doesn't know whether what you said is *accurate* law — whether you stated the rule exactly or whether it's actually a little different from what you said. For example, is the law's time element as flexible as you stated it ("an extended period"), or is it an inflexible bright-line test ("more than ten hours")? You might win if the test is flexible. Nine hours seems like an extended time under the circumstances (sleep, restroom, breakfast). But if the test turns out to be "more than ten hours," you will definitely lose because your client was held for nine hours.

"What's your authority for that, counselor?" asks the judge. She expects you to prove that the rule exists and that you have stated it accurately. If you can't prove that, you'll lose. She asked for authority because authority is the only way to prove the law.

If the rule is judge-made law, the authority would be judicial precedents that created the rule together with precedents that have enforced it. While enforcing a rule, courts often refine it by working out details about the rule's meaning. If a legislature created the rule, the authority would be a statute and as well as cases that have interpreted the statute. Other types of authority include constitutions, court rules, administrative regulations, restatements, scholarly law review articles, and respected treatises.

Although coerced confessions are forbidden in a general sense by the U.S. Constitution's Fifth Amendment,[1] the specific rules on coerced confessions are in the thousands of precedents[2] interpreting the Fifth Amendment. When you answer the judge's question, you must identify the most important and relevant of them and explain why they support your position.

Of those thousands of precedents, which are the *most* authoritative? How can you identify the very few — perhaps a dozen — that are most likely to influence the judge's decision?

This chapter explains how to choose authority. Before reading the rest of this chapter, however, return to Chapter 1 and review §1.3 (Where Law Comes From) and §1.4 (The Common Law).

§7.2   How Courts Are Organized

Because the United States has a federal system of government, we have two types of court structures — state and federal. Each state has its own courts, enforcing that state's law. And the federal government has courts throughout the country, enforcing federal law. The U.S. Constitution allocates limited responsibilities to the federal government and reserves the rest to the states. As a result, state courts adjudicate a much wider range of claims than federal courts. State courts, in fact, decide the overwhelming majority of cases.

Courts are either trial or appellate. A lawsuit starts in a trial court, which hears witness testimony and examines other evidence. After the trial court decides the case, the losing party can appeal to an appellate court, asking it to reverse the trial court's decision. Some states have only one appellate court. In those states, all appeals from trial courts go straight to the state's supreme court. The federal government and most states have two appellate levels. An appeal from a trial court goes to an intermediate appellate court. From there an appeal goes to the highest court.

---

1. "No person . . . shall be compelled in any criminal case to be a witness against himself . . . ."
2. A Westlaw search for "coerced confession" produces almost 6,000 precedents.

trial ct. → general jurisdiction

§7.2.1   State Courts

Every state has a trial court of *general jurisdiction*, which tries all cases
except those that fall within the *limited jurisdiction* of a specialized trial court.
Court names differ from state to state. In most states the general jurisdiction trial court is called the Circuit Court, the Superior Court, or the Court
of Common Pleas. Among the specialized courts might be a Family Court, a
Juvenile Court, a Small Claims Court, and others.

In some states, such as Pennsylvania and Maryland, the intermediate appellate court hears appeals from every part of the state. In others, such as California, New York, and Florida, the intermediate appellate court is divided
geographically into districts, departments, or the equivalent.   *divisions*

Court names aren't consistent from state to state. In California and many
other states, the Superior Court is the general jurisdiction trial court. But in
Pennsylvania the Superior Court is the intermediate appellate court. In many
states, the intermediate appellate court is called the Court of Appeals or a
name close to that. But in Maryland and New York, the Court of Appeals is
the highest state court. In most states, the highest state court is called the
Supreme Court. But In New York, the Supreme Court is a general jurisdiction
trial court.   *different names in each state — not uniform*

§7.2.2   Federal Courts

The federal court system is organized around a general trial court (the U.S. *diff.*
District Court), a few specialized courts (such as the Tax Court), an interme-   *courts*
diate appellate court (the Court of Appeals), and the final appellate court (the
U.S. Supreme Court).

The U.S. District Courts are organized into 94 districts. Where a state has
only one district, the court is referred to, for example, as the U.S. District Court
for the District of Montana. Some states have more than one district court.
California has four: the District Court for the Northern District of California
(at San Francisco), the Eastern District (at Sacramento), the Central District
(at Los Angeles), and the Southern District (at San Diego).   *4 districts*

The U.S. Courts of Appeals are organized into thirteen circuits. Eleven
of the circuits include various combinations of states. The Fifth Circuit, for
example, hears appeals from the district courts in Louisiana, Mississippi, and
Texas. There's also a U.S. Court of Appeals for the District of Columbia and
another for the Federal Circuit, which hears appeals from certain specialized
lower tribunals.

The U.S. Supreme Court hears appeals from the U.S. Courts of Appeals. It
also hears appeals from the highest state courts where the state court's decision has been based on federal law. But the U.S. Supreme Court's jurisdiction
is discretionary. In almost all other appellate courts, the losing party below
has a right to appellate review — a right to have to the appellate court decide

whether the lower court's decision should be reversed. The U.S. Supreme Court, however, has discretion to choose which appeals it will hear, and it chooses to hear very few.

§7.3   Types of Authority

Authority is either primary or secondary. You'll be able to follow this discussion more easily if you visualize it this way:

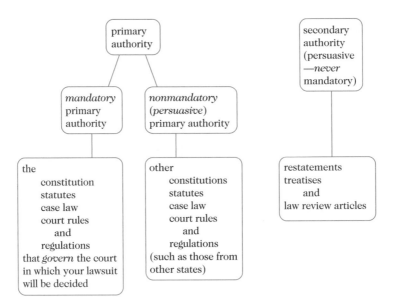

§7.3.1   Primary Authority

Primary authority includes precedent, statutes, constitutions, administrative regulations, and court rules such as the Federal Rules of Civil Procedure. Primary authority is created by legislatures, courts, and other governmental entities that have the *power to make* law. Primary authority is either mandatory or persuasive.

Mandatory authority—which must be obeyed—is primary authority that has been created by *the government whose law controls the outcome of the dispute you are working on.* For example, in a tort case being litigated in an Ohio trial court under Ohio law, mandatory authority would include relevant Ohio statutes and appellate court decisions (and, rarely, the state constitution). *Mandatory authority* and *binding authority* mean the same thing.

Nonmandatory primary authority is primary authority that your court is not required to obey. It might persuade your court even if the court isn't required to follow it. *Nonmandatory authority* and *persuasive authority* mean the same thing. Nonmandatory precedent is precedent from courts that cannot govern the dispute you are working on. If you represent a client litigating a question of Ohio law, a decision by an Indiana state court on Indiana law is primary authority. But in Ohio it is nonmandatory primary authority. Indiana courts can't create Ohio law.

How can you separate mandatory precedent from nonmandatory precedent? Look at the situation from the perspective of the judge who will rule on the dispute you are working on. Courts to which a losing party can appeal are courts that can reverse the judge's decision. Precedent from those courts is mandatory authority because, if the judge doesn't obey it, the judge's decision will be reversed. The Ohio Supreme Court can reverse other Ohio courts, either directly or indirectly. But the Indiana Supreme Court has no power to reverse an Ohio trial court.

A state's supreme court binds all lower courts in that state. A state's intermediate appellate court binds trial courts under its jurisdiction. If the state has a state-wide intermediate appellate court like the Pennsylvania Superior Court (see §7.2.1), its precedents are mandatory authority in all the state's trial courts because the Superior Court can reverse any of their decisions. If the state has a geographically segmented intermediate appellate court (again see §7.2.1), each part of that court can reverse trial courts only in its part of the state.

In federal courts, the U.S. Courts of Appeals are *coordinate* courts in relation to each other (see §7.2.2). Looking at the country as a whole, one circuit's Court of Appeals has the same rank as every other circuit's Court of Appeals. The Courts of Appeals do not bind each other. In fact, federal law can differ from one circuit to another. For example, the Second and Fifth Circuits have different tests for preliminary injunctions.

Arizona is part of the Ninth Circuit. The Ninth Circuit Court of Appeals can reverse decisions made by a U.S. District Court judge located in Arizona. Thus the Ninth Circuit Court of Appeals' decisions are mandatory authority in Arizona. They are not mandatory in New Mexico, which is in the Tenth Circuit. But if the Tenth Circuit has no precedent on a given issue, the Ninth Circuit's decisions might help a New Mexico federal court to fill the gap (see §7.5).

§7.3.2 Secondary Authority

Secondary authority is not law. It describes the law or explains it. Secondary authority might be persuasive authority, but it is never mandatory.

Secondary authority is produced by people or organizations that might by experts about the law but have no power to create it. The secondary sources most likely to be used as authority are restatements, treatises written by scholars, and articles and similar material published in law reviews. Other types exist, but these three are the ones you are most likely to encounter in the first year of law school.

A restatement is a series of black-letter common law rules organized into sections with supplemental drafters' comments. Restatements are commissioned by the American Law Institute to formulate a consensus view of (restate) the common law. Restatements have an important role in first-year Torts, Contracts, and Property courses, as well as several second- and third-year courses. When a restatement is no longer up-to-date, it is superseded by a second or third version. Thus, the Restatement (Third) of Property replaced the Restatement (Second) of Property.

The authoritativeness of a treatise depends on the reputation of its author and on whether the treatise has been kept up-to-date. Some of the outstanding treatises have been written by Wigmore (evidence), Corbin (contracts), Williston (contracts), and Prosser and Keeton (torts). Some treatises are multivolume works; some are in a single volume; some are hardbound with pocket parts or other annual supplements; and some are in looseleaf binders for easier updating.

Law reviews print two kinds of material: articles, which are written by scholars, judges, and practitioners, and notes and comments, which are written by students. If an article is thorough, insightful, or authored by a respected scholar, it may influence a court and might be strong authority. Only in the most unusual of circumstances does a student note or comment influence a court. But even where law review material will not be influential, it might help you analyze an issue, and its footnotes can help you find cases, statutes, and other authority.

§7.4   The Hierarchy of Authority

Sources of law, both primary and secondary, are ranked so that one can be chosen over another. The following are some of the basic rules for ranking authority:

Mandatory authority always outranks nonmandatory authority. On questions of Ohio law, for example, Ohio statutes and Ohio Supreme Court precedents outrank Indiana precedents as well as restatements, treatises, and law review articles.

Within the same jurisdiction, the separation and allocation of powers causes some mandatory authority to outrank other mandatory authority. A constitution prevails over an inconsistent statute. Either a constitution or a statute prevails over inconsistent case law, court rules, and administrative regulations.

This is basic civics. Constitutions create governments. A legislature, a court, or an administrative agency has only the powers granted by the applicable constitution. Although a state's courts can make common law, the legislature

[handwritten: statues → common law]

has a superior power to create law in statutes, and statutes outrank the common law.

Within the same jurisdiction, a decision from a higher court outranks a decision from a lower court—if the higher court has the power to reverse the lower court. See §7.3.1.

Within the same jurisdiction, newer mandatory authority outranks inconsistent older mandatory authority. An Ohio statute enacted last year outranks an Ohio statute fifteen years ago if the two statutes are inconsistent with each other. The newer statute also outranks precedent interpreting the older statute.

If the Ohio Supreme Court overrules one of its own precedents—or if it decides a case in a way that's in somehow inconsistent with one of its own precedents—the new precedent outranks older one.

Some secondary authority is more persuasive than other secondary authority. When secondary authority matters, many courts are most likely to be influenced by a restatement. You can find out whether a state's courts defer to a particular restatement by checking the manner and frequency with which the restatement is cited in the state's decisions. After restatements, the most influential secondary authority will usually be treatises. After treatises will be law review articles if they are thorough and written by scholars with recognized expertise.

[handwritten: treatises]

§7.5 How to Use Nonmandatory Precedent and Secondary Authority to Fill a Gap in Local Law

A gap can exist when your jurisdiction's case law doesn't have all the legal rules needed to resolve your case. Your court must decide whether to fill that gap and, if it does so, which rule to adopt. Nonmandatory precedent and secondary authority might help your court make those decisions. But be careful. Some gaps can be filled only by a legislature. Sections 1.3 and 1.4 in Chapter 1 explain the difference between court-made common law and law made by legislatures. In addition, §7.1 in this chapter includes a constitutional issue where nearly all the rules have been created through precedent. If an issue is normally reserved to legislatures, your court won't be able to create basic rules filling a gap. That's the legislature's job.

Another type of gap occurs when your jurisdiction has a rule—whether court-made or statutory—but it isn't clear how that rule should be applied to facts like yours. Nonmandatory precedent and secondary authority might help a court decide how to apply the rule. But nonmandatory authority can help only if it comes from a jurisdiction that has the same basic rule your jurisdiction has. If the other jurisdiction's courts enforce a different rule, those precedents won't help your court help your court decide how to enforce your jurisdiction's rule.

Fill a gap in two steps. Begin by laying a foundation that explains the gap. Then use nonmandatory precedent or secondary authority to fill it.

§7.5.1 Laying the Foundation

Define the gap and specify how local law doesn't resolve the issue. Local law means the law governing your dispute. For example, Ohio tort law is local law if the dispute concerns an auto accident in Ohio.

A deep gap can occur where the issue is one of *first impression* in local law. That means that local appellate courts have never before resolved it. If some local courts have ruled, the issue is no longer one of first impression, but a gap would still exist if the rulings are from lower courts and the jurisdiction's highest court has not settled the law. Or local cases might have come close to the issue without directly resolving it. Another kind of gap occurs where the local cases are so old or so poorly reasoned that they no longer represent current public policy.

To lay the foundation, do three things:

1. State the issue precisely,
2. explain what local law has decided, and
3. identify what local law has *not* decided.

The gap is what local law hasn't decided. But to understand the gap, the reader needs to know what local law *has* decided.

The following lays a foundation concisely:

> No appellate court in this state has decided whether the sale of a newly built home implies a warranty of habitability, and the legislature has enacted no statute that would resolve the issue. However, a common law warranty of habitability has been recognized, as a matter of common law, in a growing number of states. . . .

Here, the gap is total: there are no statutes and no case law.

Things usually aren't that clear cut. A few local cases might have nibbled around the edges of the issue without actually resolving it. Or some cases might have set out relevant public policy while resolving other issues — but not your issue. In situations like these, the foundation isn't complete until you have explained, in as much detail as the reader would need to agree with you, why the issue is still open.

> No reported decision has determined whether a violation of § 432 *[a local statute]* is negligence per se. But Colorado and Arizona *[neighboring states with similar conditions]* have enacted similar statutes. *[Here, you should add an*

explanation of those statutes sufficient to convince the reader that they really are similar.] Courts in those states have held . . . .

Here we have a statute, but the courts have not yet decided a certain aspect of its meaning (whether a violation is negligence per se). The foundation won't be complete until you have shown that the Colorado and Arizona statutes are so similar that they should be interpreted the same way.

The Second District Court of Appeal has permitted this type of jury instruction. But the Fourth District considers it reversible error because it confuses juries. *[Here, add explanations of the Second and Fourth District cases and show they come to opposite results.]* It is also reversible error in federal courts and in most other states that have considered the issue . . . .

Here you have in-state cases, but they disagree with each other. To complete this foundation — and before discussing the out-of-state authority — the Second and Fourth District cases would have to be explained.

The following is not a foundation:

Kansas *[the decisional state]* has not addressed this issue.

The reader hasn't been told what Kansas *has* done. Are there no analogous precedents? If not, say so. Is there nothing in Kansas law that would set out local public policy on the question? If not, say so. The reader needs to know exactly what the gap is and how deep it is.

Don't lecture the reader on basic principles of the hierarchy of authority ("since there are no reported decisions in this state on this issue, it is necessary to look to the law of other jurisdictions"). The reader long ago learned that that is the standard method for filling gaps.

§7.5.2 Filling the Gap

Once you've laid the foundation, explain the nonmandatory precedent or secondary authority or both. Show exactly how and why that authority provides good guidance.

If you're using nonmandatory precedent, choose it in approximately this order of priority:

First, did the nonmandatory precedent decide the same issue that arises in your client's case? Go back to the confession case you were arguing at the beginning of this chapter. Your issue is whether depriving a person, for an extended period, of opportunities to fulfill necessary bodily functions constitutes coercion. An entirely different issue is whether threats of violence are coercion. Because threats-of-violence precedents decide a different issue, they are barely relevant to your case and might not be relevant at all.

Second, was the nonmandatory precedent decided on facts similar or analogous to your client's facts? If the facts aren't analogous, the nonmandatory precedent is distinguishable. Chapter 9 explains why.

Third, how good is the nonmandatory precedent's reasoning? Is the logic sound? Did the court explore the issue thoroughly? Or did it just state its conclusion without much explanation?

Fourth, what kind of court decided the issue? Is it the highest court in its jurisdiction? Is it a court that has in the past influenced the courts in your jurisdiction?

Fifth, how has the precedent been treated in other cases and in secondary authority? Have other courts cited it with approval? Or has it been criticized in other courts and in scholarly treatises?

Sixth, when was the precedent was decided? Your court might treat more recent opinions as more authoritative than very old ones, simply because changing social conditions can make a rule obsolete. But don't dismiss an older opinion just because it's old. If the relevant social conditions haven't radically changed, older opinions can still be excellent law. Your casebooks are filled with older opinions that are still widely cited by courts today.

Precedent interpreting statutes in other jurisdictions is treated somewhat differently from precedent interpreting the common law. That's because precedent interpreting statutes is authority only for what *specific* words mean in *specific* statutes. That precedent has no life independent of the words interpreted.

Precedent interpreting a statute from another state can be persuasive authority, but only if the other state's statute is similar to your statute. If the two are identical, precedent from the other state can be particularly persuasive. Two statutes can be virtually identical even if there are minor differences in wording that do not affect the statutes' meaning. But where the substance of the statutes is different, precedent from the other state has more limited value. If the two statutes take radically different approaches to solving the same problem, precedent from the other state usually has little or no value.

If your state's statute is based on a model statute, such as the Uniform Commercial Code, courts can easily see the persuasiveness of precedent interpreting other states' enactments of it. But states often make changes in uniform statutes when enacting them. Be sure that the other state's version of the model statute isn't significantly different from your statute's version.

§7.6   How Courts Use Dicta

A holding is a court's ruling on an issue. A holding creates precedent because later courts must follow it through the doctrine of stare decisis. Reasoning *essential* to a court's holding is part of the precedent.

Dicta are comments in a judicial opinion that are *not* essential to a court's ruling on an issue. Dicta aren't part of courts' holdings and therefore aren't precedent. Often dicta discuss facts that are not before the court. Examples are in the next paragraph. Dicta are only nonmandatory authority and can never be mandatory authority. (Lawyers disagree about whether and when to say *dicta* or *dictum*. The footnote explains why.[3] We take no position on this, and whatever your teacher prefers is correct.)

Decisions include dicta for a variety of reasons. Sometimes dicta adds clarity. A court might want, for example, to make clear what it is *not* deciding: "If the plaintiff had presented evidence of injury to his reputation, he might be entitled to damages." A court might add dicta to justify an apparently harsh decision: "Although these facts might constitute a cause of action for defamation — which the plaintiff did not bring — they do not substantiate the invasion of privacy cause of action asserted in the complaint, which we dismiss." Or a court might use dicta to suggest something to a lower court for action on remand: "Although the parties have not raised on appeal the question of appropriate damages, that issue is likely to arise in the new trial we have ordered, and we point out that . . .").

Because dicta doesn't create precedent, lawyers rely on dicta sparingly. But on occasion they do rely on it. If the court that wrote dicta can reverse the court in which your case is being or could be litigated, the dicta, though not mandatory, becomes especially influential.

It isn't wrong to use dicta. But it is wrong to use it inappropriately. Dicta can never take the place of a holding, and it's wrong to treat dicta as though it could. If you do use dicta, identify it as such. Otherwise a reader might think that what you've written is sloppy or an attempted deception.

§7.7   Nonprecedential Opinions

For a judicial opinion to serve as precedent, a court must designate it for publication in the official case reporter. Sometimes courts issue opinions that they don't intend to be used as precedent. These opinions are called *nonprecedential*, or *unpublished*, because they aren't published in official reporters.

While researching, you might run across these cases, because they're often available through electronic legal research services and court websites. If you

---

3. This disagreement rests on Latin definitions, although few lawyers have studied Latin as a language. In Latin, *dictum* can mean either "word" or "something said" or "statement." See D.P. Simpson, Cassell's New Latin Dictionary 188 (1959). The English word *dictionary*, a book of word definitions, is derived from *dictum*'s "word" meaning. The plural is *dicta* ("words" or "statements"). In legal writing, *dictum* is short for *obiter dictum*, meaning "a statement made in passing" (singular). More often you will see the plural *obiter dicta*, meaning "words said in passing" or "statements made in passing." Because in Latin dictum can mean "statement," it is grammatically correct to use the word *dictum* to refer to a statement that is made by a court in a judicial opinion but is not part of a holding. It is also grammatically correct to use the plural *dicta* to refer to a single judicial statement because it takes more than one word to make a statement.

encounter a case that doesn't have a citation to a print reporter, always check to see whether it's nonprecedential. If the case has only an electronic citation, it's probably non-precedential. If it is nonprecedential, most electronic legal research services also note that at the top of the document. To complicate matters further, since 2001, the federal Courts of Appeals have "published" many of their nonprecedential opinions in a print reporter called the *Federal Appendix*, making "unpublished opinions" a true misnomer. Cases in the *Federal Appendix* are still nonprecedential, however.

Nonprecedential judicial opinions can never be mandatory authority because, by definition, they aren't legal precedent. Thus, even if an opinion comes from the highest court in your jurisdiction, you cannot rely on it or cite it as mandatory in a legal document. But lawyers do read nonprecedential opinions, which can play a role in your legal analysis.

If you're confused about this, you aren't alone. There's no widespread consensus on how and when nonprecedential opinions can be used. Because their status is controversial, you should cite nonprecedential opinions in writing only rarely, and even then with caution. Some courts have rules specifically prohibiting or limiting the use of nonprecedential opinions. If you are considering citing nonprecedential authority in a memo or brief to be filed in a court, check that court's rules first. In a brief you submit to a U.S. Court of Appeals, you can cite federal nonprecedential opinions issued after 2007. But even though citation is allowed, the judges can give the opinion any weight they want. Some might be persuaded by it. Others will ignore it just because of its status as nonprecedential.

Although nonprecedential opinions aren't mandatory authority, they can still be useful as persuasive authority because they do reflect a court's attempt to resolve a legal issue by applying the law to a particular set of facts, which might be similar to yours. And in predictive writing, a nonprecedential opinion might give you some indication of how judges tend to react to the issues and facts you are dealing with. Even if you wouldn't use a nonprecedential opinion in a court document, you might provide it to a supervisor in an inter-office communication, or use it yourself to help you develop your understanding. The best practice is to ask a supervisor whether the office has a policy regarding these opinions.

Exercise
The Hierarchy of Authority

You are working on a case that is now being litigated in the U.S. District Court for the District of Nevada. You have been asked to find out whether a defendant who made and lost a motion to dismiss for insufficient service of process can now subsequently move to dismiss for failure to state a claim on which relief can be granted. (Don't worry about exactly what that means. Just know that Rule 12 of the Federal Rules of Civil Procedure governs motions to dismiss in federal courts.)

You have found the following authority, all of which squarely addresses your issue. Make a preliminary ranking of the authorities solely from the information provided below. California and Nevada are both in the Ninth Circuit.

Catdog v. Amundsen — 4th Circuit, 2008

Great Basin Realty Co. v. Rand — Nevada Supreme Court, 2002

Matthewson's treatise on Federal Courts (published last year)

3 *Wilkes v. Jae Sun Trading Corp.* — 9th Circuit, 1977

2 *Pincus v. McGrath* — United States Supreme Court, 1949

1 Rule 12 of the Federal Rules of Civil Procedure (effective 1938)

Barking Pumpkins Records, Inc. v. Sepulveda — California Supreme Court, 2009

Garibaldi v. City of Boulder — 10th Circuit, 2003

Ott v. Frazier — 7th Circuit, 1931

supreme ct or circuit ct?

 Working with
Statutes

§8.1 Five Tools of Statutory Interpretation

If a statute has been interpreted by a court whose decisions are mandatory authority (Chapter 7), the statute means whatever that court says it means, and lawyers say that the statute's meaning is *settled* law. But often the meaning isn't settled, and you'll use the tools explained in this chapter.

Some statutes have never been interpreted by a mandatory appellate court, but that's unusual. More often, a mandatory appellate court has interpreted part of a statute but not all of it. If, for example, a statute has nine sections, and a mandatory appellate court has interpreted eight of them definitively, the ninth section's meaning is still unsettled law. For that ninth section, you'll need to do what some future court would do — determine meaning using some or all of the following tools for interpreting statutes:

1. the statute's *words*
2. the statute's *context*, which can show what the legislature was trying to accomplish — also known as the policy behind the statute
3. a collection of maxims known as the *canons of statutory construction*
4. *interpretations* of the statute from nonmandatory authority — lower or collateral courts, administrative agencies, and scholars
5. the statute's *legislative history*, which consists of the documents and records created by various parts of the legislature during the course of enactment

Tools for interpreting statutes

At one time, nearly every jurisdiction in the United States strictly followed the plain meaning rule, which permits use of other statutory interpretation tools only if the statute's words are ambiguous. In a strict plain meaning state, you are required to limit yourself to the statute's wording if the words have a "plain meaning," and you are permitted to use the other tools only if the words are ambiguous.

But lawyers and courts use the other tools frequently. First, statutes often are ambiguous. Some statutes are magnets for ambiguity. Second, in a number of states, the courts have modified or abolished the plain meaning rule and now search outside the statute for evidence of intent even where the statutory wording seems clear and unambiguous.

§8.2   The Statute's Words

Courts always begin with the statute's words. Some statutes define their own words. The statutes in Chapter 4 are examples. Sometimes a relatively mundane word is defined, for the purposes of the statute, in a surprising way. And a term may have different meanings in different statutes.

For example, section 6-201 ("Franchises") of the Administrative Code of the City of New York defines "the streets of the city" as

> streets, avenues, highways, boulevards, concourses, driveways, bridges, tunnels, parks, parkways, waterways, docks, bulkheads, wharves, piers, and public grounds or waters within or belonging to the city.

while the same Code's section 16-101(3) ("Department of Sanitation") defines "street" to include any

> street, avenue, road, alley, lane, highway, boulevard, concourse, driveway, culvert and crosswalk, and every class of road, square and place, and all parkways and through vehicular park drives except a road within any park or a wharf, pier, bulkhead, or slip by law committed to the custody, and control of the department of ports and terminals.

Why might a wharf be a "street" in one part of a code but not in another? In section 6-201, the word "street" stands for a place where activity might require getting a franchise from the city. In section 16-101(3), the same word stands for a place for which the Department of Sanitation has the responsibility for cleaning, sweeping, sanding, and removing ice, snow, and garbage. Because the purposes are different, the meaning is different. But the drafters couldn't invent two new words — one for each meaning. They had to use "street" in both places.

[margin handwritten note: Some statutes define their own words]

§8.3 The Statute's Context

Context might reveal policy — what the legislature was trying to accomplish — and a statute is to be interpreted consistently with its policy. Courts will not mechanically apply a statute in a literal way that would undermine the approach the legislature has taken to solving the problem in dispute.

The *statutory* context can include other sections of the same statute, the heading (name) of the section at issue, the statute's title and preamble (if any), and other statutes addressed to the same subject matter. It can also include statements of policy in the statute's preamble and in the preambles of other statutes.

The *social and economic context* might identify the events and conditions that could have motivated the legislature to act. But this would be limited to social and economic conditions that existed at the time of enactment, not later.

§8.4 Canons of Statutory Construction

A canon of statutory construction is a general guideline. Here are some examples:

A statute is to be construed in light of the harm the legislature meant to remedy.

Statutes on the same subject (in Latin, *in pari materia*) are to be construed together.

If two statutory provisions apply, the more specific provision governs over the more general one.

Where possible, statutes are to be construed so that their constitutionality is preserved.

When a statute has been interpreted by courts and the legislature has not later amended the statute, the legislature is presumed to have acquiesced in the court's interpretation.

Words used in a statute are assumed to have the meaning they already have in the law generally. But if the words are not terms of art with special meaning in the law, they are assumed to mean what ordinary dictionaries say they mean.

Penal statutes are to be narrowly construed.

Courts can't know whether legislators have enacted a particular statute with the canons in mind — or even whether legislators have ever heard of the canons of construction. It is also true that canons tend to be inconsistent with one another and that courts may invoke them to justify decisions rather than to help in making decisions.[1] But most canons of construction are useful concepts.

Canons are rules of a sort and must be proved with authority. Originally all canons were judge-made law. Many state legislatures, however, have enacted statutes governing how courts must interpret the state's statutes, and these codify or overrule some of the canons.[2] Unless the legislature has not done that, the authority for a canon is in precedents alone.

§8.5   Interpretations from Nonmandatory Authority

You might find any of the following. None are mandatory authority. Your courts might or might not be persuaded by them.

Interpretations by lower courts or collateral courts. If the interpretive precedent is from a court that cannot reverse the court where your issue would first be litigated, that precedent is not binding but might persuade your court (see Chapter 7).

Interpretations of the statute by administrative agencies charged with enforcing the statute. Courts often defer to a specialized enforcement agency, assuming that an agency that constantly deals with a statute understands it better than judges do. For example, federal courts are strongly influenced by the U.S. Environmental Protection Agency's interpretation of the Clean Air Act.

Comparison with parallel statutes in other jurisdictions. Sometimes states enact similar statutes or even identical ones such as the Uniform Commercial Code. If Iowa's courts have interpreted a certain section of the UCC and Minnesota's courts haven't, the Iowa cases might be persuasive in Minnesota although they wouldn't be binding there.

Interpretations of the statute by scholars who are recognized experts in the field. If a scholar has written books or extensive law review articles about a statute, a court might be persuaded by the scholar's expertise.

§8.6   Legislative History

You might think that the sensible thing would be to ask the legislature what it had in mind when it enacted the statute. The people who enacted it ought to know what the words mean. Actually, as a group they don't.

The collective intent of a legislature, or of any other large group of people, may simply be more a metaphysical idea than something ever provable through evidence. Most state legislatures have between 100 and 200 voting

---

1. Karl N. Llewellyn, *The Common Law Tradition: Deciding Appeals* 521-35 (1960).
2. For example, Kan. Stat. Ann. § 77-109 (1997) and Tex. Gov't Code Ann. tit. 3, subtit. B (2015)

members. Congress has 100 Senators and 435 Representatives. A legislature is just too large to be able to tell you what it — as a group — was thinking in some prior year when it enacted the statute you're interested in.

Legislatures consider such a staggering number of bills that most members aren't likely to have clear memories years later of what they thought a bill meant at the moment they voted for or against it. Many questions of statutory interpretation arise long after enactment, when few of the enacting legislators are still in office or even alive.

The only direct evidence of legislative intent is what legislators or legislative committees said and wrote *while the statute was being drafted and enacted.* This is the statute's legislative history.

Although legislative history would seem to be the most direct evidence of the legislature's purpose, it is sometimes viewed with suspicion. It is often incomplete, especially with state statutes, and, because of the chaotic nature of legislative work, it can be internally inconsistent. Parts of it can contradict other parts. It is also vulnerable to manipulation by legislators who may not share the views of a majority of their colleagues. Most legislators have no more understanding of a bill than they can get from a quick reading of it or — more likely — from reading a short synopsis of it but not the statute itself.

Some portions of the typical legislative history, however, tend to be viewed by the courts as particularly reliable. Written reports from the legislative committees that considered and drafted the statute explain to the legislature as a whole why the statute is needed and what it is meant to accomplish. If a committee report is thorough and well written, it might be the best evidence of legislative intent.

§8.7   An Example of Statutory Interpretation at Work

Below are two decisions during the same criminal case interpreting the National Motor Vehicle Theft Act, enacted by Congress in 1919.

If you want to steal something, you'll have to move it and hide it. You might be especially interested in stealing cars and other motor vehicles because their portability makes your job easier. Their whole purpose is to be moved. And you can move them fast across state lines. You can steal a car in Boston tonight and be in Chicago, five states away, by tomorrow night. The Boston police can't track you down and arrest you in Chicago. But the federal government might. That's why Congress passed the National Motor Vehicle Theft Act.

Does the statute cover aircraft? William McBoyle stole an airplane and flew it to another state. He was convicted of violating the Act and appealed to the U.S. Court of Appeals for the Tenth Circuit, arguing that an airplane isn't a "motor vehicle" under the statute. In the first decision below, the Tenth Circuit ruled against him.

After losing in the Tenth Circuit, McBoyle appealed to the U.S. Supreme Court. In the second decision below, you'll learn whether he won there or lost.

McBOYLE v. UNITED STATES
43 F.2d 273 (10th Cir. 1930)

PHILLIPS, Circuit Judge.

William W. McBoyle was convicted and sentenced for an alleged violation of the National Motor Vehicle Theft Act, section 408, title 18, U.S. Code. The indictment charged that on October 10, 1926, McBoyle caused to be transported in interstate commerce from Ottawa, Ill., to Guymon, Okl., one Waco airplane, . . . which was the property of the United States Aircraft Corporation and which had theretofore been stolen; and that McBoyle then and there knew it had been stolen. . . .

In the movies, when you hear someone say, "They've crossed the state line — call the FBI," this is the kind of statute that creates federal jurisdiction.

[handwritten: stolen airplane]

The primary question is whether an airplane comes within the purview of the National Motor Vehicle Theft Act. This act defines the term "motor vehicle," as follows:

[handwritten: "airplane" w/in the statute?]

> The term "motor vehicle" when used in this section shall include an automobile, automobile truck, automobile wagon, motor cycle, or any other self-propelled vehicle not designed for running on rails.

Counsel for McBoyle contend that the word "vehicle" includes only conveyances that travel on the ground; that an airplane is not a vehicle . . . ; and that, under the doctrine of ejusdem generis, the phrase "any other self-propelled vehicle" cannot be construed to include an airplane.

[handwritten: what "vehicle" includes in this context?]

[In a passage deleted here, the court traces various meanings ascribed to the word "vehicle" in both legal and popular usage, quoting authorities that define a vehicle as an object that travels and carries things or people. One of the definitions specifies that a ship is a vehicle; according to another, a vehicle carries things or people, "especially on land."]

A canon of construction: Where general language follows a list of specific examples, the general language's meaning is limited to the same nature [ejusdem generis] as the specific, unless there are clear indications to the contrary.

The court focuses on the words of the statute and considers the canon of ejusdem generis only long enough to decide that the court's interpretation of the statute would not offend the canon.

Both the derivation and the definition of the word "vehicle" indicate that it is sufficiently broad to include any means or device by which persons or things are carried or transported, and it is not limited to instrumentalities used for traveling on land, although the latter may be the limited or special meaning of the word. We do not think it would be inaccurate to say that a ship or vessel is a vehicle of commerce.

broad enough meaning of "vehicle"

An airplane is self-propelled [and] is designed to carry passengers and freight from place to place. It runs partly on the ground but principally in the air. It furnishes a rapid means for transporation of persons and comparatively light articles of freight and express. It therefore serves the same general purpose as an automobile, automobile truck, or motorcycle. It is of the same general kind or class as the motor vehicles specifically enumerated in the statutory definition and, therefore, construing an airplane to come within the general term, "any other self-propelled vehicle," does not offend against the maxim of ejusdem generis.

" of the same kind"

Furthermore, some meaning must be ascribed to [Congress's use of the] phrase "any other self-propelled vehicle" [immediately after Congress had specifically listed] all of the known self-propelled vehicles designed for running on land. . . .

We conclude that the phrase, "any other self-propelled vehicle," includes an airplane. . . .

Are you convinced by the court's interpretation of the statutory wording?

COTTERAL, Circuit Judge (dissenting). I feel bound to dissent on the ground that the National Motor Vehicle Theft Act should not be construed as relating to the transportation of airplanes.

DISSENT

A prevailing rule is that a penal statute is to be construed strictly against an offender and it must state clearly the persons and acts denounced. [Citations omitted.]

Another *canon of construction*. The dissenter will soon try to link this one up with *ejusdem generis*.

It would have been a simple matter in enacting the statute to insert, as descriptive words, airplanes, aircraft, or flying machines. If they

Now the dissenter takes on the *words of the statute*, but in a way the court did not. The dissenter asks what Congress could have written into the statute but chose not to.

had been in the legislative mind, the language would not have been expressed in such uncertainty as "any other self-propelled vehicle not designed for running on rails." The omission to definitely mention airplanes requires a construction that they were not included. Furthermore, by excepting vehicles running on rails, the meaning of the act is clarified. These words indicate it was meant to be confined to vehicles that *run,* but not on rails, and it did not extend to those that *fly* . . . .

The rule of ejusdem generis has special application to this statute. General words following a particular designation are usually presumed to be restricted so as to include only things or persons of the same kind, class, or nature, unless there is a clear manifestation of a contrary purpose. [Citation omitted.] The general description in this statute refers to vehicles of the same general class as those enumerated. We may assume an airplane is a vehicle, in being a means of transportation. And it has its own motive power. But is an airplane classified generally with "an automobile, automobile truck, automobile wagon, or motor cycle"? Are airplanes regarded as *other types of automobiles* and the like? A moment's reflection demonstrates the contrary.

Counsel for appellant have referred us to debates in Congress when the act was pending as persuasive of an interpretation in his favor. [Citations to the Congressional Record omitted.] . . . The discussions of the proposed measure are enlightening . . . in showing that the theft of automobiles was so prevalent over the land as to call for punitive restraint, but airplanes were never even mentioned.

It is familiar knowledge that the theft of automobiles had then become a public menace, but that airplanes had been rarely stolen if at all, and it is a most uncommon thing even at this date. The prevailing mischief sought to be corrected is an aid in the construction of a statute. [Citation omitted.]

how do we classify airplanes?

The dissenter turns to the *canon* considered in the court's opinion.

Because this question was not addressed in the reports of the committees that drafted the statute, the only relevant *legislative history* is the floor debates. Floor debates are a notoriously unreliable form of legislative history because they can include remarks by legislators who took no part in drafting the statute in committee, who might not have thought much about it, and who may not even have read it. But here the floor debates reveal surprising evidence of legislative intent: no legislator complained about a need to do something about airplane theft.

Finally, the dissenter takes up the *historical context.*

McBOYLE v. UNITED STATES
283 U.S. 25 (1931)

Mr. Justice HOLMES delivered the opinion of the Court. . . . The question is the meaning of the word "vehicle" in the phrase "any other self-propelled vehicle not designed for running on rails." No doubt etymologically it is possible to use the word to signify a conveyance working on land, water or air, and sometimes legislation extends the use in that direction, e.g., land and air, water being separately provided for, in the Tariff Act [of] 1922 [citation omitted]. But in everyday speech "vehicle" calls up the picture of a thing moving on land. Thus in Rev. Stats. § 4, intended, the Government suggests, rather to enlarge than to restrict the definition, vehicle includes every contrivance capable of being used "as a means of transportation on land." And this is repeated, expressly excluding aircraft, in the Tariff Act [of] 1930 [citation omitted]. So here, the phrase under discussion calls up the popular picture. For after including automobile truck, automobile wagon and motor cycle, the words "any other self-propelled vehicle not designed for running on rails" still indicate that a vehicle in the popular sense, that is a vehicle running on land, is the theme. It is a vehicle that runs, not something, not commonly called a vehicle, that flies. Airplanes were well known in 1919, when this statute was passed; but it is admitted that they were not mentioned in the reports or in the debates in Congress. It is impossible to read words that so carefully enumerate the different forms of motor vehicles and have no reference of any kind to aircraft, as including airplanes under a term that usage more and more confines to a different class. The counsel for the petitioner have shown that the phraseology of the statute as to motor vehicles follows that of earlier statutes of Connecticut, Delaware, Ohio,

While dissecting the words of the statute, *Holmes considers the* statutory context.

Historical context and *legislative history* are considered together.

Again, Holmes simultaneously uses two tools—this time *legislative history* and *comparison with parallel statutes.* The point is that Congress seems to have modelled the Act on statutes that clearly do not address aircraft theft. The most telling comparison—and perhaps the most enjoyable for its irony—is with a *city's* traffic regulations, which certainly could not have been meant to penalize the stealing of airplanes.

Michigan and Missouri, not to mention the late Regulations of Traffic for the District of Columbia [citation omitted], none of which can be supposed to leave the earth.

. . . When a rule of conduct is laid down in words that evoke in the common mind only the picture of vehicles moving on land, the statute should not be extended to aircraft, simply because it may seem to us that a similar policy applies, or even upon the speculation that, if the legislature had thought of it, very likely broader words would have been used. [Citation omitted.]

Judgment reversed.

As important as *policy* is, it also has its limitations. Here Holmes notes that his court is permitted to construe the statute only to accomplish the goal Congress had selected for it—and not some other goal the court might think equally valid.

---

amended statute

Unhappy with the Supreme Court's decision, Congress amended the statute so that it now punishes anyone who

transports in interstate or foreign commerce a motor vehicle, vessel, *or aircraft,* knowing the same to have been stolen.[3]

Congress later added a definition of "aircraft" so the statute could adapt to changing technology:

"Aircraft" means any contrivance now known *or hereafter invented, used, or designed* for navigation of or for flight in the air.[4]

That definition was added when airplanes were still powered by piston engines and propellers rather than by jet engines.

Would the statute today penalize knowingly moving a stolen interplanetary rocket across a state line? Look carefully the definition quoted above. To get to Mars, the rocket would have to travel for a few minutes through the atmosphere's air. But for many months afterward, it would travel through a void where there is no air (outer space). Is traveling through air the rocket's purpose or goal — the reason it was created? Its purpose is primarily to travel through outer space, and traveling through air is only incidental to that purpose (months versus minutes). Remember that an airplane travels a short

3. 18 U.S.C. § 2312 (2006) (emphasis added).
4. 18 U.S.C. § 2311 (2006) (emphasis added).

distance on land to become airborne, but the Supreme Court held in *McBoyle* that an airplane is not a motor vehicle.

There's no case law on this. But if you would like to know the answers to all these questions, you could steal an interplanetary rocket, move it across a state line, and appeal your conviction to the Supreme Court. Depending on how the Justices interpret the words "invented . . . for," you might spend many years in prison — or you might walk freely like McBoyle. Whenever a legislature enacts a statute with wording that is less than perfectly clear, we can't know for certain what it means until a court tells us while deciding a case.

§8.8 How to Present Statutory Analysis in Writing

Focus on the words of the statute because the words are what you must interpret. The crucial term or phrase should appear, inside quotation marks, when you state the issue, your conclusion, the rule on which you rely, and the most important steps in your analysis. For example, state the issue like this:

> If regularly scheduled boat service is considered one of the "streets of the city" within the meaning of section 6-201, would the Interborough Repertory Theatre need to get a franchise to offer entertainment on evening cruises using the theater's own boat?

This is a discussion about what "streets of the city" means. Focus on those words and use the tools explained in this chapter.

Because statutes are drafted to govern wide ranges of factual possibilities, a rule expressed entirely in statutory language may need to be reformulated for a specific application.

Consider a bomb-disarming robot capable of moving on its own treads. A police department might own one of these robots. If someone spots a suspicious package on a street corner, the police might clear the area, take cover themselves, and send their robot over to investigate.

Suppose your client stole a robot and took it across a state line. It's a small robot powered by a small internal battery. It can't travel very far, and it can't do anything unless it's in view of the police officer holding the remote control. You're writing a memo predicting whether your client will be convicted under the National Motor Vehicle Theft Act. Is the robot a "motor vehicle"? It's purpose isn't to travel. It's purpose is to disarm bombs. It was built to move under its own power only because no one wants to lift it up, carry it over to the bomb, and put it down. Here's the key sentence from the statute, which you already read in *McBoyle*:

> The term "motor vehicle" when used in this section shall include an automobile, automobile truck, automobile wagon, motor cycle, or any other self-propelled vehicle not designed for running on rails.

Most of this sentence is not helpful. The words "automobile," "automobile truck," "automobile wagon," and "motor cycle" are just examples of "motor vehicles." The issue isn't whether a bomb-disarming robot is one of those things.

What are the elements of the definition for "motor vehicle"? The sentence includes two of them. Something must be "self-propelled," and it must not be "designed for running on rails." In *McBoyle*, the Supreme Court decided that Congress meant to include a third element: something is a motor vehicle only if it operates primarily on land. In your memo, don't quote the entire sentence from the statute. Instead quote the words to be interpreted and write something like this:

> For the purposes of the National Motor Vehicle Theft Act, a "motor vehicle" is an object that is "self-propelled," that operates primarily on land, and that does not run on rails.

You'll have to explain to the reader that two of these elements are in the Act's words, and that the Supreme Court has held that the third element (operates primarily on land) is implied because it's inherent in what Congress did.

Exercise I
Plagiarism and the Board of Bar Examiners

This exercise is in Appendix A.

Exercise II
The Ironwood Tract

This exercise is in Appendix A.

9

Working with Precedent

§9.1 Eight Tools for Working with Precedent

Occasionally, you might have an issue that is entirely resolved by mandatory precedent on point — a case from the highest court in your jurisdiction deciding on facts identical to the ones presented by your client — but that's unusual.

More often the law is uncertain, and you must construct an answer from tangential precedent, using at least some of the following tools:

1. ranking precedent according to the hierarchy of authority and the principles derived from it;
2. formulating rules along a continuum from the broadest to the narrowest arguable from a precedent's facts and wording;
3. synthesizing fragmented authority into a unified whole and reconciling conflicting or adverse authority;
4. determining policy from precedent;
5. analogizing favorable precedent and distinguishing unfavorable precedent; and
6. testing for realism, as a judge might see your analysis.

Chapter 7 explained the first skill — *ranking precedent according to the hierarchy of authority and the principles that are derived from it.* Chapter 3 (§3.2) explained the second skill — *formulating rules along a continuum from the broadest to the narrowest.* This chapter explains the other four skills.

§9.2   Synthesis

If no single mandatory precedent settles the rule and explains how to apply it, you would need to *synthesize* several precedents together to provide a unified understanding of the rule. Synthesis is the process of finding collective meaning—what the cases as a group stand for—even though that meaning can't be found in any one individual case.

It's not a synthesis to describe Case A, describe Case B, describe Case C, and then stop. That's nothing more than an annotated list: The raw materials have been held up to view, but they have not been sewn together. To turn it into a synthesis, ask yourself what the cases really have in common under the surface. Identify the threads that appear in all three cases. Then tie the threads together. And organize the analysis around the threads themselves (rather than around the individual cases).

The reader cares more about the threads than about the cases, and an individual case is important only to the extent that it teaches something about a thread. It may turn out that Case B sets out the most convincing proof of whatever is in question; Cases A and D agree and are the only out-of-state cases to have decided the issue; and Case C is a much older decision standing for the same rule but on reasoning that is less complete than that expressed in Case B. An effective synthesis might explain Case B in full; use Cases A and D to show that foreign authority agrees; and then not use Case C at all (or only if needed to fill in a remaining gap). Make the synthesis clear to the reader. Begin by stating it in an opening sentence that includes the synthesized rule or statement of policy:

> Although the Supreme Court has not ruled on the question, the trend in the Courts of Appeal is to hold that such a prosecution is dismissable where any of four kinds of government misconduct has occurred: . . .

A synthesis like this could take several pages to prove because, typically, no case will consider more than one form of misconduct.

§9.3   Determining Policy from Precedent

Every legal rule has at least one purpose—a goal the rule is meant to accomplish. That purpose is the rule's *policy*. The policy might be to encourage something useful such as home ownership or preventative health care. Or the policy might be to reduce or prevent something harmful such as pollution or highway crashes.

A rule without policy is pointless. It accomplishes nothing useful. "It is revolting," Justice Holmes wrote, "to have no better reason for a rule of law than that so it was laid down in the time of Henry IV. It is still more revolting if the grounds upon which it was laid down have vanished long since, and the rule simply persists from blind imitation of the past."[1]

Once you know a rule's policy, you can argue that when the rule is applied to your facts, the outcome should be consistent with the policy. Sometimes a court will tell you plainly what the policy is. But more often the policy will be implied in the court's reasoning rather than openly stated. What results does the rule generally cause — directly or indirectly? Does the court seem to treat those results as worthwhile? *implied policy*

§9.4 Analogizing and Distinguishing

An *analogy* shows that two situations are so parallel that the reasoning that justified the decision in one should do the same in the other. When a court is persuaded by an analogy to precedent, the court is said to "follow" the precedent. To construct an analogy, do the following: *identical reasoning should be used*

First, be sure that the issue in the precedent is the same one you are trying to resolve. *same issue*

Second, identify the precedent's determinative facts. Don't look for mere coincidences between the precedent and your facts. Instead identify the facts that the court treated as crucial and on which it truly relied. *look at facts true court relied on*

Third, compare the precedent's determinative facts to your facts. If your facts are equivalent to the precedent's facts, you have an analogy. The facts don't need to be identical, but they must be *equivalent*. If one bank robber waved a gun and another waved a knife, the weapons aren't identical, but they are equivalent. They're both deadly weapons. *facts must be equivalent*

Distinguishing is the opposite of analogy. To distinguish a precedent is to show that two situations are so different that they need not be decided the same way. To distinguish a precedent, go through the same three steps as when analogizing, except that in the third step you would show that the facts are fundamentally dissimilar. *same steps, but show how facts are dissimilar*

§9.5 Testing for Realism

The last skill is that of *testing the result of your reasoning for its realism and reasonableness, looking at your analysis the way a judge would.*

Experience on the bench creates what Roscoe Pound called "the trained intuition of the judge"[2] — an instinct for how the law ought to treat each case to do justice to the parties and the situation. If your analysis seems unrealistic to a judge's intuition, the judge will reject what you have done, using the same

---

1. O. W. Holmes, *The Path of the Law,* 10 Harv. L. Rev. 457, 469 (1897).
2. Roscoe Pound, *The Theory of Judicial Decision,* 36 Harv. L. Rev. 940, 951 (1923).

analytical tools explained in this chapter. Karl Llewellyn wrote that "rules *guide*, but they do not *control* decision. There is no precedent that the judge may not at his need either file down to razor thinness or expand into a bludgeon."[3] Because the law is hardly ever certain, a judge can always fold back your reasoning and make other analogies, build other syntheses, and so forth — or, worse, adopt the analogies, syntheses, and other constructs proposed by your adversary.

Step back from what you are doing and ask yourself whether the result will seem reasonable and just to the typical judge. Testing for realism requires that you have some understanding of how the judicial mind operates. That may take a long time to come to know fully, but you are learning some of it now through the decisions you read in casebooks and through the writing you do in this course.

§9.6   An Example of the Precedent Skills at Work

In this example, first we describe the facts as your client has told them to you. Then we provide four precedents. And finally we explain how you can analyze the precedents.

§9.6.1   The Client's Story

Megan and Troy Hartley married 14 years ago when both were sophomores in college. Megan dropped out of school and worked for four years at various jobs as a receptionist, a delivery truck driver, and a cashier. She earned the couple's only income while Troy finished college and earned a masters degree in business finance. They have two children, twins born eight years ago and named Ariel and Jason.

Troy now earns $475,000 a year as an investment banker. Megan has a part-time job as a salesperson in an art gallery and earns, on average, about $35,000 a year. Early in the marriage, Megan asked Troy to work less and spend more time with the children so she could find a full-time job and build a career, but he refused.

For the past two years, Megan and Troy have bickered often, and she cannot stand it when the bickering turns into shouting. On three occasions during those two years, Troy struck her, once on each occasion, in the face, at the end of a shouting match.

A few years ago, Troy bought a German shepherd, which he named Debenture. Although Debenture has never, to Megan's knowledge, bitten anyone, he bares his teeth and growls when Troy shouts, and this makes Megan and the children nervous.

---

3. K. N. Llewellyn, *The Bramble Bush* 180 (1930).

Last Sunday evening, after a weekend of bitter arguing, Troy announced that he had had enough and was leaving. He packed a bag and left.

The art gallery where Megan works laid off half its staff on Monday morning. Megan was able to keep her job, but when she came home from work at six o'clock, she was depressed and worried about whether the gallery would close, throwing her out of work. The children were with Megan's parents.

Troy returned around eight o'clock and told Megan that he had consulted a lawyer and that the lawyer had drafted a separation agreement, which Troy had already signed. The agreement provided that Troy and Megan would live apart, beginning immediately, that they would have joint custody of the children, and that a divorce would be obtained as soon as possible. It provided that Megan get six months of alimony and about ten percent of the value of the couple's property.

Troy put the agreement on the kitchen table and angrily demanded that Megan sign it. Debenture was sitting in the corner, and Megan could see him perk up and become more attentive as Troy's voice became louder.

Troy told Megan that if she did not sign the agreement, he would tell the court that her "artsy friends do drugs in front of Ariel and Jason." Troy added that no one would believe her if she were to deny these accusations because it would be her word against his and he would make a much better witness than she would. Angrily and in a loud voice, Troy said that the court would therefore take the children away from her and give her none of their property. At this point, Troy was pounding the coffee table, and Debenture was on his feet, staring at Megan attentively. She expected Debenture to start growling if Troy began yelling.

Megan signed the agreement and asked Troy to leave immediately and to take Debenture with him. Troy did so. Megan's friends don't "do drugs."

Megan knows nothing about divorce law. At the time she signed the agreement, she had no idea whether Troy's predictions about divorce and the courts were accurate.

She consulted you a few days after signing the agreement. You believe that if there were no valid separation agreement, a court would probably award Megan sole custody of the children, child support, three to five years of alimony, and about fifty percent of the couple's property.

§9.6.2 Four Precedents

Prenuptial agreements and separation agreements are contracts. Duress is grounds for voiding a contract. If a court voids a contract, the contract ceases to exist.

Your state's highest court has decided the following cases.[4]

---

4. The cases are based on *Biliouris v. Biliouris*, 852 N.E.2d 687 (Mass. App. 2006); *Blejski v. Blejski*, 480 S.E.2d 462 (S.C. 1997); *Germantown Manufacturing Co. v. Rawlinson*, 491 A.2d 138 (Pa. Super. 1985); *Hall v. Hall*, 27 N.E.3d 281 (Ind. Ct. App. 2015); *Hamilton v. Hamilton*, 591 A.2d 720 (Pa. Super. 1991); and *Holler v. Holler*, 612 S.E.2d 469 (S.C. 2005).

RASCHI v. RASCHI
(2006)

Mary Raschi argues that her prenuptial agreement with Timothy Raschi is voidable because of duress.

At the time the parties began dating in mid-1991, Timothy was a physician, and Mary was a home economics teacher. Mary had a child by an earlier marriage. In October 1992, Mary learned that she was pregnant with Timothy's child, and shortly afterward she informed Timothy of the pregnancy. He told Mary that he would not marry her unless she signed an prenuptial agreement, which Timothy's lawyer drafted. Mary consulted her own lawyer, who advised her not to sign it.

She signed it anyway in December 1992. At that time, Timothy's assets were worth $986,000, and Mary's assets were worth about $100,000. Timothy's income was $332,800 per year, and Mary's income was $87,100 per year. The agreement provided that the individual property of each party remain the party's sole and exclusive property, and that neither party would have a claim to alimony from the other.

Mary and Timothy's child was born in May 1993. During the marriage, Mary was an unemployed stay-at-home mother and the primary caretaker of both children while Timothy ran his medical practice.

In November 2001, Timothy sued for divorce, asking the trial court to enforce the terms of the prenuptial agreement. Mary argued that she was coerced into signing it due to the circumstances in which she found herself: a pregnant single mother, presented with an agreement shortly before her wedding date and being told that if she did not sign the agreement there would be no wedding.

A person who enters into a contract under the influence of such fear as precludes him from exercising free will and judgment may avoid the contract on the grounds of duress. Coercion sufficient to avoid a contract need not, of course, consist of physical force or threats of it. Social or economic pressure illegally or immorally applied may be sufficient.

Mary's signing the agreement was not the product of coercion or duress. Although the circumstances presented Mary with a difficult choice, those circumstances did not divest Mary of her free will.

QUISENBERRY v. QUISENBERRY
(2015)

Michael Quisenberry argues that a written agreement between him and Susan Quisenberry is voidable because he signed it under duress.

Michael and Susan married in March 2004. A few weeks later, he was arrested for burglary. In September 2004, he was convicted and sentenced to four years' imprisonment. In December 2004, Susan visited him in prison and told him that she intended to divorce him. Michael begged her not to and offered to sign an agreement giving Susan financial protection in they divorced after he was released from prison.

Susan drafted the agreement herself, copying it from form agreements she found online. She mailed it to Michael, and he signed it and mailed it back to her, after which she signed it.

Michael was released in 2008 and returned to live with Susan. The parties separated October 2013. Susan sued for divorce in November 2013 and moved to enforce the agreement. Michael argues that he was under duress because he signed the agreement while incarcerated without access to legal counsel and because Susan threatened to divorce him while he was in prison if he did not sign the agreement.

Duress invalidates a contract if improper external pressure or influence deprived a party of free will so that the party formed the contract involuntarily. Duress does not occur if the victim has a reasonable alternative to succumbing and fails to take advantage of that alternative.

Michael was not under duress when he signed the agreement. The only way to get what he wanted — avoiding a divorce while in prison — was to sign the agreement. But a bargaining disadvantage is not the same thing as duress. He was not deprived of free will.

not deprived of free will

FIDRYCH v. SPRINGFIELD MANUFACTURING CO.
(1985)

Joan Fidrych argues that contractual documents she signed are voidable because she signed them under duress.

Robert Fidrych, her husband, was employed by the Springfield Manufacturing Co. as its assistant controller. He embezzled $327,011 from the company. On May 21, 1982, the company discovered the embezzlement and fired him. Joan testified at trial that when he told her of this, her "whole world fell apart."

On May 25, Peter Kulaski, an employee of the company's insurer, came to the Fidrych's house and spent a half-hour with them. He showed them two judgment notes, which are contractual documents, and demanded that both of the Fidrychs sign both notes. Because she had done nothing wrong, Joan was surprised to see her name on the documents. She asked Kulaski if she and her husband would need an attorney. Kulaski said that if the Fidrychs cooperated, there would be no need for an attorney and Robert would not be prosecuted. Joan signed both notes. *threat of crim prosecution*

A threat to start a criminal prosecution amounts to duress. "Experience indicates that the threat of a well-founded prosecution, likely to result in imprisonment, is usually sufficient to coerce even a brave man." 13 Samuel Williston, Williston on Contracts § 1613 (3d ed. 1970).

Kulaski included Joan's name on the judgment notes but did not tell her that he was doing so until minutes before he asked her to sign them.

Joan had already been in a weakened mental state as the result of a recent miscarriage, and was visibly upset during the meeting, having learned of her husband's embezzlement. At the meeting, she was told that if she cooperated, she would have no need for legal counsel. She understood this to mean that if she signed the notes, her husband would not go to jail. She had no reasonable alternative but to sign. Her signature was thus obtained by duress.

GRANT v. GRANT
(2012)

Alonzo Grant is a U.S. citizen and has always lived in the United States. Ludmila Grant is from Bulgaria. In 2006, the parties met online through social media. They conversed electronically and by phone and on Sept. 5, 2007, Ludmila traveled to the United States to live with Alonzo. Before that date, Ludmila had never been outside Bulgaria. She had almost no money and relied on Alonzo for financial support.

In November 2007, Ludmila became pregnant with Alonzo's child. Her visa would expire on Dec. 4, 2007, and she believed she would have to leave the country unless she married Alonzo. Alonzo showed Ludmila a premarital agreement and said he would marry her only if she signed it. Before signing it, Ludmila attempted to translate it from English into Bulgarian, but was unable to do so because, as she later testified, it "had strange technical language." She made notes while trying to translate, and her notes list words for which she could not find a translation, including "undivided," "equitable," and "pro rata." Ludmila did not hire a lawyer because she had no money to pay for one.

Ludmila signed the agreement on Nov. 25, 2007. The parties were married on December 1, 2007, three days before Ludmila's visa was to expire. The parties separated on Feb. 13, 2010. Ludmila then sued for divorce. Alonzo moved to dismiss her claims for alimony and equitable distribution, claiming they were precluded by the premarital agreement.

The central question with respect to whether a contract was executed under duress is whether, considering all the surrounding circumstances, one party to the transaction was prevented from exercising his free will by threats or the wrongful conduct of another. Whether or not duress exists in a particular case is a question of fact to be determined according to the circumstances of each case, such as the strength or weakness and age and capacity of the party threatened.

Alonzo knew that Ludmila's visa would soon expire, that she was pregnant with his child, and that she relied completely on him for financial support. We hold that Ludmila signed the agreement under duress and that it is voidable.

§9.6.3 Using the Precedent Analysis Tools

Below is a discussion of how the tools in this chapter might be used in the Hartleys' situation. At the end of the chapter is an exercise in which you will bring everything together.

Ranking precedent. Each case was decided by the highest court in your state and is thus mandatory authority. None of these cases expressly overrules another one. And no case is so inconsistent with an earlier one that the earlier case has been impliedly overruled. The cases come to different results, but that is because some of the facts differ and are distinguishable. The cases enforce rules that are either identical or at least consistent (see synthesizing and reconciling below). No case contains dicta.

Formulating rules along a continuum from the broadest to the narrowest interpretations. All the cases enforce a general three-element test for voiding a contract on the ground of duress (see synthesizing and reconciling below). For each case, it's also possible to express instead a narrow version of that rule. For example, *Fidrych* can be cited for the proposition that a contract is voidable for duress if one party threatens another with criminal prosecution.

Synthesizing and reconciling. All the cases expressly state or impliedly use the following three-element test:

A contract is voidable for duress if

1. one party threatened or pressured the other
2. the threat or pressure was *wrongful*
   Raschi: "pressure illegally or immorally applied"
   Quisenberry: "improper external pressure or influence"
   Grant: "by threats or the wrongful conduct"
3. the threatened party was thus *deprived of free will*
   Raschi: "under the influence of such fear as precludes him from exercising free will and judgment"
   Quisenberry: "deprived a party of free will so that the party formed the contract involuntarily"
   Fidrych: the Williston quote, "the threat of a well-founded prosecution, likely to result in imprisonment, is usually sufficient to coerce even a brave man"
   Grant: "prevented from exercising his free will"

Grant expressly holds that this test is to be applied to the circumstances as a whole ("to be determined according to the circumstances of each case, such as the strength or weakness and age and capacity of the party threatened"). The other cases imply the same thing by the way they explain and analyze the facts.

Quisenberry holds that a weak bargaining position — without wrongful threats — does not equal duress ("a bargaining disadvantage is not the same thing as duress" and "Duress does not occur if the victim has a reasonable alternative to succumbing and fails to take advantage of that alternative"). None of the other cases is inconsistent with this.

Determining policy.   None of the cases expressly states a policy, but you can deduce it from each case's reasoning. You already know from the offer-and-acceptance part of your Contracts course that a contract is formed by a free agreement — a meeting of the minds — between the parties.

Usually one party is stronger than the other. Your cell phone company, for example, has a stronger bargaining position than you do. Unequal bargaining shouldn't prevent enforceable contracts. If it did, few contracts would be enforceable. But in an extreme situation the inequality could become unacceptable if the stronger party has turned the weaker party into a victim unable to exercise free will.

Where the problem is created by threats or pressure, the three-element duress test identifies victims in a way that's consistent with the general policies of contract law. The threatening party must have behaved reprehensibly. The cases say "wrongfully," "illegally," "improperly," or "immorally." And the threat must have prevented a true agreement — a genuine meeting of the minds — by depriving the threatened party of free will.

Analogizing and distinguishing.   Three facts occur in all the cases and in Megan's story. First, a party or the party's lawyer drafted a contract. Second, that party demanded that the other party sign it. And third, the other party felt under pressure to sign. Beyond that, there are factual differences, which might be analogous to or distinguishable from your client Megan's story. Here they are:

The threat

Rasch :	Timothy threatened not to marry Mary.
Quisenberry:	Susan threatened to divorce Michael.
Fidrych:	Kulaski threatened to prosecute Joan's husband.
Grant:	Alonzo threatened not to marry Ludmila.

How would you describe the threat Troy made to Megan? Compared to each of the cases, is Troy's threat analogous or distinguishable?

Circumstances in which the threat was delivered

Raschi:	Mary was pregnant with Timothy's child.
Quisenberry:	Michael had just begun serving a four-year prison sentence.
Fidrych:	Kulaski demanded that Joan immediately sign documents that she had never seen before. She was already distraught

because her husband had been fired for committing a crime
and because of a recent miscarriage.

Grant: Ludmila was pregnant with Alonzo's child. She believed
that if he didn't marry her, she would be deported back to
Bulgaria. She had limited knowledge of English. She had
been in the U.S. for only two months and had never before
been outside her home country.

Compare Megan's circumstances with those in each case, as described above.
Are her circumstances analogous or distinguishable?

Economic disparity between the parties

Raschi: Timothy was in a much better position financially, but at
the time Mary signed the agreement, she was capable of
working at a job and supporting herself. *analogous*

Quisenberry: Not an issue.

Fidrych: Not treated as an issue. But the company is obviously in a
better position financially than a fired employee.

Grant: Ludmila "relied completely on [Alonzo] for financial
support."

Compare Megan and Troy's finances with each case. Is their situation analogous or distinguishable?

Opportunity to consult a lawyer

Raschi: "Mary consulted her own lawyer, who advised her not to
sign it."

Quisenberry: The court ignored the fact that Michael was "incarcerated
without access to legal counsel."

Fidrych: Kulaski told Joan that if she and Robert signed the notes,
Robert wouldn't be prosecuted, and they wouldn't need a
lawyer.

Grant: Ludmila had no money to pay a lawyer. She actually tried
diligently to translate the agreement into her native language and failed because of the technical terminology.

Obviously Megan had enough money to consult a lawyer. She hired you shortly
after signing the agreement. But did any pressure attributable to Troy discourage her from consulting with you before signing? If so, was that pressure as bad
as what happened in *Fidrych* and *Grant*?

To help you keep track of all this, you might make a matrix so you can visualize the comparisons and contrasts.

	Threat	Threat Circumstances	Economic Disparity	Opportunity to Consult Lawyer	Case Outcome
Raschi					
Quisenberry					
Fidrych					
Grant					

When you fill in the facts, the patterns become obvious. (If you do this on a computer, set up the page in landscape mode because matrices can be wide.)

Testing for realism. Based on the cases and Megan's story, you might have developed a tentative theory, based on logic, about whether the Hartleys' separation agreement is voidable for duress.

If you litigate this issue, the trial court's decision could be appealed to the same court that decided *Raschi*, *Quisenberry*, *Fidrych*, and *Grant*. Reading four cases from that court should give you some sense for how its judges instinctively feel — on a human level — about duress in family situations. Will those judges be receptive to your tentative theory? Or will they reject it as unrealistic?

Exercise I
Duress

In §9.6.2, is the Hartleys' separation agreement voidable for duress? Why or why not? Explain your reasoning in detail.

Exercise II
Emil Risberg's Diary

This exercise is in Appendix B.

Working with Facts

§10.1 What Is a Fact?

Consider the following statements:

1. *The plaintiff's complaint alleges* that, at a certain time and place, the defendant struck the plaintiff from behind with a stick.
2. At trial, *the plaintiff's principal witness testified* that, at the time and place specified in the complaint, the defendant struck the plaintiff from behind with a stick.
3. At the conclusion of the trial, *the jury found* that, at the time and place specified in the complaint, the defendant struck the plaintiff from behind with a stick.
4. At the time and place specified in the complaint, *the defendant struck the plaintiff from behind with a stick.* FACT
5. At the time and place specified in the complaint, the defendant *brutally* struck the plaintiff from behind with a stick.
6. At the time and place specified in the complaint, the defendant *accidentally* struck the plaintiff from behind with a stick.
7. At the time and place specified in the complaint, the defendant *committed a battery* on the plaintiff.

Which of these statements expresses a fact?

Statement 1 is an allegation of a fact. Statement 2 is evidence offered in proof of the allegation. Statement 3 is a procedural decision that the evidence proves the allegation. Statement 4 is the fact itself.

This sequence is inherent in litigation. Statements 1 through 3 are actually procedural events like those mentioned at the beginning of Chapter 3. The party seeking a remedy first alleges, in a pleading, facts that, if proved, would merit that remedy (Statement 1). At trial, that party submits evidence — testimony (Statement 2), documents, and other tangible evidence — to persuade the fact finder that the allegations are true. If the fact finder, in this case a jury, is persuaded, the allegations are proved (Statement 3) and become facts (Statement 4).

Statement 5 contains the word *brutally*, which is a subjective characterization. Two people might see the same action, both of them disliking it, but they might characterize it differently. One might consider it brutal. The other might consider it bad behavior but not brutal. If you haven't seen the incident yourself, you should wonder whether the word *brutally* accurately summarizes what happened, or whether it instead reflects the value judgments and preferences of the person who has characterized the incident as brutal. A characterization is not a fact. It's only an opinion about a fact.

Statement 6 includes the word *accidentally*. The defendant might have wanted to cause violence, or he might have struck the plaintiff only inadvertently and without any desire to do harm. With both possibilities, an observer might see pretty much the same actions: the stick being raised, the stick being lowered, the collision with the back. The difference between the two possibilities is in what the defendant might have been thinking or feeling when he struck the plaintiff. If you say that the defendant struck the plaintiff "accidentally," you've inferred what the defendant was thinking at the time. That's a factual inference, a conclusion derived from facts. A factual inference isn't a fact. It's the product of reasoning in which a fact is one of the raw materials.

Statement 7 is a conclusion of law and is not a fact at all. Battery is a concept defined by the law, and you can discover whether a battery occurred only by consulting one or more rules of law. A conclusion of law is the result of applying law to facts. A factual inference (Statement 6) is based on purely factual reasoning without applying law to facts. "Accidentally" is a factual inference because no rule of law defines an accident. Battery is a conclusion of law because battery is a tort with elements.

The *nonexistence of a fact* can itself be a fact. For example:

8.   At trial, *no witness has testified* that the defendant struck the plaintiff deliberately or that the plaintiff suffered any physical or psychological injury or even any indignity.

Here, the absence of certain evidence is itself a fact. Consequently, the defendant might be entitled to a directed verdict because some things have not been proved.

At first, you may have difficulties with four fact skills: (1) separating facts from other things; (2) separating determinative facts from other kinds of facts;

(3) building inferences from facts; and (4) purging your analysis of hidden and unsupportable factual assumptions. When you have mastered these skills, you will be able to make reasoned decisions about selecting and using facts. This section has explained the first skill, and the exercise at the end of this chapter develops it further. The remainder of this chapter considers each of the other skills in turn.

§10.2 Identifying Determinative Facts

Facts can be divided into three categories. The first is made up of facts that are essential to a controversy because they will determine the court's decision: if a change in a fact would have caused the court to come to a different decision, that fact is determinative. The second is a category of explanatory facts that, while not determinative, are nevertheless useful because they help make sense out of a situation that would otherwise seem disjointed. The third category includes coincidental facts that have no relevance or usefulness at all: they merely happened. In life's randomness, all three categories of facts occur mixed up together in a disorderly mess. But lawyers have to separate out the determinative facts and treat them as determinative.

You have already started learning how to do that in this and other courses, mostly through the analysis of precedent. When, for example, you're asked to formulate the rule of a case, you've begun to develop the habit of isolating the facts the court considered determinative and then reformulating those facts into a list of generalities that — when they occur together again in the future — will produce the same result that happened in the reported opinion. But when you look at a given litigation through the lens of an opinion, you're looking at it *after* a court has already decided which facts are determinative: you are explicating the text of the opinion to learn what the court thought about the facts. We're concerned here with another skill: looking at the facts at the *beginning* of the case, before they are even put to a court, and *predicting* which the court will consider determinative.

§10.3 Building Inferences from Facts

The main part of intellectual education is . . . learning how to make facts live.

— *Oliver Wendell Holmes*

Let's return for a moment to Welty and Lutz from Chapter 4 (§ 4.3).

One of the elements of burglary is the intent to commit a felony within the dwelling. In the jurisdiction where Welty and Lutz live, that element can be satisfied only if a defendant had that intent at the time that any breaking and entering might have occurred. If the defendant formed the intent for the first time after entering the dwelling, the element isn't satisfied. Assume that Welty broke and entered Lutz's apartment when she opened the door further and walked in. Did she — at the instant she stepped inside — intend to commit a felony there?

Your response may be "Well, let's ask Welty — she's the one who would really know." But things aren't so easy. If you're the prosecutor, you may find that the police have already asked her that question and that she has refused to answer or has given an answer that the police consider self-serving. In fact, you rarely have direct evidence of a person's state of mind. People don't carry electronic signboards on their foreheads on which their thoughts can be read at moments the law considers important. Instead, as the prosecutor you would have to prove Welty's state of mind through the surrounding circumstances — for example, through the things she did or didn't do, as well as the things she knew other people had or hadn't done. Although her state of mind would be easier to determine if she had appeared at Lutz's door with weapons — or, in another situation, with safecracking tools — inferences can be built from circumstances even without such dramatic displays of intent.

Even if you're Welty's defense lawyer and can freely ask her when she formed an intent to hit Lutz, you might not be much better off than the prosecutor. She might tell you something like the following:

> I don't know when I decided to punch him. I had to listen to his loud music on his four-foot concert speakers for two or three hours while I was trying to study for Civil Procedure. At least once or twice during that time, I thought that it might be nice to punch his lights out, but I don't know that I had decided then to do it. When I knocked on his door, I thought, "This guy had better be reasonable, or else" — but at that instant I don't know whether I was committed to punching him. When I pushed the door open and stepped inside, I thought that he might learn a little respect for the rest of us if something very emphatic happened to him — something that might help him remember in the future that other people have needs and that he shouldn't be so self-centered. Even then, I wasn't certain that I was going to do anything except try to reason with him. But when he ordered me out, I decked him. Nobody ever told me that I was supposed to make sure that my thoughts fit into this "state of mind" thing you're telling me about. I have no idea when I "formed an intent" to hit him. I can only tell you what my thoughts were at each step in the story. You're the lawyer. You tell me when I "formed an intent."

Now the problem is something else: a party's thoughts don't mesh nicely with the law's categories of states of mind. Welty's sequence of emotions somehow culminated in an action, but there seems to have been no magical moment at which anger crystallized into a decision that the law might recognize as "intent." A defense lawyer handles this problem in the same way that a prosecutor deals with the absence of direct evidence. Each lawyer will build inferences from the circumstances surrounding Welty's actions. As Welty sees the arguments unfold, she might conclude that the law is doing strange and perhaps arbitrary things in categorizing her thoughts. But the law must have a way of judging states of mind, and it relies heavily on circumstances.

§10.4 Identifying Hidden and Unsupportable Factual Assumptions

David Binder and Paul Bergman have pointed out that, "[i]f in medieval times there was 'trial by combat,' then today we have 'trial by inference.'"[1] Your adversary and the court will mercilessly challenge your inferential streams, looking for weaknesses in the way they were put together. You must purge your analysis of hidden assumptions that won't stand up to scrutiny when exposed. Consider the following:

> Detective Fenton Tracem rushes breathlessly into the office of the local prosecutor, Les Gettem, eager to persuade Les to issue an indictment. Fenton describes the evidence he has uncovered:
>
> Les, we've got a good case for bank robbery against Clyde. The gun the robber used and dropped at the door was originally purchased by Clyde. The owner of A-1 Guns can definitely identify Clyde as the purchaser and the teller can identify the gun. . . . Two days after the robbery Clyde moves out without giving Ness, his landlord, his two neighbors, Capone and Siegel, or the post office his new address. . . .
>
> The detective has disgorged a mass of circumstantial evidence which appears in the aggregate to be quite convincing. The prosecutor cannot, however, be content to rely on this presentation. In order to analyze the probative value of the evidence, Gettem must first expressly articulate the generalization which links each item of evidence to an element.
>
> [E]xpressly articulating generalizations is the key to determining just how strong a piece of evidence is.
>
> Consider, therefore, the generalization the prosecutor might articulate for the first piece of evidence, that the gun used and dropped by the robber was originally purchased by Clyde. The generalization might be something like, "People who have purchased a gun subsequently used in a robbery are more likely to have participated in the robbery than people who have not."[2]

How accurate is this generalization? See what happens when you compare it with either of two other strings of generalizations. Here's the first one: "Robbers don't feel morally compelled to pay for what they acquire. Because guns can be stolen, a robber has no need to pay for a gun." Here's the second

---

1. David A. Binder & Paul Bergman, *Fact Investigation: From Hypothesis to Proof* 82 (1984).
2. *Id.* at 92-93.

string: "Robbers plan their crimes. A robber can foresee the possibility of losing control of a gun during the robbery. A robber can also foresee that a gun legally purchased from a merchant might be traced back to the robber. Clyde is bright enough to have realized this." Both strings seem more believable than "People who have purchased a gun subsequently used in a robbery are more likely to have participated in the robbery than people who have not" — and *either* string might overcome and negate the generalization on which the detective relies.

> In the beginning years of practice, one must force oneself to articulate explicitly the generalizations on which one relies, for it is not a skill practiced in everyday life. In fact, there is a word for people who state the generalizations underlying all inferences they make: bores. But in the privacy of one's office, one should expressly identify the premises on which one relies [because] by articulating the underlying generalization one can consciously consider the question of how strongly it is supported by common experience. . . .
>
> [A]rticulating generalizations . . . may bring to mind potential exceptions. . . . [O]ne method of testing the degree to which common experience uniformly supports a generalization is to add "except when" to a generalization, and see how many reasonable exceptions one can identify. . . .
>
> [For example, consider] a generalization that one might make in Clyde's case: "People who move without leaving a forwarding address are usually trying to avoid detection." By adding "except when," one sees that this generalization is subject to many exceptions and is therefore less likely to be persuasive. People may be trying to avoid detection, except when they simply forget to leave a forwarding address, or except when they do not yet know the permanent address to which they will be moving, or except when they will be moving around for a time and will not have a permanent address.[3]

When you build and test your own inferences, don't commit to paper much of the analysis Binder and Bergman describe. It's thinking reserved for the privacy of your own office.

But things are different when you attack your adversary's inferences. If Clyde becomes your client, you might argue that a directed verdict should be — or, on appeal, should have been — granted because a rational jury would not be able to find guilt beyond a reasonable doubt. In a supporting memorandum or in an appellate brief, you might write, "The evidence that he moved without leaving a forwarding address does not tend to prove guilty flight. It could just as easily prove that he forgot to leave a forwarding address, or that he did not yet know his new permanent address when he moved, or that he would be moving around for a time without a permanent address."

---

3. *Id.* at 93-96.

Exercise
The Menu at the Courthouse Cafe

The following items appear on the menu at the Courthouse Cafe. Decide what is a fact, what is a characterization, and what is a conclusion of fact. (If part of an item is factual and part is not, decide exactly where the fact ends and the non-fact begins.)

Hot, steaming coffee
Healthful oat bran muffins
Pure beef hot dogs
Garden-fresh vegetables
Hand-picked huckleberries
Home-made huckleberry pie
Delicious peanut butter ice cream

ORGANIZING PROOF OF A CONCLUSION OF LAW

11 A Paradigm for Organizing Proof of a Conclusion of Law

§11.1 Why We Need to Organize Proof of a Conclusion of Law

Medwick is a first-year law student and a talented computer programmer. He is particularly good at creating web robots, which are also called bots.

A bot is software that searches for certain kinds of websites and then automatically does something — good or bad — on each site. Google uses bots to search and index websites. Every website owner welcomes this because Google's indexing brings visitors to the site. A different bot, however, might be used to attack websites. For example, sites that sell concert tickets must defend themselves against bots attempting to buy up all the best seats.

In August, just before the start of the fall semester, Medwick created a bot that finds websites that allow people to post comments. Wherever it could, the bot would post a comment that was really an advertisement for a business that paid Medwick. The ads offered to sell things like out-of-print CD's, spare parts for vintage cars, or cheap vacations in Tahiti. The bot did everything automatically. Medwick activated it from his keyboard and studied Torts or Property for hours while the bot did its work. He planned to use the income to support himself while in law school.

Many websites require a visitor to agree to "Terms & Conditions," that typically appear in a little window or can be accessed through a link. Clicking on a button labeled "I Agree" or "I Accept" allows the visitor to use the site. Almost everyone clicks "I Agree" or "I Accept" without bothering to read the terms and conditions. A website's terms and conditions are a contract if a person using the website agrees to them. These are called clickwrap or click-through contracts. Clicking on "I Agree" or "I Accept" is the electronic equivalent of a signature on the last page of a contract.

In September, a process server walked into Medwick's Civil Procedure class and silently handed him some documents that looked like they had been drafted by a lawyer. This disrupted the class. After the process server left, the Civil Procedure teacher asked to see the documents. After looking at them for a few moments, she told the class that Medwick had been served with a summons and complaint and that lawsuits begin that way. Medwick was stunned.

He is being sued by ExitRow.com, Inc., which operates a travel planning website. One part of the site has data on airlines, from which people can learn which airlines provide the most reliable service between any two cities. Another part has electronic bulletin boards where people can comment on travel issues such as improving security procedures and permitting cell phone calls during a flight.

The following sentence appears near the beginning of ExitRow.com's terms and conditions: "The User promises not to post advertising on this website or use the website for commercial purposes in any way." The terms and conditions can be viewed through a little window on ExitRow.com's home page. The only way into the site is through the home page, and the website blocks access to the rest of the site unless the user clicks on an "I Agree" button on the home page. Medwick had programmed his bot to click on every "I Agree" button it encountered. The bot cannot read or interpret contract language.

In its complaint, ExitRow.com requests damages for breach of contract and alleges that Medwick's bot posted hundreds of ads on its website. Medwick has hired your law firm to defend him. Your research shows that this dispute is governed by California law.

"I didn't agree to anything," Medwick told you. "I've never even seen their contract. I never promised not to advertise on their site. How could I agree to a contract I've never seen?"

Is Medwick bound to ExitRow.com's terms and conditions?[1]

Suppose you need to write out your legal analysis so that it could be read by another lawyer, either a supervising lawyer in your firm or a judge to whom you would argue this case. What will you say first? What will you say after that? How will you organize everything? And how much detail will you provide? Those questions are answered in this chapter and in Chapter 12.

§11.2   A Paradigm for Structuring Proof

A conclusion of law is a determination of how the law treats certain facts. In predictive writing, it can be expressed as a present statement ("Medwick is

---

1. This fact pattern benefitted from suggestions by Kenneth Chestek and David Thomson.

contractually bound by ExitRow.com's Terms and Conditions") or as a prediction ("A court will probably hold that Medwick is contractually bound . . ."). In persuasive writing, it can be expressed as a present statement or as a recommendation to the court.

In both predictive and persuasive writing (Chapter 4), you prove a conclusion of law by explaining the law and the facts in ways that convince the reader that your conclusion is the right one. Organizing what you say is essential to convincing the reader. This chapter and Chapters 12-14 explain how to organize.

A supervising lawyer who reads a predictive Discussion in an office memorandum (Chapters 4 and 16) does so in preparation for making a decision. So does a judge who reads persuasive writing in a motion memorandum or appellate brief. They will make different kinds of decisions. The lawyer will decide what to advise the client or how to handle the client's case. The judge will decide how to rule on a motion or appeal. Both look for a tightly structured analysis that makes your conclusion seem inevitable.

To the reader who must make a decision, analysis is most easily understood if it is organized into the following paradigm formula — or into some variation of it.

To prove a conclusion of law:

1. State your conclusion.
2. State the primary rule that supports the conclusion.
3. Prove and explain the rule through citation to authority, description of how the authority stands for the rule, discussion of subsidiary rules, analyses of policy, and counter-analyses.
4. Apply the rule to the facts with the aid of subsidiary rules, supporting authority, policy considerations, and counter-analyses.
5. If steps 1 through 4 are complicated, sum up by restating your conclusion.

Acronyms have been used to help students remember this kind of formula. For example, *CREAC* stands for Conclusion, *R*ule, rule *E*xplanation, rule *A*pplication, and restated *C*onclusion. Another acronym is *CRAC*: Conclusion, *R*ule, *A*pplication, and Conclusion. A third acronym is *CRuPAC*: Conclusion, *R*ule, *P*roof of Rule, *A*pplication, and Conclusion.

What do the ingredients in this formula mean?

Your conclusion is the one you are trying to prove. Some examples are in the first paragraph of this section.

The rule is the principal rule on which you rely in reaching your conclusion. Other rules might also be involved, but this is the main one on which your analysis rests.

Rule proof and explanation is a demonstration that the main rule on which you rely really is the law in the jurisdiction involved. The reader needs to know for certain that the rule exists in the jurisdiction, and that you have expressed it accurately. Both can be done through citations to authority, such as statutes and precedent, together with explanations of how that authority stands for the rule as you have stated it, explanations of policy, and counter-analyses. (This chapter and Chapters 12-13 explain how to do all that.) Subsidiary rules sometimes help explain the main rule.

Rule application is a demonstration that the rule + the facts = your conclusion. Explain your logic and use authority to show that your result is what the law has in mind. (This chapter and Chapters 12 and 13 explain how.)

Sometimes authority that you use in rule proof might reappear in rule application, but for a different purpose. For example, suppose that *Alger v. Rittenhouse* held that a boat crew that caught a shark became its owner to the exclusion of the fisherman who hooked but lost the shark an hour before. (In your client's case, neighboring ranchers trapped in their corral a wild mustang that immediately jumped over the fence and ran onto your client's land, where it was captured by your client.) In rule proof, you can use *Alger* to prove that your jurisdiction has adopted the rule that wild animals become the property of the first person to reduce them to possession. In rule application, you can use *Alger* again—this time to show that your client satisfies that rule because her position is analogous to that of the boat crew.

A *subsidiary rule* is one that guides application of the main rule or works together with it in some way necessary to your analysis. In a criminal case, the main rule would set out the elements of the crime. Among the subsidiary rules would be the one that permits conviction of any crime only on evidence that establishes guilt beyond a reasonable doubt.

A rule's *policy* is the rule's reason for being. The law doesn't create rules for the fun of it. Each rule is designed to accomplish a purpose (such as preventing a particular type of harm). When courts are unsure of what a rule means or how to apply it, they interpret the rule in the way that would be most consistent with the policy behind it. Thus, policy can be used to show what the rule is (in rule proof) and how to apply it (in rule application).

Counter-analysis is a term used by law teachers, but not by many practicing lawyers. A *counter-analysis* evaluates the arguments that could reasonably be made against your conclusion. Don't waste the reader's time by evaluating marginal or far-fetched arguments. In predictive writing, the counter-analysis is an objective evaluation of each reasonable contrary argument, with an honest report of its strengths and weaknesses. You must report whether your conclusion can withstand attack. And you must consider the possibility that other analyses might be better than the one you have selected. Like authority and policy, counter-analyses can appear both in rule proof and in rule application—but for different purposes. (In persuasive writing in a motion memo or appellate brief, a counter-analysis is called a *counter-argument*. It doesn't objectively consider contrary points of view. It argues against them, stressing their weaknesses and showing their strengths to be unconvincing.)

The paradigm formula is a tool to *help* you organize. It can be varied in many ways, although you should do so only for good reasons. This chapter explains why readers prefer that you organize your analysis this way. Chapters 12 and 13 explain how to vary the formula to suit your needs. Chapter 14 explains how to start using the formula and how to check your writing to see whether it is organized effectively.

§11.3 Why Readers Prefer This Type of Organization

Remember that all of your readers will be practical and skeptical people and will be reading your memo or brief because they must make a decision.

State your conclusion first because a practical and busy reader needs to know what you're trying to support before you start supporting it. If your conclusion is mentioned for the first time *after* your analysis (or in the middle of that analysis), some or all your reasoning seems pointless to the reader who doesn't yet know what your reasoning is supposed to prove. Effective legal writers usually state their conclusions boldly at the beginning of a Discussion or Argument ("The plaintiff has a cause of action because . . ."). This may take some getting used to. It's contrary to the way writing is often done in college. And most of us have been socialized since childhood to state a conclusion only after a proof—even in the most informal situations—to avoid appearing opinionated or confrontational.

Far from being offended, however, the reader who has to make a decision is grateful not to be kept in suspense. That kind of reader becomes frustrated and annoyed while struggling through sentences the relevance of which cannot be understood because the writer has not yet stated the proposition the sentences are intended to prove.

State the rule next because, after reading a conclusion of law, the skeptical law-trained mind instinctively wants to know what principles of law require that conclusion instead of others. After all, the whole idea of law is that things are to be done according to the rules.

Then prove and explain the rule because the reader will refuse to follow you further until you've established that the rule is what you say it is and until you've educated the reader somewhat on how the rule works. The skeptical law-trained mind won't accept a rule statement as genuine unless it has been proved with authority. And you can't apply a rule that the reader has not yet accepted and understood.

Apply the rule last because that's the only thing left. When you apply the rule to the facts, you complete the proof of a conclusion of law.

Along the way, counter-analyze opposing arguments because the skeptical law-trained mind will be able to think up many of those arguments and will want them evaluated. Almost every train of reasoning can be challenged with reasonable arguments. If you don't account for them, the reader will doubt you because it will look as though you're avoiding problems rather than solving them.

§11.4   Varying the Paradigm Formula to Suit Your Needs

The formula set out in §11.2 can be varied in three ways.

First, you can vary the sequence in which the components appear. (See §11.4.1.)

Second, in rule proof and in rule application, you can vary the depth of your explanation to suit the amount of skepticism you expect from the reader. (See §11.4.2 and Chapter 12.)

Third, you can combine separately paradigmed analyses into a unified explanation of several issues and sub-issues. (See §11.4.3 and Chapter 13.)

§11.4.1   Varying the Sequence

In some situations, you might vary the sequence of the paradigm formula's components — for example, by stating the rule first and the conclusion second — although the order should not be illogical or confusing. Think long and hard before deciding to vary the sequence in the box on page 117, and, if you do vary it, you should be able, if your teacher asks, to give a good reason for doing so. In particular, *rule proof should be completed before rule application begins.* Variations in sequence usually don't work well in office memos. They are more likely to be useful in persuasive writing in motion memoranda and appellate briefs. Pages 253-54 explain why.

§11.4.2   Varying the Depth

In rule proof and explanation, some statements about the law are complicated and others aren't. You might need many pages to explain a particular rule because many people would be skeptical about it ("*Pennoyer v. Neff* is still good law"). Or you might need only a few pages because what you say will easily be accepted.

The same is true about rule application. You need to write more analysis if the reader will be skeptical that the rule should be applied as you say and less if the reader will easily see the point.

Chapter 13 explains how to expand or contract analysis and how to decide when to expand or contract it.

§11.4.3   Combining Separately Structured Analyses

If you reach several conclusions or sub-conclusions, the reader will need a separately structured proof for each one.

For example, suppose you represent the plaintiff in a negligence lawsuit. Negligence has four elements: (1) a duty owed by the defendant to the plaintiff, (2) the defendant's breach of that duty, (3) an injury suffered by the plaintiff (4) proximately caused by the breach. To succeed at trial, you'll need to prove all of the elements. If you're writing an office memo in which you predict success at trial, you'll make four separate predictions, one for each element:

1.   We can prove a duty owed by the defendant to the plaintiff.
2.   We can prove a breach of that duty.
3.   We can prove that the plaintiff suffered an injury.
4.   We can prove that the breach proximately caused the injury.

In the memo, you'll say these more concisely, for example: "The breach proximately caused the injury." Each of these predictions is a separate conclusion of law. Each will require its own separately paradigmed proof.

You can combine separately structured proofs like these into a single unified presentation that supports an overall conclusion ("The plaintiff has a cause of action for negligence"). Chapter 12 explains how.

Exercise
Changing Planes in Little Rock

Wong sued Keating in an Arkansas state court. Wong has never lived in Arkansas, and none of the events that led to *Wong v. Keating* happened in Arkansas. The only time Keating has ever set foot on the ground in Arkansas was for 45 minutes while changing planes at the Little Rock airport. The only way for Keating to get to Shreveport, Louisiana, where she had a job interview, was to fly into Little Rock on one flight and then fly from Little Rock to Shreveport on another. During those 45 minutes, while Keating was walking in the airport from her incoming gate to her outgoing gate, a process server, acting on Wong's behalf, served Keating with a summons and complaint in *Wong v. Keating*. Keating moved to dismiss on the ground that Arkansas has no personal jurisdiction over her. Wong claims that service in Arkansas alone gives Arkansas personal jurisdiction over Keating.

Below is an analysis of this issue. Find the components of the paradigm for organizing proof of a conclusion of law. Find the writer's conclusion; the primary rule that supports that conclusion; proof and explanation of that rule; and application of that rule to the facts. Mark up the passage below to show where each of the components occurs. If you can find any counter-analyses or policy discussions, mark them, too. Finally, for each component, ask yourself whether the writer has told you enough. Are you confident that the writer is correct? If not, what kinds of additional information would you need?

Arkansas has personal jurisdiction over Keating. Under the Due Process Clause of the Fourteenth Amendment, a state is authorized to exercise personal jurisdiction over a defendant who is served with a summons while the defendant is voluntarily inside the state. *Burnham v. Superior Court*, 495 U.S. 604 (1990). That is true even if service of the summons is the only connection between the state and the plaintiff, the defendant, or the plaintiff's claim. It is true where the defendant does not reside in the state, is only traveling through the state, and has no connection to the state except for the trip during which the defendant was served. *Id.* It is also true where none of the events or circumstances alleged in the plaintiff's complaint happened in the state. *Id.*

The defendant in *Burnham* was a New Jersey resident who had traveled on business to southern California and then to northern California to visit his children. The plaintiff was the defendant's wife, who had him served in a divorce action while he was in northern California. Four justices of the Supreme Court joined in an opinion by Justice Scalia and held that, under precedent going back two centuries, a state has "the power to hale before its courts any individual who could be found within its borders." *Id.* at 610. Another four justices joined in an opinion by Justice Brennan and held that the defendant's presence in the state at the time of service was a purposeful availment that satisfies the minimum contacts requirements of *International Shoe*, 326 U.S. 310 (1945). The ninth justice (Stevens) concurred separately on the ground that both rationales are correct. Because there was no majority opinion, it is not settled which rationale supports the rule, although the rule had the unanimous support of all nine justices.

Regardless of the rationale, the effect here is that service on Keating in the Little Rock airport created personal jurisdiction in Arkansas. Keating was present in Arkansas at the moment of service. The process server's affidavit is evidence of that, and Keating concedes it. Moreover, she does not claim that she did not know she was in Arkansas or that she was in the state under duress. She bought her airline ticket knowing she would have to change planes in Little Rock, and her presence was therefore voluntary.

Keating argues, however, that she was not in Arkansas long enough to be subject to the state's jurisdiction, even if she was served in Arkansas. She points out that the *Burnham* defendant had traveled *to* California to conduct business there and visit his children, spending nights in hotels and purposely availing himself of the benefits of the state. Keating contends that this case is distinguishable from *Burnham* because her destination was Louisiana rather than Arkansas, and because she was on the ground in Arkansas for less than an hour and only for the purpose of getting to Louisiana.

This case cannot be distinguished from *Burnham*. The Scalia opinion stressed that the state's jurisdiction extends to any visitor, "no matter how fleeting his visit." *Id.* at 610. And the Brennan rationale would treat using the Little Rock airport for a connecting flight as purposeful availment supporting minimum contacts because Keating gained a benefit from Arkansas. Any other result would represent unsupportable policy in an era of modern travel. There is no practical way to craft a rule that would clearly distinguish between a presence in the state that is too short for jurisdiction and a presence that is long enough, which is why the Supreme Court held in *Burnham* that any presence is enough, if the defendant is served while present.

Moreover, Keating's presence in Arkansas was not limited to her 45 minutes inside the airport. She could have been validly served while either of the airplanes on which she flew was on the tarmac or even in the air over Arkansas. Service of process on a passenger in an airplane that flew over Arkansas but never landed in the state has been sustained because at the moment of service the passenger was inside Arkansas, even though the passenger was not on the ground. *Grace v. MacArthur*, 170 F. Supp. 442 (E.D. Ark. 1959). The *Grace* court reasoned that there is no real difference between a passenger on an airplane that passes through Arkansas airspace and a passenger who travels through the state by train or bus without disembarking. *Id.* at 447.

Thus, Arkansas has jurisdiction over Keating, and her motion to dismiss should be denied.

12 Varying the Depth of Rule Proof and Rule Application

§12.1 Introduction

Chapter 11 explained a paradigm for structuring proof of a conclusion of law. This chapter explains how to vary two parts of that paradigm — rule proof and rule application — in terms of depth.

Depending on the situation, rule proof and rule application can be very short, very long, or somewhere in between. In one instance, rule proof might need only a sentence, while rule application might require three pages. In another instance, the reverse might be true. Or each of them might be four or five pages long — or four or five sentences long. How can you tell how much depth is needed? Ask yourself three questions:

First, how much explanation will convince the reader that the conclusion is correct? That depends on the reader's level of skepticism, which in turn depends on how important the issue is to the decision the reader must make, and on how complicated the reader will think the issue to be.

Second, how much explanation will prevent the reader from studying independently the authorities you rely on? The second question poses what might be called the need-to-read test: you haven't explained enough if your reader would find it hard to agree with you without actually studying the authorities you've cited. A reader's need to go to the authorities is predicated on the context. A reader is more likely to feel that need with a critical, difficult, or obscure point than with a simple, peripheral, or routine one. A reader's need to know more is particularly great for authority that is the only support or the central basis for your conclusion.

Third, how much explanation would tell the reader those things needed to make an informed decision? Put another way, if the reader were to go to the authorities, would the reader be startled to find the things you've left out? Part of your job is to leave things out. The reader is counting on you to cut out the things that don't matter. But don't leave out so much that the reader is deprived of some of the information on which a decision would have to be based.

Don't explore an issue in more depth than a reader would need. Remember that the reader is a busy person, almost as intolerant of too much explanation as of too little. If you include much detail about peripheral issues or about routine propositions with which the reader will easily agree, the reader feels stuck in quicksand.

Be careful. Most students underestimate the skepticism of readers. If you have no idea how much to explain, err on the side of making a more complete explanation until you have gained a better sense of what must be fully proven and where proof can be at least partially implied.

Rule proof and rule application can each be explored in a way that's *conclusory*, *substantiating*, or *comprehensive*. The rest of this chapter explains how.

§12.2   Conclusory Explanations

A conclusory explanation does no more than allude to some basis for the deduction made by the writer. Here's an example from the facts in Chapter 11:

> Medwick is contractually bound to ExitRow.com's Terms and Conditions because he programmed his bot to click on the "I Agree" button on ExitRow.com's website. A contract is formed by an objective manifestation of agreement, even if a party does not read the contract before agreeing to it. *Marin Storage & Trucking, Inc. v. Benco Contracting & Eng'g, Inc.*, 107 Cal. Rptr. 2d 645, 651 (Ct. App. 2001). Programming a bot to click on an "I Agree" button is analogous to signing a contract without reading it.

Here the rule is clearly set out, but the only proof of it is a citation to a decision, without any explanation of the court's reasoning or of the facts there adjudicated. The conclusion is also plainly stated, but the only rule application is an allusion to a single fact: Medwick programmed his bot to click on the "I Agree" button on ExitRow.com's website. There are no counter-analyses and no discussion of policy.

A conclusory explanation is appropriate only where the reader will easily agree with you, or where the point isn't important to your analysis. In those situations, a detailed analysis would seem tedious to the reader. Elsewhere, however, a conclusory explanation would deprive the reader of information essential to the decision the reader must make. For example, from the example above, a supervising lawyer cannot decide how to advise Medwick. At the very least, the lawyer would want to know the facts of *Marin Storage & Trucking,* how they're analogous to website clickwrap agreements, the court's reasoning in *Marin,* and whether any cases decide whether bots can create contracts.

§12.3   Substantiating Explanations

A substantiating explanation goes more deeply into the writer's reasoning but still doesn't state the analysis completely:

> Medwick is contractually bound to ExitRow.com's Terms and Conditions. A contract is formed by an objective manifestation of agreement, even if a party does not read the contract before agreeing to it. *Marin Storage & Trucking, Inc. v. Benco Contracting & Eng'g, Inc.,* 107 Cal. Rptr. 2d 645, 651 (Ct. App. 2001). In *Marin,* a party was bound when its employees signed contractual documents without reading them. In website clickwrap contracting, a person agrees to a website's terms and conditions if he programs a bot to do something that he knows the website will interpret as agreement. *Register. com, Inc. v. Verio, Inc.,* 356 F.3d 393 (2d Cir. 2004). Medwick programmed his bot to click on "I Agree" and "I Accept" buttons automatically wherever the bot found them, which is what the bot did on ExitRow.com's website. That is analogous to signing a contract without reading it.

This passage provides more rule proof and more rule application. But it's not comprehensive.

A substantiating explanation is appropriate where the reader needs more than a conclusory explanation, but where the point being made isn't really central to your analysis. It isn't appropriate where the reader will probably be aggressively skeptical. The substantiating passage above would not satisfy the lawyer who must make difficult decisions about how to handle Medwick's case.

§12.4   Comprehensive Explanations

A comprehensive explanation includes whatever analyses are necessary to satisfy an aggressive skepticism. Rule proof and rule application can be augmented with further detail about the law and the facts, with added or expanded counter-analyses, and with policy discussions sufficient to give the skeptical reader confidence that the law's goals would be achieved through your conclusion:

Medwick is contractually bound to ExitRow.com's Terms and Conditions because he programmed his bot to agree to them.

The writer's conclusion.

A contract is formed by an objective manifestation of agreement, even if a party does not read the contract before agreeing to it. *Marin Storage & Trucking, Inc. v. Benco Contracting & Eng'g, Inc.*, 107 Cal. Rptr. 2d 645, 651 (Ct. App. 2001). Marin often supplied construction cranes to Benco at building sites. After each day, Marin's crane operator wrote the number of crane-usage hours on a form and handed it to a Benco employee, who confirmed the hours and signed the form. At the top of the form were the words "Work Authorization and Contract," and at the bottom was the sentence "This is a contract which includes all terms and conditions stated on the reverse side." There was no evidence that any of the Benco employees who signed the form ever read the reverse side. *Id.* at 649-50. The court held that Benco's employees objectively manifested agreement when they signed a document with words warning that it was contractual. *Id.* at 651. Whether they read the terms of the contract was irrelevant. *Id.*

The main rule.

Rule proof and explanation begin.

The Restatement takes the same position: "where an offer is contained in a writing either the offeror or the offeree may, without reading the writing, manifest assent to it and bind himself without knowing its terms." Restatement (Second) of Contracts, § 23, cmt. b (1979). The policy behind this rule is to protect a party who relies on the agreement from a later argument by the other party that no contract exists because the other party had not read or understood it. *Id.* cmt. e.

Policy is introduced.

Medwick is an experienced programmer and knows that websites often require users to agree contractually to terms and conditions. He could have visited ExitRow.com's website personally and read ExitRow.com's Terms and Conditions. Instead, he programmed his bot

Rule application begins.

to click on "I Agree" and "I Accept" buttons automatically wherever the bot found them, which is analogous to signing a contract without reading it.

No California court has decided a contract case involving a bot. But in a diversity case applying California law, the Second Circuit held that a website visitor is not bound to a contract the visitor has not read unless the website informs the visitor that a particular action constitutes agreement to that contract and the website allows the visitor to read the contract before agreeing to it. *Specht v. Netscape Communications Corp.*, 306 F.3d 17 (2d Cir. 2002). Netscape claimed that the plaintiffs had agreed to all of its contract by downloading Netscape's software. *Id.* at 23. Although the website gave notice of some contract terms, a visitor would have had to search the site exhaustively to discover others, including the ones at issue in the lawsuit. *Id.* at 23-24. The Second Circuit held that the plaintiffs were not bound by the additional terms because "a reasonably prudent Internet user in circumstances such as these would not have known or learned of [their] existence." *Id.* at 20.

In a later diversity case also applying California law, the Second Circuit held that a person agrees to a website's terms and conditions if he programs a bot to do something that he knows the website will interpret as agreement. *Register.com, Inc. v. Verio, Inc.*, 356 F.3d 393 (2d Cir. 2004). Verio programmed its bot to visit Register.com's website several times a day and collect web addresses, to which Verio then sent marketing solicitations. *Id.* at 396-97. Register.com's website contained this notice: "By submitting a . . . query, you agree that . . . under no circumstances will you use this data to . . . support the transmission of mass unsolicited, commercial advertising or solicitation via email." *Id.* at 396. The court

A counter-analysis begins

To show why Specht does not control, the writer explains the most analogous case.

129

held that because Verio's bot had been programmed to collect web addresses despite the
notice, Verio was contractually obligated not
to use them for email marketing. *Id.* at 404.
The court distinguished its earlier decision
in *Sprecht* on the grounds that in that case
Netscape had designed its website so that visitors would not have known they were agreeing to additional terms. *Id.* at 402.

Register.com is the only case that applies
California contract law to bots. Like Verio,
Medwick programmed his bot to behave in a
way that a website would interpret as agreement to the site's terms and conditions. He
thus agreed to and is bound by those terms
and conditions.

A wrap-up restating the conclusion.

§12.5   Cryptic Explanations

Beginners sometimes write explanations so cryptic as to be less than conclusory. The writer of a passage like the following has tried to put too much
into a small bottle:

> Medwick is contractually bound to ExitRow.com's Terms and Conditions.
> *Marin Storage & Trucking, Inc. v. Benco Contracting & Eng'g, Inc.*, 107 Cal. Rptr.
> 2d 645, 651 (Ct. App. 2001).

A cryptic explanation is never enough — even in a situation where a conclusory explanation would suffice — because a cryptic explanation omits any
statement of the rule on which the conclusion is based.

Exercise
Punitive Damages and Bedbugs

This Exercise is divided into Exercise A and Exercise B, below. To do each exercise,
you'll need the facts in *Matthias v. Accor Economy Lodging*, 347 F.3d 672 (7th Cir.
2003). Here they are, in the court's words:

> . . . The plaintiffs . . . were guests [in the defendant's Motel 6] and were bitten
> by bedbugs, which are making a comeback in the U.S. as a consequence of more
> conservative use of pesticides. . . . The jury . . . awarded each plaintiff $186,000 in
> punitive damages though only $5,000 in compensatory damages. . . .

. . . In 1998, EcoLab, the extermination service that the motel used, discovered bedbugs in several rooms in the motel and recommended that it be hired to spray every room, for which it would charge the motel only $500; the motel refused. . . . By the spring of 2000, the motel's manager "started noticing that there were refunds being given by my desk clerks and reports coming back from the guests that there were ticks in the rooms and bugs in the rooms that were biting." She looked in some of the rooms and discovered bedbugs. . . .

Further incidents of guests being bitten by insects and demanding and receiving refunds led the manager to recommend to her superior in the company that the motel be closed while every room was sprayed, but this was refused. . . .

. . . By July, the motel's management was acknowledging to EcoLab that there was a "major problem with bed bugs" and that all that was being done about it was "chasing them from room to room." . . . Rooms that the motel had placed on "Do not rent, bugs in room" status nevertheless were rented.

It was in November that the plaintiffs checked into the motel. They were given Room 504, even though the motel had classified the room as "DO NOT RENT UNTIL TREATED," and it had not been treated. . . .

Although bedbug bites are not as serious as the bites of some other insects, they are painful and unsightly. Motel 6 could not have rented any rooms at the prices it charged had it informed guests that the risk of being bitten by bedbugs was appreciable. . . .

Exercise A: Below is the court's explanation for its conclusion that Motel 6 is liable for an intentional tort. Is the court's explanation conclusory, substantiating, comprehensive, or cryptic? Did the court choose an appropriate level of explanation? (Should it have explained less or more or neither?) To answer these questions, you need to know why the court reached this conclusion. A plaintiff who has proved that a defendant has committed an intentional tort, such as fraud or battery, is eligible for punitive damages. In this appeal, the defendant raised two punitive damages issues. The first is this one (was the plaintiff eligible for punitive damages?). The second, which you'll reach in Exercise B, is whether the trial court's punitive damage award was too large.

> [Motel 6's] failure either to warn guests or to take effective measures to eliminate the bedbugs amounted to fraud and probably to battery as well (compare *Campbell Iv. A.C. Equipment Services Corp.*, 242 Ill. App. 3d 707, 610 N.E.2d 745, 748-49, 182 Ill. Dec. 876 (Ill. App. 1993); see Restatement (Second) of Torts, supra, § 18, comment c and e), as in the famous case of *Garratt v. Dailey*, 46 Wn.2d 197, 279 P.2d 1091, 1093— 94 (1955), appeal after remand, 49 Wn.2d 499, 304 P.2d 681 (Wash. 1956), which held that the defendant would be guilty of battery if he knew with substantial certainty that when he moved a chair the plaintiff would try to sit down where the chair had been and would land on the floor instead. See also *Massachusetts v. Stratton*, 114 Mass. 303 (Mass. 1873). There was, in short, sufficient evidence of "willful and wanton conduct" within the meaning

that the Illinois courts assign to the term to permit an award of punitive damages in this case.

Exercise B: Below is the court's explanation for its conclusion that the trial court did not award excessive punitive damages. Is the court's explanation conclusory, substantiating, comprehensive, or cryptic? Did the court choose an appropriate level of explanation? (Should it have explained less or more or neither?) Does the court rely on policy? Does it use counter-analyses?

. . . In arguing that $20,000 was the maximum amount of punitive damages that a jury could constitutionally have awarded each plaintiff, the defendant points to the U.S. Supreme Court's recent statement that "few awards [of punitive damages] exceeding a single-digit ratio between punitive and compensatory damages, to a significant degree, will satisfy due process." *State Farm Mutual Automobile Ins. Co. v. Campbell*, 538 U.S. 408 (2003). The Court went on to suggest that "four times the amount of compensatory damages might be close to the line of constitutional impropriety." *Id.* . . . Hence the defendant's proposed ceiling in this case of $20,000, four times the compensatory damages awarded to each plaintiff. The ratio of punitive to compensatory damages determined by the jury was, in contrast, 37.2 to 1.

The Supreme Court did not, however, lay down a 4-to-1 or single-digit-ratio rule — it said merely that "there is a presumption against an award that has a 145-to-1 ratio," . . . and it would be unreasonable to do so. We must consider why punitive damages are awarded and why the Court has decided that due process requires that such awards be limited. The second question is easier to answer than the first. The term "punitive damages" implies punishment, and a standard principle of penal theory is that "the punishment should fit the crime" in the sense of being proportional to the wrongfulness of the defendant's action, though the principle is modified when the probability of detection is very low (a familiar example is the heavy fines for littering) or the crime is potentially lucrative (as in the case of trafficking in illegal drugs). Hence, with these qualifications, which in fact will figure in our analysis of this case, punitive damages should be proportional to the wrongfulness of the defendant's actions. . . .

[O]ne function of punitive-damages awards is to relieve the pressures on an overloaded system of criminal justice by providing a civil alternative to criminal prosecution of minor crimes. An example is deliberately spitting in a person's face, a criminal assault but because minor readily deterrable by the levying of what amounts to a civil fine through a suit for damages for the tort of battery. Compensatory damages would not do the trick in such a case, and this for three reasons: because they are difficult to determine in the case of acts that inflict largely dignitary harms; because in the spitting case they would be too slight to give the victim an incentive to sue, and he might decide instead to respond with violence — and an age-old purpose of the law of torts is to provide a substitute for violent retaliation against wrongful injury — and because to limit the plaintiff to compensatory damages would enable the defendant to commit the offensive act with impunity provided that he was willing to pay, and again there would be a danger that his act would incite a breach of the peace by his victim.

When punitive damages are sought for billion-dollar oil spills and other huge economic injuries, the considerations that we have just canvassed fade. As the Court emphasized in *Campbell*, the fact that the plaintiffs in that case had been awarded very substantial compensatory damages — $1 million for a dispute over insurance coverage — greatly reduced the need for giving them a huge award of punitive damages ($145 million) as well in order to provide an effective remedy. Our case is closer to the spitting case. The defendant's behavior was outrageous but the compensable harm done was slight and at the same time difficult to quantify because a large element of it was emotional. And the defendant may well have profited from its misconduct because by concealing the infestation it was able to keep renting rooms. Refunds were frequent but may have cost less than the cost of closing the hotel for a thorough fumigation. The hotel's attempt to pass off the bedbugs as ticks, which some guests might ignorantly have thought less unhealthful, may have postponed the instituting of litigation to rectify the hotel's misconduct. The award of punitive damages in this case thus serves the additional purpose of limiting the defendant's ability to profit from its fraud by escaping detection and (private) prosecution. If a tortfeasor is "caught" only half the time he commits torts, then when he is caught he should be punished twice as heavily in order to make up for the times he gets away. . . .

All things considered, we cannot say that the award of punitive damages was excessive. . . . The judicial function is to police a range, not a point. . . .

13 Combining Proofs of Separate Conclusions of Law

§13.1 Introduction

If you reach several conclusions or sub-conclusions, the reader will need a separately structured proof for each one. You can combine separately structured proofs for several conclusions or sub-conclusions into a single unified presentation.

You'll need to do this in four situations: where more than one element of a rule is in dispute (see §13.2); where more than one claim or defense is at issue (§13.3); where you have alternative ways of proving a single conclusion (§13.4); or where you're writing about separate but related issues (§13.5).

§13.2 How to Organize Where More Than One Element Is at Issue

If you must resolve all the elements of a rule, you'll have an ultimate conclusion for the rule as a whole, together with a sub-conclusion for each element:

Ultimate Conclusion on the Ultimate Issue	"The client has a cause of action for negligence because Bevens injured the client by driving while talking on a hand-held cell phone."
	Element #1: "As a driver, Bevens owed a duty of care to others on the road, including the client."

Sub-Conclusions on Sub-Issues	Element #2:	"Bevens breached that duty by talking on a hand-held cell phone while driving."
	Element #3:	"The client suffered injuries in an auto accident."
	Element #4:	"The accident and the injuries were proximately caused by Bevens's breach of the duty of care."

If this analysis were to be written out, the opening or *umbrella* passage would state the conclusion ("The client has a cause of action for negligence") and the essence of the reason ("because Bevens injured the client by driving while talking on a hand-held cell phone"). The opening paragraph would also recite the *rule* on which it is based (the elements of negligence). If the rule is settled law, it might be proved in the opening paragraph with little more than a citation to authority. Otherwise, *rule proof* would supply whatever else is needed to show that the underlying rule is law (and perhaps to show generally how the rule is expected to work, if that would help).

Then would follow separate, paradigm-structured discussions for the elements. Each element is a sub-issue for which you have a sub-conclusion (shown above). Each element would have to be defined through a rule that provides a definition (*a declaratory or definitional rule*); the definition would have to be proved through authority (*rule proof*); and the facts would have to be analyzed in light of the definition (*rule application*).

The umbrella passage would be a single paragraph in a simple situation and a few paragraphs in a complicated one (for example, if the underlying rule is hard to prove). The umbrella passage would at first seem to be an incomplete paradigm structure because it would *not include rule application and definitions of the elements.* But this paragraph or these paragraphs actually function as an umbrella paradigm structure that covers, organizes, or incorporates the subordinate, structured proofs of each of the elements. (For illustrations, see the Discussion in the office memo in Appendix C.)

The umbrella passage also sets out a roadmap for what follows. It at least implies to the reader what issues you'll consider, their relative importance or unimportance, and sometimes the order in which you'll consider them.

After the umbrella passage, the most dispositive issues or sub-issues usually—but not always—should be addressed first. Here, if you were to determine that the client has no cause of action because talking on a hand-held cell phone did not proximately cause the accident, you could analyze the fourth element (proximate cause) before you analyze the others. The fourth element would be the most important one because it would resolve the ultimate issue (whether the client has a cause of action).

If you believe, however, that *all* the elements can be proved, you could instead analyze them in the order in which they appear in the rule. That might be easier for the reader to follow if no element takes vastly more space than another to explain. But the situation might be different if one element were to consume, for example, three-quarters of the Discussion. There, the reader might be able to follow the analysis more easily if you were to dispose of the other elements first to set up the context.

You might be tempted to focus on one element, conclude that it isn't satisfied in the facts, and then ignore the other elements as moot on the theory that the one you've analyzed disposes of the whole controversy. That won't work because it might turn out that you're wrong about the element you believe to be dispositive. Here, for example, you cannot ignore the other elements of negligence just because you believe that the fourth element (proximate cause) isn't satisfied. If you turn out to be wrong, the reader of predictive writing is entitled to know what will happen with the other elements.

The difference between a procedural rule and a substantive rule: Substantive rules create rights and liabilities from events that occur in everyday life. You've been studying substantive rules in Contracts, Torts, Property, and Criminal Law. Procedural tests govern how lawyers work in litigation and how judges and juries make decisions. You're studying some procedural rules in Civil Procedure and will study others later in Evidence and Criminal Procedure.

The two most frequent ways in which procedural and substantive rules interact are where the application of a substantive rule is governed by a procedural test and where a procedural test incorporates a substantive rule.

Where the application of a substantive rule is governed by a procedural test: When a procedural test and a substantive test are used together, the procedural test shows how to apply the substantive test to the facts.

An example happens in every criminal case: the defendant is guilty only if the prosecution proves each element of the crime beyond a reasonable doubt. The umbrella is the rule defining the crime, and the sub-issues are the elements of the crime. The procedural rule (requiring proof beyond a reasonable doubt) is not part of this structure. But, inside each issue, you use it to measure whether the substantive element has been satisfied. For example, if the issue is whether the defendant is guilty of common law burglary, the sub-issues are, "Is there proof beyond a reasonable doubt that the defendant *broke* a building?" and "Is there proof beyond a reasonable doubt that the defendant *entered* a building?" and "Is there proof beyond a reasonable doubt that the building was a *dwelling*?" and so on (see Chapter 4).

Where a procedural test incorporates a substantive rule: For example, in federal courts a party is entitled to summary judgment if (1) there is no genuine issue of material fact and (2) the party is entitled to judgment as a matter of law.[1] The second element incorporates all substantive rules on which a judgment would rest — such as the rule defining the cause of action. These two elements would be separate issues under the umbrella of the test for summary judgment. The elements of the substantive rules would be sub-issues under the second element of the test for summary judgment ("entitled to judgment as a matter of law"). There would be an umbrella (the second element, covering the elements of the substantive tests) within an umbrella (the procedural test as a whole). This happens *only* where a procedural rule incorporates a substantive test, most often with a summary judgment or a preliminary injunction. An example appears in Appendix F.

§13.3   How to Organize Where More Than One Claim or Defense Is at Issue

Suppose your supervising attorney wants to know whether the client will be awarded damages in a tort case. You need to figure out whether the client has a cause of action (one issue or collection of issues). And you anticipate that the defendant will raise the affirmative defenses of comparative negligence (another issue or collection of issues) and sovereign immunity (yet another). Although this is a more complex situation than the one where several elements of a single rule are in dispute, it's handled in the same way (see §13.2). You build an umbrella paradigm structure, and underneath it you prove the sub-conclusions through separate, subordinate paradigm-structured analyses. For example, the ultimate conclusion might be that the client will be awarded damages because she has a cause of action (the first sub-conclusion); was not comparatively negligent (the second sub-conclusion); and the claim doesn't fall within the defendant's sovereign immunity (the third sub-conclusion). Thus:

Ultimate   The client should be awarded damages.
Conclusion
on the
Ultimate
Issue

---

1. Rule 56 of the Federal Rules of Civil Procedure.

Sub-Conclusions on Sub-Issues	Sub-Issue #1:	The client has a cause of action for negligence.
	Sub-Issue #2:	She committed no comparative negligence (an affirmative defense).
	Sub-Issue #3:	Sovereign immunity does not prevent recovery here (another affirmative defense).

Because negligence has four elements, the first sub-issue could be divided further into separate proofs of each of those four elements.

§13.4 How to Organize Alternative Ways of Proving a Single Conclusion

In the first year of law school, this typically occurs in an appellate advocacy assignment where the jurisdiction has no rule on point, where it could choose between or among competing rules, and where you could argue that either of two or more competing rules will—independently of one another—justify the conclusion. It, too, is handled through the umbrella paradigm structure explained in §13.2:

Ultimate Conclusion on the Ultimate Issue	The judgment below should be reversed.

Sub-Conclusions on Sub-Issues	Sub-Issue #1:	This court should adopt rule X.
	Sub-Issue #2:	Under rule X, the judgment should be reversed.
	Sub-Issue #3:	Even under rule Y (the competing rule), the judgment should be reversed.

§13.5 How to Organize When You're Writing About Separate but Related Issues

There are still other ways in which separate issues might need to be resolved to support a single conclusion. Suppose someone sues your client, and your supervising attorney wants to know whether that lawsuit can be dismissed on forum selection grounds (on grounds that it was brought in the wrong court). You'll have to resolve some or all of the following issues: Does this court have subject matter jurisdiction over this kind of case? Does this court have personal jurisdiction over our client? Is this court the right venue for this lawsuit?

If your conclusion is that the lawsuit was brought in the right court, you'll have to show that the court has subject matter and personal jurisdiction and that venue is proper. To do that, you'll use the same umbrella paradigm structure explained in §13.2:

Ultimate Conclusion on the Ultimate Issue	This lawsuit is not dismissible on forum selection grounds.
Sub-Conclusions on Sub-Issues	Sub-Issue #1: This court has subject matter jurisdiction. Sub-Issue #2: This court has personal jurisdiction over our client. Sub-Issue #3: Venue is proper in this court.

§13.6   How to Start Working with Multi-Issue Situations

All these different ways to organize can seem confusing when you first think about them. But with some practice, they'll become second nature. Many students feel confused at this point, but within a few weeks, they begin to gain confidence in organizing this way. And within a year or two, most students instinctively think in structured proofs. This section provides some suggestions for getting to that point.

While researching and planning your writing, ask yourself how many issues you have. If you have a hard time identifying issues, ask yourself how many conclusions of law a court would need to make to rule in your favor. Then ask how many conclusions of law a court would need to make to rule in the other side's favor. Now consolidate those two lists to produce a list of issues. When you had two lists (before consolidating them), many issues will have been listed twice because they were flip sides of each other. When you consolidate, you'll often merge two issues into one. The advantage of making two lists is that it helps you avoid overlooking an issue. When you look at only your side of the case, you sometimes miss an issue that the other side will raise.

Now, figure out what kind of issues you have. Is an issue part of the cause of action, part of a defense, part of a procedural requirement, or something else? This will help you figure out which of the structures described in §§13.2 through 13.5 to use.

Choose one of the multi-issue structures explained in this chapter, and adapt it to your case. Start a document on your computer and type a list of every conclusion of law you'll make in your memo or brief, like the lists in §§13.2 through 13.5. Organize the conclusions logically — for example, elements of a cause of action first, then defenses. Treat this as the beginning of an outline. In the next chapter, §14.1 explains how to complete this outline and turn it into a memo or brief.

Use introductory or roadmap paragraphs to explain your umbrella paradigm to the reader. A roadmap paragraph lists the conclusions you'll reach. It maps out your discussion so the reader knows what to expect. If the document is a long one (such as an appellate brief), the roadmap paragraph tells the reader where to find the analysis supporting each conclusion. In a shorter document, your headings inside the document will do that. In a roadmap paragraph, state your ultimate conclusion ("The client should be awarded damages," for example) and then state the sub-conclusions that support that ultimate conclusion. If some elements of a test are at issue and others are not, the roadmap paragraph is the place to make that clear. Most judges say that a well-written roadmap paragraph is very important or essential in helping them understand what you are trying to say.[2] Here is a typical roadmap paragraph, which you might use to introduce the discussion outlined in §13.3:

> The plaintiff should be awarded damages. The evidence supports all four of the elements of negligence. The defendant owed a duty to the plaintiff to keep the loading dock clear and breached that duty by leaving explosive materials on the loading dock overnight. The plaintiff's injury, destruction of the warehouse, is uncontested. It was proximately caused by the breach when the materials exploded. Although the defendant pleaded the defense of comparative negligence, no evidence supports it. And sovereign immunity has been waived by § 419 of the Highways Code.

Use headings to show your reader where your analysis of each issue begins. Lawyers and judges won't read your work from beginning to end. They'll read parts of it at a time, and headings help them find the parts they need. If you're writing a predictive memo, look at the way headings are used in Appendix C. If you are writing a persuasive memo or a brief, you will write point headings, which are explained in Chapter 26.

---

2. Kristen K. Robbins-Tiscione, *The Inside Scoop: What Federal Judges Really Think about the Way Lawyers Write*, 8 J. Legal Writing Inst. 257, 273 (2002).

Working with the Paradigm

§14.1 Using the Paradigm Formula to Outline and to Begin Your First Draft

Think of the paradigm formula for organizing proof of a conclusion of law (from Chapters 11, 12, and 13) as a tool to *help* you organize. It will also keep your material from getting out of control. Here it is again:

To prove a conclusion of law:

1. State your conclusion.
2. State the primary rule that supports the conclusion.
3. Prove and explain the rule through citation to authority, description of how the authority stands for the rule, discussion of subsidiary rules, analyses of policy, and counter-analyses. (*This is rule proof and explanation, or simply rule proof.*)
4. Apply the rule to the facts with the aid of subsidiary rules, supporting authority, policy considerations, and counter-analyses. (*This is rule application.*)
5. If steps 1 through 4 are complicated, sum up by restating your conclusion.

This section describes one method of starting to work with the formula. It's only a suggestion for the first time you write. If you develop a different procedure that works better for you, use that instead.

In the method described here, label everything so that you know where it goes. Then just plug it into whatever variant of the formula best fits your situation. The first time you try this, it might seem a little awkward if you've never done anything like it before. But the second or third time it will feel more natural because it fits the way people instinctively work and because it takes less effort than other methods of organizing.

Begin by figuring out how many issues and sub-issues you have. Each one will be analyzed through a separate paradigm structure.

For each issue or sub-issue, identify the rule that's central to and governs the answer. (You might also use other rules, but for the moment focus on the rule that — more than any other — compels your answer.)

Now, inventory your raw materials. For each issue or sub-issue, sort everything you have into two categories: rule proof and rule application. Some methods of sorting seem to work better than others. Dividing your notes into two piles, for example, doesn't seem to work very well — nor does copying and pasting all your research into one big document.

A better method is to go through your notes and write "RP" in the margin next to everything that you might use to prove your rule and explain it and "RA" next to everything that might help the reader understand how to apply the rule. Some ideas or authorities might do both and get a notation of "RP/RA." If you have several issues or sub-issues, you can work out a method of marking them separately, such as "#3RP" for "rule proof on issue 3" or "#1RA" for "rule application on issue 1." If you have printed the cases, write these notations next to each part of the case that you'll use. Go through your facts, too, marking the ones that are important enough to talk about during rule application. If you've been thinking about ideas that aren't in your notes, write them down and note where they go.

Now, think about how all these things add up. If you haven't yet drawn a conclusion, do it now. If you decided previously on a conclusion, check it against your raw materials to see whether it still seems like the best conclusion.

Ask yourself whether a reasonable argument could be made against any part of your analysis. If so, make a note of it and of where it goes. Decide whether that argument is so attractive that it would probably persuade a judge. And decide exactly *why* a judge would — or would not — be persuaded. If you decide that the argument is likely to persuade, modify your analysis accordingly. (If you can't find any arguments at all that might work against your analysis, you may be avoiding problems that your reader will later see.)

Your notes are now complete enough to be organized into an outline based on some variation of the paradigm formula.

To make a fluid outline, just assemble everything. For each issue or sub-issue, take a piece of paper and write four abbreviated headings on it (for example: "concl" or "sub-concl," "rule," "RP," and "RA"). (You can do this on a computer instead, if you feel more comfortable typing than writing.) Some students find it helpful to lay out this information in a chart or diagram. Under "concl" or "sub-concl," write your conclusion or sub-conclusion for that issue in whatever shorthand will remind you later of what your thinking is (for example: "no diversity — Wharton/citizen of Maine"). Under "rule," do something similar. Under "RP," list your raw materials for rule proof. For each item listed, don't write a lot — just enough so that later you'll be able to see at a glance everything you have. If you're listing something found in a case, a catch-phrase and a reference to a page in the case might be enough (for example: "intent to return — *Wiggins* p.352"). Under "RA," do the same for rule application. Make sure that everything you have on that issue is listed in an appropriate place on that page.

Assume that for rule proof on a certain issue you've listed six resources (cases, facts, and so on). You haven' t yet decided the order in which you will discuss them when you prove the rule. In most situations, the decision will be easier and more apt if you do *not* make it while outlining. The best time to decide is just before you write that issue's rule proof in your first draft. (*You don't need to know exactly where everything will go before you start the first draft.*) When you decide, just write a number next to each item ("1" next to the first one you'll discuss, and so on).

When you write the first draft (Chapter 5), you probably won't use everything that you previously marked into one category or another. Inevitably, some material won't seem as useful while you're writing as it did when you were sorting, and you will discard it.

Keep track of what you're doing by checking off or crossing out each item in the outline as you put it into the first draft. When everything has been checked off or crossed out, you have completed the first draft of your Discussion in an office memo (or Argument if you're writing a motion memo or appellate brief).

So far, you have concentrated on making sure that all worthwhile raw materials get into your first draft. During rewriting, your focus will change. While you rewrite (Chapter 5), look to see where things are. If you find conclusions at the end of analysis, for example, move them to the beginning. While rewriting, ask yourself the questions in §14.2 below.

§14.2 Rewriting: How to Test Your Writing for Effective Organization

A well-organized presentation of analysis is immediately recognizable. Issues and sub-issues are handled separately, and each issue is clearly resolved before the next is taken up. Inside each issue and each sub-issue, the material is organized around the elements of the controlling rule or rules, and not around individual court decisions. Rule proof is always completed before rule application begins. Each issue and each sub-issue is explored through a well-chosen variation of the formula explained in this chapter. The reader is given neither too little nor too much explanation, but instead is able to read quickly and finish confident that the writer's conclusion is correct. Authority is discussed in the order of its logical importance, not necessarily in the chronological order in which it developed. Finally, the writer's organization is apparent throughout: the reader always knows where she is and how everything fits together. These things all come from sound *architecture:* from a wisely chosen building plan that the writer can explain and justify if asked to do so.

To figure out whether you have accomplished these things, ask yourself the following questions after you have written a first draft.[1]

> **14-A**   **Have you stated your *conclusion* for each issue? If so, where?** State it precisely, succinctly, and in such a way that the reader knows from the very beginning what you intend to demonstrate. Some lawyers express a prediction openly ("Kolchak will not be convicted of robbery"), while others imply the prediction by stating the conclusion on which it is based ("The evidence does not establish beyond a reasonable doubt that Kolchak is guilty of robbery").

> **14-B**   **Have you stated the *rule* or rules on which your conclusion is based? If so, where?**   If the cases on which you rely haven't formulated an explicit statement of the rule, you might be tempted just to describe the cases and let the reader decide what rule they stand for. If you feel that temptation, you probably haven't yet figured out exactly what the rule is. And if you haven't done it, the reader won't do it for you. Formulate a credible rule, and prove it by analyzing the authority at hand.

> **14-C**   **For each issue, have you *proved and explained* the rule in an appropriate amount of depth?**   Is your rule proof conclusory, substantiating, or comprehensive? How did you decide how much depth to use? If you were in the decision-maker's position, would you need more rule proof? Less? Is policy accounted for? If the rule seems arbitrary, the reader will resist agreeing that it's the correct one to use. The reader will more easily agree if you at least allude to the policy behind the rule and the social benefits the rule causes. Have you counter-analyzed attractive arguments that might challenge your choice or formulation of the rule?

> **14-D**   **For each issue, have you *applied* the rule to the facts in an appropriate amount of depth?**   Have you relied, where possible,

---

1. When marking up your work, your teacher might refer to these questions by using the number-letter codes that appear next to each question here.

on analogies to cases with favorable outcomes? Have you distinguished factually similar cases with unfavorable outcomes?

Is your rule application conclusory, substantiating, or comprehensive? How did you decide how much depth to use? If you were in the decision-maker's position, would you need more rule application? Less? Have you accounted for policy? Have you counter-analyzed attractive arguments that might challenge your application of the rule?

14-E **Have you completed rule proof and explanation before starting rule application?** If you let the material get out of control, the result may be a little rule proof, followed by a little rule application, followed by a little more rule proof, followed by a little more rule application — and so on, back and forth and back and forth. Finish proving the rule before you start applying it. If you start to apply a rule before you have finished proving it, the reader will refuse to agree with what you're doing.

14-F **Have you varied the paradigm formula's sequence only where truly necessary?** If you have varied the sequence of the components of the formula, why? Was your goal more valuable than any clarity you might have sacrificed by varying the sequence? (It might have been, but your decision should be a conscious one.)

14-G **Have you organized a multi-issue presentation so the reader understands how everything fits together?** If you have combined separately structured explanations, did you identify separate sub-conclusions? Are the combined paradigms covered by an umbrella paradigm? Is the result crystal-clear to the reader? If not, how could it be made so? (If you are writing a persuasive motion memo or appellate brief, see pages 253-54.)

14-H **Have you organized around tests and elements rather than around cases?** Your goal isn't to dump before the reader the cases you found doing research. The law is the rules themselves. A case merely proves a rule's existence and accuracy. The cases are raw materials, and your job isn't complete until you have built them into a coherent discussion organized around the applicable tests and their elements. A mere list of relevant cases, with discussion of each, isn't helpful to a decision-maker, who needs to understand how the rules affect the facts. This fault is called case-by-case-itis. It's easy to spot in a student's paper: the reader sees an unconnected series of paragraphs, each of which is devoted to discussion of a single case. The impression made is sometimes called "show-and-tell" because the writer seems to be doing nothing more than holding up newly found possessions. A student not making this mistake might use five cases to analyze the first element of a test, one case — if it's dispositive — to analyze the second, three for the third, and so on, deploying cases where they will do what is needed.

14-I **Have you avoided presenting authority in chronological order unless you have a special need to do so?** The reader wants to know what the current law is and how it governs the facts at hand. A little history might be useful somewhere in the discussion. But you'll waste the reader's time if you begin with the kind of historical background typical of a college essay. Unless there's some special need to do otherwise, present authority in the order of its logical importance, not the order in which it came to be.

14-J **Have you collected closely related ideas rather than scattering them?** If there are three reasons why the defendant will not be convicted, list them and then explain each in turn. The reader looking for the big picture can't follow you if you introduce the first reason on page 1; mention the second for the first time on page 4; and surprise the reader with the third on page 6. If you have more than one item or idea, listing them at the beginning helps the reader keep things in perspective. It also forces you to organize and evaluate your thoughts. Sometimes, in the act of listing, you may find that there are really fewer or more reasons — or whatever else you are listing — than you had originally thought.

Exercise
Teddy Washburn's Gun

This exercise takes you through the ground work needed to make a prediction and helps you organize raw materials — rules, facts, statutes, cases — into an outline that tracks the components of the paradigm. After the fact narrative below, you'll find two statutes and three cases, followed by questions for you to answer.

Facts

In his prime, Gorilla Morrell was often on the bill at Friday Night Wrestling. Now he is reduced to hanging around Washburn's Weights Room & Gym, which is next door to Washburn's Bar & Grill. Gorilla is good for Teddy Washburn's business because customers in the Weights Room try to take Gorilla on. When this happens, customers from the Bar wander into the Weights Room to watch. There they order more drinks, which Washburn passes through a hole he has cut through the wall. Afterward, Gorilla, his adversary, and the spectators tend to adjourn back to the Bar, where the spirit of conviviality usually leads to games of billiards accompanied by further orders of food and drink.

Washburn has let Gorilla build up a bill of $283.62, dating back over several weeks. Last night, they had words over the matter. Gorilla took a swing at Washburn, who came out from behind the bar and chased Gorilla out into the street. There Gorilla took another swing at Washburn, and Washburn, demanding his money, pulled out a gun (which he bought and for which he has a license).

Gorilla grabbed for the gun, but it fell out of Washburn's hand, sliding five or six feet along the sidewalk and coming to rest at the feet of Snare Drum Bennett, a mechanic who was returning from work. Bennett happened onto this scene only in time to hear Washburn demand money and to see him pull out the gun and have it knocked from his hand.

Bennett, Washburn, and Gorilla looked at the gun, then at each other, and then at the gun again. Finally, Bennett crouched down, picked up the gun, checked to make sure the safety was on, and put it in her coat pocket. "Washburn," she said, "you haven't paid *me* yet for the front end work I did on your car."

"I will," said Washburn.

"It's $575," said Bennett, "and it's been three weeks. I think you should go back inside. You ought to pay your own debts before you accuse other people of welshing out on you."

"How can I pay you," exclaimed Washburn, "if he won't pay me?"

"That's your problem," said Bennett, "I'm holding onto the gun. You can't seem to handle it right now, and I want my money."

At that point, Gorilla clobbered Washburn in the face and sent him staggering. Bennett turned around, walked a half-dozen steps, and began to turn into a dark alley. Washburn started to get up, called out "Hey, you!" and took a step in Bennett's direction. Bennett took the gun from her coat, pointed it at Washburn, smiled, and said, "Back off, bucko."

Washburn froze, and Bennett walked into the alley. As soon as she was out of sight, she dropped the gun into an open but full trash dumpster. The dumpster belongs to a grocery store and is about five feet inside the alley, which in turn is about twenty feet from the front door of Washburn's bar.

An hour or so later, the police came to Bennett's home and arrested her for robbing Washburn of his gun. Bennett told them where she had dropped it. The police went straight to the dumpster but found nothing inside, not even the trash that had muffled the gun's fall. *dumpster emptied*

Statutes

Criminal Code § 10: No person shall be convicted of a crime except on evidence proving guilt beyond a reasonable doubt.

Criminal Code § 302: A person commits robbery by taking, with the intent to steal, the property of another, from the other's person or in the other's presence, and through violence or intimidation. A person does not commit robbery if the intent to steal was formed after the taking.

intent to steal post-taking?

Cases

BUTTS v. STATE

The defendant had worked for the Royal Guano company for two and a half days when he was fired. He demanded his wages but was told that he would have to wait until Saturday, which was payday. He was ordered off the premises and left. After a few hours, he returned with a gun, found the shift foreman, and demanded his wages again. The foreman told him to come back on Saturday. (The company agrees that it owed the defendant wages, but insists that he wait until payday to receive them.) When the foreman refused, the defendant showed the gun and demanded again. The foreman then paid the amount the defendant requested.

An intent to steal is an intent to deprive the owner permanently of his property. There is no intent to steal if the defendant in good faith believes that the property taken is the defendant's own property and not the property of somebody else.

The defendant could reasonably have supposed that he was entitled to his pay when his connection with the company was severed. He was wrong because the money was the property of the company until the company paid it to him. But he acted in good faith and therefore did not have the intent to steal (although he may be guilty of crimes other than robbery).

GREEN v. STATE

We reverse the defendant's conviction for robbing Mrs. Lillie Priddy.

Although there was evidence that the defendant assaulted Mrs. Priddy, that alone does not prove robbery. Mrs. Priddy testified as follows: She was walking along a road and came upon the defendant, who struck her so that she lost consciousness. After a minute or two, her mind cleared, and she saw the defendant standing in the road and her purse on the ground about five feet from each of them. The contents of the purse were spilled out on the ground. She kicked him and ran, never seeing her purse again.

The issue is whether there was a "taking" sufficient to support a charge of robbery. A taking is the securing dominion over or absolute control of the property. Absolute control must exist at some time, even if only for a moment.

If Mrs. Priddy was unconscious, she could not know whether the defendant ever had control of her purse, or whether it simply fell to the ground and was later taken away by someone else. None of its contents were found in the defendant's home. The testimony showed a very violent assault and battery upon her by the defendant, but does not establish a robbery.

STATE v. SMITH & JORDAN

The defendants overpowered and disarmed the complainant of his knife. He had surprised them after they broke into his gas station. With the complainant's knife (but not the complainant), they got into their car and drove off. Later, the police found the defendants standing by their wrecked car. The complainant's knife was on the ground nearby. The defendants were convicted of robbery.

To convict for robbery, the defendant must have intended permanently to deprive the complainant of the taken property. If a defendant takes another's property for the taker's immediate and temporary use with no intent permanently to deprive the owner of his property, he is not guilty of robbery.

It would be unreasonable to assume that the defendants, fleeing from arrest for the crime of breaking into the gas station, had any expectation of returning the knife. They would have been captured if they had tried. For the purpose of decision here, we assume that defendant took the knife "for temporary use" and that after it had served the purpose of escape, they intended to abandon it at the first opportunity lest it lead to their detection. That, however, would leave the complainant's recovery of his knife to mere chance and thus constitute a reckless exposure to loss that is consistent with an intent permanently to deprive the owner of his property. In abandoning it, the defendants put it beyond their power to return the knife. When, in order to serve a temporary purpose of one's own, one takes property (1) with the specific intent wholly and permanently to deprive the owner of it, or (2) under circumstances which render it unlikely that the owner will ever recover his property and which disclose the taker's total indifference to his rights, one takes with the intent to steal.

Analyzing and Organizing

Exercise II-A: You have been asked to determine whether Bennett is likely to be convicted of robbing Washburn of his gun. Make a list of the issues.

Exercise II-B: For each issue, take a separate piece of paper and, using the process described in §14.1, answer the following questions:

1. What rule from the cases above disposes of the issue? (If you can't find a rule that would dispose of the issue, say so. If that's true, it means that additional authority is needed.)
2. What passages from these authorities prove the rule?
3. What facts in Bennett's story would be determinative for the issue?
4. What passages from these authorities would guide you in applying the rule to those determinative facts? (If you find none for a given issue, say so. Again, if you're right, more authority is needed.)
5. What cases would you analogize to or need to distinguish? Why? How would you do it?

Exercise II-C: In Exercise II-B, you started creating an outline from which to write. If there are any holes in this outline, list them. How will you fill them in?

PREDICTIVE
ANALYSIS
DOCUMENTS

15 Interviewing the Client

Client representation starts with an interview. A person who wants a lawyer's help calls to make an appointment. The secretary finds a convenient time and asks what the subject of the interview will be. The person calling says, "I've just been charged with a crime" or "I signed a contract to buy a house and now the owner won't sell." At the time of the appointment, that person and the lawyer sit down and talk. If the visitor has confidence in the lawyer, the visitor may become a client.

During that conversation, the lawyer learns what problem the prospective client wants solved, the client's goals in getting it solved, and what the client knows factually about the problem. The lawyer also learns about the client as a person and gives the client a reciprocal opportunity to learn about the lawyer. Then or later, the lawyer and client also negotiate the contract through which the client hires the lawyer, but here we focus on the main parts of the interview: building a relationship with the client and fact-gathering.

§15.1 Clients and Lawyers

Most clients are not really interested in hiring "a lawyer." They want to hire a genuine and caring human being who can do lawyer work well.

You probably dislike it when a doctor treats you as a case of flu, rather than as a person who has the flu. The problem is more than unpleasantness. A doctor who treats you as a human being with flu-like symptoms might spend enough time with you to learn that you also have other symptoms inconsistent with the flu, and that you have a different disease, which should be treated differently. If you have not yourself been a client, you can imagine what clients experience during lawyer interviews simply by remembering how you have experienced contact with professionals such as doctors.

Treating the client as a person is called "client-centered lawyering,"[1] which means focusing your efforts around what the client wants rather than what you assume the client should want. Your client has hired you to accomplish the *client's* goal. And many clients can collaborate actively with you along the way, brainstorming with you how to solve problems.

You are obligated to keep secret whatever the client tells you in private, which is the lawyer's *duty of confidentiality*.[2] There are exceptions. For example, a lawyer may reveal the client's confidences to other people with the client's permission. And a lawyer may reveal the client's confidences to prevent the client from committing a serious crime. States differ in how they define these and other exceptions to the duty of confidentiality.

§15.2   The Interview

After the sort of pleasantries that people exchange when meeting each other, the lawyer says something like, "How can I help you?" or "Let's talk about what brings you here today" or "My secretary tells me the bank has threatened to foreclose on your mortgage. You're probably worried. Where shall we begin?"

§15.2.1   Learning What the Client Knows

Do not label the problem in your own mind until you have heard most of the facts. A client who starts by telling you about a dispute with a landlord might have defamation and assault claims rather than breach of a lease obligation.

Do not leap in with questions as soon as the client has told you the nature of the problem. Give the client a full opportunity to tell you whatever the client wants to talk about before you intervene. Many clients want to make sure from the beginning that you hear certain things about which the client feels deeply. If you obstruct this, you will seem remote, even bureaucratic, to the client. And if you listen to what the client wants to tell you, you may learn a lot about the client as a person and about how the client views the problem.

In the beginning, encourage the client to present the facts in the way the client thinks best. After a while (sometimes pretty quickly), the client will want you to take the lead.

Most clients will not mind your taking notes on a pad of paper, if you first explain that you want to be sure to remember everything the client tells you. But keep listening while you write, and make eye contact often. You might feel

---

1. David A. Binder, Paul Bergman, Susan C. Price & Paul R. Tremblay, *Lawyers as Counselors: A Client-Centered Approach* (2d ed. 2004).
2. ABA Model Rules of Professional Conduct, Rule 1.6.

comfortable taking notes on your laptop, but consider whether your client would feel comfortable as well. The screen places a barrier between you and your client at a time when you want to encourage interaction.

§15.2.2 Questions

Explore the various aspects of the problem in detail. On each topic, start with broad questions ("Tell me what happened the night the nuclear reactor melted down") and gradually work your way toward narrow ones ("Just before you ran from the control panel, what number on that dial was the needle pointing to?"). But do this gradually. If you jump too quickly to the narrow questions, you will miss a lot of information because the broad questions show you what to explore. Ask broad questions until you are not getting useful information anymore. Then go back and ask narrow questions about the facts the client did not cover. While the client is answering the broad questions, you can note on a pad the topics you will need to explore later using narrow questions.

When you start exploring various aspects of the problem in detail, try to take up each topic separately. Too much skipping around confuses you and the client.

Word your questions carefully. How you ask them has a lot to do with the quality and quantity of the information you get. A good question does not confuse, does not provoke resistance, and does not distort memory. *One of the marks of an effective lawyer is the ability to ask the right questions in the most productive way.*

What makes a question work well? First, it seeks information that really does need to be known. Second, a good question is phrased in a way most likely to produce valuable information. Some words help find information and encourage answers, while other words confuse, cloud memory, or provoke resistance. Third, a good question is asked in a useful sequence with other questions. Sometimes other questions have to be asked and answered first. And ask one question at a time. If you ask two at a time, only one of them will be answered.

Keep asking questions until you have all the details: when, where, who, how, and why. Get them precisely. "Last week" is not good enough. You need "Thursday, at about 11 A.M., in the truckstop parking lot." If the client tells you about a conversation, ask who else was present, what else was discussed, how long the conversation lasted, how it started, how it ended, what words each participant used, and so on. You are going to need these details to analyze the situation. In nonprofessional life, vagueness and approximation are usually enough in conversations. But experienced lawyers know that, in representing clients, only precision works.

Before the interview ends, make sure you understand the timeline of events from beginning to end: What happened first, what happened next, what happened just after that, and so on.

§15.2.3   Listening and Talking

The ability to listen well is as important in the practice of law as the ability to talk well. The popular image of a lawyer is of a person talking — to juries, to judges, to adversaries, to reporters. But in the end, the lawyer who succeeds is the one who also knows how to listen. If you do not listen carefully, you might as well not have asked the question, and you will not know what to ask about next. Knowledge is strength, and in the practice of law one of the most important means of gaining knowledge is to listen carefully.

When communicating with clients, talk and write in plain English. If you have to use a term of art, explain its meaning in an uncondescending way. Use concrete, precise language and not vague generalities. Behave in ways that encourage clients to tell you things that you need to know and to ask questions about things that make the client anxious.

§15.2.4   How to Conclude

Clients often want the lawyer to predict immediately whether the client will win or lose. Do not even try to make that prediction. You must first research the law. The client might need to supply information or documents that were not brought to the interview. Nearly always, the client does not know all the facts, and you and the client will need to investigate them further. And you need to think about it. Hasty predictions are often inaccurate.

But clients want assurance. What can you give them? Usually, it is enough to explain what work you will do. A client might not realize that lawyers do not know all the answers right away. But we do know how to find the answers. You can convey to your client that you take the problem very seriously and want to do something about the issues. You can also explain specifically what you will do next.

As a client leaves your office, two questions are typically running through the client's mind: Will this lawyer be able to accomplish what I want? And did this lawyer truly *hear me* and *understand me*? The law and the facts might prevent you from accomplishing what the client wants. But nothing should prevent you from hearing the client deeply and understanding the client as a person.

16 Office Memoranda

§16.1 Office Memorandum Format

Form follows function.

— motto of the Bauhaus school of architecture

An office memorandum predicts how the law will treat the client. Chapter 4, which you should review now, explains predictive analysis.

The memo might be read many times over a period of months or years by several different lawyers, including the one who wrote the memo. It might be used as a resource long after it was written. For example, a memo might be written after a client asks whether it would be worthwhile to start a lawsuit. If the answer is yes, and the client decides to sue, the memo might be used again to help a lawyer — perhaps you or your supervisor — draft the complaint. It might be used a third time when the lawyer responds to a motion to dismiss, and so on.

Writing predictive memos can make your predictions, on average, more accurate. That's because *writing is thinking*. When you start writing a memo, you might believe that this particular client has a cause of action. But as you try to explain that, you might discover that the explanations don't hold water and that the client actually has no cause of action. Writers often change their mind while writing because writing causes them to rethink what they thought they knew.

Who should you imagine your reader to be? When you start working at a job, there will be nothing to imagine because most of the time your reader will be your supervisor. But in law school, your assignments are hypothetical. Imagine that you're writing to the typical partner or supervising lawyer described in §6.2. This person will be busy and by nature skeptical and careful. She will be reading your memo for the purpose of making a decision and will probably be under some kind of pressure (especially time pressure) while reading.

Format varies from law office to law office and from case to case, but a typical office memo includes some combination of the following:

1. A memorandum heading
2. The Issue or Issues
3. A Brief Answer
4. The Facts
5. A Discussion
6. A Conclusion

In some offices and for some purposes, the Brief Answer might be combined with the Issue or Issues. In a relatively uncomplicated situation, the Brief Answer or the Conclusion (but not both) might be omitted.

Think of memos as manuals to guide the reader's decision-making. They aren't necessarily read from beginning to end. The reader might open up a particular memo or brief on several different occasions, and the reader's purpose at any given time determines the portions of the document that will be read and the order in which they'll be read. These documents are very much like your car's owner's manual. The reader's need at the moment may be limited (*"How do I change this flat tire?"*), and it can be satisfied without having to read the entire document.

The rest of this chapter is easier to follow if you look to the memo in Appendix C for illustration as you read the description below of each of these components.

The **memorandum heading** simply identifies the writer, the recipient, the date on which the memo is completed, and the subject.

> To: *[supervising lawyer]*
> From: *[you]*
> Date: *[today]*
> Re: *[subject, including client's name]*

The "Re:" line should specify enough context that the reader knows what aspect of the client's representation the memo addresses. For example:

> To: Theresa Wycoff
> From: Christine Chopin
> Date: March 1, 2017
> Re: Eli Goslin's Claim for a Constructive Trust

Another method would be to use a separate line for identifying the client:

To: Theresa Wycoff
From: Christine Chopin
Date: March 1, 2017
Client: Eli Goslin
Re: Claim for a Constructive Trust

The **Issue** (or Issues) states the question (or questions) that the memo resolves. The Issue also itemizes the inner core of facts that you think crucial to the answer. You can phrase the Issue as a question about whether a legal test has been satisfied or how the law treats a particular problem (*"Does driving at twice the speed limit constitute reckless endangerment under Penal Code § 786?"*). Or you can ask a question about how the courts would rule in a particular dispute (*"Is Mr. Maglie likely to be convicted of reckless endangerment under Penal Code §786 for driving at twice the speed limit?"*).

Notice how the examples in the preceding ask for the prediction — one explicitly and the other implicitly:

implicitly predictive Issue: Does driving at twice the speed limit constitute reckless endangerment under Penal Code § 786?

explicitly predictive Issue: Is Mr. Maglie likely to be convicted of reckless endangerment under Penal Code § 786 for driving at twice the speed limit?

These are essentially the same question. Answering *yes* to one of them is the same as answering *yes* to the other.

Which version should you use? Choose the one that works better for the circumstances. In one memo, the implicit version might be more appropriate, and in another the explicit one might work better. And in the office where you work, local custom might favor one over the other.

An Issue includes its context — both the governing body of law and the crucial facts.

If the issue is statutory, refer to the statute. In the examples above, Penal Code § 786 governs. If the issue is one of common law, refer to the jurisdiction and the common law doctrine (*"negligence under Wyoming law"*). The Appendix C memo's Issue refers to New York's version of the common law constructive trust.

The Issue also refers the essential facts. In the examples above, only one fact is essential: the client drove at twice the posted speed limit. The Appendix C memo addresses a more complicated factual situation.

The **Brief Answer** states the writer's prediction and summarizes concisely why it's likely to happen. This usually involves at least an allusion to the determinative facts and rules, together with some expression of how the facts and rules come together to cause the predicted result. The complete analysis occurs in the Discussion.

For the reader in a hurry, the Brief Answer should set out the bottom-line response in the most accessible way. Compare two Brief Answers, both of which respond to the following Issue:

Issue

Did the District Attorney act unethically in announcing an indictment at a press conference where the defendant's criminal record was recited, an alleged tape-recorded confession was played, ballistics tests on an alleged murder weapon were described, and the defendant was produced for photographers without the knowledge of her lawyer?

Brief Answer
(Example 1)

Under Rule 3.6 of the Rules of Professional Conduct, it is unethical for a prosecutor before trial to publicize, among other things, any criminal record the defendant might have, any confession she might allegedly have made, or the results of any tests the government might have undertaken. Under Rule 8.4(d), it is also unethical to engage in conduct "prejudicial to the administration of justice." That has occurred here if the press conference — and particularly the presentation of the defendant for photographers — created so much pretrial publicity that the jury pool has been prejudiced. Therefore, the District Attorney violated Rule 3.6 and may have violated Rule 8.4(d).

Brief Answer
(Example 2)

Yes. Except for the production of the defendant for photographers, all the actions listed in the Issue are specifically prohibited by Rule 3.6 of the Rules of Professional Conduct. In addition, if producing the defendant for photographers tainted the jury pool, it was unethical under Rule 8.4(d), which prohibits conduct "prejudicial to the administration of justice."

Example 1 is closer to the way you might think through the Brief Answer in a first draft. But to make it useful to the reader you would rewrite it to be something like Example 2, which can be more quickly read and understood.

The **Facts** set out the events and circumstances on which the prediction is based. Usually, the Facts are a story narrative, but sometimes organizing them by topic works better — for example if different things happened in different places at the same time. Include dates only if they are determinative or needed to avoid confusion. A date could be determinative if the issue is based on time, such as a statute of limitations.

One way to begin the fact statement is to introduce the most important character or characters, as in the Appendix C memo. Another is to summarize the most important event or events (*"Mr. Goslin deeded his home to his nephew, assuming he would be able to continue living there, and now the nephew is trying to force him to leave"*). A third way of beginning is to state why the memo is being written (*"Mr. Goslin wants to know whether he can regain ownership, or at least exclusive possession, of his home"*). Choose the method that would be most helpful in the case at hand to the reader who will probably make the most use of the memo.

Include all facts you consider determinative, together with any explanatory facts needed to help the story make sense. If your reader is already familiar with the factual background, this part of the memo might be abruptly short — much shorter than the fact statement in Appendix C — because your purpose will be to remind the reader about the essential facts, rather than to make a detailed record of them, which already be in your office's file for this client.

For example, if over the past few days you and your supervisor have spent several hours working together on the Appendix C case — and your supervisor therefore is already familiar with the facts — you might use a condensed fact statement something like this:

> The client is elderly, retired, arthritic, and a widower. His only asset is his home, and he has no other place to live. His only income is from social security.
>
> Last year, when the client could no longer pay his mortgage, his nephew offered to make the remaining $11,500 in payments as they became due. Seventeen years ago, the client contributed $3,200 to the nephew's college tuition, but the nephew did not say he was now reciprocating.
>
> The client, without stating his purpose to anyone, then gave a deed to the house to the nephew. The client has told us, "At the time, it seemed like the right thing to do. He was going to pay the mortgage, and after a certain point — maybe after I'm gone — the place would become his. I didn't think it would end up like this." The nephew did not ask for a deed.
>
> A few weeks ago, the nephew unexpectedly moved into the house and ordered the client to move out. The client refused, and the nephew has become verbally and physically abusive.

Compare this condensed version with the one in the Appendix C memo, where the writer knows that the reader is less familiar with the factual details.

The **Discussion** is the largest and most complex part of the memo. It proves the conclusion set out in the Brief Answer. If the discussion is highly detailed or analyzes several issues, it can be broken up with subheadings to help the reader locate the portions that might be needed at any given time.

When writing a Discussion, you will use rules to predict what a court will do; organize proof of your conclusion; select authority to back up your conclusion; and work with precedent, statutes, and facts.

The **Conclusion** summarizes the discussion in a bit more detail than the Brief Answer does. The Brief Answer is for the reader who needs to know the bottom line but has no time to read more. The Conclusion is for the reader who needs and has time for more detail, but not as much as the Discussion offers. The Conclusion or Brief Answer can also provide an overview for the reader about to plunge into the Discussion.

Here and in the Brief Answer, carefully choose the words that will tell the reader how much confidence to ascribe to your predictions. Attached to many of your predictions will be the words "probably," "probably not," "likely," or "unlikely." If you think the odds are very high that you are right, you can say something like "almost certainly." If the Issue is framed as a question about whether a test has been satisfied (*"Did the District Attorney act unethically...?"*), a simple "yes" or "no" will be understood as the equivalent of "almost certainly yes" or "almost certainly no," and you do not need to add the extra words.

Prediction can be expressed (*"the client will almost certainly lose a lawsuit"*) or implied (*"the client does not have a cause of action"*). But make a prediction, not a guess. When you make a prediction conditioned on a fact not yet known, specify the condition (*"if producing the defendant for television cameras tainted the jury pool, it was unethical"*).

Although the Brief Answer is limited to responding to the Issue, the Conclusion is an appropriate place to explain what lawyering tasks need to be done, to suggest methods of solving the client's problem, or to evaluate options already under consideration. If any of these things would be complicated, they can be accomplished in a **Recommendations** section added after the Conclusion.

§16.2   Writing an Office Memo

Some lawyers tend to write the Discussion before writing anything else because the other components of the memo will be shaped in part by insights gained while putting the Discussion together. Other lawyers start by writing the Facts because those seem easier to describe. (Lawyers who write the Discussion first would say that they cannot start by writing the Facts because, until they have worked out the Discussion, they don't know which facts are determinative.) Other lawyers are flexible. They start with whatever component begins to "jell" first, and they often draft two or more components simultaneously.

§16.3 How to Test Your Writing for Predictiveness

After you have written a first draft — and before you start on later drafts — ask yourself the following questions.

16-A   **Have you edited out waffling?**   Vague waffling, using words like "seems to," "appears," and their synonyms, makes your advice less useful to clients and supervising lawyers. If it happens that someone disagrees with you, lightning will not strike you down on the spot. On the contrary, supervisors and judges are grateful for forthrightness and are impatient with hedging. But it's not waffling to say that "the plaintiff *probably* will win an appeal" or "is *likely* to win an appeal." No prediction can be a certainty.

16-B   **Have you said or implied whether your prediction is qualified?**   Is the law unsettled because courts disagree with each other or because a statute is so new that it hasn't yet been interpreted by courts? If so, make sure the reader understands that. Overt qualifications of accuracy are usually not necessary, since the prediction can be stated in a way that implies your degree of confidence in it. The implication comes not from "weasel words" like "seems to" or "perhaps" (see item 16-A), but instead from a precise statement of the variables on which the prediction is based (*"The defendant will probably prevail unless . . ."*).

16-C   **Have you accounted for gaps in the law?**   Sometimes the law has gaps — holes that have not yet been filled in by legislation or by precedent (see §7.5 in Chapter 7). If the law you're dealing with is unsettled or incomplete, have you identified the gaps for the reader? And have you predicted how the courts will fill them?

16-D   **Have you solved a problem rather than written a college essay?**   A college essay is a forum for academic analysis — analysis to satisfy curiosity — rather than for practical problem-solving. In a college essay, you can reason in any logical manner toward any sensible goal you select, even at whim. But legal writing is practical work. Your Discussion should focus on resolving specific questions. Sentences not helpful in resolving those questions should be cut.

17 Email Communication

Lawyers spend a lot of time writing email. They write to coworkers, clients, opposing counsel, courts, and many others. They email for many different purposes: to set up meetings, ask and answer questions, attach documents, and communicate legal analysis. A lawyer with a busy practice receives a high volume of email every day.

As a new lawyer, your goal should be to make sure you use email professionally and effectively. Experienced lawyers frequently complain that recent law school graduates don't know how to use email appropriately. Although you may have been writing email nearly all your life, you probably haven't done so in a professional context.

Writing professional email is a skill. This chapter explains how to do it and how to communicate legal analysis precisely in an email.

§17.1   Email Pitfalls

Used properly, email enhances law practice by facilitating quick and easy communication. But if not used carefully, email can embarrass you and, worse, adversely affect clients and other lawyers. When preparing to write an email, start by asking yourself whether an email is appropriate. Is this a matter better handled with a phone conversation? Is what you are going to say too complicated for the short email format? Do you really need to contact your recipient at all, or is it an issue you can resolve yourself?

Lawyers are critical readers with high standards. Experienced lawyers often complain that recent law school graduates are too informal in their use of email, showing a lack professionalism. To avoid embarrassment, spell every-thing perfectly and use proper grammar. Write complete sentences, not frag-ments. Avoid slang. Address your reader with respect. Although email is more informal than other types of legal writing, it is still a professional communi-cation and requires a professional tone. Assume that every email you write might later appear as an exhibit in a lawsuit and be read by a judge and jury. Write your emails so carefully and professionally that you wouldn't be embar-rassed if that were to happen.

Experienced lawyers complain about the frequency and timeliness of emails written by new lawyers. Because email transmits immediately, other lawyers and your clients will expect prompt replies. Try to respond to every email within 24 hours, even if just to acknowledge the message and say you are work-ing on the answer. Don't send hasty or thoughtless messages. Busy lawyers are flooded with email and don't want to see any more than is necessary. Because email is easy to send, junior lawyers tend to send frequent and multiple emails to supervisors. Stop and think before sending. Is the email really necessary? Have you gathered all of your questions and comments into a single message, rather than sending multiple messages? Have you paused and reflected rather than sent an email in haste or anger? These are common mistakes to avoid.

Email can easily lead to misunderstandings because the recipient sees only your words on a screen with none of the clues — voice tone and body lan-guage — that communicate nonverbal meaning. Suppose you and another lawyer are negotiating a contract. You represent the buyer; the other lawyer represents the seller. You telephone the other lawyer and speak these words:

> My client needs the contract signed by Thursday. Will you be able to do it by then?

Say these two sentences — out loud — in the tone you would use if you were asking the other lawyer, as a favor to you and your client, to speed things up even though you know that will be inconvenient for the other lawyer and her client.

Now say them again. But this time you aren't asking a favor. You're demand-ing something. The second sentence communicates that you want the other lawyer to concede that she must do what the first sentence requires. When you speak the words, use your voice tone to communicate that you expect to be obeyed.

Email is a cold medium. Words you intend to be friendly can often look unfriendly. If you were to put those two sentences in an email, many lawyers would assume that you're making a demand. To prevent misunderstanding, sometimes you'll need to express in words things that in conversation you would communicate by voice tone. For example, if in an email you mean to ask a favor, you might need to write something like this:

My client needs the contract signed by Thursday. I realize that this might be a problem for you and your client. But is there any way you can do it by then?

To the other lawyer, there's a big difference between this and the original version.

§17.2 Email and Confidentiality Problems

A lawyer's work is governed by a number of ethics rules, which you will learn in detail in your second- or third-year course in Professional Responsibility. One of a lawyer's ethical duties is to keep confidential everything the lawyer knows about the client and the client's situation unless the client authorizes the lawyer to reveal those confidences. (There are other exceptions, but they aren't relevant here.)

Nearly all states have adopted the ABA Model Rules of Professional Conduct. Here are excepts from the rule on confidentiality:

Rule 1.6 Confidentiality of Information

(a) A lawyer shall not reveal information relating to the representation of a client unless the client gives informed consent, the disclosure is impliedly authorized in order to carry out the representation or the disclosure is permitted by paragraph (b).
[Paragraph (b) lists various exceptions to the duty.]
(c) A lawyer shall make reasonable efforts to prevent the inadvertent or unauthorized disclosure of, or unauthorized access to, information relating to the representation of a client.

Official Comments 5 and 19 relate to email even though they don't mention email:

Comment 5

... Lawyers in a firm may, in the course of the firm's practice, disclose to each other information relating to a client of the firm, unless the client has instructed that particular information be confined to specified lawyers.

Comment 19

When transmitting a communication that includes information relating to the representation of a client, the lawyer must take reasonable precautions to prevent the information from coming into the hands of unintended recipients.

Much of your email will include confidential information. Much of it will contain attorney work product, which is covered in the discovery part of your course on Civil Procedure. And much of it can affect the attorney-client privilege, which you will learn about in your second- or third-year course on Evidence.

If you handle email badly, you migh breach your ethical duty of confidentiality; create work product and discovery issues; inadvertently waive your client's attorney-client privilege; or do two or even all three of these. In other words, you can cause a lot of damage if your email ends up on the wrong person's computer screen.

Be careful to make sure your email is clearly addressed to the correct recipient. And be careful with email programs that autocomplete or autofill addresses. Autocomplete might be your friend because it saves keystrokes, but it's also your enemy. Unless you pay careful attention what it puts into your emails' *TO* field, your email can be delivered to the wrong person. Also, make sure you haven't inadvertently chosen the *REPLY-ALL* option when you mean to reply to the sender alone and not to the people whom the sender cc'd. If you have attached a document, double-check to make sure it's the one you intend to send.

If you accidentally send an email or an attachment with confidential information to someone who shouldn't see it, you are required to notify your superiors and, in some instances, your client. You are also required to do your best to mitigate any damage that is caused.

Many lawyers and law firms include boilerplate language at the end of every email, stating that the email's contents are confidential. But that wording is not sufficient to protect the email's confidentiality. If the wrong person has seen an email, the boilerplate language can't erase information from that person's memory.

§17.3   Professional Tone and Appearance

When writing an email in a law practice context, your primary goal should be to meet the needs of your reader (as in all legal writing). You can accomplish this by being mindful of both maintaining a professional tone and making your writing easy to read on a screen. While these may not be things you have thought about before when writing email, as a lawyer, they should become second nature to you. As you read through this section, refer to Appendix D, which provides an example of a professional email.

§17.3.1   Keeping It Professional

Being professional in email does not mean being stiff and overly formal. Email tends to be more informal than memoranda of law (Chapter 16) and letters (Chapter 19). In an email, it is acceptable to be conversational, as long as you remember that this is a professional communication and not a quick note to a friend. Each component of the email should be clear, direct, and focused, without extraneous information. When you start a new job, ask to see a sample or two of email that would illustrate that office's expectations concerning form and tone.

Subject line.　Assume that your reader is busy, with an inbox full of messages. The subject line should clearly communicate the purpose of the email so the recipient doesn't overlook it. If the email refers to a client or a case, include the name but also the email's specific subject. For example, "A v. B" provides much less informative than "A v. B., custody hearing." If you are replying to a message, don't change the subject line unless the topic of the message has shifted to something different. Think about how your reader might search for the message, and use language that is distinct and easy to find.

Salutation.　In most cases, begin the email with a salutation. If the email is part of a back-and-forth exchange, use your judgment about whether a salutation is necessary every time. Starting with a greeting lets your reader know that the message is intended for them, and helps you to maintain a professional approach to the email. How you begin depends on the relationship you have with your reader and the environment in which you are writing. In a very formal law firm, you might be expected to start an email to a partner with "Dear Ms. Khan," while in a more casual environment you might write "Hi, Sofia." First names may or may not be appropriate, depending on how well you know the person you are writing to and the nature of the relationship.

Body of the message.　The content of the message obviously depends on its purpose. Regardless of the content, however, the principles of good legal writing apply. You don't need to be overly formal in your use of language, but your writing should be clear, concise, and direct. Look back at what you have written and edit it. Don't assume that you can use sloppy or wordy language just because you are sending an informal email. Decide on an appropriate level of detail and omit anything extra.

Get to the point quickly. While a greeting is important, spending too much time on pleasantries may irritate a busy reader. In addition, keep the email focused on one subject. Don't mix personal business, such as making plans for lunch, with answering a legal question.

Signature.　Your email address will likely tell your reader who you are, so a signature is not necessary for that purpose. But signatures are expected in professional communications. They reinforce that you are attaching your name to your message and stand behind what you have said. In addition, you should have an automatic signature block that makes it easy for your reader to get in touch with you for follow-up questions. The signature block should include your position — Are you an intern? An associate? A staff attorney? — as well as the firm or organization you work for, a street address, a phone number, and a clickable email address.

§17.3.2   Making the Email Easy to Read

In addition to adopting a professional tone, your email should be professional in appearance and easy for your reader to follow. It is as likely that your email will be viewed on a mobile device, such as a phone or tablet, as on the larger screen of a laptop or desktop computer. It's difficult to read large blocks of text on a small screen. What looks like a few lines on a laptop screen may make for a lot of scrolling on a phone. One good way to get a sense of how easy your email is to read would be to send it to yourself and view it on different devices.

How do you deal with the problem of endless scrolling when you have to write a legal analysis of a complex question? You can use several techniques. First, write concisely as possible, and do not include extraneous information. Second, break the text up into smaller units, using headings, subheadings, and bullet points to make it easier for the reader to follow your organization and not get lost. You can also use different systems of headings, numbering, and bullets to indicate the hierarchy of information in an email, and to communicate the relationship between concepts.

Be aware of font and typeface. You might not have control over how your email is viewed. Thus, use with caution techniques such as varying the font type, size, and color. Changing font color could also be perceived as unprofessional, and some colors may be hard to read. Steer away from these methods of differentiating text unless you are very confident that you know how your email will be viewed.

§17.4   Communicating Legal Analysis in an Email Memo

Often you'll be asked to answer a legal question and to deliver your answer and reasoning in an email. You will write an *email memo* — an email that functions somewhat like an office memorandum, but scaled down drastically to email proportions. The chief differences between an email memo and a formal, full-scale memorandum are that (1) there is no standard format for communicating legal analysis in email and (2) email works better for short and simple questions but usually isn't the appropriate vehicle for long and complex legal analysis.

Writing a memo-like email is challenging because you must compress sophisticated legal analysis into the body of an email. And it's challenging because you must do everything quickly. Your supervisor asked for an email because she needs your answer fast.

Once you have made sure that you fully understand the legal question or questions you are addressing and have all of the relevant facts, go about the analysis in much the same way you would if you were writing a formal full-scale memorandum of law.

Organization.   Although an email has a much less formal structure than a memorandum and doesn't have separate sections for issues presented, brief answer, statement of facts, etc., you should still analyze your issue and organize your response using the paradigm outlined in Chapter 11. While the level of depth may vary in an email, the basic principle of stating your conclusion, explaining and citing your legal authority, and applying that authority to the facts, is important in any kind of legal analysis.

You don't need a formal question presented, but you should start the email with a quick review of the issue you are addressing together with your bottom-line answer. This quick overview will help to focus the email and let your reader know what to expect.

To figure out how much detail to include in the paradigm rule explanation and application (Chapter 11), first go through all the analytical steps yourself to make sure you fully understand the issues. Then make decisions about what to highlight and how much to include for your reader (see Chapter 12). If an issue is clear and not complicated, you can be more conclusory. If an issue is complex and confusing, provide more depth. You might decide to simplify the rule explanation by providing less detail about a judicial opinion. Consider using parenthetical explanations with case citations as a means of efficiently explaining precedent. Or you might present a more conclusory application of law to fact, highlighting the outcome more than the reasoning. You can't make those decisions until you have fully thought out the analysis for yourself, however, and determined how much will be lost if you cut down on detailed explanation. If you decide the analysis is too long and complex to be easily read in an email, you might make the choice to write a longer document and attach it to the email, providing your reader with just a summary in the email itself.

You don't need to end the email with a reiteration of your conclusion. In an email, this should be obvious and unnecessary. If your analysis has revealed further questions to explore or next steps to be taking, identify them and ask your supervisor whether you should proceed. Otherwise just wrap up and sign off.

Citation to legal authority.   Remember that you are writing to a critical legal reader, who will want to know how you supported your analysis, even in an email. That means providing your reader with easy access to the legal authority you relied on. This is particularly important if you have presented the highlights of a case holding without an in-depth discussion of the reasoning. It is good practice, if you are writing to a supervisor, to ask, before writing the email, about her preferences regarding how authority to provide. Some lawyers might be satisfied with a citation they can look up. Others might want hyperlinks, although if you use this option, make sure you are clear on what source to link — a commercial service or a free website. Another good option, which many lawyers prefer, is attaching PDF files of the cases and other authorities you have relied on. Your goal should be to provide your busy reader with the easiest and most efficient way to check on the authority that you have relied on.

Writing the email. You'll find it easier to do the writing in a word-processing program — for most people, that's Microsoft Word — and then copy and paste your work into the email. Word-processing software has features to facilitate writing. Email programs have few or none of those features.

Some of your formatting might be lost when you copy and paste. Before hitting *Send*, read your work one last time and make sure the headings are where you want them and, if you numbered paragraphs, that the numbers survived the journey from copying to pasting.

The *last* thing to do before sending is typing the recipient's name in the *To* field. If you do that earlier, and you accidentally hit *Send* before finishing the message or adding any attachments, the recipient will receive an unfinished message. Even though you'll realize your mistake and send a corrected message soon after, the recipient will have an overloaded inbox, will probably confuse the two messages, and will be puzzled about what you're communicating — to your embarrassment.

§17.5   How to Test Your Emails for Professional Effectiveness

Before hitting *Send*, ask yourself the following questions:[1]

17-A   Is your email addressed to the right person? Have you checked to make sure you haven't hit reply-all or that your email system hasn't autofilled the wrong address?

17-B   Is the subject line clear so the reader can easily identify your email's purpose?

17-C   Have you included an appropriate greeting and signature?

---

1. When marking up your work, your teacher might refer to these questions by using the number-letter codes that appear next to each question here.

17-D Is the email clear and concise, with a professional but not overly formal tone, so that a busy reader can quickly and easily read through it?

17-E Have you used headings, bullet points, and other devices to make the organization easy to see and to keep the email readable on small screens?

17-F Have you clearly organized the legal analysis in enough depth for the reader to feel confident in your analysis, but without being overwhelmed?

17-G Have you asked for information or identified next steps, where appropriate?

17-H Have you included attachments or links or otherwise provided access to the information you relied on in developing your answer?

17-I Have you proofread for errors and clarity?

18 Oral Presentations to Your Supervising Lawyer

For lawyers, time is quite literally money. In addition to busy law work, a lawyer must cultivate clients, and those clients are cost-conscious. For these reasons, as well as for convenience and the advantages of personal interaction, the modern practice of law increasingly requires junior lawyers to report their research results orally. For many issues, a full, formal memorandum would not be efficient or necessary. And an oral presentation gives the supervising lawyer an opportunity to discuss the issue with the junior lawyer and ask questions so that both lawyers, talking together, can test ideas and brainstorm.

Usually the junior lawyer meets with the senior lawyer in person, but this can sometimes happen on the telephone. The junior lawyer should be prepared to give an initial summary of her research. The summary should be as brief as possible given the complexity of the legal problem. The summary's most important characteristic is that it should get immediately to the point. You might start by saying something along the lines of "you asked this question; the answer is this; here is why."

This chapter lays out the best practices for giving an oral presentation of research. In sum: (1) Prepare a short overall presentation of the conclusion and analysis, akin to the brief answer in the memorandum or the short email answer; and (2) prepare to answer key questions about the analysis and authorities, as well as the path of your research.

§18.1   Preparing

§18.1.1   Getting the Assignment

As a preliminary matter, make sure you and your supervisor are on the same page in terms of what she wants you to do. With any assignment, show up with something that allows you to take notes. While this can be a legal pad, tablet, or laptop, just be sure it is something that allows you to write quickly. The important thing is that you write down the issue or assignment as explained by the supervisor, and then before leaving, read it back to your supervisor. You can say, "I just want to be certain that I'm supposed to research whether our client has a reasonable expectation of privacy while he's in his business office," or the like. Make sure you understand which jurisdiction's law governs. And be sure to ask approximately how much time you should spend on the assignment. Time is a budgeted resource.

§18.1.2   Researching

While doing your research, keep your focus on the precise question so you don't waste your time (and anyone's money) digging up law that will ultimately not be relevant. A useful technique is to have a research "bull's-eye" or target that you keep written down, near you while you research so that you can periodically remind yourself. Start with a narrow target and move away from it in small steps only to the extent you determine that there is no law on the initial target. Especially with online research, which allows you to follow link after link, it is too easy to lose your way and go far from your original target.

Secondary sources are a useful place to start your research for many reasons. They can give you a comprehensive "big picture" understanding of the issue, and that will help in all phases of the presentation: making a conclusion, analyzing difficult law, and answering questions from your supervisor.

§18.1.3 Writing Out Your Analysis

Before the meeting you should read and synthesize the law. Organize this synthesis, as you would any legal analysis, using the paradigm (Chapter 11) and a level of depth appropriate to the situation (Chapter 12). Begin with your conclusion, briefly summarize the key law or rules you rely on, note your key authority, and then apply the law to your client's facts.

Prepare for the oral presentation by drafting something in writing. This is the best way to prepare to speak cogently and effectively. It will help you organize your thoughts and work out any problem areas ahead of time. You do not want to go into the presentation without a fully formed idea of your answer and your reasoning. Approach the presentation just as you would the discussion of authority in a formal memorandum, without the added step of having to polish your writing.

Writing your analysis in advance will prevent you from floundering about or rambling during the meeting—both of which are real dangers with this type of report and are irritating to a busy senior lawyer. You might also find that your analysis changes or evolves as you write. It's best for this kind of evolution to happen *before* the meeting with your supervisor rather than in front of him. It's dangerous to go into a meeting with a stack of cases and no idea what to make of all of them. It's like bringing a bag of puzzle pieces to your boss and asking her to assemble the puzzle. That's not her job. It's *your* job.

§18.1.4 Whittling Down the Analysis to the Initial Summary

When you have reached a conclusion and analysis in which you are fairly confident, then you can start whittling your analysis down to its essentials. The essentials will be your initial summary. Two good starting points for organizing and compiling the initial summary are the "brief answer" for an office memo (Chapter 16) or an email answer (Chapter 17). As always, you should start with your conclusion, summarize the relevant rules on which you rely and apply it to the client's facts. But the "rule explanation" part will be quite abbreviated, expanding or contracting as necessary depending on the complexity of the issue. Think of describing your authority in terms of quick explanatory parentheticals as opposed to paragraph-long descriptions. Again, the key here is to be as direct and brief as possible given the nature of the issue. Your initial summary is really an entrée into the real purpose of the meeting, which is the discussion led by questions from your supervisor.

§18.2 Questions from Your Supervisor During the Meeting

After you finish stating your summary, you should expect questions from your supervisor. Lawyers are skeptical and probing by training. They are excellent at finding weaknesses and holes in a legal analysis. One lawyer we know says that the toughest oral argument she ever did wasn't in any courtroom—it was in the office of a senior partner at her law firm. The questions may be tough, but try to look at them as an important step in the collaborative brainstorming process. You are both on the same side and are trying to do the best work for the client.

Because you will likely get questions, particularly about your legal authority, it is very important that you go into the presentation with materials that will help you answer the questions quickly and accurately. First, have clear, easy-to-follow notes about your research path. This is especially important if you have little or no "on point" authority and if your reasoning is built on analogies and other statute and precedent analysis tools (Chapters 8 and 9). Your supervisor will want to make sure that you checked all potential avenues for authority. You should be able to explain your research path in a coherent, organized way. Be prepared to discuss not only where you looked, but what searches you used and what results they achieved. If you chose not to look at certain authorities, be prepared to say why.

Second, be prepared to discuss the substance of the authority. It's a good idea to have copies of the key cases with important language highlighted (either electronic or hard copy). You may want to ask your supervisor ahead of time whether she would like the key authority sent to her in advance by email or instead provided at the meeting in hard copy (or both). If you provide hard copy, highlight and annotate the essential party to make it easier for her to find the key language when you refer to it.

But you will need more than copies of the cases. No one expects you to have memorized the case law, but you don't want to be flipping through stacks of cases searching for the answer. This is anxiety-producing, embarrassing, and inefficient. Instead, find a way to organize a "cheat sheet" of your cases that you can refer to quickly and easily. One way is a case chart or matrix. This can be done in a Word table or in Excel or another charting program. The left column is your list of cases and other columns are for key facts, holdings, and relevant reasoning. Try to keep this chart to one page, or perhaps two in very complicated cases. A simple one looks something like this:

Case	Facts	Holding	Reasoning
State v. Brown, 660 A.2d 1221 (N.J. Super. App. Div. 1995)	Police found evidence of a murder in defendant's duffel bag hidden in storage room in basement of apartment building. Other tenants of the building and super had keys to room.	4th Amendment did not bar search.	Defendant had no reasonable expectation of privacy in duffel bag stored in storage room to which others had keys.
People v. Duvall, 428 N.W.2d 746 (Mich. App. 1988).	Police searched desk of sheriff's deputy and found evidence of a crime. Sheriff's deputy shared desk with others.	Sheriff's deputy had no standing to object to search.	Defendant had no reasonable expectation of privacy in desk others shared.

§18.3 Typical Questions

A supervisor's questions will vary with the legal issue, of course. Try to anticipate questions ahead of time and prepare answers to them. Look for holes or weaknesses in your analysis and identify the reasons why they don't change your conclusion. Distinguish or otherwise address adverse law or facts. Here are some typical questions supervising lawyers may ask:

- What is our best authority? Why is it the best? Is it mandatory or non-mandatory? If nonmandatory, why do you think the court in our case will follow it? Are there any distinguishing facts that the other side could use to diminish the value of the case? What are they and how would we handle that argument?
- What authority hurts us the most? Why is it the worst? Why doesn't it change your conclusion? How can we handle it?

You might not be able to answer every question definitively, but that's okay. Again, you and your supervisor are on the same side, and this is a discussion. Be forthright about weaknesses in the client's position. Don't sugarcoat weakness or try to hide it. If your conclusion is that the client probably won't prevail, be clear about that.

If you find that you cannot answer a question, be honest about that, too. You can always offer to do additional research to look into a question that arises. One way to prepare to handle tough questions is to look at secondary sources like treatises or practitioner manuals. Secondary sources can often be the first step in a research project anyway. In an oral presentation, secondary sources can be very helpful in allowing you to predict an answer when the law does not definitively answer the question.

For example, if you read in a treatise on defamation that "courts generally take the position that '[c]artoons are rhetorical hyperbole' . . . which cannot be reasonably construed as literal depictions of actual situations" then you might be able to make an informed prediction about a defamation action against your cartoonist client even if there is no law in your jurisdiction.[1] Similarly, if you know that historically, courts have uniformly denied punitive damages where a civil plaintiff can't establish a right to compensatory damages, but that recently, some courts have allowed punitive damages in those cases, you know something about the modern trend of the law and can make a prediction even if there is a gap in your law, or even law against you in your jurisdiction.[2] This kind of general, overarching knowledge is essential to the researcher and will help you answer questions even if you have no on-point authority.

---

1. David A. Elder, *Defamation: A Lawyer's Guide* § 8:45 (2016).
2. Automobile Liability Insurance 4th, § 27:20 (2016).

§18.4   The Most Essential Points

Prepare ahead of time so that you have fully synthesized your authority and are confident in your conclusion and analysis.

Prepare a short, direct summary of your conclusion and analysis, which is the oral equivalent of the email answer or brief answer.

Prepare to answer questions while explaining your conclusion and analysis.

To help you answer questions knowledgeably, use a case chart and secondary sources so you have a comprehensive overview of the issue.

Your supervisor's time is a very limited resource. Use it *efficiently*. When you begin, get straight to the point and be brief.

§18.5   Mistakes to Avoid

Imagine the scene through your supervisor's eyes. You don't want her to see you

- being long-winded or rambling,
- showing up with a pile of cases and no plan,
- losing focus and spending too much time on cases that are not relevant, or
- hiding weaknesses in the case or painting an unrealistically rosy a picture of the client's position.

Client Advice Letters

§19.1   Advice in Writing

Advice is explaining to a client how the law treats the client's situation. When you do that in writing, you'll write a *client advice letter*. This chapter explains how. A sample client advice letter is in Appendix E.

Client advice letters are about halfway between a conversation with the client and an office memo. They record the essence of what you would say to the client during a meeting in your office. And often they summarize ideas you worked out in detail earlier while writing an office memo.

If the client is an individual, you should probably give the advice, at least preliminarily, in person or over the telephone. Advice given only by letter might seem cold to the client. Conversation, on the other hand, promotes questions as well as brainstorming with the client about how to solve the problem. But an advice letter can be a useful supplement to advice you've already given in person. For example, if a client has a complicated or difficult decision to make, the client might want a written explanation to refer to while thinking things over.

If the client is an organization, a larger proportion of the advice will be given solely by letter. For the most part, the problems are more complex, and the people in the organization need conversation less because they're more experienced than individual clients are at dealing with the problems at hand.

§19.2   Style and Tone in a Client Advice Letter

Perhaps the biggest challenge in writing a client advice letter is explaining complicated legal concepts to a reader who knows little or nothing about law. Some lawyers say that you don't really understand the law until you can explain it to a nonlawyer. To do that, identify the core concepts and then find everyday language that precisely expresses them.

The tone of a client letter should be professionally precise and at least implicitly supportive. In choosing a tone, ask yourself these questions:

What does the situation call for?
What would this client want from a professional?
What are you comfortable with in terms of your own style?
How do you want to present yourself to clients?

The second question — *What would this client want from a professional?* — may be the most complex. Consider the client's level of sophistication (education, occupation, experience with lawyers). And consider the client's feelings. Is the client experiencing anxiety, grief, or anger? Even in positive situations, such as buying property, happiness can be mixed with anxiety. Or is this transaction, from the client's point of view, pure business? It probably is if the client is an organization or a businessperson, if you have been hired on a matter the client considers routine, and if the client has a lot of experience with lawyers.

Contractions ("don't," "won't") are fine in a letter, although not in a memo or brief.

§19.3   How to Organize a Client Advice Letter

Client letter format resembles in some ways the format of an office memo: issue, brief answer, facts, discussion, and conclusion. (See Chapter 16.)

In fact, sometimes you will write a client advice letter from an office memo. You'll research and write the memo to establish how the law treats the client's situation. If the client needs advice in writing, you'll condense the memo, removing most of the detail about the law, and then rewrite what's left into a letter that includes what the client needs to know in language the client can easily understand. When you do this, you need to change everything for a new reader. You wrote the memo for a supervising lawyer. Now write the letter for a client who knows little or nothing about the law.

A client letter has these parts:

1.   the beginning formalities
2.   one or two opening paragraphs, stating the problem and summarizing your advice

3. one or two paragraphs reviewing the key facts
4. your advice in detail
5. one or two closure paragraphs
6. the ending formalities

If the letter is complex, you might use headings to break it up, although you should adapt the wording in the headings to the client and the situation. The client advice letter in Appendix E is simple enough to need only a few headings.

1. The beginning formalities. These are (1) the letterhead, which is already printed on the law office's stationery; (2) a confidentiality warning; (3) the date; (4) the client's name and address; (5) perhaps a reference to the letter's subject; and (6) the salutation.

A confidentiality warning generally reminds the client not to show the letter to other people without a good reason. It also suggests to others who accidentally see the letter that they are not to read it.

If the client is an organization, a "RE:" line might be helpful. It comes between the client's address and the salutation, is positioned close to the right-hand margin, and might include a number that would help the client identify its own records on the matter.

The salutation (*"Dear Ms. Naguchi:"*) always ends with a colon, never a comma. Here's an example:

[letterhead]

CONFIDENTIAL

ATTORNEY-CLIENT COMMUNICATION

AND WORK PRODUCT

Monica Naguchi

Standard Insurance Co.

4 Cornell Street

Claremont, CA 91711

RE: Cucamonga Forwarders, Inc.

Your file # 98-326

Dear Ms. Naguchi:

---

2. One or two opening paragraphs, stating the problem about which the client has sought your advice, and a brief summary of what your advice will be.   This corresponds to the issue and brief answer in an office memo. If you have bad news, this is where the client will learn that it's bad. Think long and hard about the words you use to convey that bad news. Reading words on a page can be a cold experience for the client.

3. One or more paragraphs reviewing the key facts on which the advice is based, as you understand those facts.   You might think it wastes words to tell the client the client's own facts, but there are several good reasons for doing it.

First, if you've misunderstood any of the facts and the client knows better, the client can correct what's wrong. Many lawyers add a sentence asking the client to do that: "If I have described any of the facts inaccurately, please call me."

Second, a fact recitation limits the advice to the facts recited, and that can be important in the future if the facts change. A tenant who doesn't have a claim against the landlord for a filthy lobby might have one next week if the lobby ceiling caves in.

Third, you might recently have learned of some facts the client doesn't yet know about. If so, describe the newly found facts in words that tell the client they are new: "Since we last spoke, I have discovered that the 1996 deed was never properly recorded in the county clerk's office."

And finally, a fact recitation is a good, professional transition into the advice itself.

4. The advice, which can be structured in either of two ways.   First, if the client wants to know how the law treats a situation — "Would my company violate the law if we import this product?" — you'll predict how a court would rule or you'll report the client's or other people's rights and obligations. The client asked a specific question, and you're answering it.

Alternately, if the client must make a decision, you'll counsel in the letter by suggesting the options from which the client can choose and, for each option, explaining the factors that might make a given choice attractive or unattractive. In the advice portion of the letter, list the options and explain their advantages, costs, risks, and chances of success. When you estimate risks and chances of success, you are making predictions. Costs are not limited to money. The cost of suing includes not only legal fees and other litigation expenses, but also the time and energy the client would have to invest in the lawsuit and the stress most litigants suffer while the suit is in progress.

Be especially careful about the words you use to communicate the degree of confidence you have in your advice. When you write, "We have a reasonably good chance of winning at trial," you might mean that you believe the client will probably win although the risk of loss is significant. But many clients would read those words to mean that victory is nearly assured. That's because it's only human for a client who has suffered a wrong to assume that forces of justice will resolutely correct it. Don't, through vagueness, imply unjustified optimism. Find ordinary, everyday words that the client you're writing to will understand exactly as you mean them.

Conversely, if the news truly is bad, don't cushion it so much that the client will not appreciate it. Don't say, "Our chances in litigation are problematic," if what you really mean is, "It's very unlikely that such a lawsuit would succeed."

Use lawyer talk as little as possible. If a technical term has a good equivalent in ordinary English, use the ordinary word even if it does not convey 100 percent of the meaning of the technical term. Eighty percent is good enough, unless the missing 20 percent is relevant to the client's situation. If you use a technical term, define it. By talking law with other students and in class, you might forget that people outside law school don't understand what you have been studying so hard to understand.

When you translate lawyer talk into ordinary English, do it respectfully. Imagine writing the letter to one of your grandparents. This isn't just good communication, it's also good business. People often distrust a stereotyped lawyer who talks to everyone in legalese. But clients can like and trust a good human being who can explain things clearly and respectfully and who does a good job of being their lawyer.

Write simply but don't oversimplify. If the law is unsettled, in flux, or unclear, explain that. The client will want to know why your advice is qualified by uncertainty in the law itself. Discuss authority only if it's central to the issue, such as a recent appellate case that changes everything you've told the client in the past.

Reciting the law can be cold and confusing (*"in this state, tax must be paid by the property owner on each lien against real property recorded in the county clerk's office"*). Describing its effect on the client is warm and often eliminates the need to recite the law (*"if you refinance the mortgage on your home, you'll have to pay $1,250 in mortgage tax"*).

Unlike all your other readers, your client assumes that the law is exactly what you say it is. You don't need to recite rules of law or cite and explain authority the same way you would in a memo or a brief. But you do need to know what you're talking about. Lawyers aren't perfect at predicting, but if you're so wrong as to not know what you're talking about, you'll lose clients and learn a lot about the details of malpractice law.

Organize the material in any way that helps the client understand it. Often that isn't through the paradigm formula described in Chapter 11. You aren't writing for the skeptical senior partner or judge to whom everything must be proved. You're writing for a lay person who won't easily understand what you know.

5. One or two closure paragraphs.   Sum up your advice in two or three sentences. Specify what can or should be done next, who should do it, and when it should be done.

If the client must make a decision, set the stage for that. List the options from which the client will choose. Invite the client to telephone you. If extended conversation would be better, suggest that the client make an appointment to see you.

This is also a good place to note the extent to which your advice is conditioned on facts not yet known or events that haven't yet occurred. In some offices, the closure paragraphs include boilerplate sentences pointing out that the advice is limited to the facts recited earlier and to current law, which might change, and so on. Other offices don't include this kind of thing, on the assumption that it alienates clients.

6. The ending formalities.   Place your signature over your typed name and under a parting phrase like, "Sincerely Yours" or "Best Regards" — whatever words are customary in your office.

VI

GENERAL WRITING SKILLS

Paragraphing

§20.1 How Paragraphing Reveals Your Organization

In college, you might have organized your paragraphs by writing until you seemed to have written a lot, stopping, starting a new paragraph, and then going through the cycle again and again. But in law, paragraphs put together that way will confound and annoy readers who must find your meaning quickly.

Most readers unconsciously use paragraph divisions to learn how a writer's thoughts fit together. They assume that each paragraph substantiates or explores a separate and distinct idea or subject. They also assume that the first or second sentence in each paragraph states or implies that idea or subject and, if necessary, shows how it's related to matters already discussed. To the extent that you frustrate these assumptions, your writing will be less helpful to the reader and therefore less influential.

Paragraphing has three goals. The most obvious is to break your material up into digestible chunks. The second is to help you discipline yourself to confront and develop each theme inherent in the material. The third is to tell the reader where she or he is in your logic, how that place was arrived at, and where you are headed — in other words, to make your organization apparent. If the reader feels lost or doesn't immediately know what the paragraph's thesis or topic is or how it differs from that of the preceding paragraph, there's something wrong with the paragraph's length or structure or with the wording of individual sentences. As you'll see in §20.4, the paragraph's first sentence is the one most often botched.

How can you tell the difference between a paragraph that accomplishes these goals and one that does not? An effective paragraph has five characteristics. First, it has *unity*. It proves one proposition or covers one subject. Material more relevant to other propositions or subjects has been placed elsewhere.

Second, an effective paragraph has *completeness.* It includes whatever is necessary to prove the proposition (or some part of it) or cover the subject. Third, an effective paragraph has *internal coherence.* Ideas are expressed in a logical sequence that the reader can easily follow. Fourth, an effective paragraph is of *readable length.* It's neither so long that the reader gets lost nor so short that valuable material is underdeveloped or trivialized. Fifth, an effective paragraph *announces or implies its purpose* at the out-set. Its first or second sentence states or implies its thesis or topic and, if necessary, makes a transition from the preceding material. Ineffective paragraphing is related to incomplete analysis. When you set out to fix problem paragraphs, you will often find yourself fixing analytical problems as well.

§20.2   Probative Paragraphs and Descriptive Paragraphs

Some paragraphs merely *describe* conditions or events; they convey information without analysis. But in legal writing, most paragraphs are expected to do more than that: they *prove* propositions that help resolve issues. In descriptive writing, the paragraph states information, and the first or second sentence tells the reader the paragraph's topic or theme, if that isn't already evident from the context. In probative writing, the paragraph exists to prove its first or second sentence, which states the paragraph's *thesis.*

A topic is merely a category of information ("weather in Death Valley"). A thesis is a proposition capable of proof or disproof ("the climate of Death Valley is brutal"):

Descriptive

In January in Death Valley, the average high temperature is about 65°, and the average low is about 37°. Spring and fall temperatures approximate summer temperatures elsewhere. In April and in October, for example, the average high is about 90°, and the average low about 60°. July is the hottest month, with an average high of about 116°

Probative

The climate in Death Valley is brutal. At Furnace Creek Ranch, the highest summer temperature each year reaches at least 120° and in many years at least 125°. The highest temperature recorded in Death Valley — 134° — is also the highest recorded anywhere on the earth. In an average year, only 1½ inches of rain fall. In the summer sun, a

and an average low of about 87°. The highest temperature ever recorded in Death Valley was 134 on July 10, 1913. Average annual rainfall is about 1½ inches.

person can lose four gallons of perspiration a day and — in 3% humidity — die of dehydration.

A confused reader of descriptive writing might ask, "What is this paragraph about?" But a confused reader of probative writing asks instead, "What is this writer trying to prove?"

In a college essay, you might have written many descriptive paragraphs describing abundant raw materials and then concluded with a short passage expressing some inferences that the raw materials support. In law, that kind of organization will frustrate your readers. The law-trained reader wants to learn at the beginning what you intend to prove and wants to be told, at each step along the way, how the raw materials support the proposition you are trying to prove. Recitation of raw materials is not a proof. Proof is an explanation of *how* the data support the inference.

Probative and descriptive writing can occur in the same document. But in a Discussion (or Argument in a motion memo or appellate brief), the writing should be largely probative, with only occasional digressions into description. Some other parts of a memo or brief, however, are predominantly description. The best examples are the Statement of Facts in an office memo and the Preliminary Statement in a motion memo or appellate brief.

§20.3   Thesis Sentences, Topic Sentences, and Transition Sentences

A probative paragraph states its thesis in its first or second sentence, and that sentence is the *thesis sentence*.[1] A descriptive paragraph does the same with its *topic* unless the topic is implied by the context. Although in descriptive writing a topic can often be implied, in probative writing the thesis should be expressly stated. (Remember that a practical reader needs to know your purpose in saying things before you start saying them.) With either type of paragraph, a *transition sentence* helps show the reader how the paragraph is connected to the material before it or the material after it.

Thesis, topic, and transition sentences can be worked into a paragraph in several different ways. A transition sentence most often appears at the

---

1. In college, "thesis sentence" is sometimes used to refer to a sentence that sums up the meaning of an entire essay. Here, it has a different meaning.

beginning of a paragraph, less often at the end (as a bridge into the next paragraph), rarely in the middle, and not at all if a transition is unnecessary. The first sentence in a paragraph can often do double duty. It might both state a thesis or topic and make a transition. Or a transition sentence at the beginning of a paragraph can imply a topic while making a transition from the previous paragraph. If the paragraph begins with a transition sentence that does not also state a thesis or state or imply a topic, the paragraph's second sentence can express either. Where a paragraph's thesis or topic is complex, the paragraph might end with a closure sentence that ties up loose ends.

§20.4   The Two Most Common Ways of Botching a Paragraph's Beginning

The two most common ways of botching the beginning of a paragraph are (1) omitting entirely any statement of the thesis or topic, and (2) using a topic sentence to begin a probative paragraph (which should have a thesis sentence instead). Either problem can force a supervisor or judge to read the paragraph two or three times to figure out its purpose, unless that is clear from the context.

1. *Botching the beginning by omitting any indication of the thesis or topic:* The habit of announcing or implying a paragraph's purpose at the beginning is a kind of self-discipline. Because it forces you to articulate the paragraph's reason for being, it will encourage you — especially during rewriting — to limit the paragraph to one thesis or topic (unity), to do whatever is necessary inside the paragraph to prove that thesis or cover that topic (completeness), and to express the ideas in the paragraph in a sequence appropriate to the thesis or topic (coherence). If a statement of the topic or thesis is missing, that often means that you don't yet know what the paragraph is supposed to accomplish — which can lead to conversations like this:

(a) Instructor identifies a murky paragraph in student writing.

(b) Instructor asks student, "Tell me in a sentence what you are trying to say in this paragraph."

(c) Student reads paragraph — ponders — and, generally, comes up with a one-sentence statement.

(d) Instructor says, "Well, would it help the reader if you *said that* at the front end of the paragraph?"

(e) Light bulb flashes over student's head.

(f) Instructor then asks, "Now if that's your main idea, how does *this* sentence [indicating one whose function is unclear] tie in to that idea?"

(g) If the student suggests a function, the instructor asks, "Is there any way you could make that function clearer to the reader?"

(h) If the student does not see a function, the instructor asks, "Does that sentence belong in the paragraph?"

As the author of this familiar scene concludes, "There is no reason why you, the writer, cannot carry on that conversation inside your own head as you [rewrite]."[2]

2. *Botching the beginning by using a topic sentence to begin a probative paragraph:* Consider this probative paragraph, which begins with an unhelpful topic sentence:

> The federal bank robbery statute penalizes obtaining anything of value from a bank "by force and violence, or by intimidation." 18 U.S.C. § 2113 (2000). Several cases have defined the term "intimidation." For example, a defendant takes by intimidation when he hands a bank teller a note reading "Put all your money in this bag and nobody will get hurt." *United States v. Epps,* 438 F.2d 1192 (4th Cir. 1971). The same is true where a defendant, while holding his hand in his pocket to suggest that he has a weapon, hands a teller a note reading, "This is a holdup." *United States v. Harris,* 530 F.2d 576 (4th Cir. 1976). And even where a teller never sees a weapon, intimidation is proved where a defendant produces a note stating, "I have a gun. Give me all the bills or I will shoot you." *United States v. Jacquillon,* 469 F.2d 380 (5th Cir. 1972).

This is *not* a descriptive paragraph. Its purpose is to prove a definition of "intimidation." But the first sentence doesn't tell you what the definition is and therefore it isn't a thesis sentence. The first sentence announces only a topic — the federal bank robbery statute — and thus doesn't communicate what the paragraph is meant to prove. In fact, *no* sentence in the paragraph sets out the definition that the paragraph is intended to prove. To the reader who needs to know what "intimidation" is, a paragraph like this one is frustrating to the point of impatience. Not only does the reader need to know exactly what you're trying to prove, but he needs to know it *before proof begins.* Most of the problem could be solved with an accurate thesis sentence like this:

> Under the federal bank robbery statute, 18 U.S.C. § 2113 — which penalizes obtaining anything of value from a bank "by force and violence, or by intimidation" — the courts have defined "intimidation" as conduct reasonably calculated to produce fear, even in the complete absence of physical violence. . . .

The last fourteen words of this sentence give the whole paragraph meaning because they synthesize the holdings of the cases into a definition that the paragraph proves to be accurate.

Once you've replaced a topic sentence with a thesis sentence, some rewording and reordering of other sentences might be needed to give the paragraph coherence — to show, in other words, *how* the rest of the paragraph proves the thesis. Notice how the earlier version has been changed below so that it now seems to flow straight from the new thesis sentence:

---

2. Peter W. Gross, *California Western Law School's First-Year Course in Legal Skills,* 44 Alb. L. Rev. 369, 389–90 (1980).

Under the federal bank robbery statute, 18 U.S.C. § 2113 — which penalizes obtaining anything of value from a bank "by force and violence, or by intimidation" — the courts have defined "intimidation" as conduct reasonably calculated to produce fear, even in the complete absence of physical violence. For example, even where a teller never actually sees a weapon, intimidation is proved where a defendant produces a note stating, "I have a gun. Give me all the bills or I will shoot you." *United States v. Jacquillon,* 469 F.2d 380 (5th Cir. 1972). More vaguely expressed threats are treated the same way. A defendant takes by intimidation when he hands a bank teller a note reading, "Put all your money in this bag and nobody will get hurt." *United States v. Epps,* 438 F.2d 1192 (4th Cir. 1971). And the result is the same even where the threat is entirely implied — for example, where a defendant, while holding his hand in his pocket to suggest that he has a weapon, hands a teller a note reading, "This is a holdup." *United States v. Harris,* 530 F.2d 576 (4th Cir. 1976).

If your prior writing experience has primarily been descriptive — and that's true of most law students — you'll need to discipline yourself to see the difference between a descriptive paragraph and a probative one. And you'll have to be careful to begin probative paragraphs with thesis sentences. You will probably find that this kind of self-discipline forces you to make your meaning more clear to the reader throughout the paragraph — and that consequently you'll analyze more deeply.

When you begin a probative paragraph with a topic sentence — or when you write a paragraph that doesn't state or imply a thesis or topic — in all likelihood you didn't know when you began to write the paragraph what you intended to prove or describe within it. In a first draft, that's okay. The purpose of a first draft is to get the material out in the open so you can finish analyzing it. But during rewriting, when you find a topic sentence atop a probative paragraph — or when you find a paragraph with no thesis or topic sentence at all — that's often a clue that you have not yet begun to articulate *even to yourself* what you are trying to accomplish in the paragraph. But this problem isn't hard to solve. Merely asking yourself "What am I trying to prove here?" often produces almost instantly a thesis sentence that gives the whole paragraph meaning and relevance.

§20.5   How to Test Your Writing for Effective Paragraphing

In first drafts, paragraphs are seldom put together well. Instead, the work of paragraphing generally occurs during re-writing. To identify the paragraphs in need of rehabilitation, ask yourself the following questions.[3]

---

3. When marking up your work, your teacher might refer to these questions by using the number-letter codes that appear next to each question here.

20-A **Have you stated or implied, near the beginning of each paragraph, the paragraph's thesis (if the paragraph is probative) or its topic (if the paragraph is descriptive)?** If the reader does not learn the paragraph thesis or topic at the beginning, the reader will have to read the paragraph two or three times to figure out its purpose. The only time you're exempt from this requirement is when the context clearly implies the topic or thesis.

20-B **Have you gotten rid of throat-clearing introductory sentences, which bump into the paragraph's thesis or topic backward?** For example:

> The district court considered this question in *Pickett*. There, the court showed limited patience with the way the parties referred to themselves and each other. It did agree to call one defendant Guitar Maker Oswald Who Lives in Germany. But it refused to call another The Artist Formerly Known as Prince, or even just "the Artist," and it refused to allow that defendant to use his guitar symbol in place of his name in the captions of pleadings and motions. Instead, the court just called him Nelson.

You can combine the first two sentences into a single thesis or topic sentence that goes straight to the point:

> In *Pickett*, the district court showed limited patience with the way the parties referred to themselves and each other. . . .

20-C **Have you given each paragraph a unified purpose?** Prove one proposition or cover as much of one subject as is digestible in one paragraph. Remove and place elsewhere material that is more relevant to other propositions or subjects.

20-D **Within each paragraph, have you expressed your ideas in a logical and effective sequence?** Where a paragraph is confusing but nothing is wrong with its size or with the wording of individual sentences, the problem is usually that the paragraph lacks internal coherence. That happens when ideas within the paragraph are presented in a sequence that makes it hard for the reader to understand them or how they fit together to prove the thesis or illuminate the topic.

20-E **Have you broken up paragraphs that were so large that the reader would have gotten lost?** Although no set rules govern paragraph length, paragraphs that wander aimlessly or endlessly don't accomplish the goals of paragraphing. Where that happens, you have probably tried to develop two or more complex and separable themes in a single paragraph, perhaps without being aware of it. The cure is to identify the individual themes and then break up the material accordingly into digestible chunks (which become separate paragraphs).

20-F **Have you rewritten paragraphs that were so short that no thesis or topic is developed?**   Generally, one- and two-sentence paragraphs are ineffective unless you have a special reason for emphasizing something or for separating out uncomplicated material. One- or two-sentence paragraphs can be used to good effect in clearing up matters that are preliminary (such as identifying the procedural posture) or ancillary (such as identifying issues that aren't presently before the court). When used carefully, short paragraphs can also emphasize some memorable aspect of the material. In many other situations, however, a short paragraph leaves the reader hungry for a more satisfying explanation of some important point. If a paragraph is so short that no thesis or topic is developed, ask yourself whether (1) you might have missed the complexities of the thesis or topic, or (2) the thesis or topic might be so simple that it doesn't merit treatment in a separate paragraph because it's actually part of some other thesis or topic.

20-G **Have you stated or implied how each paragraph is related to the surrounding material?**   There are several ways of doing this. The paragraph can begin with a transition sentence. Or it can begin with a sentence that both makes a transition and states a thesis or topic. Or the last sentence of the preceding paragraph can build a bridge between the two paragraphs. That sentence can raise an expectation, for example, that the second paragraph satisfies.

Exercise I
The First Weeks of Law School (Probative and Descriptive Paragraphs)

Write two paragraphs — one descriptive and the other probative — about the first weeks of law school.

Descriptive paragraph: Summarize what happened during your first weeks in law school. Describe only things you saw, heard, read, and wrote. Do not try to prove any belief you might have about the first weeks of law school.

Probative paragraph: The opening sentence of this paragraph should be "The first weeks of law school are hard" (or "puzzling" or "exciting" or "cruel" or "challenging" or any other characterization you choose) "because" — and here you complete the sentence by stating whatever you believe to be the cause of your characterization. The rest of the paragraph should prove the thesis expressed in this sentence.

Exercise II
Escape from Prison (Paragraph Unity, Coherence, and Length)

Is the paragraph below limited to proving a single proposition or covering a single subject? If not, what material is extraneous? Is the paragraph of appropriate size? If you believe it's too long, how should the problem be solved? Are the ideas expressed in a sequence that enables you to understand the meaning of the paragraph without reading it twice? If not, what sequence would be better? Edit the paragraph in light of your answers to these questions. Add any thesis, topic, or transition sentences that you think are needed. (Each sentence is preceded by a letter in brackets so that you can refer to it in class without having to read the sentence aloud.)

[A] A prisoner who leaves a prison without permission is guilty of a crime of escape. [B] Until relatively recently, the defense of necessity was not available in California to a prisoner who claimed that prison conditions were so intolerable as to require escape. [C] An early case, for example, affirmed a conviction for escape, conceding that "if the facts were as stated by the defendant, he was subjected to brutal treatment of extreme atrocity" in a "remote" mountain prison camp far from any authorities to whom he might complain. *People v. Whipple*, 100 Cal. App. 261, 266, 279 P.2d 1008, 1010 (2d Dist. 1929). [D] And a more recent case affirmed a conviction where the defendant offered evidence that other prisoners had threatened to kill him, and that prison guards had refused to protect him. *People v. Richardson*, 269 Cal. App. 2d 768, 75 Cal. Rptr. 597 (1st Dist. 1969). [E] Both *Whipple* and *Richardson* cited 1 Hale P.C. 611 for the proposition that escape from prison can be excused only to avoid death as immediate as that threatened when the prison itself is engulfed in fire. [F] But drawing on decisions from other jurisdictions, the Court of Appeal for the Fourth District has held that, through a "limited defense of necessity," a prisoner can defeat a prosecution for escape if the prisoner can demonstrate (1) that she or he was "faced with a specific threat of death, forcible sexual attack or substantial bodily injury in the immediate future, "(2) that a complaint to the authorities would have been futile or not possible, (3) that the same was true regarding resort to the courts, (4) that the prisoner used no "force or violence" in escaping, and (5) that the prisoner surrendered to the authorities "when he [had] attained a position of safety from the immediate threat." *People v. Lovercamp*, 43 Cal. App. 3d 823, 831-32, 118 Cal. Rptr. 110, 115 (4th Dist. 1974). [G] Even under this test, Victor Minskov does not have a defense to the charge of escape. [H] He had been beaten twice by a group of prisoners who threatened to attack him as long as he remained in the same prison. [I] He scaled the prison wall at 4 A.M. immediately after the second beating and while being chased by the same group. [J] After the first beating, he had complained to prison guards, who laughed at him, and during the second beating his cries for help brought no response. [K] The courts would not have been able to protect him from such an assault, and he used no force or violence in escaping. [L] But after leaving the prison he hid under an assumed name for 16 months and was finally captured at the Los Angeles airport trying to leave the country. [M] Thus, he will not be able to show that he complied with the last element of the *Lovercamp* test by surrendering to the authorities upon attaining "a position of safety from the immediate threat."

Effective Style

§21.1 Clarity and Vividness

The difference between the *almost* right word and the right word is . . . the difference between the lightning bug and the lightning.

— *Mark Twain*

Modern English was created through the merger of two languages, Anglo-Saxon Old English and Norman French, and it has borrowed liberally from other languages, especially Latin and Greek. Because it has such a huge vocabulary, English can express with precision a very wide range of nuance — if you can find the "right" word. But with so many similar words to choose from, it's easy to choose the "wrong" one — the word that blurs meaning, rather than sharpening it.

Important-sounding words tend to be less vivid and less precise than simple and straightforward ones. The following doesn't say as much as it should: "The victim *indicated* that the defendant had held the gun." Did the writer mean "The victim *said* that the defendant had held the gun"? Or did she mean "The victim *pointed* at the defendant when asked who had held the gun"? To the reader who needs to know exactly what happened, *indicated* obscures the truth rather than communicating it. The simpler word often says more than the more dignified one. And the dignified word is often euphemistic and fuzzy rather than crisp and vivid.[1]

You might be tempted to try to sound like a lawyer but fail to *communicate* like one — for example by writing *ingested* (an impressive but vague word) instead of something that would tell exactly what happened, such as *ate*,

---

1. Both tendencies are described in George Orwell's most famous essay, *Politics and the English Language.*

drank, or *swallowed*. Judges and senior lawyers want to read straightforward English. They are frustrated and confused by pretentiously vague writing, which they treat as evidence of mediocrity. Law depends on clarity, precision, and readability.

In one study, appellate judges and their law clerks were asked to appraise material written in a contorted style that might be called "legalese," while other judges and their law clerks were asked to evaluate the same material rewritten into straightforward "plain English." They thought the original legalese "substantively weaker and less persuasive than the plain English versions."[2] And the judges and law clerks assumed that the traditional legalese had been written by lawyers working in low-prestige jobs.[3]

Don't write like this:

> The above captioned appeal is maintained by the defendant as a direct result of

Instead, write like this:

> The defendant appeals because

The longer version ("the above captioned appeal . . .") might sound fancy, but a reader won't as easily understand it. Figure out exactly what should be said and then say exactly that.

To understand the importance of clarity in law, remember two things. First, you must prove everything you say, because the legal reader considers every unsupported assertion to be the equivalent of an untruth. Second, no matter how important the issue, your reader can spare only a very limited amount of time to ponder what you write. The more time the reader must spend trying to figure out what you mean, the less time the reader has to consider agreeing with you. Where poor writing obscures the message or makes the reading troublesome, you may get rejection even where you should have gotten agreement. "[A] cardinal principle of good writing [is] that no one should ever have to read a sentence twice because of the way it is put together."[4]

When it comes to clarity, you will never get the benefit of the doubt. The reader is always right: "If the reader thinks something you wrote is unclear, then it is, by definition. Quit arguing."[5]

---

2. Robert W. Benson & Joan B. Kessler, *Legalese v. Plain English: An Empirical Study of Persuasion and Credibility in Appellate Brief Writing*, 20 Loyola L.A. L. Rev. 301, 301 (1987). Other research has produced similar results. *See, e.g.,* Sean Flammer, *Persuading Judges: An Empirical Analysis of Writing Style, Persuasion, and the Use of Plain English*, 16 J. Legal Writing 183 (2010).

3. Benson & Kessler, *supra* n.2, at 301-02.

4. Wilson Follett, *Modern American Usage* 480 (1974).

5. Donald McCloskey, *The Writing of Economics* 7 (1987).

§21.2 Conciseness

The present letter is a very long one simply because I had no time to make it shorter.

— Pascal

Most first drafts use too many words to communicate a given idea effectively. Part of rewriting is disciplining yourself to trim your words down to something easily read and quickly understood. Compare two explanations of *Sherwood v. Walker,* a mutual-mistake-of-fact case that appears in most Contracts casebooks. The first draft is on the left. The rewrite, on the right, uses fewer words to express the same concept both concisely and more clearly.

It is important to note that, at the time when the parties entered into the agreement of purchase and sale, neither of them had knowledge of the cow's pregnant condition.	When the parties agreed to the sale, neither knew the cow was pregnant.
Because of the fact that the cow, previous to the contract, had not become pregnant, despite planned and observed exposure to bulls whose reproductive capacities had been demonstrated through past experience, the seller had made the assumption that the cow would not be able to produce offspring.	The seller had assumed that the cow was infertile because she had not become pregnant when he tried to breed her with bulls.
Due to the fact that the seller had made a statement to the buyer describing the cow's opportunities to reproduce and the failures thereof, there would have been, in the buyer's thinking, no purpose to any further investigation or inspection he might have considered making.	Because the seller had told the buyer about the cow's history, the buyer did not investigate further.
For these reasons, the contract did not include a provision for an upward modification in the payments to be made by the buyer to the seller in the event that the cow should later prove to be capable of reproduction.	Thus, the contract did not provide for an increase in the purchase price if the cow should turn out to be fertile.

How did the writer convert the verbose first draft on the left into the concise final draft on the right?

First, the writer rewrote some sentences so that a person or a thing *did* something. Although the verbose draft is weighted down with modifiers, the concise version focuses on well-chosen nouns and verbs, and many modifiers became unnecessary as the writer incorporated their meaning into those nouns and verbs (and sometimes into more succinct modifiers):

the cow's pregnant condition	*became*	the cow was pregnant
despite planned and observed exposure to bulls whose reproductive capacities had been demonstrated through past experience	*became*	when he tried to breed her with bulls
there would have been, in the buyer's thinking, no purpose to any further investigation or inspection he might have considered making	*became*	the buyer did not investigate further

Second, the writer eliminated phrases that didn't add any meaning:

It is important to note that	*was deleted because the "importance" is communicated by the sentence's placement and, ironically, by the rewritten version's brevity*
previous to the contract	*was deleted because it's communicated by the context*

Third, the writer weighed each word and phrase to see if the same thing could be said in fewer words:

at the time when	*became*	when
entered into the agreement of purchase and sale	*became*	agreed to the sale
neither of them	*became*	neither
had knowledge of	*became*	knew
Because of the fact that	*became*	because

had made the assumption	*became*	assumed
would not be able to produce offspring	*became*	was infertile
Due to the fact	*became*	Because
had made a statement to	*became*	told
describing the cow's opportunities to reproduce and the failures thereof	*became*	about the cow's history
For these reasons	*became*	Thus
include a provision for	*became*	provide for
an upward modification in the payment to be made by the buyer to the seller	*became*	an increase in the purchase price
in the event that	*became*	if
the cow should later prove to be capable of reproducing	*became*	the cow should turn out to be fertile

Be careful, however, not to edit out needed meaning. It would be folly to eliminate so much verbiage that a reader wouldn't know that the cow was pregnant when sold; that the parties didn't know of the pregnancy at the time; that the contract didn't provide for an adjusted price; and why it didn't do so.

§21.3   Forcefulness

Forceful writing *engages* the writer.[6] Forceful writing leads the reader through ideas by specifying their relationships with one another and by identifying the ideas that are most important or compelling.

---

6. Mark K. Osbeck, *What Is "Good Legal Writing" and Why Does It Matter?*, 4 Drexel L. Rev. 417 (2012).

Specify relationships. Transitional words and phrases, such as the following, can very economically show relationships between ideas:

accordingly	in fact
additionally	(in order) to
although	in spite of
analogously	in that event
as a result	instead
because	moreover
but	nevertheless
consequently	not only . . . , but also
conversely	on the contrary
despite	the other hand
even if	on these facts
even though	rather
finally	similarly
for example	since
for instance	specifically
for that reason	such as
furthermore	there
hence	therefore
here	thus
however	under these circumstances
in addition (to)	while
in contrast	

Some transitional words and phrases are stronger than others. Choose those that accurately represent the relationship.

For example, some words are better than others at showing causation. *Because* and *since* do a much better job than *as* and *so.* Both *as* and *so* can confuse a reader who sees them used much more often — and much more effectively — to join contemporaneous events ("the muggles gasped as Harry flew past on his Nimbus 2000") or to emphasize the abundance of some fact ("they were so astonished that . . .").

The word *since* is an acceptable synonym for *because,* especially in passages where one word or the other must be used several times. But *since* is the weaker of the two. It confuses a reader who wouldn't know immediately from the context whether it refers to causation or to time:

> Because the defendant spent the marital assets on extravagances, the plaintiff has no money for attorney's fees.

If this had begun with *since,* you wouldn't have known until near the end of the sentence whether the dependent clause introduced causation or marked a point in time ("Since the defendant spent . . .").

Some words and sentence structures show contrast better than others do. Consider this:

> The Court of Appeal has held that the objection is waived if not made at trial, but it has also held that, even without an objection, a conviction should be reversed where a prosecutor's conduct was as inflammatory as it was here.

The word *but,* buried in the middle of a long sentence, only weakly tells the reader that one idea (the rule about waiver) is being knocked down by another (the exception for inflammatory prosecutorial conduct). Everybody writes this kind of thing in first drafts, but you should recognize and fix it during rewriting:

> Although the Court of Appeal has held that the objection is waived if not made at trial, it has also held that, even without an objection, a conviction should be reversed where a prosecutor's conduct was as inflammatory as it was here.

Although tells the reader from the very beginning of the sentence that the first clause, however damning, will be shown soon not to matter. If handled carefully, however, *but* can still do the job well:

> The Court of Appeal has held that the objection is waived if not made at trial. But it has also held that, even without an objection, a conviction should be reversed where a prosecutor's conduct was as inflammatory as it was here.

This solves the problem in a different way. The sentence has been broken in two, and the new second sentence begins with *But.* (Despite common belief, no rule of grammar forbids starting a sentence with a conjunction.)

When you discuss several ideas together, you can make that clear to the reader through some sort of textual list. The list need not be diagrammed. In fact, it's usually more economical to incorporate a list into the text with a transition sentence ("There are four reasons why . . ."), followed by sentences or paragraphs coordinated to the transition sentence ("First . . ." or "The first reason . . .").

Identify the most important ideas. There are several methods. One is simply to say it:

> This attorney's most reprehensible act was to make a motion for a preliminary injunction where his clients were not in any way threatened with harm.

Other methods are more subtle. You can put an emphasized idea at the beginning of a sentence, paragraph, or passage, where it will be most quickly noticed. Or, as in the paragraph below, you can write a series of sentences that lead up to one that succinctly conveys the emphasized idea:

This attorney served and filed a pleading alleging extremely unlikely facts without making any factual investigation.

He made numerous frivolous motions, including one for a preliminary injunction when his clients were not threatened with harm. He has now brought an appeal without any basis in statute or precedent, and he has submitted a record and brief not in compliance with the court's rules. He has thoroughly disregarded the professional obligations of an attorney.

§21.4   Punctuation and Other Rules of Grammar

In re HAWKINS
502 N.W.2d 770 (Minn. 1978)

[The Lawyers Professional Responsibility Board petitioned the court for an order disciplining the respondent lawyer for unethical conduct.]

The referee . . . found that respondent's failure to comply with [certain court rules] and his repeated filing of documents rendered unintelligible by numerous spelling, grammatical, and typographical errors were sufficiently serious that they amounted to incompetent representation. . . .

It is apparent to us that [respondent's] repeated disregard of [court rules], coupled with the incomprehensibility of his correspondence and documentation, constitutes a violation of Rule 1.1 of the Minnesota Rules of Professional Conduct. . . .

. . . Public confidence in the legal system is shaken when lawyers disregard the rules of court and when a lawyer's correspondence and legal documents are so filled with spelling, grammatical, and typographical errors that they are virtually incomprehensible. . . .

Respondent . . . is hereby publicly reprimanded for unprofessional conduct [and ordered, among other things, to participate in a program of writing instruction].

In another case, a trucking company and the Interstate Commerce Commission battled for 19 years over the confusion caused by the absence of a single comma in an administrative order.[7] And the Maine Supreme Court had to write a two-thousand word decision to untangle the mess created by two commas that somehow ended up in the wrong place in a statute.[8]

Correct punctuation makes writing clear and easier to understand. It's not mere decoration. A lawyer can't excuse a poorly punctuated sentence by arguing that the reader would be able to understand it if she or he would think about it. A lawyer's job is to make meaning so plain that the reader doesn't need to read the sentence twice.

---

7. *T. I. Mccormack Trucking Co. v. United States*, 298 F. Supp. 39 (D.N.J. 1969).
8. *Sawyer v. State*, 382 A.2d 1039 (Me. 1978).

Punctuation and other grammar skills have an important effect on your credibility and reputation. Readers — including graders of law school exams — will question your analytical abilities and general competence if you don't observe the accepted rules of English grammar. "Where lumps and infelicities occur," the novelist John Gardner wrote, "the sensitive reader shrinks away a little, as we do when an interesting conversationalist picks his nose."[9]

§21.5 How to Test Your Writing for Effective Style

[I]t is a struggle to make a sentence say exactly what you mean.

— *Arthur Koestler*

In first drafts — even by the best writers — style is usually pretty awful. Effective style is really achieved through rewriting, as you spot style problems and fix them. While rewriting, ask yourself the following questions.[10]

| 21-A | **Do your nouns and verbs let the reader see the action?** As you write and rewrite, ask yourself what words will *engage* the reader.[11] What words will bring the reader into your thinking? For example:

wrong:	In *Smith*, there was no withdrawal of the guilty plea, based on the court's determination of a lack of evidence of coercion.
right:	In *Smith*, the court denied the defendant's motion to withdraw her guilty plea because she submitted no evidence that the plea had been coerced.
wrong:	There is a possibility of action in the near future by the EPA to remove these pesticides from the market.
right:	The EPA might soon prohibit these pesticides.

In the "wrong" examples, you can barely tell who has done what because the ponderous tone obscures the action, and because the nouns and verbs are vague and lazy. They don't stand out, take charge, and create action. The "right" examples are more vivid and easier to understand. You immediately know what's going on and don't need to read the same words twice.

In law, people do things to ideas, objects, and other people. The only way to describe that clearly is with relatively plain and simple nouns and verbs. As with so many other legal writing problems, rewriting is the key to solving this one.

---

9. John Gardner, *The Art of Fiction: Notes on Craft for Young Writers* 99 (Knopf 1984).
10. When marking up your work, your teacher might refer to these questions by using the number-letter codes that appear next to each question here.
11. Osbeck, *supra* note 6.

Your early drafts might have sentences like the "wrong" examples above, but your final drafts should more closely resemble the "right" ones. Here is how to do it:

Nouns: As you rewrite, figure out who is doing things and make those people and organizations the subjects of sentences and clauses. Grammatically, only the subject gets to act. In the first two examples above, the main event was what the court did, which is why the court had to become the subject of the sentence. But the defendant did something, too, (or, more accurately, failed to do something), and she thus became the subject of a clause inside the sentence.

Verbs: As you rewrite, do two things.

First, wherever possible, replace the verb *to be* with an action verb. The verb *to be* includes *is, are, am, was, were,* and *will be.* They do a good job of describing condition or status ("the defendant is guilty"). But they aren't verbs of action. In fact, they obscure action. If somebody is doing something, find an action verb to express it. In particular, find ways of eliminating variations on *there is* (such as *there were* and *it is*). Sometimes these constructions are helpful or even unavoidable ("there are four reasons why the plaintiff will not be able to recover. . . ."). At other times, however, they hide your message in a fog of excess verbiage ("inside the locker there was a loaded gun" should become "a loaded gun was in the locker").

Fixing this isn't hard. During rewriting (Chapter 5, §5.7), use the find feature in your word processor to search for *are, is,* and *was.* Every time you find one, consider replacing it with an action verb. In some instances, that will strengthen your writing, and in others it won't. Sometimes the only way to express an idea is to use the verb *to be.* Decide one way or the other. If you have been overusing the verb *to be,* replacing it with action verbs can transform your writing so that it immediately becomes more lively and vivid.

Second, replace nominalizations with genuine verbs. A nominalization is a phrase that converts a simple verb into a complicated noun or noun-phrase. "The search *was a violation of* the defendant's rights" should become "the search *violated* the defendant's rights." The nominalized phrase *was a violation of* is weaker and wordier than the blunt and vivid verb *violated.* The same problem occurs when you ask an adjective to do a verb's job ("was violative of"). Some other examples:

delete these	*and replace them with these*
is able to	can
enter into an agreement	agree
make the argument that	argue that
make the assumption that	assume that
is aware of	knows
is binding on	binds
give consideration to	consider
make a determination	determine
make an objection	object
make payment to	pay
make provision	provide

21-B **Have you used verbs that show the precise relationship between subjects and objects?** For example:

wrong: The court *dealt with* common law larceny.

What did the court do to larceny? Define it? Define only one of the elements? Clarify the difference between larceny and false pretenses? Decide that that offense no longer exists because the legislature has replaced it with the statutory crime of theft? The sentence would be much better with a verb that tells the reader precisely what happened.

wrong: The Freedom of Information Act *applies* to this case.

Does the Act require that the document at issue be published in the Federal Register? Does it require that the document be given to anyone who asks for a copy? Does it require that the document be available for photocopying, but not at government expense? Or does it give the government permission to refuse to do any of these things? We would know more if *applies* were replaced with a verb that communicates exactly what the Act really does.

wrong: Section 452(a) *involves* the Rule Against Perpetuities.

Here, *involves* communicates only that § 452(a) has some connection with the Rule Against Perpetuities. Has § 452(a) codified the Rule? Modified it? Abolished it?

The three verbs illustrated here — *deal with, apply*, and *involve* — rarely communicate a precise relationship between a subject and an object.

21-C **Have you brought the reader to the verb quickly?** Consider this:

The defendant's solicitation of contributions through an organization with a misleading name, immediate deposit of the funds in a bank account in the Bahamas, and eventual use of the money to buy a vacation home in his own name constitutes fraud.

The verb is what ties an English sentence together. In fact, an English sentence is incomprehensible until the reader has identified both a subject *and* a verb. And the most easily understood sentences bring the reader to the verb as quickly as possible. The example above can't be understood in a single reading because it's front-loaded. The reader doesn't reach the verb and object ("constitutes fraud") until after plowing through a 39-word subject.

Sentences like that are caused by automatically making whatever you want to talk about the subject of the sentence. "What shall I talk about next?" you ask yourself and then write down the answer. That becomes the subject of a sentence, no matter how unreadable the result. In first drafts, you can't avoid doing this, but in later drafts you should recognize the problem and fix it.

Front-loaded sentences can be fixed in either of two ways. The first is to simplify the subject so you can bring the reader to the verb quickly:

> The defendant committed fraud by soliciting contributions through an organization with a misleading name, immediately depositing them in a Bahamian bank account, and eventually using the money to buy a vacation home in his own name.

The other cure is to break the original sentence in two:

> The defendant solicited contributions through an organization with a misleading name, immediately deposited them in a Bahamian bank account, and eventually used the money to buy a vacation home in his own name. This was fraud.

You'll lose control of your sentences if you just let them happen. Each sentence must be *built*.

21-D **Have you put the verb near the subject and the object near the verb?** A sentence is hard to understand if you insert a clause or phrase between a subject and a verb or between a verb and an object:

> Grateful Dead Productions, despite the Dead's reputation for tolerating and even encouraging bootleg tapings of concerts when they were still giving them, has several times sued for copyright infringement when the band's albums have been bootlegged.

The solution is to move the clause or phrase to the end or to the beginning of the sentence, leaving the subject and verb (or the verb and object) relatively close together.

move phrase or clause to the END of the sentence	Grateful Dead Productions has several times sued for copyright infringement when the Dead's albums have been bootlegged, despite the band's reputation for tolerating and even encouraging bootleg tapings of concerts when they were still giving them.
move phrase or clause to the BEGINNING of the sentence:	Despite the Grateful Dead's reputation for tolerating and even encouraging bootleg tapings of concerts when they were still giving them, Grateful Dead Productions has several times sued for copyright infringement when the band's albums have been bootlegged.

The clause or phrase should begin the sentence only if you want to emphasize it.

21-E **Have you used transitional words and phrases to show how ideas are related?** Beginners often underestimate the reader's need to be told explicitly how ideas fit together or contrast with one another. You can do this economically with transitional words and phrases. See the ones listed in §21.3.

21-F **Have you streamlined wordy phrases?** Good rewriting pares a convoluted phrase down to something straight-forward:

delete these	*and replace them with these*
because of the fact that	because
during such time as	during
for the purpose of	to
for the reason that	because
in the situation where	where
in the case of	in
in the event that	if
make a motion	move
subsequent to	after
take into consideration	consider
until such time as	until
with regard to	regarding
with the exception of	except

21-G **Have you deleted throat-clearing phrases (also known as "long windups")?** Phrases like the following waste words, divert the reader from your real message, and introduce a shade of doubt and an impression of insecurity:

> It is significant that . . .
>
> The defendant submits that . . .
>
> It is important to note that . . .
>
> The next issue is . . .

Of the two examples below, why would the plaintiff's lawyer feel more comfortable writing the first than the second?

The plaintiff submits that the judgment should be reversed because . . .

The judgment should be reversed because . . .

The unnecessary words in the first example shift emphasis from the idea propounded and to the obvious but irrelevant fact that the writer is the one doing the propounding. (But it is *not* ineffectual to begin an attack on an adversary's argument by beginning with phrasing like "Although the defendant has argued . . .")

21-H | **Have you broken up or streamlined unnecessarily long sentences?** If a sentence is too long to be understood easily on the first reading, express the sentence's ideas in fewer words, or split the sentence into two (or more) shorter sentences, or do both. If you decide to reduce the sentence's verbiage, see questions 21-A, 21-F, and 21-G and review §21.2. If you decide to break up the sentence, be sure to avoid the "sing-songy" style described in question 21-I.

21-I | **Have you rewritten sing-songy sentences?** For example:

> The defendant solicited contributions through an organization with a misleading name. He immediately deposited the funds in a bank account in the Bahamas. Eventually, he used them to buy a vacation home in his own name. This was fraud.

These are four simple sentences, three of them beginning with a subject. The passage sounds naive and probably will bore the reader. The cause is a tendency to write down one thing at a time, without describing the relationships between or among the things mentioned. At its most extreme, the result is a series of simple sentences, all beginning with the subject.

There are two kinds of cure. One is to focus on the relationships, especially causal ones, using some of the transitional words and phrases listed in §21.3:

> Not only did the defendant solicit contributions through an organization with a misleading name, but he immediately deposited the funds in a bank account in the Bahamas. Moreover, he used them to buy a vacation home in his own name. Therefore, he has comitted fraud.

The other cure is to vary three things periodically: the types of sentences (some simple, some compound, some complex); the lengths of sentences (some long, some short, some medium); and the way sentences begin (some with the subject, some with a prefatory word or phrase, some with a dependent clause). Closely related material can be combined into fewer sentences, where the sentence structure itself can demonstrate relationships between ideas:

> Having solicited contributions through an organization with a misleading name and deposited them in a Bahamian bank account, the defendant used the funds to buy a vacation home in his own name. This was fraud.

This example uses a subordinate sentence element ("Having solicited . . . bank account") to achieve the desired effect.

You can avoid the sing-songy effect by understanding and using the full range of sentence structures available in English.

| 21-J | **Have you avoided the passive voice unless you have a good reason for using it?** In the active voice, the subject of the sentence acts (*"Maguire sued Schultz"*). In the passive voice the subject of the sentence is acted upon (*"Schultz was sued by Maguire"*).

The passive voice has three disadvantages. It's often more verbose. It tends to vagueness. And it's usually weaker and more boring to read. Most sentences should be in the active voice.

But the passive may be the more effective voice when you don't know who acted, when you think the identity of the actor is not important, or when you want to deemphasize the actor's identity. For example, compare the following:

> Ms. Blitzstein's aid-to-dependent-family benefits have been wrongfully terminated fourteen times in the last six years.
>
> The Department of Public Welfare has wrongfully terminated Ms. Blitzstein's aid-to-dependent-family benefits fourteen times in the last six years.

Here the passive is actually more concise. Depending on the context, the passive might not be vague because the reader would know that the Department is the only agency capable of terminating aid-to-dependent-family benefits, or at least that the Department is being accused of doing so in this instance.

And, again depending on the context, the passive sentence may be the stronger and more interesting of the two. If the reader is a judge who's being asked to order the Department to stop this nonsense, the passive will be the stronger sentence because it emphasizes the more appealing idea. Generally, a judge is more likely to sympathize with a victim of bureaucratic snafus than to condemn a government agency for viciousness or incompetence.

Sometimes, the passive voice is a good way of avoiding sexist pronouns. See question 21-S.

| 21-K | **Have you placed modifiers close to what they modify?** When people talk, modifiers sometimes wander all over sentences, regardless of what they're intended to modify. But formal writing requires more precision. These sentences all mean different things:

> The police are authorized to arrest *only* the person named in the warrant.
>
> [*They aren't authorized to arrest anyone else.*]

The police are authorized *only* to arrest the person named in the warrant.
   [*They aren't authorized to torture or deport him.*]

The police are *only* authorized to arrest the person named in the warrant.
   [*They have the right to arrest him, but they don't have to. The warrant gives them some discretion.*]

Only the police are authorized to arrest the person named in the warrant.
   [*Civilians aren't authorized.*]

Make sure that the modifier's placement communicates what you really want to say, and don't assume that a busy reader can figure out the meaning from the context.

21-L **Have you used parallel constructions when expressing a list?** Even implied lists should be expressed in some sort of consistent structure. Each item or idea must be phrased in the same grammatical format. Consider the following:

> This attorney should be disbarred because of his neglect of a matter entrusted to him, for pleading guilty to the felony of suborning perjury, and because he disclosed a client's confidences without the client's consent.

Here, the first listed item is expressed as a noun possessed by a pronoun ("his neglect"); the second as an unpossessed gerund ("for pleading"); and the third as a dependent clause, complete with subject, verb, and object ("because he disclosed confidences"). Although the first and third items are preceded by the word "because," the second is not. Isolated from the others, each form alone would be grammatical. But the inconsistencies among them make the whole sentence sound inarticulate. That would not have been true if each item in the list were expressed in the same format:

> This attorney should be disbarred because he neglected a matter entrusted to him, pleaded guilty to the felony of suborning perjury, and disclosed a client's confidences without the client's consent.

21-M **Have you used terms of art where appropriate?** Where an idea peculiar to the law is usually expressed through a term of art, that term should be used because it conveys the idea as precisely as the law can manage and because it often makes long and convoluted explanations unnecessary. Don't write "the plaintiff asked the court to tell the defendants to stop building the highway." It is much more precise to write "the plaintiff moved for an order preliminarily enjoining. . . ."

But don't confuse terms of art with legal argot. A term of art is the law's symbol for an idea that usually cannot be expressed with precision in any other way. Legal argot, on the other hand, has no special meaning peculiar to the law. It's just pretentious wording used for everyday concepts. (See question 21-O.)

21-N | **Have you edited out inappropriately used terms of art?** Terms of art ought to be used only to convey the precise meaning the law holds for them. Where you use a term of art (perhaps because it sounds lawyer-like) but don't really intend to communicate the idea the term of art stands for, the reader will assume that you don't know what you are talking about.

21-O | **Have you edited out imitations of lawyer noises?** Said noises found in and about a lawyer's writing have heretofore caused, resulted in, and led to grievous injury with respect to said lawyer's readers, clients, and/or repute, to wit: by compelling the aforesaid readers to suffer confusion and/or consternation at the expense of the aforementioned clients and consequently rendering said repute to become null, void, and nugatory.

Thinking like a lawyer is not the same as imitating lawyer noises like the ones in the preceding paragraph. Expressions like "to wit," "hereinbefore," and "aforesaid" are argot — not terms of art (see question 17-M) — and they do not convey anything that ordinary English cannot communicate more clearly and less awkwardly. The most valuable memos and the most persuasive briefs are written in the real English language. For example:

just fine:	Elvis has left the building.
bad:	Elvis has departed from the premises.
worse:	It would be accurate to say that Elvis has departed from the premises.
meaningless:	Elvis has clearly and unequivocably left the building.
meaningful:	There is uncontroverted evidence that Elvis has left the building.

Why is "clearly and unequivocably" meaningless? Elvis could not unclearly or equivocally leave the building. Either he has, or he hasn't. Writing something like "clearly and unequivocably" pounds the table without adding meaning. But "uncontroverted evidence" is meaningful because it says that there's evidence that Elvis has left and no evidence that he hasn't. We expect to read in the next sentence about the 27 witnesses who will testify that they saw Elvis go through the stage door, step into a stretch limousine, and disappear into the night.

21-P | **Have you edited out contractions and other conversational language?** Conversational language — the kind you'd use in a casual email to a friend — doesn't belong in most professional documents.

Professional practice, however, has been evolving on the question of contractions — merging two words with an apostrophe (such as "don't" for "do not"). Contractions do not belong in documents filed in court. But lawyers routinely use contractions in professional email (Chapter 17) and in client letters (Chapter 19). Office memos are a middle ground. Some law firms discourage contractions in office memos. Other firms have no preference one way or the other. (No contractions appeared in the first edition of this book. But because professional practice has been evolving, contractions appear frequently in the edition you're reading now.)

21-Q | **Have you edited out inappropriate abbreviations?** In formal documents, a lawyer doesn't write "the N.C. Supreme Court has held . . . ." Spell words out unless the abbreviation is generally used at least as often as the full name (for example, "NAACP" and "FCC"). Otherwise, abbreviate only in citations.

21-R | **Have you avoided rhetorical questions?** They don't work. Your job is to lead — not jab — the reader.

21-S | **Have you avoided sexist wording?** In the way all languages evolve, English is now shedding many centuries of sexist phrasing. Perhaps a decade or two from now, English might settle into phrasings that are both gender-neutral and fluid. In the meantime, writers must struggle a bit.

The thorniest problem is English's use of the pronouns *he, his,* and *him* to refer generally to people of either sex. The problem wouldn't exist if English had a pronoun that meant "any person," regardless of sex. But English lacks that. The ersatz pronoun *s/he* irritates most readers. The ritual incantations *he or she, his or her,* and *him or her* are wordy and, if repeated often, tedious.

The best solution is to eliminate the need for a pronoun. If that can't be done, recast both the pronoun *and* its noun in the plural. That might also make the writing more concise:

	To calendar a motion, an attorney must file *his* motion with the clerk.
pronoun replaced with "the"	To calendar a motion, an attorney must file *the* motion with the clerk.
actor made plural	To calendar motions, attorneys must file *their* motions with the clerk.
actor eliminated from sentence	A motion is calendared by filing it with the clerk.

As a last resort, you might fall back on *he or she, his or her,* or *him or her.* But these phrases pose another problem. Suppose the sentence reads this way:

To calendar a motion, an attorney must file his or her moving papers with the clerk.

Our eye hits the word *his,* and we imagine a male lawyer, maybe in a dark blue suit, handing documents over a counter to a court clerk. (For most readers, words create images — and the more specific the words, the more detailed the image.) Our eye continues through the words *or her,* and for a split-second we allow for the possibility that this attorney with moving papers might be female. We do this for a split-second because the other image got there first (and maybe because of assumptions about sex-based roles). And after that split-second is over, we go back to thinking about motions and clerks and what happens when things are not calendared properly — and if we are imagining anything, it's probably still the male lawyer in the blue suit.

Sex-biased nouns are usually easier to avoid. The "reasonable man" in negligence law can as easily be the "reasonable person"; and, depending on the context, "manpower" might be replaced with "effort," "personnel," "workers," or something else. Some nouns, such as "businessman," are harder, however. Unless sex truly matters ("the corporation specializes in the manufacture of businesswomen's clothing"), it is sexist to refer to a woman in business as a "businesswoman." (She is a person in business. What does her sex have to do with it?) Unless the awkward term "businessperson" gains acceptance, the only solution is to rephrase the sentence so that you don't need a word like "businessman" or "businesswoman."

Exercise
Kalmar's Driveway

Rewrite the following sentences around nouns and verbs that describe action. Make sure that each sentence is of comprehensible length. Eliminate throat-clearing phrases,

and replace nominalizations, unnecessary passives, and unnecessarily wordy constructions. You'll find this easier if you read the whole exercise before starting to rewrite.

1. It is evident that Kalmar is likely to be convicted of accepting a bribe because
    all the elements of bribery are susceptible of proof beyond a reasonable
    doubt.
2. A person is guilty of accepting a bribe if that person is an employee of the
    government and "requests or receives from any other person anything of
    value, knowing it to be a reward or inducement for an official act," Crim. Code
    § 702, and a conviction may occur only if evidence is presented by the prose-
    cution that persuades the finder of fact beyond a reasonable doubt that the
    defendant is guilty.
3. The initial element that can be established is that Kalmar is an employee of
    the government.
4. The facts indicate that in his capacity as Roads Commissioner, Kalmar had
    occasion from time to time to purchase, on behalf of the government, quan-
    tities of cement, asphalt, and other road construction materials from Phelps,
    who caused these materials to be delivered to road-repair sites on trucks
    owned by Phelps.
5. Kalmar had need for a new driveway at his own home, and he made a request
    to Phelps for a recommendation of a contractor who would do a good job at
    a reasonable price.
6. Phelps told Kalmar that she would look into the matter, but, without Kalmar's
    knowledge, a new driveway was built at his home by her employees the
    next day.
7. The circumstances fit into a pattern showing that Kalmar had knowledge
    that he was being offered a reward or inducement by Phelps for official acts
    directly relating to his job, and although the statute does not specify that
    a defendant must know at the time the thing of value is actually delivered
    or physically taken that it is a reward for official acts, Kalmar both accepted
    and continued to receive the bribe when, according to the facts, he did not
    undertake any effort to compensate Phelps for the cost of the driveway.
8. Because the cost involved is such that it could not have been accidentally
    overlooked by Kalmar, there can be no innocent explanation for the fact
    that he had an opportunity every day to see that he had a new driveway for
    which nothing had been paid, and there is therefore no reasonable doubt
    about his guilt.

Quotations

Section 22.1 explains the complex rules on quotation format. Section 22.2 explains how to avoid faults like overquoting, unnecessarily long quotations, and quoting out of context.

§22.1   Quotation Format

Bluebook rule 5 governs the format of quotations. Here are the most essential requirements:

Use brackets to enclose additions and substitutions that you place inside a quotation, including conversion of a lowercase letter into a capital or vice versa (Bluebook rule 5.2). Use brackets, not parentheses. On your computer keyboard, brackets are at the right end of the row under the numbers.

If you incorporate a quote beginning with a capitalized word into a sentence of your own, the capital letter must be reduced to a lowercase letter unless the capital denotes a proper name. Use brackets to show that you have changed the original. For example:

wrong: The court held **that** "**Not** so long ago, in a studio far, far away from the policymakers in Washington, D.C., George Lucas conceived of an imaginary galaxy," but his trademark is not infringed when politicians refer to a proposed missile defense system as Star Wars. *Lucasfilm Ltd. v. High Frontier*, 622 F. Supp. 931, 932, 935 (D.D.C. 1985).

right: The court held **that** "[n]ot so long ago, . . ."

Under Bluebook rule 5.3, if you delete words (other than a citation) from a quote, you must indicate that by an ellipsis (". . ."). When the final words of a sentence are omitted, the sentence ends with *four* periods—three for the ellipsis and one to end the sentence. There are two exceptions.

First, where you incorporate a quotation into a sentence of your own composition—as in the Star Wars example above—don't place an ellipsis at the beginning or the end of the quotation. Incorporating the quote into your own sentence already suggests that part of it might have been chopped off.

Second, don't place an ellipsis at the beginning of a quotation, even if you intend the quote to stand on its own as a complete sentence. If the quote isn't incorporated into a sentence you have written and if the first letter of the quote wasn't capitalized in the original, capitalize that letter and place it in brackets to indicate an alteration.

If the quotation is 50 words or more, you must put it in a block quote, separated from your text with extra white space above, below, and on the sides. To add extra space above and below, skip an extra line in each place. To add it on the sides, use the indent function in your word processor's *Layout* or *Format* menu.

Don't use quotation marks at the beginning and end of a block quote. The extra white space around the quote tells the reader that you're quoting. And don't put the citation inside the quotation block.

Instead, put the cite in your text, at the beginning of the next line you write. The first example below is wrong on *both* counts:

wrong: Judge Kozinski disagreed:

> "Where does [Vanna] White get this right to control our thoughts? The majority's creation goes way beyond the protection given a trademark or a copyrighted work, or a person's name or likeness. . . . For better or worse, we *are* the Court of Appeals for the Hollywood Circuit. Millions of people toil in the shadow of the law we make, and much of their livelihood is made possible by the existence of intellectual property rights." *White v. Samsung Electronics Am., Inc.*, 989 F.2d 1512, 1519, 1521 (9th Cir. 1993) (Kozinski, J., dissenting) (emphasis in original).

> Based on this reasoning, the client should be able to . . . .

right: Judge Kozinski disagreed:

> Where does [Vanna] White get this right to control our thoughts? The majority's creation goes way beyond the protection given a trademark or a copyrighted work, or a person's name or likeness. . . . For better or worse, we *are* the Court of Appeals for the Hollywood Circuit. Millions of people toil in the shadow of the law we make, and much of their livelihood is made possible by the existence of intellectual property rights.
>
> *White v. Samsung Electronics Am., Inc.,* 989 F.2d 1512, 1519, 1521 (9th Cir. 1993) (Kozinski, J., dissenting) (emphasis in original). Based on this reasoning, the client should be able to . . . .

But you should block-quote rarely — if ever. See question 22-B in §22.2.

§22.2 How to Test Your Writing for Effective Use of Quotations

While writing — and rewriting — ask yourself the following questions.[1]

> **22-A**   **Have you quoted and cited every time you use other people's words?**   Other people's words must have quotation marks around them and a citation to the source. If you don't do this, you will be treated as a plagiarist. See §6.5 in Chapter 6. It doesn't matter whether you do it out of sloppiness or out of an intent to deceive. An idea that you get from a written source must be attributed to that source with a citation, even if you express the idea in your own words.

> **22-B**   **Have you quoted only the essential words?**   Don't quote unless the quoted words fit into at least one of the following categories:

1. words that must be *interpreted* in order to resolve the issue, such as a statute's key words (see §8.8 in Chapter 8);
2. words that are so closely identified with the topic under discussion that they are *inseparable* from it;
3. words that, *with remarkable economy,* put the reader in touch with the thinking of a court, legislature, or expert in the field; or
4. words that are *the most eloquent and succinct conceivable* expression of an important idea.

---

1. When marking up your work, your teacher might refer to these questions by using the number-letter codes that appear next to each question here.

Beginners are too quick to think that words, merely because they're printed in a book, can satisfy the third or fourth criterion. That kind of awe results in a sentence like the following:

> The court relied on "[w]ell-established jurisprudence of our sister states . . . holding that baseball is a strenuous game involving danger to . . . players . . . and that one who, with full knowledge of this danger, attends . . . and places himself in a position of danger, assumes the risks inherent in the game." *Gaspard v. Grain Dealers Mut. Ins. Co.*, 131 So. 2d 831, 834 (La. Ct. App. 1961).

Although the writer of the sentence above did some editing, the only words really worth quoting are the ones in quotes below:

> Relying on "[w]ell-established" precedent in other states holding baseball to be a dangerous game, the court concluded that anyone who knows of that danger and nevertheless plays baseball "assumes the risks inherent in the game." *Gaspard v. Grain Dealers Mut. Ins. Co.*, 131 So. 2d 831, 834 (La. Ct. App. 1961).

Which sentence is easier to read and understand — the first one with a big quotation (44 words) or the second one with two short quotes (totaling 9 quoted words)? Which sentence more clearly focuses on the relevant ideas?

The most convincing descriptions of authority are written almost entirely in your own words with very few and very short quotations that convey the essence of the court's approach.

Block quotations are especially troublesome. Busy readers skim over or refuse to read large quotations because, in their experience, only a few of the quoted words really matter, and it may take too much effort to find them. Readers feel that block quotations are obstacles that have to be climbed over. The more of them you use, the more quickly a reader will decide not to read any of them. Judges and supervising attorneys view large quotations as evidence of a writer's laziness. They believe that your job is to find the essential words, isolate them, and concisely paraphrase the rest. When you throw a big block quotation at a reader, you're asking the reader to do some of your work.

How do you cut a block quotation down to size? Assume that you have written the following in a first draft:

> In *Roth* the Supreme Court held that a government could, without satisfying the traditional clear-and-present-danger test, restrict public distriution of obscene material. But it came to the opposite conclusion when faced with a statute that punished private possession of obscene materials in one's own home:
>
>> It is true that in *Roth* this Court rejected the necessity of proving that exposure to obscene material would create a clear and present danger of antisocial conduct or would probably induce its recipients to such conduct. . . . But that case dealt with public distribution of obscene materials

> and such distribution is subject to different objections. For example, there is always the danger that obscene material might fall into the hands of children . . . or that it might intrude upon the sensibilities or privacy of the general public.

Stanley v. Georgia, 394 U.S. 557, 567 (1969). A number of the Court's later right-to-privacy rulings have been based in part on *Stanley.*

First drafts are full of passages like this, and in a first draft they cause no harm. But in later drafts, you should realize that the block quote will repel the reader. Ask yourself "Why do I want this quote? What words inside it satisfy one or more of the four criteria?"

Your answer might be that no words in the quote satisfy those criteria, but that the quote does contain ideas that you want the reader to know about. If so, *rewrite all of it in your own words.* If you do this well — and it does require effort — your words will be better than the original quote because your words will *fit* better.

On the other hand, the answer might be that some words are too valuable to give up. Here, "might fall into the hands of children" creates an image that economically reflects the Court's thinking (criterion 3), and "intrude upon the sensibilities or privacy of the general public" sets out a standard that will need to be interpreted (criterion 1). Isolate words like that, and rewrite everything else, condensing in the process. You might come up with something much more readable, like this:

> In *Roth* the Supreme Court held that a government could, without satisfying the traditional clear-and-present-danger test, restrict public distribution of obscene material. But it came to the opposite conclusion when faced with a statute that punished private possession of obscene materials in one's own home. In *Stanley v. Georgia,* 394 U.S. 557 (1969), the Court struck down such a statute and distinguished *Roth* because publicly distributed pornography "might fall into the hands of children" or "intrude upon the sensibilities or privacy of the general public." *Id.* at 567. A number of the court's later right-to-privacy rulings have been based in part on *Stanley.*

This is shorter; it flows better; and it makes the meaning much clearer than the block quote did. The reader's attention is taken straight to the essential words, which stand out when integrated into your own text.

To accomplish this you don't need to be a better writer than a Supreme Court justice was. The justice who wrote *Stanley* had the task of justifying a significant decision of constitutional law. The writer of the passage above had a smaller job: explaining, as concisely as possible, the difference between *Roth* and *Stanley.* The smaller job takes fewer words.

At the opposite extreme is the problem of too many short quotations rather than quotations that are too long, although the effect on the reader is similar.

This is called snippetizing, and it might take the form of a quote from and cite to case A, followed by a quote from and cite to case B, followed by a quote from and cite to case C, and so on, without much discussion of any of the cases or of the ideas expressed in the quotes. Strings of snippet quotations give the reader a feeling of sliding over the surface of complex ideas, which the writer refuses to explain. Explain the cases.

A writer who quotes too much is sometimes called a "cut-and-paste artist" because the product is not really writing at all. Little thought goes into it, and readers have no confidence in it. What they want is *your* analysis, which comes only with hard mental work — not finding quotable words and typing them into your document.

22-C | **Have you avoided quoting out of context?** Sometimes words mean something different in context than they do when quoted out of context. Assume that a reader will check the source from which you quote. Readers often do that to learn more or to make sure that your reasoning is correct. Suppose a reader understands the words, as you have quoted them, to mean one thing, but, when checking your source, the reader discovers that in context they mean something completely different. Not only have you done the reader a disservice, but now the reader distrusts you.

22-D | **Have you quoted accurately?** Suppose you see language in a case that you want to quote. You type it into your draft, but — although you don't realize it at the time — some of the words you type into your document aren't the same as those that appear in the case. Supervisors, judges, and teachers can easily spot this. When they do, they'll lose some confidence in you because it suggests that you haven't been careful. We all tend, at least a little bit, to rewrite quotes unconsciously into our own style while copying them. The only way to prevent this is to proofread your work with the sources in front of you. Don't try to do this by toggling back and forth on your computer between the source and your draft. Instead, print your draft and compare it to the source, which you can bring up on your screen. That's the safest way to compare the two word for word.

22-E | **Have you placed quotation marks exactly where they belong?** The most common problems are (1) omitting the quotation marks that close a quotation, even though the opening quotation marks are included ("Where does the quote end?" writes the teacher in the margin); (2) omitting the quotation marks that open a quotation, even though the closing marks are present ("Where does the quote begin?" asks the teacher); and (3) where there's a quote within a quote, forgetting to change the double quotation marks of the original to single marks.

Exercise
The First Amendment

1. You are in the midst of writing a memorandum involving the right-of-assembly clause — and no other part of the First Amendment. You intend to quote the words to be interpreted. This is the text of the entire amendment:

> Congress shall make no law respecting an establishment of religion, or prohibiting the free exercise thereof; or abridging the freedom of speech, or of the press; or the right of the people peaceably to assemble, and to petition the Government for a redress of grievances.

Using words from the Amendment, complete the following sentence: "The First Amendment provides . . . "

2. Do the same for a memorandum involving the freedom-of-speech clause.

THE SHIFT TO PERSUASION

23 Developing a Persuasive Theory

Persuasive writing aims to convince judges to do what your client wants. Whether you are writing a motion memorandum or an appellate brief, the ability to persuade centers on three skills: developing a persuasive theory (explained in this chapter), developing persuasive arguments (Chapter 24), and telling the client's story (Chapter 27).

§23.1 Strategic Thinking

A strategy is a plan for reaching a goal. A teacher, a client, or a supervisor might ask you, "How can you win? What's your *plan*?" You won't be able to answer that question until you're well into researching and writing your motion memo or appellate brief. But at some point, you should have an answer.

In litigation writing, a lawyer plans by identifying goals (such as persuading a court to adopt rule X or to find fact Y) and then by generating a list of possible methods of accomplishing each goal. In imagining these alternative strategies, ask yourself, "What would *cause* a court to decide in my favor?" After predicting each strategy's risks and chances of success, the lawyer selects the best one for each goal.

If you're asked why you did a particular thing and can answer only "I guess it seemed like a good idea at the time," people will assume that you didn't really think through the problem. In post-mortems of your work, a supervising lawyer or a teacher might ask you a litany of questions about strategy:

What was your goal?
What was your strategy?
What other possible strategies did you consider and reject?
For each rejected strategy, why was it inferior to the one you did choose?
What led you to believe that the strategy you chose would actually achieve the ultimate goal?
Did you do all the things necessary to execute the strategy you chose?

Supervisors and teachers ask these questions because a lawyer's job is *to make desired things happen.*

§23.2   Theories: Of the Case, of the Motion, of the Appeal

To make their decisions, judges need more than raw information about the law and the facts. They make decisions by *choosing between theories,* and you'll lose if your adversary's theory is more attractive than yours.

Think back to a major decision you had to make — perhaps the choice of which apartment to rent or which car to buy. If your decision-making was conscious and deliberative — as judges hope their decisions are — you can probably recall an idea — or a small number of related ideas — that caused you to choose one apartment over another or one car over another. And if your decision-making was conscious and deliberative, there was probably a moment when you first identified and appreciated this idea (or small group of ideas). At that moment, you probably also realized that one of the alternatives had become inevitable. Some people who specialize in sales work call this moment the "selling point" because the decision to buy becomes inevitable once the selling idea is fully appreciated by the buyer.

Persuading is selling, and judges have accurately been described as "professional buyers of ideas."[1] Judges have their selling points, and both lawyers and judges use the word *theory* to refer to the collection of ideas that, in a given case, a lawyer offers for purchase. At trial, each lawyer propounds a *theory*

---

1. Girvan Peck, *Strategy of the Brief,* Litigation, Winter 1984, at 26, 27.

of the case. If the court is to decide a motion or an appeal, the phrases *theory of the motion* or *theory of the appeal* might be used instead. Each lawyer proposes a theory, and the court chooses between them.

A theory is an idea on which a decision can be based — a way of looking at the controversy. A persuasive theory is a view of the facts and law — intertwined together — that justifies a decision in the client's favor and motivates a court to make that decision. A persuasive theory "explains not only *what* happened but also *why*" through a compelling story that "has both rational and psychological appeal" and thus is "persuasive both to the mind and to the heart."[2]

§23.3   Developing a Theory

> Luck is the residue of design.
>
> — *Branch Rickey*

Before the memo in Appendix C was written, Goslin undoubtedly showed his lawyer a deed that, on its surface, seemed to give the nephew every right to have Goslin and his belongings removed. A lawyer who lacks the skill of theory design might say something like this to such a client: "Well, Mr. Goslin, you made a mistake. In the future, don't give a deed without securing some rights for yourself, either by making a collateral contract or by taking payment for your equity. In the meantime, I think you'll have to move out."

Another — and better — lawyer might look under the surface for possibilities. At the time of the deed, did Goslin believe he was giving up all his property rights? Did he think he was going to continue to live in the house? Had the nephew said or done anything that would show that he thought Goslin was making a gift or was going to move out? Is there anything in the history of this uncle and this nephew on which some sort of reliance theory might be based? Since people don't usually negotiate with their relatives at arm's-length or with written contracts, and since people can turn on each other even in family relationships, might some part of the law go so far as to enforce understandings between relatives, even if those understandings have never been spoken or written down?

---

2. David Binder & Paul Bergman, *Fact Investigation: From Hypothesis to Proof* 140, 184 (West 1984).

Notice the technique. First, open doors to factual possibilities. Then find out how the law treats those possibilities. And discover whether evidence can prove them.

A theory won't spring forth in final form from your mind. Instead, a germ first occurs and then grows as new information is learned and more law researched. Although research guides the growth of the theory, the theory also guides the course of the research, each filling in the gaps of the other. Sometimes, there is rapid progress. At other times, it may be painfully slow.

How do you develop a theory?

First, narrow your focus to the issues. What will really matter to the court? Every case has some aspects that have distressed the client but will be greeted in court with profound boredom. Certain kinds of suffering — for good reasons or bad — have no effect whatever on the typical judge. Some suffering can be dismissed on the ground that it's too small to merit judicial intervention, or that it's as much the client's own fault as anybody else's, or that it represents problems courts can't solve. Conversely, every case has some aspects that both client and lawyer would like to forget but will nevertheless strongly influence a judge. The client might have suffered a wrong, for example, but only while doing something that judges find unacceptable. Or the other side might enjoy one of the traditional advantages in court. It might, for instance, be engaged in one of those industries that courts like to protect. Every theory has to take these kinds of things into account.

Second, list your case's strengths and weaknesses and the other side's strengths and weaknesses. What are your best facts? Conversely, what facts make you worry? What are your best and worst authorities and rules of law? What are the human equities of the situation? Be realistic about the people in the courthouse and the way they are likely to deal with your case.

Third, think of a way of looking at the case that, if believed, would make your client the winner.

Fourth, compare your theory to the criteria for effectiveness explained in §23.7. To the extent that your theory falls short of effectiveness, can you fix it?

Finally, once you have an effective theory, write the motion memo or appellate brief that will present it.

It can help to develop contradictory theories together — to develop, in other words, your adversary's most likely theory while creating your own. If you look at the case as your adversary will see it, and if you hypothetically work up a theory for your adversary to argue, you'll be able to identify the weaknesses in your theory. Otherwise, you will look at the controversy onesidedly, and your theories will reflect wishful thinking and be too onedimensional to withstand attack.

§23.4 The Power of Stories to Grip and Involve a Writer's Audience

[E]very lawsuit is a story. I don't care if it's about a dry contract interpretation. You've got two people who want to accomplish something and they're coming together. That's a story. And you've got to tell a good story [with] some sense of drama, some building up to . . . the legal arguments. . . . [C]ertainly here at the Supreme Court and in the courts of appeals you're looking for a couple of hooks in the facts that hopefully are going to be repeated in one form or another later on in the legal argument, but also are going to catch somebody's interest.

— *Chief Justice John Roberts*

Robert McKee[3] has taught many of the best screenwriters in Hollywood how to write stories. So many screenwriters are in his debt that he was actually portrayed in that role in the movie, *Adaptation*. Nicholas Cage plays a screenwriter who asks McKee for help overcoming writer's block.

McKee also teaches businesspeople how to persuade by telling stories. In a typical business situation, a young start-up company has developed a valuable idea, such as a drug that will prevent heart attacks, and the company needs venture capitalists to lend money or buy stock so the company can finish the job and get the drug to market. This resembles the situation lawyers are in when they ask a court for relief. A person who wants something (a lawyer or a company's executives) tries to persuade a decision-maker (a judge or an investment banker) who has very rational criteria for making the decision (rules of law or the math of whether an investment will make a profit).

If the company's chief executive officer meets with the investment bankers and makes only a logical presentation with PowerPoint slides, based on statistics and sales projections, the "bankers would nod politely and stifle yawns while thinking of all the other companies better positioned" to bring this drug to market.

But if the CEO tells a compelling story about how the company overcame obstacles to develop the drug, get it patented, and get regulatory approval, but now it has to overcome one final hurdle — financing — to put the drug on sale, that causes "great suspense" and the possibility that "the story might not have a happy ending." The CEO has the bankers "on the edges of their seats, and he says, 'We won the race, we got the patent, we're poised to go public and save a quarter-million lives a year.' And the bankers just throw money at him."

---

3. The quotes from McKee and the material about him are from *Storytelling That Moves People: A Conversation with Screenwriting Coach Robert McKee*, 81 Harv. Bus. Rev. 51-57 (June 2003).

Why? Nothing should be more rational than finance. If the numbers on the PowerPoint slides show that this project will produce a profit without too much risk, the bankers should invest in it — but typically they won't unless they feel enthusiasm, unless they have been captured by the story. If you challenge McKee on this, he'll say, "I know the storytelling method works, because after I consulted with a dozen corporations whose principals told exciting stories to Wall Street, they all got their money."

In a law school classroom, making the most logical argument is everything. That is as it should be. Legal argumentation is difficult to master, and legal education devotes a lot of effort to teaching students how to argue well.

But in the real world, when you make purely logical arguments to decision-makers like judges, as Mckee points out, "they are arguing with you in their heads" — because logic and argument naturally arouse skepticism — and "if you do persuade them, you've done so only on an intellectual basis. That's not good enough because people are not inspired to act by reason alone." A story, he says, persuades "by uniting an idea with an emotion."

Every case has a story. You've been reading them in the casebooks in other courses. Actually, every case has at least two stories — one for each side. The one you read in the court's opinion is the winning story. Sometimes, you read the losing story in a dissenting opinion.

Nearly all good stories have tension. The stories lawyers tell courts have tension because they involve conflict. When we start to hear or read a story like that — and if the story is well told — we naturally start asking questions like these: Who's the good person? Who's the bad person? What bad thing did the bad person do? How did it affect the good person? (We're worried.) What happens next? How will the story end?

§23.5   Imagery in Theory Development

A picture held us captive.

— Wittgenstein

Imagery has a powerful effect in stories and theories. Thinking in images will help you find new ways of looking at facts.

A truck runs off the highway, through a farmer's fence, and over the farmer's cow. The truck driver's insurance company wants to pay as little as possible for this cow, and the farmer, of course, wants much more money.

The insurance company's lawyer will tell a story in which the cow is "a unit of livestock" or "a farm asset," as though the issue is how much money the farmer should get to replace a machine-like object that consumes grass as fuel to produce milk and an occasional calf. The story will focus on numbers from the farmer's books that show the productivity of this object, its acquisition costs, depreciation, useful life remaining at the time of its destruction, and so forth. The insurance company's lawyer will use this story because the numbers show the cow to be an unexceptional object.

The farmer's lawyer looks for a different story to tell. "Tell me about the cow," she asks the farmer. "That wasn't just any cow," replies the farmer,

> That was Bessie! She was the only Guernsey cow left in this county. She didn't give that thin milk you get out of a Holstein that people buy in the grocery store. She gave the thickest, most flavorful milk you ever tasted. We didn't sell it to the dairy. They wouldn't pay a decent price for it anyway because dairies care about quantity, not quality. We drank it ourselves and made the best butter and cheese out of it. And Guernseys are smaller cows. They're friendly, like pets, and Bessie was part of our family.

Imagery that you can "see" in your mind creates the persuasive weight of each of these stories. The farmer's lawyer wants the judge to see a big pair of eyes in a Guernsey head nudging the farmer with affection — a loss to the farmer's family that exceeds the loss of a grass-to-milk machine. The insurance company's lawyer, on the other hand, wants us to see the farmer's balance sheet, where a certain item of livestock is carried as an asset valued at a certain number of dollars.

In any writing that grows out of this controversy, the farmer's lawyer probably won't mention Bessie's head nudging the farmer, and the insurance company's lawyer probably won't mention the balance sheet. Those things aren't, strictly speaking, relevant to the legal issues. But if the lawyers are good writers, they'll include enough detail so that the reader will see, in the reader's own mind, something like those scenes.

Imagery is part of storytelling, and it influences how readers, including judges, feel about the legal issues. Vividness not only helps the reader remember the story, but it makes the story more believable. Imagery makes a story real.

If you develop an eye for revealing detail, your stories will much more quickly come to life as vivid and compelling. Word choice is critical. The right words help the judge see the image. The wrong ones don't.

§23.6 Finding and Developing the Story

Facts aren't the story. They're the raw materials for the story.

A client sits in your office, describing in detail a problem that the client wants you to solve. These details are the facts. The client isn't telling you a persuasive story. Clients typically don't know how to do that. They hire lawyers to do it for them. The client can tell you only facts — "I got this letter in the mail," "Smith told me the company was going bankrupt," "I can't pay my bills."

In a law school writing assignment, you might get these details as part of your assignment.

Regardless of how you get the facts, they aren't yet a story. The story is hidden in the facts. You have to find it there. Look for details that reveal character. Look for details that lend themselves to persuasive imagery. Assemble these into a story that fulfills the four purposes of storytelling — (1) to motivate the judge to act, (2) to communicate who your client and witnesses are, (3) to communicate who the other side and their witnesses are, and (4) to neutralize the unfavorable facts.

While you are doing this, try telling the story to a friend or relative whose thinking you respect and who doesn't know the case you are working on. Telling the story orally helps you refine it and test it out before you start writing it. Speaking it aloud helps you understand and improve it. Then, ask how your friend or relative feels about the story. Does it motivate? Do the characters seem realistic? And so on.

After you've worked out the story, ask yourself whether you can summarize its essence persuasively in two or three sentences. If you can't, either the story is too complicated or you haven't identified the core facts. If the story is too complicated, your reader will get lost. If you don't know the core facts, you won't be able to focus on them when you tell the story. And you'll need to focus on them at the very beginning in the Statement of the Case or Statement of Facts. Despite its name, the Statement is where you tell the story. As you'll learn in Chapter 27, the Statement should begin with a paragraph or two that summarizes your story's core facts.

Finally, will the judge care? If not, the story won't work. Nor will the theory on which the story is based.

§23.7   How to Evaluate Your Theory

To figure out whether your theory stands a significant chance of persuading a court, ask yourself the following questions.[4]

| 23-A | **Does your theory "[a]ccount for or explain all of . . . the unfavorable facts"?**[5]   When a judge or jury first looks at the case, if your theory is inconsistent with an undeniable fact, one of the two will be considered wrong — and it will not be the undeniable fact. Ambiguous evidence and debatable inferences are usually resolved in whatever way is most consistent with the evidence that cannot be questioned. When the time for

---

4. When marking your work, your teacher might refer to these questions by using the number-letter codes that appear next to each question.
5. David M. Malone & Peter T. Hoffman, *The Effective Deposition* 53 (2d ed., 1996).

decision arrives, the adjudicator's natural tendency is to say, "Let's start with what we know already and unquestionably."

| 23-B | **Does your theory "explain away in a plausible manner as many unfavorable facts as it can"?**[6] It's not enough to build on the ev- |

idence you like. Your theory should also explain why the evidence you *dislike* should not prevent a decision in your favor. Is it overcome by other evidence in your favor? Does it prove facts that aren't as important under the law as other facts that your evidence has proved?

| 23-C | **Does your theory "[e]xplain why people acted in the way they did"?**[7] If your theory doesn't do that, some significant part of the |

case will still seem mysterious to the judge or jury. As long as that mystery remains, a judge or jury will feel that your theory hasn't "solved" the controversy. If a theory assumes that the actors behaved differently from the way people normally do in similar circumstances, the theory isn't persuasive unless it includes a compelling reason for the difference. Theories that impute deceit to objective witnesses, for example, are less attractive than those that suggest honest mistakes. Innocent misunderstandings are much more common in life than lying or stealing.

| 23-D | **Does your theory have a solid basis in fact?** Are your interpretations of the statutes and cases reasonable? When a court exam- |

ines your legal arguments, will the court be persuaded?

| 23-E | **Does your theory seem "consistent with common sense and . . . plausible?"**[8] All else being equal, a simple theory is more |

down-to-earth than a complex one, although even a simple theory must address all the facts. A theory has a commonsense appeal if its internal logic is consistent, if it's realistic, if its explanations are compatible with the judge or jury's experiences in life, and if it reflects their values and the values of the community to which they feel responsible. The most easily sold theories are those that are based on easily believable interpretations of the evidence and the authorities; that would lead to reasonable results; that don't ask a judge or jury to believe that people have behaved in improbable ways; and that ask for narrow decisions rather than earth-shaking ones.

Like any other kind of consumer, a judge buys only when struck with a feeling of confidence that the purchase will turn out well, without causing injustice or embarrassment on appeal or before the public. Like most people who have had substantial opportunity to observe human nature, judges

---

6. George Vetter, *Successful Civil Litigation* 30-31 (1977).
7. Malone & Hoffman, *supra* n. 6, at 53.
8. *Id.*

can be astute at surmising how various kinds of people would behave under given circumstances. And like most people with substantial responsibilities, judges believe things work out better when people are reasonable rather than extreme. Judges feel safer when they can make narrow decisions, rather than earth-shaking ones, because narrow decisions are less likely to create new problems and controversies. (A judge would much rather find that your client is not guilty on the facts than hold that the statute defining the crime is unconstitutional.)

A theory that sells in an appellate court has a flavor different from one that seems attractive to a trial court. That's because trial judges and appellate judges don't see their work in precisely the same way. A trial court is a place of routine, and trial judges want to make decisions the way they are usually made and not in ways that would change the world. Although trial judges sometimes try to avoid the full impact of appellate authority, the rulings of the courts to which a trial judge's decision could be appealed are like orders from a superior, and the trial judge needs and wants to know — through those rulings — what the supervising courts expect.

In contrast, appellate judges are conscious of their responsibility to see the bigger picture and to keep the law as a whole fair and reasonable, even if that requires modifying the common law now and then to fit changes in society. Judicial circumspection and the doctrine of stare decisis keep these changes to a minimum, however, and appellate courts generally presume the decision below to be correct, reversing only if deeply troubled by what happened in the lower court. Generally, theories presented to high appellate courts are more policy-oriented than theories presented to trial courts.

Exercise
Escape from Prison? (Developing a Theory)

Orville Bradwyn is charged with the crime of escape from prison. The state's sole witness was Benjamin Tunmeyer, a prison guard, who testified as follows.

Q: Please tell the court what you observed and did at 6:30 in the evening on the sixth of July.

A: I was checking prisoners in the dinner line. Prisoners are required to be in there at that time, and any prisoner who hasn't shown up for dinner is considered missing. The defendant didn't appear. I then checked his cell. Some material had been put in his bed, bunched up so that it looked like somebody was asleep there. His radio had been left on. But he was gone.

Q: What did you do?

A: We searched the grounds outside the prison. We didn't find the defendant there, so we searched inside the prison — first the perimeter, and then the inside of buildings and containers where someone might hide. We finally found him in the laundry room at 7:39 P.M.

Q: What did he have with him?

A: All of his clothing.

Q: Does the prison wash the laundry of any other institution?

A: Yes, we do the laundry for the state hospital down the road. It's done in the same laundry room where we found the defendant.

Q: How is the hospital's laundry transported to and from the prison?

A: By truck. The hospital's truck brings in it in the morning and picks it up at about 8 P.M.

Q: Are prisoners permitted in the laundry room in the evening?

A: No prisoner is allowed in that room after 5 P.M. Hiding in one of the hospital's laundry bags is an obvious way to escape from the prison.

Q: What precautions are taken to prevent that?

A: At 5 P.M., a guard makes sure all prisoners assigned to work in the laundry have left, and then the door is locked. In addition, the guard opens up each laundry bag that goes to the state hospital and makes sure it has only laundry in it. Then he locks up the room and locks another door on the corridor leading to the laundry room. Nobody is inside those doors until the hospital's truck arrives about three hours later.

Q: What guard was assigned that responsibility on the night in question?

A: Me. I sent out all the prisoners and satisfactorily inspected the state hospital's bags. Then, I locked the doors and left.

Q: Was Mr. Bradwyn assigned to work in the laundry?

A: Yes. But he was not scheduled to work in the laundry room on the day in question.

Cross-examination:

Q: Are you familiar with Mr. Bradwyn's reputation among other prisoners and among corrections officers?

A: He is an exceptionally tidy person.

Q: Were there any prior occasions on which you and Mr. Bradwyn had shouting matches?

A: Yes. It's almost impossible to inspect his cell. He starts yelling the minute you touch any of his things. He says he doesn't like them moved.

Q: What was the defendant doing when you found him?

A: He was washing his clothes. No, actually, he was drying them. They were in the dryer.

Q: What items of clothing were in the dryer?

A: Both of his prison uniforms — prisoners are issued two — socks, undershirts, undershorts. They were still wet.

Q: What did you find when you searched Mr. Bradwyn's cell?

A: Letters from his family, personal photographs, letters from his lawyer, an address book.

Q: Before dinner, prisoners are free to move about outside their cells; aren't they?

A: Yes.

Q: And the same is true after dinner, isn't it?

A: Until 7:30.

After this testimony, the prosecution rested. Before any defense witnesses testified, Bradwyn moved to dismiss on the ground that the prosecution had presented insufficient evidence to convict.

Develop two theories that satisfy the criteria in §23.7. One theory should support Bradwyn and his motion. The other should support the prosecution and oppose the motion. Use the method outlined in this chapter.

The relevant statute and cases interpreting it appear below:

CRIMINAL CODE § 745

If any person committed to prison shall break and escape therefrom or shall escape or leave without authority any building, camp, or any place whatsoever in which he is placed or to which he is directed to go or in which he is allowed to be, he shall be deemed guilty of an escape and shall be punished by imprisonment for a term not to exceed five years, to commence immediately upon the expiration of the term of his previous sentence.

STATE v. HORSTMAN

The crime of escape is established by proof that the defendant was confined in a prison and escaped from such confinement or departed without authority from a place to which she or he was duly assigned. Unauthorized departure is the gravamen of the offense.

STATE v. CAHILL

While incarcerated, the defendant was placed in solitary confinement for fighting with another prisoner. A guard inadvertently left the cell door unlocked. The defendant got out and was apprehended on top of the prison wall.

The defendant argues that the evidence does not prove that he committed the crime of escape because there is no evidence that he escaped from the custody of the Department of Prisons. He argues that, at most, he is guilty of the lesser crime of attempted escape.

The crime of escape was complete, however, when the defendant got out of his cell. The crime can be committed without leaving the prison as a whole. It is enough that the defendant left a place where he was confined within the prison.

STATE v. LIGGETT

The defendant was incarcerated and assigned to work in the prison shop manufacturing auto license plates. On the day in question, the defendant was reported absent from his shift in the license plate shop. After a prolonged search, he was found inside a machine in the prison cannery, using a pillow, and reading a novel.

The evidence does not prove beyond a reasonable doubt that the defendant committed the crime of escape. He failed to report for work in one part of the prison and, without authorization, spent the time in another part. That might violate prison rules and merit internal prison discipline, but it is not the crime of escape.

24. Developing Persuasive Arguments

§24.1 What Is an Argument?

An argument is a group of ideas arranged logically to convince a reader or listener to do a particular thing or to adopt a particular belief.

That doesn't include belligerent comments between drivers after a fender-bender accident in a parking lot. The drivers are really venting anger, neither of them having any hope of persuading the other. Nor does it include aggressive expression of one's view's on politics, fashion, or sports. Many people are eager to state their opinions so that you know what they think — and not with the intent of changing your mind. But if they are truly trying to persuade you, they're making a genuine argument.

Uncapitalized, the word *argument* means a contention designed to persuade. Capitalized, an *Argument* is the largest portion of a motion memo or appellate brief. An Argument might include many arguments.

In designing an argument, your initial question should be "What will make the reader or listener *want* to agree with me?" A good argument will *affect* the audience. It leads readers or listeners through reasoning so convincingly that, at the end, they are pleased to be persuaded.

Most disputes are two-sided in the sense that each side can make credible arguments, and it takes real work for the judge or jury to choose between them. Here is an example from a nonlitigation setting: hypothetical testimony before a Congressional committee on whether to impose a tariff on shoelaces:[1]

---

1. A tariff is a tax on imported products. It makes the import more expensive when sold to the consumer. Arguments like these have been made whenever Congress has considered tariff and trade bills. (The examples here were vaguely inspired by testimony regarding the 1962 Trade Expansion Act but not about shoelaces.) This is a hypothetical. Please do not assume that imported shoelaces are now specially taxed, or that the domestic shoelace industry has any trouble competing with imports, or that a domestic shoelace industry even exists. The parallel block quotes are just examples of how arguments work against each other.

A new and stiff tariff should be imposed on imported shoelaces. We do not ask for a ban on the import of foreign shoelaces. All we ask for is a chance to compete fairly. Foreign shoelace manufacturers pay their workers only a fraction of what workers in our shoelace factories are paid, and that is why their shoelaces are so much cheaper than ours. Unless imported shoelaces are taxed on the boat or at the border, they will become so cheap that our own domestic shoelace manufacturers will be driven into bankruptcy. Our own hard-working employees will lose their jobs, adding to the unemployment problem. And if our own domestic shoelace manufacturing industry disappears, our country will become completely dependent on imported shoelaces. If imported shoelaces were cut off during international conflicts, we would have no source of new shoelaces, which means that eventually most shoes would become unwearable. Every soldier has to lace up boots to go into combat. Most office and factory workers have to tie shoelaces to get to work in the morning. Please do not let our domestic shoelace industry become extinct.

Imported shoelaces should not be subject to a tariff. The American consumer already pays too much for shoelaces. If they are so essential that everyone needs them, they should cost less. We cannot protect every domestic industry that faces hard foreign competition. If we tried, the cost of living to the American consumer would go up because it is impossible for people to live without buying imported goods. A tariff might save some American jobs, but it would destroy others because some people make their living importing shoelaces and other goods. If the American shoelace manufacturers cannot compete without the help of a tariff, their industry should become extinct and its resources directed toward some business that Americans really can do better than foreign producers. And the country is not going to be brought to its knees because it doesn't have shoelaces. It is extremely difficult to imagine any international conflict that could cut off a supply of imported shoelaces. And if an international conflict ever did that, it would also cut off the supply of so many other imports that shoelaces would be the least of our worries.

Your job is to make your arguments better than the adversary's, or to make the adversary's arguments worse by finding their weak points, or — preferably — to do both of these things. This chapter explains how.

§24.2   What Judges Expect from Written Argumentation

Judges are busy people who view any assertion skeptically and who must make many decisions in short periods of time. Thus, they need complete but concise arguments that can be quickly understood.

Judges are evaluated on their skill at the *art* of judging — not on whether they know all the law. They know a great deal about rules of procedure, which they use constantly, but they usually know much less about individual rules of substantive law. In most courts, judges cannot specialize in particular areas of substantive law: they must decide any case you bring before them. Unless a case turns on parts of the law about which a judge has thought deeply lately, the judge will depend on you to explain what the law is and how it governs the case. And a judge knows nothing at all about the facts of a case except for what can be learned through the lawyers and their evidence.

Judges will want you to *teach* them your case. Think of a motion memo or appellate brief as a *manual on how to make a particular decision* (and on how to write the opinion that justifies that decision). A lawyer who can show the court how the decision should be made, laying out all the steps of logic, stands a much better chance of winning.

If done in a respectful tone, this is not as presumptuous as you might think. If you have prepared properly, you'll know much more about the decision than the judge will. But teach the court without insulting its intelligence, and do so in the clearest and most concise manner possible. Judges find it hard to rule in your favor if you are condescending or waste their time.

§24.3   How to Evaluate Your Arguments

> A carefully prepared, carefully stated, lawyer-like written argument is a work of art and a joy forever.
>
> — *E. Barrett Prettyman*

A convincing argument isn't just a random collection of stray comments that sound good for the client. Those kinds of comments might be useful raw materials. But they become an argument only when they coalesce into a coherent presentation that influences the audience to do what you want. To evaluate whether your arguments are persuasive, ask yourself the following questions.[2]

---

2. When marking your work, your teacher might refer to these questions by using the number-letter codes that appear next to each question.

24-A | **Have you designed a compelling theory and backed it up with compelling arguments?**   Until you provide proof, a judge won't believe anything you say. Proof is a well-argued theory that compels a decision favorable to your client. You can develop a theory through the process described in Chapter 23.

A persuasive argument is neither extravagant nor belligerent. To a judge, extreme statements sound unreliable. Because judges are experienced, professional skeptics, they are rarely fooled by inaccurate or farfetched statements, and when they find such a statement in an argument, a dust of untrustworthiness settles over the theory and the lawyer involved. Judges usually have what the novelist Ernest Hemingway, in another context, called "a built-in, shockproof, shit detector."[3] You need to be similarly equipped so that you can examine — with a judge's skepticism — each statement you contemplate making. It helps to have a good understanding of human nature.

Good arguments are reasonable and accurate, appear reliable, and make your client's victory appear *inevitable* — either because the higher courts will reverse any other result, or because it's the only right thing to do, or both. The feeling of inevitability is a judge's selling point. It's reached by laying out for the judge every step of logic so that your conclusion becomes more and more irresistible as the argument proceeds. A judge knows when the selling point approaches, because the job of deciding seems to grow easier.

24-B | **Have you made both motivating arguments and justifying arguments?**   Both are needed to persuade.

A *motivating argument* causes a judge to *want* to decide in your favor. It causes the judge to feel that any other decision would be unwise or unjust. Motivating arguments tend to be centered on facts or a combination of facts and policy. This is how you might express the main motivating argument in the Appendix F motion memo:

> The defendant created a risk of irreversible harm to the health of 130 children by mishandling a toxic substance, which he could have handled safely using standard techniques.

A *justifying argument* shows that the law requires or at least permits the result you want. Justifying arguments are centered on legal rules or on a combination of rules and policy. Again oversimplified, this is the main justifying argument in the Appendix F motion memo:

> The evidence satisfies the test for summary judgment in a negligence case.

---

3. *Writers At Work: The Paris Review Interviews, Second Series* 239 (George Plimpton ed., 1965).

The first year of law school is designed to teach you how to make justifying arguments. You probably understood something of motivating arguments even before you came to law school, although you will learn more now about making them.

In judicial opinions, justifying arguments are usually developed in much detail while motivating arguments are only hinted at. The hints are found most often in the court's recitations of the facts. Have you had the feeling, while reading the first few paragraphs of an opinion, that you knew how the case would be decided before the court had told you — and even before the court had begun to discuss the law? If so, it was probably because you noticed in the fact recitation clues about which facts had motivated the court.

Why do you need both motivating arguments and justifying arguments?

A motivating argument alone isn't enough because even a motivated judge isn't supposed to act without a solid legal justification. Judges understandably want to feel that they're doing a professional job of judging, and they can be reversed on appeal if they fail to justify their actions within the law.

Unless coupled with a motivating argument, a justifying argument alone will not persuade. The law can usually be interpreted in more than one reasonable way. When a judge is given a choice between two conflicting justifying arguments, each of which is reasonable, the judge will take the one she or he is motivated to take. (Judges are, after all, human.) Remember what Karl Llewellyn wrote: "rules *guide*, but they do not *control* decision. There is no precedent the judge may not at his need either file down to razor thinness or expand into a bludgeon."[4]

Many beginners have more difficulty developing motivating arguments than they do with justifying arguments. Before starting law school most of us have already had a fair amount of experience justifying our own beliefs. But that is not the same as getting inside another person's head and *causing* that person to *want* to do something. To motivate, we need to learn not only a new argument style but also a new *process* of creating arguments. That's because the process of creating justifying arguments is different from the process of creating motivating arguments.

> [In a college course, Kathleen wrote a paper on the] question "Is American Sign language (ASL) a 'foreign language' for purposes of meeting the university's foreign language requirement?" Kathleen had taken two years of ASL at a community college. When she transferred to a four-year college, the chair of the foreign languages department at her new college would not allow her ASL proficiency to count for the foreign language requirement. ASL isn't a "language," the chair said summarily. "It's not equivalent to learning French, German, or Japanese."[5]

4. K. N. Llewellyn, *The Bramble Bush* 180 (1930).
5. Kathleen's story is from John D. Ramage & John C. Bean, *Writing Arguments: A Rhetoric with Readings* 10-11 (4th ed. 1998).

Is this really why the department chair rejects Kathleen's request? If yes, Kathleen will be able to change his mind if she can prove that ASL is a real language, equivalent to French, German, or Japanese. But if it isn't really why he refuses, it's only a rationalization for his decision — a statement he can use to justify saying no. If it's only his rationalization, then his motivation — the true cause of the refusal — remains hidden. If he's rationalizing, he might not even be aware of his own motives.

Kathleen wasn't satisfied with the department chair's decision, and in a different college course she decided to write a paper on this issue.

> While doing research, she focused almost entirely on subject matter, searching for what linguists, brain neurologists, cognitive psychologists, and sociologists had said about the language of deaf people. Immersed in her subject matter, she was [not very] concerned with her audience, whom she thought of primarily as her classmates and the professor [who taught the class in which she was writing the paper. They] were friendly to her views and interested in her experiences with the deaf community. She wrote a well-documented paper, citing several scholarly articles, that made a good case to her classmates (and the professor) that ASL was indeed a distinct language.
>
> Proud of the big red A the professor had placed on her paper, Kathleen returned to the chair of the foreign language department with a new request to count ASL for her language requirement. The chair read her paper, congratulated her on her good writing, but said her argument was not persuasive. He disagreed with several of the linguists she cited and with the general definition of "language" that her paper assumed. He then gave her some additional (and to her fuzzy) reasons that the college would not accept ASL as a foreign language.

Kathleen addressed the concerns the department chair had expressed earlier. But rather than reacting sympathetically to her argument, he nitpicks it and offers new reasons that he hadn't mentioned before. Something else — which he hasn't specified — must be motivating him. Because Kathleen hasn't discovered the real cause of his refusal, she made an argument that only challenged his rationalizations instead of one that addressed his true motivations. That is why she has not persuaded him.

This is a common experience when justifying insights are used in an attempt — often unsuccessful — to influence real-world decision-making. The ideas that made sense while researching and sounded wonderful to colleagues are ignored by the person who makes a decision, whether that person is an administrator (as here) or a judge.

It would be easy for Kathleen to dismiss the chair of the foreign language department as a numskull, but for two reasons she cannot and should not do that. First, she can't get around the fact that he has the power of decision. The only way she can get her ASL work to count for the foreign language requirement is *to change his mind*. For this issue, he's the judge.

Second, he might have sincere and reasonable concerns that deserve to be addressed. At this point, Kathleen doesn't know what they are. Her paper focused on the issue itself, and the only audience she imagined was a friendly one. She avoided thinking about the skeptical audience, even though that audience — the department chair — is the only one that can make the decision.

You might want to forget about the skeptical audience because it's not pleasant when people doubt what you say. But if you want action, you must concentrate on that audience.

How can Kathleen find out what the department chair's concerns might be? How can she address them?

> Spurred by what she considered the chair's too-easy dismissal of her argument, Kathleen decided . . . to write a second paper on ASL — but this time aiming it directly at the chair of foreign languages. Now her writing task falls closer to the persuasive end of our continuum. Kathleen once again immersed herself in research, but this time it focused not on subject matter (whether ASL is a distinct language) but on audience. She researched the history of the foreign language requirement at her college and discovered some of the politics behind it (an old foreign language requirement had been dropped in the 1970's and reinstituted in the 1990's, partly — a math professor told her — to boost enrollments in foreign language courses). She also interviewed foreign language teachers to find out what they knew and didn't know about ASL. She discovered that many teachers [inaccurately] thought ASL was "easy to learn," so that accepting ASL would allow students a Mickey Mouse way to avoid the rigors of a real foreign language class. Additionally, she learned that foreign language teachers valued immersing students in a foreign culture; in fact, the foreign language requirement was part of her college's effort to create a multicultural curriculum.

Now Kathleen begins to understand what's really going on. She has gained insights into what the department chair is worried about, and she can write arguments that really might influence him.

> This new understanding of her target audience helped Kathleen totally reconceptualize her argument. She condensed and abridged her original paper . . . . She added sections showing the difficulty of learning ASL (to counter her audience's belief that learning ASL was easy), and literature (to show how ASL met the goals of multiculturalism), and showing that the number of transfer students with ASL credits would be negligibly small (to allay fears that accepting ASL would threaten enrollments in language classes). She ended her argument with an appeal to her college's public emphasis (declared boldly in its mission statement) on eradicating social injustice and reaching out to the oppressed. She described the isolation of deaf people in a world where almost no hearing people learn ASL and argued that the deaf community on her campus could be integrated more fully into campus life if more students could "talk" with them [in their own language]. Thus, the ideas included in her new argument, the reasons

selected, the evidence used, the arrangement and tone all were determined by her primary focus on persuasion.[6]

Kathleen's first paper was limited to justifying arguments because it did no more than provide a logical rationale that could support a decision in her favor — if the department chair were inclined to rule as she wanted. It lacked motivating arguments because it did not address the concerns of the department chair.

The second paper was good lawyering because it included both kinds of arguments. She got inside the decision-maker's thinking and showed him that his own values and needs would benefit from doing what she wanted. She kept her justifying arguments in her second paper — because they were needed to justify a decision in her favor — but they receded in importance and were joined by policy arguments with which the department chair could sympathize as well as arguments that addressed genuine practical problems that had made him skeptical.

| 24-C | **Have you limited your contentions to those that have a reasonable chance of persuading the court?** You might be tempted to throw in every good thing you can think of about your theory and every bad thing about your adversary's theory, assuming that all this can't hurt and might help. That is *shotgun writing*, and it hurts more than it helps.

Instead, focus sharply on the strong contentions. Develop them fully, and leave out the weak ones. As Holmes put it: "strike for the jugular and let the rest go."[7] That creates a document that is more compact but explores more deeply the ideas on which the decision will be based.

A good argument begins by subduing the judge's skepticism into a general feeling of *confidence* that the theory can be relied on, and then, on that foundation of confidence, it builds a feeling that your client is the *inevitable* winner. Weak contentions interfere with this. They excite skepticism, rather than quieting it. If a judge believes that you have indiscriminately mixed unreliable contentions with seemingly attractive ones, the judge's natural temptation is to dismiss the whole lot as not worthy of confidence, for the same reason that a person considering the purchase of a house justifiably suspects the integrity of the entire structure after cracked beams are found in the attic. Just as it's the builder's job to select only sturdy materials, so it's the lawyer's job — and not the judge's — to separate out the weak ideas before the memo or brief is submitted. A judge has neither the time nor the inclination to delete all the suspect material and then reassemble the remainder into something sturdier.

When you determine whether a contention has a reasonable chance to persuade, you are, of course, making a predictive judgment. A "reasonable chance"

---

6. *Id.* at 11.
7. Oliver Wendell Holmes, *Speeches* 77 (1934).

doesn't mean certainty and, in a case where you have nothing better, it might not even mean probability. To be worth making, however, a contention should have the capacity to seem tempting and attractive to a judge.

24-D **Have you organized to emphasize the ideas that are most likely to persuade?** Remember that you will make both motivating arguments and justifying arguments. Justifying arguments can be organized through the paradigm formula because they are proofs of a conclusion of law. See Chapters 11-14.

Motivating arguments, on the other hand, are more often appeals to a human sense of justice or pragmatic policy needs. When you add motivating arguments, you may vary the paradigm formula in radical ways (many of which would not work in predictive writing). In part, that's because motivating arguments should be introduced very early in a presentation, preferably in the first paragraph.

To merge motivating and justifying arguments, do this: First, write a justifying argument structured in the paradigm format. Then start adding motivating arguments wherever they seem relevant to what you have already written. Finally, write an introductory passage that sums up your motivating arguments. (This is illustrated in the motion memo in Appendix F and in the appellate briefs in Appendices G and H.) With more experience, you'll be able to write motivating and justifying arguments at the same time, or even to write the motivating argument before you write the justifying argument.

The passage that introduces the motivating argument should precede all statements of rules, proof of those rules, and rule application. Why is it so important to introduce the motivating arguments first? It tracks the way many judges think. They act on what motivates them (unless it can't be justified). Motivation is established first, the need to justify afterward. And early impressions tend to color how later material is read, and, like most people, a judge reads most carefully at the beginning. In addition, because judges are so busy, they expect the strongest material first. If they find themselves reading weak material early, they assume that nothing better follows and then stop reading altogether.

(You probably read a newspaper or online article in the same way. You expect the most important or most entertaining material near the beginning of a story, and when you have had enough, you stop reading and go on to something else. Editors know that, and articles are written with the least valuable material at the end, so readers can decide how much of a story to read. Just as your method of reading would be thrown off if the most valuable material were strewn randomly throughout the article, so a judge's method of reading a memo or brief would become muddled if the strongest arguments might appear anywhere.)

Thus, judges will expect you to get immediately to the point. A judge quickly becomes impatient with long prefatory passages of historical background because that kind of material usually doesn't help in making a decision. Even in a constitutional case where the issue is the drafters' intent one or two centuries ago, the historical material is part of the argument, not a preface to it.

The "best strategy is to strike quickly, establish momentum, and maintain the advantage through a forceful presentation of contentions selected for their persuasive effect."[8] Focus the reader's thoughts on the ideas that can cause you to win.

Present first the issues on which you are most likely to win. Within issues, make your strongest arguments first. Within arguments, make your strongest contentions and use your best authority first.

For example, if your adversary must prove that a five-element test has been satisfied, and if you think that your adversary's proof is weakest on element number three, don't argue the elements in the order in which they're listed in the controlling statute. Argue element three first because as far as you're concerned, it's the controlling element. (Your adversary, however, might do either of two things. She might argue them in exactly the order listed in the statute, to build a feeling of cumulating persuasion. Or if some elements are extremely easy to prove, she might get them out of the way first and then concentrate on the ones where the battle is concentrated.)

Sometimes, however, the logic of the dispute requires that the strongest material be delayed to avoid confusing the court. Some arguments are simply hard to understand unless preceded by less punchy material. In these situations, you must weigh your need for clarity against your need to show merit from the start.

24-E | **Have you made your organization obvious?** Don't let the judge grope for clues about how your contentions are related to each other. Instead, use the techniques of forceful writing to help the judge see your focus. Very soon after you begin to discuss each issue, tell the judge exactly what your theory is. Use a thesis sentence to state each contention before you begin to prove it. And use transitional words and phrases to show how your contentions are cumulative:

There are three reasons why . . . First, . . . Second, . . . And finally, . . .

Not only has the defendant violated . . . , but she has also . . .

8. Michael R. Fontham, *Written and Oral Advocacy* 108 (1985).

24-F | **Have you given the court a clear statement of the rule or rules on which the case turns?** That rule might not be exactly as stated in the cases to which you cite. In fact, the cases might enforce the rule without stating it at all, and you might have to figure out what the rule is from the court's reasoning, particularly the way it treats the facts.

In appellate courts, judges know that they will have to write an opinion justifying their decision and that the opinion should be as convincing as possible to the parties, to the bar, to the public, and to any higher court to which the decision could be appealed. That is a hard task where a gap in the law must be filled. The judge who asks in oral argument in a gap-filling case, "Counselor, what rule would you have us enforce?" really wants to know how — if the lawyer prevails — the court should word the second component of the paradigm formula when it writes the opinion.

24-G | **Have you relied on an appropriate amount of authority with an appropriate amount of explanation?** To rule in your favor, a court would need to believe that you have provided sufficient authority, although the typical judge is unwilling to tolerate an exhaustive explanation of every case you cite. How do you steer a middle course between underciting and overciting and between underexplaining and overexplaining?

Begin by predicting the amount of citation and explanation a skeptical but busy judge would need. Then carefully study the available authorities. Place in a "major authority" category those that will probably *influence* the court and in a "peripheral" category those that are merely somewhat related to the issue. Think in terms of cause and effect. If you had to make the judge's decision, which authorities would probably have an effect on you, *even an effect adverse to your client's position*? Those are the authorities you must discuss, and many of them are best discussed in detail. Peripheral authorities should eventually be discarded unless they're needed to fill holes in your argument not settled by the major authorities.

The quantity of authority and the volume of explanation will depend on how much is needed to clarify the issue involved, how disputed that issue is, and how important it is to your theory. At one extreme, an idea may be so complex, so disputed, and so critical that it must be supported by a comprehensive explanation, filling many pages, of major authorities. At the other extreme, if the court is apt to be satisfied with a mere conclusory explanation, you should limit citation to one or, at the very most, two cases. If an idea is undisputed and routine, such as an uncontested procedural test, it should be enough to cite, with little or no explanation, the most recent decision from the highest court in the jurisdiction that has invoked the test. (For example, notice how the test for summary judgment is proved in the memo in Appendix F.)

Give the court confidence that you are right without tiring its patience.

24-H | **Have you explained exactly and in detail how the law governs the facts?** A court rules for one party over another not merely because the law is abstractly favorable, but, more importantly, because the law and facts *combine* favorably. The judge often reaches the selling point only where the law and facts are finally combined — woven together — to show that what the writer wants is inevitable. Beginners sometimes devote so much attention to the law that they overlook the final step of arguing the facts — weaving the law into the facts to show the court precisely how the decision should be made. After all the work of explaining the law, a beginner might assume that the application to the facts is obvious, but it hardly ever is. Don't assume that merely mentioning the facts is enough: *show* the court exactly how the determinative facts require the decision you seek.

24-I | **Have you helped the facts and the people involved come alive?** Show the judge more than a chronological recitation of events. You want the judge to see something that reveals character and causation. An illustration of the difference between those two is from the novelist E. M. Forster's classic lectures on fiction.[9] When we read "The king died, and then the queen died," we might see in the mind's eye either no image or at best an image of stick-like figures without personality. But when we read "The king died, and then the queen died of grief," we see instead an image of at least one real human being: she may be wearing fairytale-like clothing, but she is genuinely suffering as real people do.

When a judge, reading an argument, visualizes stick figures or no image at all, the case seems boring and unimportant, and the judge isn't motivated to rule in your favor. But the judge begins to take sides if she can visualize real people doing real things to each other.

Before you begin to write, make a list of the determinative facts. You'll have to discuss those facts to make your argument, and that's where your opportunities occur. For each fact, ask yourself what it illustrates about the *people* involved: does it show who is an innocent victim, who is predatory, who is inexcusably foolish, and so forth. For each fact, ask yourself further what the fact illustrates about *what happened*: does it show the events to have been accidental, caused by one person's carelessness, the result of another's greed and cunning, and so on. Only by knowing what each fact reveals can you tell the client's story in a compelling way.

When you describe these facts in your writing, don't characterize them with emotion-laden words. Although a fact is determinative because the law coldly makes it so, a judge can form a human reaction to it, simply because judges prefer to make decisions that are fundamentally fair. On the other hand, a judge's professional self-image is naturally offended by an argument that reads

---

9. E. M. Forster, *Aspects of the Novel* 86 (1927).

like political oratory. *Vividness* isn't the same as luridness, which demeans an argument and the judge who reads it. If a fact will seem compelling to a court, that fact will speak for itself. All you will need is a calm description of the fact, in simple words and with enough detail to make the picture vivid. When reading the Argument in the Appendix F memo, you might have thought that the painter was irresponsible — but the writer never called him that. Instead, the writer simply described what happened so that *you* formed that opinion. (Forster didn't say that the queen loved the king. He only told you why she died.)

24-J **Have you made persuasive policy arguments?** "Tell the judge exactly what will happen in the real world if he decides for you or for your opponent."[10] Explain how the parties have been affected by the dispute, how they would be affected by the relief you seek, or how in some other way what you seek is fundamentally fair. But also go beyond that and demonstrate that what you want will produce the best result in future cases as well, remembering that the decision will become precedent. If a court must choose between competing rules, for example, show that the rule you urge is better than others. If you win, the decision will stand for that rule.

Prove policy with authority. Some policy is openly announced in decisions and statutes, but more often it's implied. For example, courts like solutions that are easily enforceable, promote clarity in the law, are not needlessly complex, and do not allow true wrongdoers to profit from illegal acts. Other policy considerations may differ from state to state. In Arizona, for example, public policy disfavors solutions that interfere with development of land for homes and industry, while in Vermont policy prefers conservation, the environment, and preservation of agriculture. Some states favor providing tort remedies even at some risk to judicial efficiency, although in others the reverse is true. Still other policy considerations differ from era to era. Some activities once greatly favored in the law — such as the building and operation of railroads in the nineteenth century — now enjoy no special treatment, while other things — such as a woman's reproductive control over her own body — are now protected in a way they once were not.

Lawyers tend to introduce policy-based arguments with phrasings like the following:

> This court should reject the rule urged by the defendant because it would cause . . .
>
> Automobile rental companies [or some other category of litigants] should bear the risk of loss because . . .
>
> Not only is the order requested by the plaintiff not sanctioned by this state's case law, but such an order would violate public policy because . . .

---

10. Hollis T. Hurd, *Writing for Lawyers* 61 (1982).

Remember, however, that policy arguments are used to reinforce argument from authority. Only where authority is unusually sparse should policy arguments play the predominant role in a theory.

24-K **Have you reinforced your theory with carefully chosen wording?** Choose words in part for the effect they should have on the reader. Simple, concrete words can paint the pictures on which your theory is based. In the Appendix F memo, notice how facts are described almost entirely in short, everyday words with very specific meanings. And notice how the word *toxic* is used to remind the reader that although lead paint seems innocuous, it is not.

Readers see scenes where writers have given concrete descriptions to build on. The knack is, first, to isolate the very few facts that are essential to the scene because they will motivate the reader or are determinative under the law, and then to describe those facts in words that are simple and concrete enough for the desired image to come quickly into the reader's mind. This is *not* simple and concrete:

> Where contamination has occurred, lead dust can be ingested by young children through frequent and unpredictable hand-mouth contact during play.

But this is:

> If the floor inside a building or the soil outside is contaminated with lead dust, young children can literally eat lead because they frequently and unexpectedly put their hands and other things in their mouths while playing.

Did you see a more vivid image when you read the second example?

You can do harm with words that claim too much. The first example below is actually less persuasive than the second:

> It is obvious, therefore, that the defendant clearly understood the consequences of his acts.
> Therefore, the defendant understood the consequences of his acts.

In the first example, "It is obvious" and "clearly" supply no extra meaning. Instead, they divert the reader's attention from the message of the sentence. Judges can assume that expressions like these are used to cover up a lack of logical proof.

Your references to the parties should be clear to the reader, but the way you refer to the parties can also advance your theory. For example, suppose Eli Goslin, the client in the Appendix C office memo, were to sue Herbert Skeffington. In a later motion memo or appellate brief, the plaintiff's lawyer would refer to his client with dignity as "Mr. Goslin." Even if his neighbors might know him to treat people and pets vilely and to have vicious opinions that offend all decent-minded folk, he can be a sympathetic figure in litigation as long as the court knows him as "Mr. Goslin," the elderly widower who only wants to live out his last days in his own home. And Goslin's lawyer might frequently refer to Skeffington as "the nephew" or "the defendant," with no dignity other than his role as nephew and with no personality other than what he reveals about himself through the way he treats his uncle. As the shadowy "nephew," it's easier to think him capable of deceit, greed, and cold-bloodedness. But if the judge were to think of him as Mr. Skeffington—and to think of the other interlopers as Mr. Skeffington's wife Amelia and their children Wendy and Tom, aged respectively eight and four—it's a little harder to think badly of them.

It can work the opposite way, too. In the Appendix F motion memo, the plaintiff's lawyer always refers to the defendant with dignity as "Mr. Raucher." The defendant's conduct is criticized, but he is never demeaned personally. And this refusal to demean can make his conduct look more starkly unacceptable because the issue is what he *did* and not him. That is not so in Goslin's situation: the issue there really is the nephew and his character.

But when referring to parties, your first obligation is to do so in a way the court will understand. In general, you have three ways: by name ("Trans-Continental Airlines"), generically by the party's out-of-court role ("the airline"), or by the party's in-court role ("the defendant").

Once the reader knows who has sued whom, the clearest references are by name. Most modern courts write their own opinions that way. If you represent a person in conflict with a large organization, it might help humanize your client to use the client's name while referring to the opponent generically ("Ms. DiMateo asked the airline for an earlier flight"), but only after introducing the organization by name and telling the reader that you'll be using a generic designation: "Ms. DiMateo sued Trans-Continental Airlines ('the airline') after . . . ." But if Trans-Continental has a terrible reputation for service, its name might do more to create sympathy for your client than a generic reference would.

In trial courts, the parties' litigation roles ("plaintiff," "defendant") are usually clear to the reader but lifeless. Appellate courts, on the other hand, will become confused if you refer to the parties as "the appellant" or "the appellee," and many prohibit it, preferring instead references to the parties' roles in the trial court ("plaintiff," "defendant") or their out-of-court roles ("the taxpayer," "the employee").[11]

> **24-L** **Have you confronted openly your weaknesses and your adversary's strengths?** Hiding from problems will not make them go away. You have to confront and defeat them. "Be truthful in exposing . . . the

---

11. *See, e.g.*, Rule 28(d) of the Federal Rules of Appellate Procedure.

difficulties in your case," an appellate judge has written. "Tell us what they are and how you expect to deal with them."[12] If you don't do that, the court will assume that you have no arguments worth making on the subject.

Ask yourself four questions. First, which cases and statutes favor your adversary? Second, which facts work to your adversary's advantage? Third, what are your adversary's strongest arguments? (Your adversary *does* have strong arguments. Otherwise, the case would not be worth litigating.) And fourth, what will your adversary say to fight against your arguments? The answers to these questions identify your adversary's strengths. After you know what those strengths are, read §24.5 to find out what to do about them.

| 24-M | **Have you enhanced your credibility through careful editing and through the appearance of your memo or brief?** Help the judge to trust you. Judges don't trust easily. Their decisions are important ones, and you will always face at least one opposing attorney with another theory to sell. A judge will more readily trust you if you appear to be careful, thorough, and professional. For that reason, a document is more persuasive if its appearance is flawless.

A well-written memo or brief can earn warm gratitude and respect from a judge. For examples, see the footnote at the end of this sentence.[13] Where one side in a case has produced fine writing and the other has done the opposite, a court can draw invidious comparisons and be influenced accordingly:

> If counsel for Phipps had asked us to direct dismissal of the complaint, we might well have done so, as we could do even [now] in the absence of such a request. . . . However, in light of counsel's inadequate and intemperate brief, . . . we shall not do so. In contrast, we compliment counsel for Mrs. Lopez on her excellent and helpful brief . . . .[14]

Beginners in law often underestimate how bad writing upsets judges. To give you a flavor of how strongly judges feel about this, read the explanatory parentheticals in the footnote at the end of this sentence.[15]

---

12. Roger J. Miner, *Twenty-five "Dos" for Appellate Brief Writers*, 3 Scribes J. Legal. Writing 19, 24 (1992).

13. "We express our appreciation to Ellen M. Burgraff, Esq., . . . for her excellent brief and argument in this case." *Swanger v. Zimmerman*, 750 F.2d 291, 294 n. 3 (3d Cir. 1984). "As Mr. Nevin [appellant's lawyer] says in his excellent brief . . ." *United States v. Moore*, 109 F.3d 1456, 1465 (9th Cir. 1997). "The court expresses its appreciation to appellant's counsel for submitting excellent briefs on this appeal." *Johnson v. Stark*, 717 F.2d 1550, 1551 n. 2 (8th Cir. 1983). "We commend assigned counsel for his excellent briefs and argument." *United States v. 4492 South Livonia Rd.*, 889 F.2d 1258, 1271 (2d Cir. 1989).

14. *Lopez v. Henry Phipps Plaza South, Inc.*, 498 F.2d 937, 946 n. 8 (2d Cir. 1974).

15. The following are only a few of the many cases in which judges have embarrassed or punished lawyers for poor writing or violating court rules on briefs or memoranda: *Jorgenson v. Volusia County*, 846 F.2d 1350, 1351 (11th Cir. 1988) (punishing a lawyer "for failing to cite adverse, controlling precedent"); *Gardner v. Investors Diversified Capital, Inc.*, 805 F. Supp. 874, 875 (D. Colo. 1992) ("The amended complaint . . . is replete with misspellings, grammatical aberrations, non sequiturs. . . ."); *P. M. F. Services, Inc. v. Grady*, 681 F. Supp. 549, 550-51 n. 1 (N.D. Ill. 1988) ("With callous disregard for the reader, plaintiff's counsel" refers

Edit out every form of intellectual sloppiness: inaccuracies; imprecision; incorrectly used terms of art; errors with citations and other matters of format and layout; mistakes with the English language, its spelling and punctuation; typographical errors; and empty remarks that don't advance the argument (such as rhetorical questions and irrelevant histories of the law). Any of those would suggest a lawyer who can't be relied on — and judges will be quick to draw that inference.

Judges are overburdened with so many cases that you should assume a certain amount of fatigue. If a memo or brief is frustrating, at least some of it will be ignored. Think about the problems a judge would have with the document, and solve them before submission. The font and type size should be easy to read. Margins should be large enough that each page doesn't look oppressively dense. Headings should look like headings (and not like part of the text). A visually inviting document is more likely to be read with care.

§24.4 Argumentation Ethics

The rules of professional ethics place limits on what you're permitted to do in argument.

First and most basically, you're forbidden to "knowingly . . . make a false statement of law or fact" to a court.[16] The whole system of adjudication would break down if lawyers did not speak honestly to courts.

Second, you must inform a court of "legal authority in the controlling jurisdiction" that you know "to be directly adverse to the position of [your] client and not disclosed by opposing counsel."[17] You aren't required to disclose out-of-state authority. You're required to disclose authority in your jurisdiction that's "directly adverse" to your arguments if your adversary hasn't disclosed it. Judges usually don't do their own research. They depend on the lawyers to inform them.

Third, you may not advance a theory or argument that is "frivolous" except that you may make a "good faith argument for an extension, modification or reversal of existing law."[18] In a legal system like ours, where "the law is not always clear and never is static," the rules of ethics permit you to advance

---

to the parties in confusing ways and "uses possessives without apostrophes, leaving the reader to guess whether he intends a singular or plural possessive, etc. Such sloppy pleading and briefing are inexcusable"); *Green v. Green*, 261 Cal. Rptr. 294, 302 n. 11 (Cal. App. 1st Dist. 1989) (ordering appellant to pay appellee's attorney's fees in part because of "the slap-dash quality of [his] briefs"); *In re Hawkins*, 502 N.W.2d 770, 770-72 (Minn. 1993) (publicly reprimanding lawyer and ordering him to attend remedial instruction because of, among other things, "his repeated filing of documents rendered unintelligible by numerous spelling, grammatical, and typographical errors"); *Slater v. Gallman*, 339 N.E.2d 863, 865 (N.Y. 1975) (imposing costs on appellant because of a verbose and unfocused brief); *Frazier v. Columbus Bd. of Educ.*, 638 N.E.2d 581, 582 (Ohio 1994) (dismissing appeal because appellant's jurisdictional memo exceeded page limit).

16. Rule 3.3(a)(1) of the ABA Model Rules of Professional Conduct.

17. Rule 3.3(a)(2) of the ABA Model Rules of Professional Conduct.

18. Rule 3.1 of the ABA Model Rules of Professional Conduct.

theories and arguments that take advantage "of the law's ambiguities and potential for change."[19] But a frivolous theory or argument — one that stands little chance of being adopted by a court — is unfair to courts and to opposing parties because it wastes their time, effort, and resources.

Separate court rules — procedural, rather than ethical in nature — also punish lawyers who make frivolous arguments. In federal trial courts, for example, every "pleading, written motion, and other paper" must be signed by an lawyer, whose signature certifies "that to the best of the [signer's] knowledge, information, and belief, formed after inquiry reasonable under the circumstances . . . the claims, defenses, and other legal contentions are warranted by existing law or by a nonfrivolous argument for extending, modifying, or reversing existing law or establishing new law."[20] Where that standard is violated, the court has the power to impose monetary fines on the offending lawyer.[21] Similar rules govern in appellate courts.[22]

§24.5 How to Handle Adverse Authority and Arguments

Which authorities most strongly favor your adversary? (Make a list.) What is your adversary's strongest argument? Her second strongest argument? If you're having a hard time answering these questions, you haven't begun to see the case as a whole.

Ignoring adverse authority won't make it go away. If the court doesn't find it, opposing counsel probably will. There are, in fact, a number of reasons for you to address adverse authority. First, as §24.4 explains, the ethical rules require it. Second, a lawyer who ignores adverse authority is seen by courts as unreliable and unpersuasive, while a lawyer who speaks with candor is more easily trusted and respected by the bench. Third, a lawyer who ignores adverse authority throws away the opportunity — often the only opportunity — to give the court reasons for not following it.

If the adverse authority is a statute, court rule, or administrative regulation, you must show that the provision was not intended to govern the controversy, or that it was intended to govern it but without harm to your client's case. Although it may seem tempting to argue that a statute you don't like is unconstitutional, courts rarely sustain such attacks. In fact, if a statute or similar provision is susceptible to more than one meaning, courts are obliged to choose one that would not violate a controlling constitution. You should

---

19. Comment to Rule 3.1 of the ABA Model Rules of Professional Conduct.
20. Fed. R. Civ. P. 11.
21. *Id.*
22. For example: "If a court of appeals determines that an appeal is frivolous, it may . . . award just damages and single or double costs to the appellee." Fed. R. App. P. 38.

frontally attack a statute only if there's significant doubt — shared by respected lawyers — about its validity.

If the adverse authority is precedent, try to weaken it, using the techniques described in Chapter 9. Consider distinguishing the precedent, focusing on significant — and not merely coincidental — differences between the precedent and your case. Be careful. The differences on which you rely should be important enough to impress a skeptical judge. Hypertechnical discrepancies and minor factual variations won't persuade because they seem arbitrary rather than a basis for a just decision. Another approach might be to reconcile the precedent with your case, showing that — although the precedent seems superficially adverse — its underlying policy would actually be furthered by the ruling you want from the court. Still another approach is to attack the precedent head-on, challenging its validity on the grounds that it is poorly reasoned or that changes in society or in public policy have made it unworkable.

Although the doctrine of stare decisis doesn't absolutely forbid the overruling of precedent, a frontal attack on mandatory case law is nearly always an uphill fight, to be attempted only when there's very serious doubt — again shared by at least some respected lawyers — about the precedent's viability. In general, don't ask a court to overrule mandatory authority if you can win through distinguishing, reconciliation, or some other skill of precedent analysis. Judges prefer distinguishing and reconciling precedent to overruling it.

But things are different where local law has a gap and where the challenged authority isn't mandatory. If a judge must choose between competing out-of-state rules, she won't be able to decide without rejecting at least some precedent as ill-founded.

With both precedent and statutes, consider taking more than one approach, arguing in the alternative — but only if neither alternative would weaken the persuasive force of the other. It's not illogical, for example, to argue, first, that a statute wasn't intended to govern the facts before the court and, alternatively, that, if the statute is interpreted otherwise, it should be held unconstitutional.

Attack an opposing argument if it has been made by your adversary, or if there is a reasonable possibility that the court might think of it and be persuaded by it. Otherwise, the court will assume that you have no defense to such an argument.

But make your own arguments first. You'll win more easily if the court's dominant impression is that you deserve to win, rather than that your adversary deserves to lose. A defensive tone can undermine an otherwise worthwhile argument. And your theory will be more easily understood if you argue it before you attack opposing arguments.

How much emphasis should you give to an attack on an adverse argument or authority? Give it as much emphasis as necessary to convince the judge not to rule against you. Little treatment is necessary if the point is minor and if the argument or authority is easily rebutted. Say more if the point is more significant or if your counter-analysis is more complex. You can't reduce the force of adverse arguments and authorities by giving them minimal treatment in your own writing. They have lives and voices of their own.

Beginners often have difficulty writing the transition and thesis sentences that introduce attacks on opposing arguments. In responsive writing, when you've already seen the other side's memo or brief, it's enough to refer to what opposing counsel has said and then to get on with the counter-argument. Here are some examples:

> The plaintiff misconstrues § 401(d)(1). Four other circuits have already decided that § 401(d)(1) provides for X and not, as the plaintiff contends, for Y. [*Follow with an analysis of the circuit cases.*]
>
> No appellate court has held to the contrary, and the few district court decisions cited by the plaintiff are all distinguishable. [*Follow with an analysis of the district court cases.*]
>
> The legislative history also demonstrates that Congress intended to provide for X and not for Y. [*Follow with an analysis of the legislative history.*]

These opening sentences are written so that opposing counsel's contention is surrounded by the writer's counter-contention and the beginning of the counter-contention's proof. The effect is to argue affirmatively and not defensively. The following is much weaker:

> The plaintiff has argued that § 401(d)(1) provides for Y, but . . .

In nonresponsive situations — where you have *not* already read your adversary's memo or brief — begin simply by denying the contention while emphasizing your counter-contention, as in the example below:

> Section 401(d)(1) provides for X and not for Y.

Don't write defensively:

> Opposing counsel might argue that § 401(d)(1) provides for Y, but . . .

Opposing counsel might never argue that.

An although clause can be useful in thesis and transition sentences:

> Although the House Judiciary Committee report states that its bill would have provided for Y, the Senate Judiciary Committee actually drafted § 401(d)(1). Both that committee's report and the conference committee report flatly state that § 401(d)(1) provides for X.

25 Motion Memoranda

§25.1 Motion Memorandum Format

A motion is a request to a court for an order, such as a preliminary injunction, or for a judgment, such as summary judgment or judgment as a matter of law. An order is a court's command during a lawsuit. A judgment terminates a lawsuit.

One party to a lawsuit may move for an order or for judgment. The other party might oppose the motion. (Motion is the noun. Move is the verb.)

When a motion is made, each party submits a memorandum of law. A defendant moving for an order dismissing a complaint, for example, submits a document that might be titled "Memorandum in Support of Defendant's Motion to Dismiss." The opposing party's document might be titled "Memorandum in Opposition to Defendant's Motion to Dismiss." This chapter describes the format of a motion memo and the process of writing one.

Like the reader of an office memo, the judge (and the judge's law clerk) may look at each memo more than once. Depending on the judge's work habits and on the nature of the motion, at least some part of the memorandum might be read once in preparation for a hearing or oral argument on the motion, again while deciding the motion, and a third time while writing an opinion. You can't assume that a memo will be read from front to back or at one sitting.

And you can't assume that a long memo will be read in its entirety. To the judge, your case is one of dozens or hundreds on a docket that might be overwhelming. In an uncongested court, a trial judge might have about 10 to 15 minutes to read your memo. In a congested one, the judge might give your memo less than five minutes. You have to make your point both quickly and well, or lose.

Few court rules govern the content of motion memos, and customs among lawyers differ from one jurisdiction to the next. The following *might* be found in a motion memo, although very few memos include them all:

1. a cover page
2. a Table of Contents, if the memo is long or if you want to gain the persuasive effect of showing all the point headings and subheadings in one place
3. a Table of Authorities — but only if the memo is long and many authorities have been cited
4. a Preliminary Statement, also called an Introduction or Summary
5. a Statement of Facts or just Facts, also called a Statement of the Case
6. an Argument, broken up by point headings
7. a Conclusion
8. an indorsement

In practice, you can shape the format to suit your case and in the most persuasive way to present your theory.

The rest of this chapter is easier to follow if you look to the memorandum in Appendix F for illustration as you read the description below of each of these components.

The **cover page** includes a caption and title, which correspond to the memorandum heading at the beginning of an office memorandum. The caption identifies the court and the parties, specifying their procedural designations (plaintiff, defendant, etc.). In a criminal case, the prosecution is called, depending on the jurisdiction, "State," "Commonwealth," "People," or "United States," and no procedural designation follows those terms in the caption. (The prosecution is not a "plaintiff.") The title identifies the memorandum and the purpose of its submission ("Memorandum in Opposition to Defendant's Motion to Dismiss").

A **Table of Contents** begins on the page after the cover page. If a **Table of Authorities** is included (and it usually is not), it appears on the first page after the Table of Contents. The tables are put together and paginated just as they would be in an appellate brief. They are explained in Chapter 29 (on appellate brief writing) because they're often omitted from law school memo assignments. Although it is optional, a Table of Contents can help you persuade by compiling all your point headings and subheadings in one place so the reader can see a broad overview of your Argument. Point headings are explained in Chapter 26. Some lawyers add a Table of Contents to a medium- or large-sized motion memo to gain that advantage. A Table of Authorities, however, is needed only in an exceptionally large motion memo, approaching the size of an appellate brief.

The **Preliminary Statement** or **Introduction** or **Summary** briefly sets out the case's procedural posture by identifying the parties; explaining the nature of the litigation; and describing the motion before the court and the relief sought through the motion. If it can be done very concisely, the Preliminary Statement might also summarize the parties' contentions, emphasizing the writer's theory of the motion. The point is to tell the judge why the matter is before the court and to define the type of decision the judge is being asked to make. That can usually be done in less than a page.

The **Statement of Facts** or **Facts** or **Statement of the Case** corresponds to the Facts in an office memo, but there are differences in substance and in drafting technique. Chapter 27 explains how to write a Statement of the Facts.

The **Argument** corresponds to the Discussion in an office memo, but here the goal is to persuade as well as to explain. An Argument is organized into *points*, each of which is a single, complete, and independent ground for relief. Each point has a heading and may be divided by subheadings, all of which are reproduced verbatim in the table of contents. Chapter 26 explains how to construct point headings and subheadings. The Argument is the most complex component of a motion memorandum, but you have already learned many of the skills required. Additionally, you will need to know how to develop theories (Chapter 23) and arguments (Chapter 24).

The **Conclusion** is intended only to remind the reader of what you seek (or oppose), with an allusion to your theory, if that can be compressed into one or two sentences. Compare the following:

Conclusion

For all these reasons, this court should preliminarily enjoin construction of the logging roads here at issue.

Conclusion

Thus, the Forest Service's authorization of these logging roads violates the National Environmental Policy Act, the Administrative Procedure Act, and the enabling legislation of the Forest Service. The harm would be irreparable, and an injunction would promote the public interest. This court should therefore preliminarily enjoin the Forest Service from building the roads.

The second example does a much better job of reminding the court, in just a few sentences, of precisely what the writer wants and why it should be done.

The **indorsement** appears under a line reading "Respectfully submitted." The indorsement includes the lawyer's name, an indication of which party she represents, and her office address and telephone number. In some jurisdictions, the attorney also signs the memo.[1]

§25.2   Writing a Motion Memorandum

As with office memos, lawyers differ about which part of a motion memorandum they draft first. But lawyers modify their habits somewhat from document to document, simply because a practice that works well in one instance might not work well in another.

Many lawyers start by writing the Preliminary Statement because it's not hard to do and is a convenient way to get going. Then they turn to the heart of the job, which is the Statement of Facts and the Argument.

Some lawyers write the Argument before they write the Statement of Facts because writing the Argument shows them what to do with the facts. Other lawyers might write the Argument and the Statement of Facts simultaneously. Some might outline the Statement of Facts while writing the Argument.

Some lawyers write the point headings and subheadings before starting to write the Argument. Others might write an outline of the Argument and gradually convert the outline into headings and subheadings. (In a finished memorandum, the headings and subheadings *are* an outline of the Argument.)

The Conclusion, the Tables, and the indorsement are best done last. The cover page can be done at any time.

While putting the memo through further drafts, ask yourself the questions in the checklists on the inside front and back covers of this book.

---

1. *See, e.g.,* Rule 11 of the Federal Rules of Civil Procedure.

26 Point Headings and Subheadings

§26.1 How Points and Headings Work

In a motion memo or appellate brief, the Argument is divided into points. Each point is given a heading and may be divided by subheadings. You'll understand this chapter more easily if, before reading it, you read the point headings and subheadings in the Tables of Contents of the motion memo in Appendix F and the briefs in Appendices G and H.

A point is an independent, complete, and free-standing ground for a ruling in your favor. If only one ground would support a favorable ruling, you have only one point and only one point heading, although the point itself could be broken up into subheadings to the extent that would help the reader. If, on the other hand, you have two or more favorable theories, each of which could stand alone as a *complete* and *independent* ground for relief, each theory is a separate point and is to be summarized in a separate heading. (Points and point headings can be organized differently in some situations involving complicated tests. For why and how, see question 26-B later in this chapter.)

How could you have more than one complete and independent reason for a ruling in your favor? Take a motion to dismiss at the beginning of a lawsuit. As they would appear in the Table of Contents, the movant's point headings might read as follows:

> **I.   The complaint should be dismissed for failure to state a cause of action.**

II. **The action should be dismissed because the summons was improperly served on the defendant.**

III. **The action should be dismissed on the ground of res judicata.**

IV. **The action should be dismissed on the ground that the plaintiff's time to sue has expired.**

If true, any one of these should justify granting the motion. A complaint that fails to set out a cause of action should be dismissed even if properly served and even if the action is not barred by res judicata or the statute of limitations. An action should be dismissed if the summons was not properly served, even if the complaint does state a cause of action — and so on.

Subheadings can be used to develop a point heading:

I. **The complaint should be dismissed for failure to state a cause of action.**

A. *The plaintiff claims only that the defendant School District did not "adequately" teach him.*

B. *Virtually every jurisdiction that has considered the question has refused to recognize a tort of "educational malpractice."*

C. *Because an education is the result of the efforts of both student and teachers, a failure to learn cannot be attributed solely to the school.*

D. *A tort of "educational malpractice" would disrupt the public schools.*

1. Scarce educational resources would be diverted to pay damages or insurance premiums.

2. A litigious atmosphere would interfere with teaching and learning.

The number of independent grounds for ruling in a party's favor can differ depending on the party's role in the same litigation. For example, in the motion memo in Appendix F, the plaintiff is entitled to summary judgment if it can prove both elements of the test for summary judgment: (1) that there's no genuine dispute of a material fact and (2) that it (the plaintiff) is entitled to judgment as a matter of law. The plaintiff has only one point because it must prove both elements to win. If it proves one but not the other, it would lose for failure to carry the whole burden. Proving one of the elements alone is therefore not a freestanding, independent ground for winning.

The Appendix F defendant would submit a memo in opposition to the plaintiff's motion. That memo is not in this book's appendices. But if you were to read it, you might find two points because the defendant can win a denial of the motion if he can prevent the plaintiff from proving *either* of the elements of the test for summary judgment.

Because the plaintiff must prove both elements, the defendant might have two ways to win. He can win if there's a genuine dispute of a material fact. Or he can win if the plaintiff isn't entitled to judgment as a matter of law. Either is good enough.

The numbering and lettering sequence for headings is the same as with a formal outline:

     I.   [point heading]

        A. [subheading]

        B. [subheading]

    II.   [point heading]

Subheadings are subdivisions of a point. Dividing something produces at least two subdivisions. Thus, it's illogical to have only one subheading. The minimum number is two.

Before completing your research, you can start to outline the Argument by rough-drafting the point headings and subheadings. In fact, your rough draft of the headings can be part of your outline.

When you set up headings and subheadings in a Table of Contents and in an Argument, study the examples in Appendices F, G, and H for format. In an Argument (but not in a Table of Contents), point headings appear in bold type. In both places, all headings and subheadings are single-spaced. In the Argument, headings and subheadings are centered with extra margins on both sides and white space above and below. Headings and subheadings should be obvious to a reader who is skimming.

If you have only an inch or two left at the bottom of a page in the Argument, don't put a heading there; put it instead at the top of the next page. For the same reason that newspaper headlines don't appear at the bottom of a newspaper page, point headings and subheadings look strange if they appear at the bottom of an Argument page without any text underneath.

§26.2 How to Evaluate Your Headings and Subheadings for Effectiveness

To figure out whether you have drafted effective point headings and sub-headings, ask yourself the following questions.[1]

26-A **Do your headings lay out a complete and persuasive outline of your Argument? Do they convey your theory?** Many legal readers, including judges, read point headings in the Table of Contents before any other part of the brief. Although a judge needs to read your Argument to fully understand it, she should be able to see in your headings the significant steps of logic on which your argument is based. Headings may include legal reasoning, anticipated counter-arguments, and policy arguments.

Notice how that's done with the headings and subheadings earlier in this chapter. If you draft the headings after you write the Argument, be sure that the headings and subheadings present a complete and coherent picture of your theory when they're isolated in the Table of Contents. When you compile the headings and subheadings in the Table of Contents, you may find that you need to redraft them because only then might you discover gaps or inconsistencies not apparent when the headings are scattered in the Argument.

Look at the Tables of Contents of the memorandum in Appendix F and in the briefs in Appendices G and H. Read the headings and subheadings there as a judge would on first opening each document. From the headings, can you understand each writer's theory? Why or why not?

26-B **Is each point an independent and complete ground for a ruling in your favor?** A point stands on its own if the court could rule in your favor based entirely on the arguments under that heading.

There's an exception to the general principle that a point should be an independent and complete ground for a ruling in your favor. *If your client must satisfy an especially complicated test, you can organize your point headings around the test's elements or factors.*

For example, a preliminary injunction is a trial court order commanding the parties to do, or refrain from doing, certain things specified in the injunction until the court can hold a trial. Preliminary injunctions tend to be granted

---

1. When marking your work, your teacher might refer to these questions by using the number-letter codes that appear next to each question.

early in a lawsuit, and they might last for years during discovery and other pretrial work until eventually the case reaches trial. In the U.S. Fourth Circuit, a district court may grant a preliminary injunction if all the following elements are satisfied: (1) the party seeking the injunction is likely to succeed on the merits eventually at trial, (2) that party would suffer irreparable harm before trial unless protected by an injunction, (3) the balance of hardships weighs in that party's favor, and (4) an injunction would be in the public interest.[2] Each of these elements is complicated. And the test as a whole is extraordinarily complicated.

See the appellant's brief in Appendix G. The plaintiff there sued asserting two claims, one under Title IX of the Education Amendments Act of 1972 and another under the Equal Protection Clause of the Fourteenth Amendment to the U.S. Constitution. The trial court denied his motion for a preliminary injunction, and he appealed to the U.S. Court of Appeals for the Fourth Circuit, filing the Appendix G brief there.

Here are the points in that brief:

ARGUMENT

I. **Preliminary Injunction Standard.**

II. **G. Has Established a Likelihood of Success on His Title IX Claim.**

    A. Excluding Transgender Students from Using the Same Restrooms as Other Students Discriminates Against G. on the Basis of Sex.

    B. Excluding G. from Using the Same Restrooms as Other Students Deprives Him of Equal Access to Educational Opportunity.

III. **G. Has Established a Likelihood of Success on His Equal Protection Claim.**

IV. **G. Has Satisfied the Remaining Preliminary Injunction Factors.**

    A. An Injunction Is Necessary to Prevent Irreparable Harm to G.

---

2. *League of Women Voters of N.C. v. North Carolina*, 769 F.3d 224, 235 (4th Cir. 2014). (Some other circuits, such as the Second Circuit, follow a different test.)

> B. The Balance of Hardships Weighs in Favor of an
>   Injunction.
>
> C. An Injunction Is in the Public Interest.

Rule 28(a)(8)(B) of the Federal Rules of Appellate Procedure require an appellant to explain the relevant standard of review. Here, Point I does that for the complicated test for a preliminary injunction. The other points address the test's elements. This brief thus illustrates the principle that if your client must satisfy an especially complicated test, you can organize your point headings around the test's elements or factors.

26-C   **Do your headings avoid assuming information that a judge wouldn't have when reading the Table of Contents for the first time?**   Put yourself in the judge's position. When turning to the Table of Contents for the first time, the judge knows nothing of the case. How would you react to this heading?

> **I.**   **The motion to quash because of the First
>   Amendment should be denied.**

Quash what? What does the First Amendment have to do with this? The following is better:

> **I.**   **The defendant's motion to quash a
>   deposition subpoena should be denied because
>   the subpoena does not violate the journalist
>   witness's First Amendment right to maintain the
>   confidentiality of his sources.**

26-D   **Is the number of subheadings for each point based on the logic of that point's arguments?**   For each point, the number of subheadings should equal the number of *significant* steps of logic inherent in the argument. For example, the failure-to-state-a-cause-of-action point earlier in this chapter depends on the following steps of logic:

- The complaint alleges only educational malpractice. Because the complaint cannot be interpreted to allege any other kind of claim, it can survive a motion to dismiss only if this state were to recognize a cause of action for educational malpractice.
- The idea of recovering for educational malpractice has been scorned by other courts.

- Such a tort is impractical because a court would not be able to deter-mine how much of the fault was the student's and how much was the school's.
- Such a tort would damage schools by disrupting the educational process.

These are the very steps represented in the subheadings in the first part of this chapter. More subheadings would have fragmented the argument so much that the reader would not quickly see how it fits together. Fewer subheadings would have hidden the logic.

26-E **Is each heading and subheading a single sentence that can be immediately understood?** Don't try to put everything in the point heading; save some of it for the subheadings. Conciseness in headings is the key to their success. For example:

> I. **The deposition subpoena should be quashed because the evidence sought is not confidential and is therefore not protected by this state's media shield law.**
>
> A. *Art. 9, § 765, permits a litigant to obtain information that the media has not treated as confidential.*
>
> B. *The appellant journalist concedes that he did not promise confidentiality to his sources.*

Each of these sentences can be understood. Don't write this:

> I. **Because this state's shield law provides no explicit protection for the media against revealing nonconfidential information or sources and because the legislative history is silent, the scope of art. 9, § 765, is limited to pro-tecting only confidential information or sources, and this court should therefore quash a sub-poena that sought information that the movant, a newspaper reporter, had obtained through conversations in which he had not promised to keep his informants' identities in confidence.**

26-F **Does each point heading identify the ruling you want?** Point headings, but not subheadings, should tell judges what you want them to do. They rarely grant relief not expressly requested. In a trial court, you can ask a judge to grant or deny a motion. On appeal, you might argue that the lower court's order granting the motion should be affirmed or reversed. For example:

> I. **The defendant's motion for summary judgment should be granted because the parties never formed a contract to merge.**
>
>   A. *There is no genuine dispute about the non-existence of a written contract.*
>
>   B. *The defendant is entitled to judgment as a matter of law because there was no written contract and no evidence of an oral understanding that could survive the Statute of Frauds.*

Don't write this:

> I. **The parties never formed a contract to merge.**
>
>   A. *There is no written contract.*
>
>   B. *There was no written contract and no evidence of an oral understanding that could survive the Statute of Frauds.*

This would leave a judge wondering, "What does this lawyer want me to do about it?"

26-G **Do your headings identify the controlling legal rules and the determinative facts?** The controlling rule of law should be identified in each point heading. Subheadings can be used to articulate more detailed law such as elements or factors. Use words such as "because" and "since" to incorporate the law into your headings. Also, include one, two, or three determinative facts that pin down for the reader how the rules of law entitle you to what you want. For example:

> I. **The defendant's motion for summary judgment should be granted because the parties never formed a contract to merge.**
>
>   A. *There is no genuine dispute about the non-existence of a written contract.*
>
>   B. *The defendant is entitled to judgment as a matter of law because there was no written contract and no evidence of an oral understanding that could survive the Statute of Frauds.*

The following refers to no facts:

    I.   The defendant's motion for summary judgment should be granted.

        A. There is no genuine dispute of a material fact.

        B. Defendant is entitled to judgment as a matter of law.

Even though both examples contain controlling rules of law, the first example effectively demonstrates how the rules of law apply to the facts of this case.

26-H   **Are your headings forceful and argumentative?** Your headings and subheadings should state an essential idea in an assertive way from your client's point of view. For example:

    I.   The defendant's motion for summary judgment should be granted because the parties never formed a contract to merge.

        A. There is no genuine dispute about the non-existence of a written contract.

        B. The defendant is entitled to judgment as a matter of law because there was no written contract and no evidence of an oral understanding that could survive the Statute of Frauds.

Don't write this:

    I.   Motions for summary judgment are not appropriate unless there is no genuine dispute of a material fact and the moving party is entitled to judgment as a matter of law.

        A. Genuine issue of disputed fact.

        B. Judgment as a matter of law.

These headings don't advance the client's case. The point heading just recites the law without advancing the client's theory. And the subheadings are labels rather than assertions.

27

Telling Your Client's Story in a Statement of the Case (or Facts)

§27.1 What Happens in a Statement of the Case (or Statement of Facts)

When I was an attorney . . . , I realized after much trial and error that in a courtroom whoever tells the best story wins.

> — *John Quincy Adams (fictionally)*
> *in the movie,* Amistad

There is nothing more horrible than the murder of a beautiful theory by a brutal gang of facts.

> — *La Rochefoucauld*

"It may sound paradoxical," wrote Justice Jackson, "but most contentions of law are won or lost on the facts."[1] In a motion memo or an appellate brief, the judge learns of the facts in the Statement of the Case, which has two purposes. One is to summarize the factual record relevant to the decision the court has been asked to make. The other purpose is to imply your motivating arguments

---

1. Robert H. Jackson, *Advocacy Before the Supreme Court: Suggestions for Effective Case Presentations,* 37 A.B.A. J. 801, 803 (1951).

through the way you present the facts. Motivating arguments, after all, grow out of the facts. See §24.3 in Chapter 24.

You'll understand this chapter more easily if you first review Chapter 10 on fact analysis and Chapter 23 on stories and imagery. Also read the Statements of Facts in the Appendix F motion memo and the Statements of the Case in the Appendices G and H appellate briefs.

In the U.S. Supreme Court, the factual part of an appellate brief is called the *Statement of the Case*.[2] The U.S. Courts of Appeals also use the term *Statement of the Case*.[3] *Statement of Facts* is also a commonly used name, especially in trial courts, which is why it's used in the Appendix F motion memo. In some states, it's also used in appellate briefs. But it doesn't entirely reflect what the reader will find there. Facts are what happened between the parties *before* one of them sued the other. As Chapter 10 explains, courts know only the allegations and evidence, from which they must infer the facts. Inferences belong in the Argument because they're *argued from* the allegations and evidence.

In the types of memos and briefs you'll write in law school, you must recite in the Statement all facts that you mention elsewhere in the document. You must also recite in the statement all facts on which your adversary relies. The judge is entitled to a place in the document where all the legally significant facts can be seen together.

You must provide a citation to a page in the record for every fact in the Statement. See §27.4, later in this chapter. The judge is entitled to an easy method of checking what you say.

You aren't allowed to argue, analyze law, or draw factual inferences in the Statement. Facts are *stated* there and analyzed in the Argument. You're allowed, however, to report the inferences witnesses drew and the characterizations they spoke. And you're allowed to state inferences that your adversary won't contest. An undisputed inference will be treated as a fact.

You aren't allowed to discuss facts that are outside the record. See §27.4. A Statement of Facts describes only procedural facts: allegations in pleadings, testimony, other evidence, and so on. Other facts must be excluded, a process called *limiting the Statement to the record*. The only facts allowed are the ones that have been put before the court through appropriate procedural means. However, the *absence* from the record of a particular allegation or piece of evidence can itself be a fact. And you can describe such a gap in the record ("no witness identified the defendant") if it demonstrates that the opposing party has failed to allege something. See Chapter 10.

And you aren't allowed to misrepresent the facts, either overtly or by omission. See §27.3, later in this chapter.

---

2. U.S. Sup. Ct. R. 24(1)(g).
3. Fed. R. App. P. 28(a)(6).

If you cannot argue, characterize, or state inferences in a Statement, how can you persuade there? The most effective Statements persuade through organization that emphasizes favorable facts and through word choice that affects the reader while saying nothing that the adversary could reasonably claim to be inaccurate. In other words, a persuasive Statement is *descriptive in form but probative in substance.*

Consider two examples, each the beginning passage of a Statement of Facts. Assume that the plaintiffs are suing a backcountry hiking guide for negligence after the guide led them into disaster. (Citations to the record have been deleted.)

On June 11, the plaintiffs asked in Stove Pipe Springs whether a backcountry guide could lead them through certain parts of Death Valley. After some discussion, they hired the defendant to take them on a full-day hike the next day.

When they started out, the defendant carried a compass and map. Each plaintiff carried sunglasses, a large-brim hat, and a quart of water.

At trial, a climatologist testified about the climate in Death Valley. Occasionally, winter temperatures fall below freezing, but there is no water to freeze. Spring and fall temperatures approximate summer temperatures elsewhere. July is the hottest month, with an average high of about 116° and an average low of about 87°. The highest temperature ever recorded in Death Valley was 134°. Reports by early explorers of temperatures above 150° have not been confirmed or repeated through official measurements. Average annual rainfall is about 1½ inches, and the number of days on which precipitation falls in an average year is eight.

The climate in Death Valley is one of the hottest and driest known. The highest temperature recorded each year reaches at least 120° and in many years at least 125°. The highest temperature recorded in Death Valley — 134° — is also the highest recorded anywhere on earth. The rainfall is only 1½ inches per year — the lowest in the Western Hemisphere — and in a few years no rain falls at all.

In the summer sun there, a person can lose four gallons of perspiration a day and — in 3% humidity — die of dehydration unless the lost water is quickly replaced. A person becomes delirious after two gallons are lost. At that heat and humidity, unprotected wood can split open spontaneously.

The defendant advertised himself as a professional and experienced backcountry guide. He was hired by the plaintiffs and then took them into Death Valley for a full-day hike on a June day with a quart of water each.

After reading the example on the right, you're probably ready to believe that this hike was madness, and that the guide was responsible for it. But in early drafts, many beginners instinctively produce a Statement like the one on the left, which doesn't convince you that the guide did anything alarming. It fails because it's descriptive *both* in form and in substance. After you complete your first-draft Statement, your goal will be to rewrite it until you have something that more closely approximates the example on the right, which is descriptive in form but *probative in substance*.

How did the example on the right persuade you?

First, the writer included no marginal facts — such as the temperatures in other months or the unverified reports by explorers — that would have obscured the critical information that persuades. You weren't even told the precise date because only the month or season matters. And each fact was given a prominence corresponding to the fact's value.

Second, the writer selected facts that would illustrate the theory: you will lose four gallons of water a day in such a place. After two gallons, you will become delirious. This was a full-day hike. The plaintiffs had a quart of water each. The defendant claimed to be a professional and experienced guide. As each of these facts is added, the logic of the theory unfolds.

Third, the relationship between each fact and the theory was pointed out to you. You were told, for example, why these temperatures should have suggested caution to the guide: they were "the highest recorded anywhere on earth."

Finally, you were given the kind of vivid details that make a theory come alive: the delirium, for example, and the wood splitting open.

But the example on the right *looks* like just a description of the relevant facts. Nothing in it could reasonably be challenged as untrue by an adversary. Each fact is objectively verifiable in the record. The only characterization ("one of the hottest and driest known") is scientifically verified. And — most importantly — the writer never expressed inferences. *You drew them all yourself.*

Litigators become story-tellers. That does not mean that they recite facts. Facts are just a collection of events and circumstances. Reciting them is usually boring. A *story*, on the other hand, touches us in the heart and in the mind because the people in it come alive so that we sympathize with one person, are offended by another, worry about a third, are impressed with a fourth, and so on. A litigator has to *find* the story in the facts and develop it so that it affects the reader. Finding the story means figuring out how the facts can come together to make a plot — like the plot of a novel — that touches the reader.

When you're writing a Statement, you can develop your story-finding and telling skills by explaining the story to a friend who doesn't know the case you are working on. As you tell the story orally, it will improve if you consciously try to use the techniques described in this chapter. Then, when you are satisfied with it, write the Statement.

§27.2   How to Evaluate Your Storytelling in a Statement of the Case (or Statement of the Facts)

If you want to win a case, paint the judge a *picture* and keep it simple.

— *John W. Davis*

While writing and rewriting your Statements, ask yourself the following questions:[5]

27-A | **Have you implied your motivating arguments and reflected your theory throughout the Statement?**   Tightly focus your Statement on facts that advance your theory. Doing that implies the motivating arguments that you'll make explicitly in the Argument (Chapter 24, §24.3). If the Statement wanders aimlessly and indiscriminately through the facts, the reader won't grasp your theory and may not even understand the story. Every word should be selected to make the theory more clear.

If you focus the Statement in this way, it might be surprisingly concise. For example, consider the following from one of Cardozo's opinions (surely, a model of brevity):

A radiator placed about ten or twelve inches from the edge of an unprotected hoistway and parallel thereto fell down the shaft and killed a man below.[6]

After reading this, we are prepared to hold liable whoever was careless enough to have put the radiator there, whoever knocked it over, and whoever failed to put a protective screen over the top of the shaft. Just tell us who they are so we can enter a judgment against them. Imagine the facts *not* mentioned: why the radiator was put there, where it came from, where it was supposed to go afterward, why the man was below, and so on. None would have advanced the theory, and all would have distracted the reader.

Throughout the Statement, the reader should be conscious — from the way the facts are cast — of whom you represent. If the reader wonders about that, even for a paragraph or two, you have probably written an unpersuasive Statement.

27-B | **Have you breathed life into the facts by telling a compelling story about people?**   You can make the story come alive by setting out the facts that show who has behaved properly and who has not, letting

---

5. When marking your work, your teacher might refer to these questions by using the number-letter codes that appear next to each question.
6. *DeHaen v. Rockwood Sprinkler Co.*, 179 N.E. 764, 765 (N.Y. 1932).

the facts themselves make your case. A simple narrative with vivid nouns and verbs does this best. For example, the U.S. Supreme Court case *Hatahley v. United States*[7]

> involved, on its face, cold jurisdictional and legal problems: Were rights under the Taylor Grazing Act, a federal law, affected by a state law regulating abandoned horses? Had there in any event been compliance with the state statute's terms? Did the Federal Torts Claims Act cover intentional trespasses within the scope of federal agents' authority? The injuries for which redress were sought were the carrying off of horses and mules belonging to the plaintiffs, who were Navaho Indians.
> . . . Here is how the facts were set forth in [the plaintiffs'] brief:

>> The animals were rounded up on the range and were either driven or hauled in trucks to a Government-owned or controlled corral 45 miles away. Horses which could not be so handled were shot and killed by the Government's agents on the spot. [T]he horses were so jammed together in the trucks that some died as a result, and, in one instance, the leg of a horse that inconveniently protruded through the truck body was sawed off by a federal employee. . . . (Fdg. 23, 25; R. 33-34.) Later, the animals were taken in trucks to Provo, Utah, a distance of 350 miles, where they were sold to a glue factory and horse meat plant for about $1,700 — at about 3 cents a pound (R. 93, 293) — no part of which was received by petitioners (Fdg. 24; R. 34).[8]

The Supreme Court held that "[t]hese acts were wrongful trespasses not involving discretion on the part of the agents, and they do give rise to a claim compensable under the Federal Tort Claims Act."[9] After reading the plaintiff's fact description, does the result surprise you?

After reading a movant's or appellant's Statement, the judge should be left with the feeling that something unacceptably wrong has happened. The movant or the appellant, after all, wants the judge to *do* something about those facts. But after reading the Statement of an appellee or a party opposing a motion, the judge should instead believe the facts are fair and just — or at least that they are not so unjust as to call for judicial intervention. One way to arouse those feelings is to show how the facts are vividly, even interestingly, just or unjust.

Can you still see in your mind trucks, horses, a corral, a man with a saw? Does that scene sum up what *Hatahley* was all about?

---

7. 351 U.S. 173 (1956).

8. Frederick Bernays Wiener, *Briefing and Arguing Federal Appeals* 58-59 (1967). (The references to "Fdg." and to "R." are citations to the record. Section 26.4 explains what a record is and how to cite to it.)

9. *Hatahley,* 351 U.S. at 181.

27-C | **Have you organized to tell the story most persuasively?**   The first step in organizing a Statement is to make a list of the facts that are — according to your theory — determinative. Add explanatory facts only if needed to avoid confusion or to tell the story coherently. Omit the coincidental facts. See Chapter 10, §10.2 for more on determinative facts, explanatory facts, and coincidental facts.

Include dates only if they're determinative or are needed to avoid confusion. Beginners tend to include every available date because dates are the easiest of all facts to state. But irrelevant dates clutter up the Statement and thus obscure the truly important facts. And if time isn't an issue, dates can mislead the reader by implying that it is. For example, where the first sentence in a Statement is "The summons and complaint were served on February 1, 2012," the reader will get the impression that the issue is about a statute of limitations or some other issue involving time.

Include the identity of a witness only if that truly adds to the story. Identifying all the witnesses by name clutters up the Statement and gets in the way of the story you want to tell. For instance, the identity of a witness could be valuable if the fact is an admission ("the plaintiff himself admitted that he was not wearing his seat belt"); if the witness is impressively authoritative ("four professors of engineering testified about why the dam collapsed"); or if the fact is part of the witness's state of mind ("the defendant testified that she intended to sell only the frame and not the painting"). And if the fact is contested — for example, one witness said the traffic light was green while another said it was red — you probably need to identify them because you'll try to show that one is more credible than the other.

You can also point to inconsistencies in the evidence and things that are missing from the record:

> Although Officer Joyner testified that Ms. Leyland was assaulted by another prisoner in her cell (T. at 178), he could not name or describe that prisoner (T. at 187), and there is no evidence anywhere in the record that another prisoner was at any point assigned to or given access to her cell. Moreover, although the warden of the county jail testified that arresting officers are not normally permitted in cell blocks (T. at 245), Officer Joyner was the sole witness who claimed to have seen an assault in Ms. Leyland's cell.

Who do you think beat up Leyland? Every word in this passage is value-neutral, and none of the evidence is interpreted or characterized. Although it persuades, the passage sounds clinically objective. The writer has merely brought together facts that had been scattered about in the record. And the writer has refrained from stating inferences — such as "Officer Joyner should not be believed" — that should be left for the Argument.

The second step is to make an outline that would set out the determinative and explanatory facts in a sequence both persuasive and easily understandable.

Sometimes — but not often — the most effective sequence is chronological. More frequently, a topical organization works better because you can use the way you organize the facts to imply the logical relationships between them. In some cases, you might try a topical organization that becomes a chronological narrative where it is important for the reader to understand the sequence in which events happened. Often, the Statement can be made more accessible by breaking it up with headings that are reprinted verbatim in the table of contents.

27-D   **Have you started with a punch?.**   Begin the Statement with a short passage — one or two paragraphs — summarizing your most compelling facts so that the judge understands the heart of your theory. Then tell the whole story, explaining along the way and in detail the facts that you summarized at the beginning. Never begin the Statement with neutral facts, unfavorable facts, or unimportant facts.

The opening passage is the most important part of the Statement. If written well, it puts the judge in a receptive frame of mind; tells the judge what facts to look for later; and creates a lasting impression. The opening passage is usually the hardest part of the Statement to write. But the extra time and effort are an excellent investment.

Imagine a judge who reads this short opening passage wondering, "Why should I *care* about this party and this story? Why should I even continue to read this Statement carefully when there's much else that I must do before the end of the day?" Write the passage to engage the judge so that she really begins to care and *wants* to read the rest of the story.

What will you say in that passage? How will you say it? Imagine that you're starting to tell the story orally to a friend, that you want your friend to listen to the whole story with rapt attention, and that you're allowed to tell only the facts, with no characterizations ("my client is a good person, and the other party is a greedy nitwit"), no factual inferences ("my client is telling the truth"), and no legal conclusions ("the other party embezzled my client's money"). You're not allowed to do those things anywhere in the fact statement. What are the first half-dozen sentences you would say to your friend? The answer to that question is the first draft of your opening passage.

27-E   **Have you emphasized favorable facts?**   That can be done through organization. Readers are most attentive at the beginning, less attentive at the end, and least attentive in the middle. It can also be done by describing favorable facts in detail and by omitting unnecessary facts that cloud the picture you want the reader to see. Notice, for example, that the name of the warden is missing from the example in question 26-C. The essential fact is the warden's official position, and his name would have no effect on the court. Compare these:

At 2:10 A.M., on Tuesday, September 2, 1986, Officer Joyner was told by his dispatcher to investigate a disturbance on the fourth floor of the building at 642 Sutherland Street. (T. at 162.) There he took a complaint from Kenneth Novak, a tenant in apartment 4-C, and, as a result, arrested Ms. Leyland, who lives in apartment 4-E. (T. at 163-65.) Officer Joyner was not able to leave the building with Ms. Leyland until 2:45 A.M. because she had been asleep and needed to dress. (T. at 166-67.) Ms. Leyland testified that she was so tired that she fell asleep in the police car during the drive to the precinct station. (T. at 14.) Cynthia Scollard, a police booking clerk, testified that she was on duty at about 3:05 A.M. on September 2, when she heard a commotion in the precinct parking lot. (T. at 145.) Ms. Scollard further testified that she noticed Ms. Leyland's injuries as soon as Officer Joyner turned Ms. Leyland over to her, and that Ms. Leyland appeared to be very tired at the time. (T. at 147-49.)

Ms. Leyland was awakened and arrested by Officer Joyner at her apartment shortly after 2 A.M. on the day she was beaten. (T. at 162-67.) A police booking clerk testified that she heard "a man yelling in the parking lot" just before Officer Joyner brought Ms. Leyland into the precinct station. (T. at 145.) The booking clerk also testified that she immediately noticed bleeding from Ms. Leyland's lip and from the side of her head (T. at 147-48), and that Ms. Leyland's face began to swell during booking (T. at 148-49.)

In the passage on the left, the following are all clutter: the date, the address, the precise times, the booking clerk's name, and the details about Leyland's tired state. The passage on the right omits the unnecessary facts, opening up room to dwell on the details that are truly essential. And the carefully edited quotation in the passage on the right brings the story to life.

27-F **Have you neutralized unfavorable facts?** The most effective method is to juxtapose an unfavorable fact with other facts that explain, counterbalance, or justify it:

Even though the booking clerk testified that Ms. Leyland did not complain to her that she had been beaten by Officer Joyner, the booking clerk also testified

that Officer Joyner stood next to Ms. Leyland throughout the booking procedure. (T. at 166-69.) Ms. Leyland testified that she had no memory of being
booked (T. at 32), and Dr. Charbonneau testified that persons who suffer a head
injury like Ms. Leyland's are often "stunned and impassive" immediately afterward. (T. at 104.)

The most effective juxtapositions are often found in sentences structured
around an "even though" contrast like the first sentence in the paragraph above.
A far less effective method is to de-emphasize an unfavorable fact by tucking
it into an obscure part of the Statement and summarizing it without much
detail. Hiding an unfavorable fact won't make it go away. And if you seem to
be trying to ignore the fact, you won't be viewed as credible and reliable. If you
don't try to neutralize it, you forfeit an opportunity to persuade.

| 27-G | **Have you humanized your client?** Be careful about how you refer to the parties. In an appellate brief, you only cause confusion

if you refer to them continually as "appellant" and "appellee" because these
designations tell the reader nothing more than who lost below.[10] The procedural designations from the trial court are more clear: "the plaintiff" and "the
defendant" in a civil case or, in a criminal case, "the defendant" and "the State"
(or "the People," "the Government," or "the Commonwealth"). More still can be
communicated by using some generic factual designation related to the issues:
"the buyer" and "the seller" in a commercial dispute or "the employer" and "the
employee" in a discrimination case.

But your client's real name is often the best tactical choice. The passages on
the preceding pages would lose much of their liveliness if "Ms. Leyland" were
reduced to "the plaintiff." The same thing would happen if Officer Joyner were
to become anonymous as "the arresting officer," although in many other cases
a depersonalized opposing party would seem easier to dislike ("the insurance
company," "the hospital").

§27.3   Story Ethics

As you know, a lawyer is forbidden to "[k]nowingly make a false statement
of material fact or law" to a court.[11]

Three kinds of false statements will incur the fury of a court. One is a flat-
out misrepresentation: making a statement about a fact that is unsupported
by the actual record. The second is misrepresentation by omission: presenting

---

10. In many courts, you are not permitted to use these designations in the body of the brief, although
they will naturally appear on the cover page. *See, e.g.,* Rule 28(d) of the Federal Rules of Appellate Procedure.
11. Rule 3.3(a)(1) of the Model Rules of Professional Conduct.

a version of the record that ignores facts favoring the opposing party.[12] The third is misrepresentation by describing your own inferences as though they were facts. In the Argument, you may draw inferences from the facts. But they should be presented as that — and argued because the court can reject them and draw contrary inferences.

Even if it weren't unethical, factual misrepresentation never fools a court and hurts the lawyer and that lawyer's client. Misrepresentations are quickly spotted by opposing lawyers, and once a misrepresentation is pointed out to a court, the entire memo or brief is treated with deep suspicion.

§27.4   The Record

Court rules require that each fact be cited to a specific page or paragraph in the record — not only when you recite the fact in the Statement, but also when you analyze it in the Argument.[13] The judge shouldn't have to go back to the Statement to find the citation. But the opening passage, where you start with a punch (question 27-D earlier in this chapter), is usually considered exempt from this requirement if the facts summarized there will be explained in detail later in the Statement.

Court rules aside, citations have a persuasive effect of their own. Thorough citations, by their appearance alone, create confidence that every fact recited in the Statement is fully supported in the record, while spotty or absent citations arouse a court's skepticism. And thorough record citations add to your own credibility by creating an impression of carefulness.

The record might include any or all of the following: (1) the pleadings; (2) evidence in the form of transcribed testimony, affidavits, and exhibits; and (3) prior court orders, judicial opinions, and, on appeal, the judgment below. Pleadings aren't evidence. If the issue before the court is whether a complaint should be dismissed, the complaint is the only source of "facts," and the "facts" must be described as allegations. You do not, however, have to begin every sentence with "The complaint alleges." It's enough to begin the Statement of Facts with the words "The complaint alleges the following:".

In a motion memo, cite to specific documents within the record, such as "Compl. ¶22" (complaint at paragraph 22), "Senten. Hrg. Tr. at 98" (sentencing hearing transcript at page 98), or "Kristen Myers Aff. ¶12 (Feb. 2, 2012)" (Affidavit of Kristen Myers, dated February 2, 2012, at paragraph 12). On appeal, cite to the record as a whole ("R. at 393") or to the joint appendix ("J.A. at 99"). If the full cite is long, a shorter form can be used after the full cite has been given once.

---

12. "[T]he court is not impressed by a statement of facts which completely ignores the evidence produced by the other side." *Manteca Veal Co. v. Corbari*, 116 Cal. App. 2d 896, 898, 254 P.2d 884, 885 (1st Dist. 1953).

13. *See, e.g.*, Rule 28(a)(7) of the Federal Rules of Appellate Procedure.

Local rules and custom usually allow some latitude in the use of abbreviations when citing to the record. The Bluebook provides guidance. The citation is placed in a parenthetical:

> The plaintiff alleged only that the goods were not delivered on time. (Compl. ¶22.)

A citation proves no more than the sentence that precedes it. If the citation is placed inside a sentence, the citation proves only the portion of the sentence that precedes it.

> Although Officer Joyner wrote in an incident report that Ms. Leyland was injured when she resisted arrest (R. at 98), he testified at trial that she was injured when assaulted by another prisoner in her cell (R. at 178).

As the examples show, the citation ends with a period if it stands alone as a citation sentence but not if you insert it into a sentence you write.

Exercise I
Topical Organization v. Chronological Organization

For each Statement of the Case in Appendices F, G, and H, decide whether the organization is topical, chronological, or a combination. For each, is the organization effective or ineffective? Why?

Exercise II
Escape from Prison? (Rewriting Fact Statements)

Orville Bradwyn is being tried for attempted escape from prison. Below is a Statement of Facts for the prosecution, followed by one for the defense. (Citations to the record have been omitted.)
Rewrite each Statement.

For the prosecution:

The defendant is a prisoner at the Simmonsville Penitentiary. On July 6, he was not in the dinner line where he was required to be, and Sgt. Tunmeyer, the prosecution's sole witness, organized a search for him. According to Sgt. Tunmeyer, no prisoner is allowed in the laundry room after 5 P.M., and the defendant was found in the laundry room at 7:39 P.M. The reason for this rule is that the laundry room is an obvious place from which to escape. The prison does the laundry of the state hospital nearby, and hospital trucks pick up hospital laundry directly from the prison laundry room. At 5 P.M., Sgt. Tunmeyer checked the laundry room thoroughly, did not see anyone, and subsequently locked the door. Even though the defendant had been assigned to work in the laundry, he was not on duty when he was found in the laundry. Before and after dinner, prisoners are free to move about outside their cells. When the defendant's cell was checked, many of his personal belongings were found. In fact, the defendant had a reputation for being tidy and was drying all of his clothes when found in the laundry at 7:39 P.M. However, when his cell was checked his radio had been left on, and some material had been left under the covers of his bed to make it look like someone was asleep there.

For the defendant:

Mr. Bradwyn is an inmate at the Simmonsville Penitentiary. At this prison, inmates are free to move about outside the cells before and after dinner, which is from 6:00 to 7:00 P.M. The prisoners are counted each day in the dinner line, and when Mr. Bradwyn was not present, he was considered missing. Prisoners are not allowed in the laundry after 5 P.M. because the laundry room provides an obvious escape route on the truck the state hospital sends at 8 P.M. each night to pick up its laundry. Sgt. Tunmeyer testified that he checked the laundry at 5 P.M. and locked it up without seeing Mr. Bradwyn there.

When Mr. Bradwyn was discovered to be absent from the dinner line, Sgt. Tunmeyer organized a search and found him in the laundry room at 7:39 P.M., where Mr. Bradwyn was drying his prison uniforms. There was no testimony about how Mr. Bradwyn could have entered the laundry room, which Sgt. Tunmeyer claims to have locked. Mr. Bradwyn is one of the prisoners assigned to work in the laundry. Sgt. Tunmeyer admits to past quarrels with Mr. Bradwyn, and that Mr. Bradwyn had filed a complaint against him for beating him. He also admitted that Mr. Bradwyn is an unusually tidy person who does not like other people to touch his things, and that at 7:39 P.M. all of Mr. Bradwyn's clothing was in a dryer.

The state has not introduced any evidence that Mr. Bradwyn was not on duty earlier in the day. Nor has it introduced any evidence that Mr. Bradwyn could not have been locked in the laundry room accidentally by Sgt. Tunmeyer at 5 P.M.

28 Handling the Procedural Posture

§28.1 Why Procedural Postures Matter

The procedural posture is the procedural event or events — such as a motion — that places an issue before the court.

In trial courts, a lawyer requests a judicial order by making a motion for it, and most procedural postures are defined in terms of the motion that has been made. Each type of motion is governed by rules on how the motion is to be decided. If you move for summary judgment, for example, you must satisfy the test for summary judgment, and your arguments ought to be designed to satisfy that test.

In a motion memorandum or an appellate brief, the procedural posture governs the arguments you can make. It also governs how you use and describe facts. That's because courts see the facts through filters that differ from one posture to another.

§28.2 Types of Procedural Postures

Trial court motions fall into four very generalized categories: (1) motions that challenge the quality of an adversary's allegations (in a pleading); (2) other motions that challenge the manner in which the litigation began; (3) motions that challenge the quality of a party's evidence; and (4) a large, catch-all category of miscellaneous case management motions. When a trial court's decision is appealed, the case moves into yet another procedural posture, where the trial judge's decision is evaluated according to a standard of review.

Rules governing how motions are decided may differ from state to state. Check the rules that govern the court for which you are writing a memorandum or brief, as well as the precedent interpreting those rules. That takes time and thought in the library. Guessing about local rules frequently leads to grief.

§28.2.1   Motions Challenging the Quality of a Party's Allegations

The *burden of pleading* is a party's obligation to allege, in its pleading, facts that, if proven, would entitle the party to the judgment it seeks. In a civil case, the plaintiff's complaint must allege facts that, if proven, would constitute a cause of action. If a defendant pleads a counterclaim or an affirmative defense in the answer, that answer must allege facts that, if proven, would substantiate a counterclaim or affirmative defense. And in a criminal case, the government's indictment or information must allege facts that, if proven, would be a crime.

In a civil action, a defendant can, before answering a complaint, move to dismiss it for failure to state a cause of action. Because this motion tests the sufficiency of allegations (and nothing more), the record is limited to the four corners of the complaint. The question isn't whether either party has proved anything. Instead, the court assumes — for the purpose of the motion only — that the factual allegations in the complaint can be proven, and the court then decides whether, if proven, those allegations would amount to a cause of action. If the court concludes that they could not, it strikes the cause of action from the pleading. If the court strikes all the causes of action pleaded in a complaint, the complaint itself is dismissed and the litigation is terminated unless the plaintiff can serve and file an amended complaint with additional or reformulated allegations that would survive a motion to dismiss.

Similarly, a plaintiff can move to dismiss a counterclaim or an affirmative defense pleaded in the defendant's answer. And in a criminal case a defendant can move to dismiss one or more counts in the indictment or information, or the entire indictment or information.

Because, at this stage in litigation, no evidence has been submitted, lawyers do not describe the "facts" alleged in the pleadings as things that actually happened. Until it receives evidence later in the case, the court has no idea whether the alleged "facts" happened, and the "facts" therefore are described purely as allegations:

> Although the plaintiff has alleged that the defendant struck him from behind with a stick, he has not alleged that the defendant intended to injure him.

In this procedural posture, you cannot accurately write the following:

> Although the defendant struck the plaintiff from behind with a stick, the defendant did not intend to injure the plaintiff.

We'll find out later — after evidence has been produced — whether the defendant struck the plaintiff or intended to cause injury.

There is an exception to all this. If the defendant admits, in the answer, an allegation made in the complaint, the allegation is considered established without need of evidence. The event alleged and admitted might be described as a fact ("The defendant struck the plaintiff") because the admission makes it as good as proved. Or it might be described as a conceded allegation ("The defendant admits that he struck the plaintiff").

§28.2.2   Motions Challenging Other Aspects of the Way in Which the Litigation Began

A defendant might move to dismiss an action on the ground that the court lacks jurisdiction over the subject matter, or that it lacks personal jurisdiction over the defendant, or that venue is improper, or that the summons did not include all the information required, or that it was improperly served, or that some persons who must be made parties have not been,[1] and so on.

Like motions challenging the quality of allegations, these seek dismissal of the action, and they're made after the plaintiff serves a summons and complaint and before the defendant serves an answer. These motions aren't limited to the contents of the complaint. In fact, the contents of the complaint might be irrelevant to the motion. If the defendant asserts that the summons was improperly served, for example, the court would ignore the contents of the complaint and would instead hear testimony from the process server and from the defendant about how the summons was delivered to the defendant.

§28.2.3   Motions Challenging the Quality of a Party's Evidence

These include (1) motions for summary judgment; (2) motions for directed verdict (or in federal courts, motions for judgment as a matter of law); and (3) motions for judgment notwithstanding the verdict (in federal courts, renewed motions for judgment as a matter of law). In contrast to the motions testing allegations in pleadings, these require the court to decide whether a party has carried a burden of production. There are also (4) motions for a new trial, which are analytically different from the other three (and therefore explained near the end of this section).

---

1. *See* Rule 12(b)(1)-(5) and (7) of the Federal Rules of Civil Procedure.

The burden of production (often called the burden of going forward) is the threshold obligation to satisfy the judge (even in cases where the actual trier of fact is a jury) that the party who must shoulder the burden can provide enough evidence that a rational fact finder — a jury — could decide in that party's favor.

The burden of production requires a party to come forward with a minimum, threshold quantum of evidence, defined by the relevant rules of procedure and by the case law interpreting those rules. The question of whether a party has carried a burden of production is generally put to a judge through one of the three motions that challenge the quality of the other party's evidence.

Motions for summary judgment,[2] for directed verdict,[3] and for judgment notwithstanding the verdict[4] exist so that parties, lawyers, and judges can avoid, where possible and appropriate, the effort and expense of trial, as well as the perils of juries. A motion for summary judgment can be made before trial. A motion for a directed verdict can be made during trial, after the adversary has rested (finished presenting evidence) and before the jury has begun to deliberate. And a motion for judgment notwithstanding the verdict is made — as its name suggests — after the jury has returned a verdict. In criminal cases, there are no summary judgments, and only the defendant can move for a directed verdict or for judgment notwithstanding the verdict.

Although these motions are governed by different procedural rules, all three are decided according to approximately the same logic: the motion should be granted if (1) the opposing party has failed to satisfy a burden of production and (2) the law is such that the movant is entitled to a favorable judgment.

The second of these two element incorporates the relevant substantive rules at issue — primarily the rules defining the cause of action and any affirmative defenses — because the only way a court can determine whether a party is entitled to judgment as a matter of law is to apply the substantive rules that define the parties' rights and obligations. If you move for summary judgment in a products liability case, the second element incorporates every part of the law of products liability that happens to be relevant to your case.

Unlike the three motions just described, the motion for a new trial doesn't test whether a party has carried a burden of production. A new trial can be granted on two kinds of grounds: (1) the jury's verdict is seriously tainted through procedural faults such as erroneously admitted evidence or inaccurate jury instructions, or (2) the verdict was against the overwhelming weight

---

2. *See* Rule 56 of the Federal Rules of Civil Procedure.
3. *See* Rule 50(a) of the Federal Rules of Civil Procedure (motion for judgment as a matter of law).
4. *See* Rule 50(b) of the Federal Rules of Civil Procedure (renewed motion for judgment as a matter of law).

of the evidence. The first category obviously doesn't test the quality of a party's evidence. The second does but it does so by examining the extent to which a burden of persuasion (rather than a burden of production) has been carried. A new trial isn't granted merely because the judge would have come to a different verdict if she had been the trier of fact. But it can be granted if the overwhelming weight of the evidence is on one side of the case and the jury returned a verdict for the other side.

In any of these procedural postures, a description of the facts is framed in terms of the evidence submitted:

> The plaintiff testified that he was struck in the back and that the defendant was the only person who was behind him at the time. The defendant does not deny that he struck the plaintiff or that he used a stick to do it. Aside from the stick, the only evidence that might conceivably show that the defendant intended to cause injury is a letter, dated two days before the incident, in which the defendant complained that the plaintiff "had better keep his cattle off my land or I'll have to do something."

Notice how each claimed fact is connected with evidence so that the reader can judge whether the evidence really proves it. That is because the provability of facts is at issue. In these procedural postures, the only facts that can accurately be stated without any reference to evidence are those that are "true" because the parties do not disagree about them.

§28.2.4 Miscellaneous Case Management Motions

These are housekeeping motions, used to manage the progress of litigation, such as motions in discovery; motions for preliminary injunctions; and suppression motions in criminal cases. What makes these motions different from the ones you've just read about is that the granting of a management motion doesn't terminate the litigation; instead, management motions regulate the litigation's progress.

For example, before trial, a criminal defendant who gave the police a confession might move to suppress it, arguing that the police wrongfully obtained the statement by failing to inform him of his constitutional right to remain silent. If the court grants the motion, the statement cannot be used as evidence at trial.

And a judge always instructs a jury on the law before the jury deliberates. A lawyer "requests" jury instructions rather than moving for them.

§28.2.5 Appeal

On appeal, a standard of review is applied to the decision below. Standards of review are explained in §31.3.

§28.3   Writing in a Procedural Posture

You will understand this section more easily if you read the Appendix F motion memo first.

Because most of a legal education is spent studying the substantive law of torts, property, and so on, you might tend to view issues in the abstract ("should the plaintiff win?"). But judges see issues in terms of the motion context in which issues are raised.

If, for example, a plaintiff moves for summary judgment, you're wrong if you define the issue as whether the plaintiff should win the case. The issues are whether there is a material dispute of fact and whether the plaintiff is entitled to judgment as a matter of law (the test for summary judgment). Compare the following Questions Presented:

> Is a painting contractor negligent where he power-sands large amounts of lead paint from the exterior of a building and thus spreads lead paint debris over most of an adjacent preschool, which is then closed and deleaded at great expense because of the overwhelming scientific evidence that lead is toxic?

> Is a painting contractor negligent *as a matter of law where it is undisputed* that he power-sanded large amounts of lead paint from the exterior of a building and thus spread lead paint debris over most of an adjacent preschool, which was then closed and deleaded at great expense because of the overwhelming scientific evidence that lead is toxic?

The italicized words in the second example aren't throwaway jargon. They reflect the test for summary judgment and are the core of the decision the court must make. If any of the itemized facts is disputed, the first element of the test for summary judgment isn't satisfied. If on those undisputed facts, the painter's negligence isn't so clear as to be a matter of law, the second element isn't satisfied.

Similarly, on appeal the question isn't whether the appellant should have won in the trial court, but instead whether the trial court's ruling was error as defined by the applicable standard of review. (See §31.3.)

Because the procedural posture and the rules governing it control the way the judge will make the decision, you must show the judge how to decide within those procedural rules. How can you do that in writing?

First, remember that in a motion or appeal the threshold rule isn't the rule of substantive law that provides the remedy sued for. The threshold rules are procedural. In a trial court, the threshold rules are the rules that govern how the motion is to be decided. On appeal, the threshold rules are the ones that govern the trial court's decision plus the appellate court's standard of review.

For example, the memo in Appendix F has been submitted by Tulta Preschool, Inc., in support of a motion for a summary judgment. In deciding the motion, the court will evaluate the record in terms of the elements of the test for summary judgment: whether there is a genuine dispute about a material fact and whether on the undisputed facts the movant is entitled to judgment as a matter of law. That test is invoked very early in Tulta Preschool's Argument.

Second, some but not many procedural tests contain an element that incorporates the underlying substantive rules on which the litigation as a whole is based (causes of action, affirmative defenses, and so on). In the test for a summary judgment, that happens through the element requiring entitlement to judgment as a matter of law. In the test for a preliminary injunction, it's done through the element requiring likelihood of success on the merits. In these situations, the court makes a procedural decision, but part of that decision is substantive.

Third, organize your paradigm variations around the procedural test. See Chapter 13. If the procedural test incorporates a substantive test, the substantive test operates as a sub-rule. To see how that's done, read carefully the Argument in Appendix F, which includes several paradigmed proofs inside the organization of an umbrella paradigm. The umbrella structure — through which the entire Argument is organized — is built on the test for a summary judgment. Because the second summary judgment element (entitlement to judgment as a matter of law) incorporates a rule of substantive law (the test for negligence), proof of the second summary judgment element includes separate paradigmed proofs for each element of the test for negligence.

Although that may all sound complicated, it's the precise sequence of logic that a judge would go through in order to decide whether Tulta Preschool should be granted a summary judgment. The judge would have to decide whether Tulta Preschool has proved each of the elements of the test for summary judgment — including all the elements of negligence, which is incorporated into the element of entitlement to judgment as a matter of law. An argument carefully organized in this way can systematically demolish a judge's skepticism because it demonstrates, element by element, how a party has carried — or, if you are arguing the other side, failed to carry — a burden.

Finally, don't go overboard in citing to authority for the procedural test. Most procedural tests are so commonly invoked that judges know them by heart. A conclusory explanation (§12.2) is usually sufficient for rule proof. (And that's all that was needed at the beginning of Tulta Preschool's Argument in Appendix F. Can you find the sentence and cite where it happens?) You should provide more only in two situations. The first is where authority will help you guide the court in rule application. And the second is where the parties disagree about the proper formulation of a procedural rule.

§28.4   Researching to Account for Your Case's Procedural Posture

You're looking for two kinds of rules:

First, you are, of course, searching for the rules that govern the *substance* of the controversy — definitions of causes of action, crimes, affirmative defenses, and other forms of rights and obligations like the ones you've already studied in the courses on torts, property, contracts, and criminal law. This is by far the larger research task in nearly all instances.

Second, you're looking for the *procedural* rules that govern how the court's decision is to be made. Some examples are —

1. rules setting out the tests for granting various motions ("Summary judgment is appropriate if there is no genuine issue of material fact and if the moving party is entitled to judgment as a matter of law");
2. rules controlling how the court must evaluate the record before it on the motion to be decided ("In deciding a motion for summary judgment, the court views the evidence in the light most favorable to the party opposing the motion"); and
3. if an appeal has been taken, the rule defining the standard of review in the appellate court ("On appeal, a grant of summary judgment is reviewed de novo").

A court evaluates the factual record differently for different types of motions. And the standard of review differs from one kind of appeal to another.

You can save a lot of research time if you first identify the type of motion involved and then look in the procedural statutes and court rules and in the cases for procedural rules that govern the motion's disposition. For any given motion, you'll probably find part of the procedural law in a statute or court rule and the rest in interpretive case law.

If you find the procedural rules in a procedural statute or court rule, the language may be subtle, but it won't be terribly hard to recognize. The section heading alone will usually announce that you have arrived at the right place — for example, "Rule 56. Summary Judgment."

In case law, when a court mentions the rules governing how a motion is to be decided, it usually does so immediately after reciting the facts and immediately before beginning the legal analysis (just as it was done in Tulta Preschool's memo in Appendix F). That is because the procedural rules are a threshold through which the court must pass in order to begin the analysis. This is typical of the kind of language you'll find:

> A complaint should not be dismissed for failure to state a claim unless it
> appears beyond a doubt that plaintiffs can prove no set of facts in support of

their claim which would entitle them to relief. [Citations omitted.] The allegations of plaintiffs' complaint must be assumed to be true, and further, must be construed in [the plaintiffs'] favor. [Citations omitted.] The issue is not whether plaintiffs will ultimately prevail, but rather whether they are entitled to offer evidence in support of their claims. [Citation omitted.][5]

The first sentence is the test that must be satisfied before the motion can be granted. The rest are some of the rules that govern how the court is to evaluate the record before it on this particular type of motion.

---

5. *United States v. Aceto Agric. Chems. Corp.*, 872 F.2d 1373, 1376 (8th Cir. 1989).

APPELLATE BRIEFS

29 Appellate Practice

§29.1 Introduction to Appeals

A *judgment*—or in equity, a *decree*—is the document through which a court terminates a lawsuit and decides the parties' rights and obligations. The judgment might award damages or grant an injunction, for example. An *order*, on the other hand, is a court's command during the lawsuit that something be done, or not be done, while the litigation is still in progress. A judgment can be appealed. Some orders can be appealed.

The appellate process performs two functions. One is correcting errors made by trial courts. The other is making new law and clarifying existing law by creating precedents. Lower appellate courts make law but concentrate mostly on error correction. Higher appellate courts view their work as mostly making and clarifying law.

The party who appeals will be called the *appellant* or the *petitioner*, and the opposing party the *appellee* or *respondent*, depending on local court rules and the type of appeal. Before writing a brief, check the court's rules for the terms appropriate to your type of appeal. If you can't find the answer, see how the parties are referred to in a reported case in the same court that *procedurally* resembles your own.

In the U.S. Supreme Court and in the highest court of every state, all the judges meet together to hear and decide appeals. In some intermediate appellate courts, appeals are heard by panels, rather than by the full court. In the U.S. Courts of Appeals, for example, decisions are made by panels of three judges; only in rare cases can a party who has lost before a panel persuade the full court en banc to review the panel's decision.

§29.2   What Happens During an Appeal

Although practice varies from court to court, these are the significant events in an appeal:

First, the appellant *serves and files whatever document is required by law to begin the appeal.* If the appellant has a right to appeal, the document is a notice of appeal, an uncomplicated paper that is usually no longer than a page and need not specify grounds for the appeal. If leave to appeal is required, as to the U.S. Supreme Court, the appellant must petition for it, specifying errors and arguing their importance. The notice of appeal is short and simple because it's a mere declaration that the appellant is doing what a losing party has a right to do. But the petition for discretionary review *asks* for permission to appeal and is therefore far more complex.

The second step in the appeal is the *transmittal of the record* from the court below to the court above. Although one might imagine this to be an easy matter of the clerk of one court locating a file and sending it to the clerk of another court, it happens that way only in cases where the record is very simple. A record can be simple, for example, where the appeal is from an order dismissing a complaint for failure to state a cause of action. There the record might not include much more than the complaint, the papers submitted by both parties in connection with the defendant's motion to dismiss, and the court's order.

Most appeals, however, arise only later in the litigation, and in those cases the preparation and transmittal of the record can delay matters for months and add thousands of dollars to the cost of the appeal. Wherever the trial court has held a hearing or trial, one or more court reporters will have to type up a transcript from stenographic notes, a time-consuming process that can produce literally volumes of material.

The third step — required in some jurisdictions and optional in others — is the assembling of an abbreviated version of the record called the *joint appendix* or the *record appendix.* At the appealing party's expense, it is printed in sufficient quantity that a copy can be given to each judge who will hear the appeal. The appellate judges need the joint appendix because the full record can be gargantuan, and the appellate court will have only one copy of it. Even if all the judges hearing an appeal were to work in the same building, it would be impractical to ask them to share a single copy, which may be bound into several bulky volumes.

The fourth step is *drafting briefs,* which each lawyer files with the appellate court and serves on opposing counsel. Chapters 30-32 explain brief writing.

The fifth step is *oral argument*. Each lawyer is allotted a predetermined period, such as fifteen minutes, to speak in open court with the judges, who might ask many questions or only a few. Oral argument is the lawyer's only chance to speak directly with the judges about the problems and issues raised by the appeal. Where the judges and the attorneys are perceptive and well-prepared, oral argument can be the most scholarly type of conversation known to the practice of law. It's the subject of Chapter 33.

After oral argument, the judges confer and discuss the merits of the appeal. In some courts, this conference occurs on the same day as argument; in others, it may happen several days later. One judge is selected to write the court's opinion. In some courts, the assignment is made by chance rotation, but in others it is made by the presiding judge. In the U.S. Supreme Court, the assignment is made by the most senior judge among the majority. The assigned judge drafts an opinion and circulates it to the other judges, who might suggest changes or might draft and circulate concurring or dissenting opinions of their own. In routine appeals, the draft majority opinion is often quickly approved, and concurrences and dissents may be held to a minimum. But in more complex and troubling cases, views can change, and an opinion originally written as a dissent might be transformed into the court's opinion, while the original majority draft is demoted into a dissent.

§29.3 The Roles of the Brief and of Oral Argument

To understand the different roles of the brief and oral argument, you must be able to visualize the effect of increasingly crowded dockets on the work of appellate judges.

Depending on the court, an appellate judge might in a month hear oral arguments and confer with colleagues on several dozen appeals, and in many courts substantially more than a hundred. For each appeal, the judge will have to read at least two briefs and in multiparty cases a half-dozen briefs or more, together with portions of the record. The judge will have to write majority opinions in a proportion of the appeals. On a five-judge court, for example, each judge is assigned one-fifth of the majority opinions. In addition, the judge may feel obligated to write several concurring or dissenting opinions.

The judge will also have to read opinions drafted by other judges and at times will write memoranda to colleagues suggesting changes in those opinions. And the judge will spend a fair amount of time reading some of the cases and statutes cited to in all these briefs and draft opinions. With all this work, the typical appellate judge would find it a luxury to spend as much as an hour reading the average brief. The time available is often no more than half an hour per brief. That's why briefs must be carefully written to persuade while demanding the least possible time and effort from the reader. Judges spend more time on briefs where the appeal raises deeply troubling issues than on briefs in more routine cases. And a judge who writes an opinion might read the briefs more thoroughly than one who does not.

The brief and oral argument perform different functions. Each is crucial, but in a different way.

In a brief, you can tell the client's story and make the client's arguments in detail. A successful brief not only persuades the judge that your client should win, but it can also be used as a manual, explaining to the judge exactly how to make the decision and how to justify it in an opinion. A judge may use the brief to prepare for oral argument, in deciding whether to reverse or affirm, to prepare for the conference with other judges, and while writing the opinion.

Oral argument can do two things better than a brief can. First, in oral argument you can more immediately motivate the court by focusing on the most important ideas — the few facts, rules, and policies — that most make your case compelling. Second, in oral argument you can try to discover, through the bench's questions, each judge's doubts. And on the spot you can explain exactly why those doubts shouldn't prevent a ruling in your favor. Oral argument, in fact, is your only opportunity to learn directly from the judges the problems they have with your arguments. But oral argument also has a significant disadvantage. Oral argument lasts only a few minutes, and memories of it can fade. The brief, on the other hand, has permanence. It's always among the judge's working materials, and it "speaks from the time it is filed and continues through oral argument, conference, and opinion writing."[1]

Detail is communicated best in writing, which can be studied. But the spontaneity of conversation encourages dialogue and lends itself to the broad sweep of underlying ideas.

§29.4   Limitations on Appellate Review

Appellate courts will reverse an order or judgment only if it's based on *reversible error.* An appellate court will affirm unless the appellant can point to a specific error by the trial court that the law considers ground for reversal. Be careful of two kinds of situations, neither of which will lead to a reversal. In the first, the result below seems unfortunate, but no error by the court below can be identified. In the absence of reversible error, an appellate court must affirm what the trial court did. That's because an appeal is only a review for the kind of mistake the law categorizes as error. In the second situation, error can be identified, but it didn't cause the order or judgment appealed from. Even if the result below was unfortunate, and even if the court below committed error, an appellate court will reverse only if the result below is traceable to

---

1. Herbert Funk Goodrich, "A Case on Appeal — A Judge's View," in *A Case on Appeal* 10-1 (1967).

the error. Error that affected the result below is called *material* or *prejudicial*. Error without such an effect is called *harmless*.

To identify error, and to figure out whether it was material or harmless, start with the procedural posture in the trial court. For example, assume that the plaintiff has requested a particular jury instruction; that the trial court denied the request and instead gave another instruction; that the jury returned a verdict for the defendant; and that, on the basis of the verdict, the trial judge entered a judgment for the defendant. The issue on appeal cannot be whether the plaintiff should have won below; rather, it is whether the trial court so erroneously instructed the jury that the entire case should be tried again to a jury properly instructed. If the instruction was error, but if the record shows that the error was not so material as to lead the jury astray, the error was harmless and won't be reversed. The error would be harmless, for example, if the evidence in support of the verdict was so overwhelming that a properly instructed jury would have returned the same verdict.

Appellate review is limited to issues that are actually *raised on appeal*. An appellate court doesn't survey the record below looking for error: in the adversary system, that's the job of the appellant's lawyer.

Appellate courts generally refuse to consider facts that don't appear in the trial court's record (also called the *record below*). You can determine whether a fact is in the record by focusing on the procedural posture in the trial court. If the order appealed from is one dismissing a complaint for failure to state a cause of action, a fact is in the record if it's alleged in the complaint. That's because, for the purpose of deciding a motion to dismiss a complaint, all facts properly pleaded are treated as though they could be proved later at trial. (And, of course, on such a motion the only factual record before the trial court is the complaint itself.)

But the situation is different where the motion in the trial court challenged a party's evidence rather than allegations. For example, assume that the appeal is from a summary judgment. If a fact appears as an allegation in a pleading but doesn't appear in any evidentiary form, it's not "a fact in the record" because the motion below tested evidence and not allegations.

There are two exceptions to the rule against considering facts outside the record. One involves the doctrine of judicial notice, through which a court—trial or appellate—will, without evidence, accept as proven certain facts that are beyond dispute. Do not make more of this than it really is. The following are examples of the kinds of indisputable facts of which courts will take judicial notice: A meter equals 39.37 inches. Cleveland is in Cuyahoga County, Ohio. October 11, 2012, was a Thursday.

The other exception is for what are called "legislative facts," which are generalized social, economic, or scientific information that guides a court in the development of law—as opposed to the "case facts" or "adjudicatory facts," which are the specific events that transpired between the parties. Legislative facts can include empirical data on the detrimental effects of racial segregation, or on the national deterioration of groundwater quality, or on the ways consumers use smartphones — all useful in determining public policy. Although the adversary system isn't very efficient at collecting legislative facts, appellate courts need them when making or changing law.

Although legislative facts can be placed in the trial record, a lawyer called in to handle an appeal sometimes needs to put before the appellate court legislative facts not developed in the record below. The appellate lawyer might include in the brief published empirical research that complements but does not crowd out the legal analysis that is the core of argument. Empirical material added on appeal doesn't need to be set out in the Statement of the Case because it's not part of the record below. Rather, it appears, with citations, in the Argument, most often in support of policy contentions.

The law presumes an order or judgment to be correct unless an appellant demonstrates that the appropriate *standard of review* has been violated. The standard of review will vary from one kind of appeal to another. Think of it as a formula of deference. Depending on the type of decision made below, the appellate court may defer — to a specified degree — to the decision of the trial court judge. Some types of decisions, for example, will be reversed if "erroneous"; others only if "clearly erroneous"; and yet others only if "an abuse of discretion." Standards of review are explained in detail in §31.3.

Finally, appellate courts are temperamentally "affirmance-prone." Unless deeply troubled by what happened below, an appellate judge will be inclined to affirm for several reasons. The trial judge handled the problem first-hand and might know more than distant appellate judges reading a cold transcript of the testimony. Because many trial decisions must be made instantly "in the heat of battle," it's unrealistic to expect perfection from a trial judge. Every reversal disturbs the status quo, and careful people like judges aren't comfortable disturbing the status quo unless it's truly necessary. And reversals impose tangible costs, which can be large, such as retrials.

30 Appellate Briefs

§30.1 Appellate Brief Format

Although rules on format differ from court to court, the required structure might commonly include the following:[1]

1. a cover page containing a caption and other information required by local rules;
2. a Table of Contents;
3. a Table of Authorities;
4. where the appeal rests on the interpretation of a constitutional provision, statute, administrative regulation, or court rule, a reprinting of the relevant material;
5. a Preliminary Statement, sometimes called an Introduction;
6. a Question Presented or Questions Presented or Statement of Issues;
7. a Statement of the Case or Statement of Facts;
8. a Summary of Argument;
9. an Argument, broken up with point headings;
10. a Conclusion; and
11. an indorsement.

---

1. Some courts require additional material, such as a statement specifying how the court acquired jurisdiction over the appeal in question.

As you read the description below of each of these components, compare the sample briefs in Appendices G and H.

The **cover page** includes the caption, followed by the document's title (such as "BRIEF FOR APPELLANT") and the name, address, and telephone number of the lawyer submitting the brief. The caption includes the name of the appellate court, the appellate court's docket number, and the names of the parties and their procedural designations (appellant, appellee, etc.) in the appellate court. Many courts require that the caption also include the parties' procedural designations in the trial court.[2] In federal appellate courts, the appellant is listed first in the caption, but in most state appellate courts the parties appear in the same order in which their names appeared in captions in the trial court. The cover page does not have a page number.

The **Table of Contents** begins on the page after the cover page. It lists all of the components of the brief (except the cover page and the Table of Contents itself); reproduces the point headings and subheadings from the Argument; and sets out the page on which each component, point, or subpoint begins. Because the point headings and subheadings are reproduced verbatim in the Table of Contents, a reader can look there for an outline of the argument and for a quick grasp of the lawyer's theory of the appeal. When read together in the Table of Contents, the point headings and subheadings should express the theory persuasively and coherently. See Chapter 26.

The **Table of Authorities** appears on the first page after the Table of Contents. It indexes the cases, statutes, constitutional provisions, court rules, administrative regulations, treatises, and law review articles cited in the argument, together with references to the pages in the brief where each authority is cited. In the Table, every authority is listed in a complete citation conforming to citation rules, and an asterisk is placed to the left of those citations that form the core of your theory. A footnote identifies those citations as "authorities chiefly relied on" or similar words to the same effect.

The Table of Authorities is broken down into three sections headed "Cases," "Statutes," and "Miscellaneous." Cases are listed in alphabetical order. If constitutional provisions, court rules, or administrative regulations are cited, they are listed with statutes, and the heading is reworded to accommodate them. (In a brief where all of these materials are cited, the heading would read "Constitutional Provisions, Statutes, Court Rules, and Administrative Regulations.") Under the heading, the citations appear in the following order: federal constitutional provisions, state constitutional provisions, federal statutes, state statutes, court rules, federal administrative regulations, and state administrative regulations.

---

2. In a criminal case, the prosecution's trial court procedural designation is always implied and never expressed. For the accused, the trial court procedural designation is, of course, "defendant" — as in "Merritt Bresnahan, defendant." But it would seem silly to write "People of the State of New York, Prosecution." Phrases like "State v. Bresnahan," "People v. Bresnahan," "Commonwealth v. Bresnahan," and "United States v. Bresnahan" unambiguously communicate that Bresnahan is being prosecuted by whatever government customarily uses the designation that precedes the "v."

"Miscellaneous" is reserved for secondary authority, such as restatements, treatises, and law review articles, and they are usually listed there in that order.

For pagination purposes, a brief is broken down into two parts. The two Tables (sometimes called the "front matter") are paginated together in lowercase roman numerals. The rest of the brief (the "body") is paginated separately in arabic numbers, beginning with "1," on the first page after the Tables. Although this may seem odd, it has a very practical purpose. Because the Tables must include page references to the body, the body is typed before the Tables are. And because you can't know how many pages the Tables will occupy until they are typed, the body must begin on page 1. The only efficient solution is to use two separate paginations: lowercase roman for the Tables and arabic for the body.

The **Constitutional Provisions, Statutes, Regulations, and Court Rules Involved** is the easiest part of the brief to draft. It is a place where the court can learn two things.

The first is a list of the codified or promulgated law (as opposed to precedent) that is *critical* to the decision the court is asked to make. A provision is critical to the decision if the parties disagree about its meaning and if the court cannot dispose of the appeal without resolving the disagreement. A court rule that merely provides for the type of motion made below is not critical to the decision unless the parties disagree about the rule's meaning and the court has been asked to resolve the disagreement. Although custom requires the use of the misleading word "Involved" in the heading to this portion of the brief, the only provisions printed under the heading are those that are *at the heart of* the issues before the court. They are much more than "Involved."

The second thing the court can learn from this part of the brief is either the precise wording of those relevant portions or — if the relevant portions are extensive — an indication that they are reproduced in an appendix to the brief. If the material is complicated enough to warrant an appendix, the reference to it could read something like this:

> The following statutes and court rules are set out in the Appendix: Sections 362 and 363 of title I of the Bankruptcy Reform Act of 1978, *as amended,* 11 U.S.C. §§ 362, 363 (2000), together with Bankruptcy Rules 1002 and 1003.

On the other hand, if the provisions are short, this portion of the brief might be written in a manner somewhat like the following:

> The First Amendment to the United States Constitution provides, in pertinent part, as follows:
>
>> Congress shall make no law . . . abridging the freedom of speech or of the press; or the right of the people . . . to petition the Government for a redress of grievances.

A reasonable editing of the relevant provisions aids the court. Be careful to indicate deletions, as you would with any other quote. See Chapter 22 on quoting.

The **Preliminary Statement (or Introduction)** briefly sets out the appeal's procedural posture by identifying the parties, listing the relevant procedural events, and describing the order or judgment appealed from. The Preliminary Statement might also describe the reasoning of the court below and identify the grounds on which the decision below is challenged on appeal. The point is to tell the court why the matter is before it and to specify the type of decision the court will have to make. That can usually be done in less than a page.

Many lawyers use this part of the brief to introduce the court to their theory of the appeal as well as their motivating arguments. See §24.3 in Chapter 24 and the examples in Appendices G and H.

A persuasive **Question Presented (or Issue)** is explained in Chapter 32.

The **Statement of the Case** is explained in Chapter 27.

A **Summary of the Argument** is what its name implies. The point headings and subheadings, as they appear in the Table of Contents, outline the argument. But the Summary does more: it condenses the argument into a few paragraphs — usually one paragraph per issue — with more meat in them than can be put into headings. The Summary should not repeat the point headings.

The **Argument** (Chapter 24) can be divided into points. Points and point headings are explained in Chapter 26.

Although some lawyers use the **Conclusion** to reargue and resummarize the theory of the appeal, the better practice is to limit the conclusion to a very short reiteration of the relief desired, together with an unamplified identification of the ground on which the relief would be based. For example:

> For all the foregoing reasons, the order of the Circuit Court for Albemarle County should be affirmed on the ground that the complaint does not state a cause of action.

A judge should be able to find in the Conclusion exactly what you want the court to do. This is particularly important where there are cross-appeals:

> For the foregoing reasons, the District Court's order should be affirmed insofar as it enjoins enforcement of Glendale Ordinance 88162, and in all other respects the District Court's order should be reversed.

or where an appellant seeks alternative relief:

> For the foregoing reasons, Mr. Merkle's conviction should be reversed because the Superior Court admitted into evidence a "confession" coerced in violation of his Fifth Amendment rights, or, in the alternative, this matter should be

remanded to the Superior Court for resentencing because the original sentence exceeds the statutory maximum.

The **indorsement** is similar to the indorsement in a motion memorandum. (See Chapter 25.)

Every court has rules governing the contents of briefs and other submitted documents. The rules are designed to make briefs easier for judges to use, and judges understandably become exasperated when the rules are ignored. Egregious violations of court rules can result in the court's striking the brief, in financial penalties imposed on the lawyer, and even in dismissal of the appeal.

§30.2   How Judges Read Appellate Briefs

How does a judge read a brief? The answer may vary considerably from judge to judge, but the following isn't unusual:

> Usually I first read both parties' statements of the questions presented; then I read the appellant's statement of the general nature of the controversy. Then I look at his outline of argument to see what points he makes. Then I look at the appellee's outline of argument to see what he is going to do in reply. Then I go to the joint appendix to see what the trial court or the administrative agency did. Then I read the appellant's statement of the facts and the appellee's statement. Thereafter I examine the two briefs one point at a time, first the appellant's and then the appellee's, on the first point; then both briefs on the second point, etc. If the point is an obvious one, or if one side or the other seems to be wholly without strength on it, I do not spend too much time on that point in my first study. On the really contested points I study both sides, read the cases, and, if facts are critical check the record references. The briefs on the critical points are often reread and reread.[3]

Other judges might read the parts of a brief in a different sequence — perhaps reading the point headings before anything else — and a given judge might vary the sequence from case to case. But the following observations generally describe the use to which a brief is put:

First, you must write for several different readers. Depending on the court, an appeal might be decided by three to nine judges. And briefs are also read by law clerks or research attorneys who assist judges by studying the briefs and recommending decisions.

Second, briefs — like memos — aren't read from beginning to end at a single sitting. They're read in chunks, at different times, depending on the needs of

---

3. E. Barrett Prettyman, *Some Observations Concerning Appellate Advocacy,* 39 Va. L. Rev. 285, 296 (1953).

the reader. (You probably read an appliance or automobile owner's manual in pretty much the same way, and a brief is a manual for making a decision.)

Third, a brief is read for differing reasons, depending on who is reading and when, and the brief must be constructed to satisfy all of these uses without frustrating the reader. The judges will also either scan or study the brief in preparation for oral argument, and afterward they'll read it again to decide how to vote. One judge will be assigned to write the court's opinion, and while doing that will reread various portions of the brief several times, looking for the detail needed to justify and explain the decision. And all along the way, the judges will be assisted by law clerks who check up on the details of the brief while the judges focus on the broader principles. Each segment of the brief must be written to satisfy all of these purposes.

Finally, a brief must include several different places where a judge can "enter" the brief by learning what the appeal is about. A judge will go first to a part of the brief that reveals the fundamental issues in the appeal and your theory on each issue. A judge ought to be able to find that material plainly set out in four different places: the point headings and subheadings (collected in the Table of Contents); the Questions Presented; the Summary of Argument; and the Statement of the Case (read together with the Preliminary Statement). Each judge has a favorite starting place. Not only do you have no way of knowing when you write the brief where a given judge prefers to begin, but you're writing for several judges and must accommodate them all. Thus, you must draft these four components so that each can separately be a self-sufficient and self-explanatory entry point for any reader.

31 Writing the Appellate Brief

§31.1 Developing a Theory of the Appeal

An effective appellate theory has some qualities beyond those explained in Chapter 23.

First, a persuasive theory of the appeal is grounded in the procedural context and limitations on appellate review explained in this chapter. For the lawyer who wants the decision below reversed, the theory is one of *reversible error*. For the lawyer who wants an affirmance, the theory is one of the *absence of reversible error*.

Second, a persuasive appellate theory does not ignore any of the limitations on appellate review described in §29.4. An appellate court will reject a theory that would violate restrictions on the court's own power to act.

Third, a persuasive appellate theory goes beyond a technical analysis and addresses the judges' concern about a fair and just result. An appellant must show both error and injustice: "If you can convince the appellate judges that the court below is wrong as an intellectual matter, but leave them with the impression that no worthwhile damage was done, the prior result will be affirmed."[1] Although an appellee might succeed by showing either an absence of error or an absence of harm, the wiser strategy is to try to show both, if that can credibly be argued.

---

1. Edward J. Lampron, *Observations on Appellate Advocacy,* 14 N.H. B.J. (No. 3) 105, 106 (Winter 1973).

Fourth, a persuasive appellate theory is soundly grounded in public policy. When judges make or change law, they're understandably concerned about the wider consequences of what they do. How would the precedent the court will create in your case affect others in the future?

Fifth, a persuasive appellate theory asks the court to make no more law than is necessary to the lawyer's goal. Most judges don't believe that their purpose on the bench is to change society in fundamental ways, and you'll have a better chance to win if your theory asks only for those changes that are truly necessary to the result you want.

Finally, a persuasive appellant's theory raises no more than two, three, or at the very most four claims of error. A theory is damaged, not strengthened, by adding additional but weaker grounds to the two or three best ones available. The weaker grounds by their mere assertion cheapen the stronger ones and take up room in the brief that is better used to more fully develop the grounds most likely to cause reversal. Effective theory development requires the good judgment to choose the strongest grounds, the selfdiscipline to focus the court's attention on them alone, and the courage to ignore other grounds that may seem tempting but, in the end, are unlikely to persuade.

§31.2   The Process of Writing a Brief

Before you begin to write, digest the record, do a significant amount — but *not all* — of the research, and develop the basic shape of your theory.

Digesting the record is more than merely reading it: study the record to identify potential reversible error by the trial court and to find every fact that could be used either to prove error or to defend what the trial court did. Look for both kinds of facts — regardless of whom you represent. Facts favorable to your position will, of course, become ammunition. But your theory must also show the appellate court why and how the facts that favor your opponent should not become determinative.

Just as a judge doesn't read a brief from beginning to end, neither does a lawyer write it that way. The Table of Contents and Table of Authorities are always done last, after the rest of the brief has already been written. The order in which the other parts are written differs from lawyer to lawyer and from appeal to appeal because one lawyer's work habits aren't necessarily effective for someone else and because an effective lawyer adapts to the individual task at hand. Eventually, you'll settle into a range of work habits that are effective for you, and your first brief is an opportunity to begin to define yourself in that way.

To help you start, consider two very different methods of writing a brief.

Order in Which a First Draft Might Be Written	
Model I	*Model II*
1. point headings	1. Questions Presented
2. Argument	2. Statement of the Case
3. Statement of the Case	3. point headings
4. Questions Presented	4. Argument
5. rest of brief	5. rest of brief

A lawyer who uses Model I outlines the Argument by composing the point headings and subheadings and by listing under each heading the material to be covered there when the Argument is written. The logical next step is drafting the Argument itself. This lawyer might draft the Statement of the Case after the Argument on the ground that the value of specific facts isn't fully understood until after the Argument is written. The Questions Presented would be written afterward because the lawyer identifies the most determinative facts — the ones recited in the Questions — while working out the Argument and the Statement.

Conversely, a lawyer using Model II would begin the first draft by writing the Questions Presented on the theory that the other parts of the brief will be more focused if the issues are first precisely defined. A lawyer who uses this model writes the Statement of the Case next, using it to work out the details of the theory of the appeal (which the Model I lawyer does while writing the Argument). Both lawyers draft the point headings before the Argument because the Argument is easier to write in segments (which the headings create).

A lawyer with flexible work habits might use Model I in an appeal where the authority and issues are difficult and complex and Model II in a more fact-sensitive appeal. Some lawyers write the Questions Presented and the Statement of the Case (and sometimes even the Argument) simultaneously, moving back and forth from one pad to another (or from one word processing file to another).

Start writing before you finish the research. "I can't start writing yet," you might say. "I haven't found all the cases." But waiting until you find all the cases can feed procrastination. And if you don't start writing, you won't know what kind of cases you should be looking for. Researching like a vacuum cleaner is inefficient. Research takes less time and effort if you know what you're looking for. A good way to find out what you should be looking for is to start writing before you finish the research. Start writing as soon as you have enough research to know roughly what your theory will be. Because writing and thinking are inseparable, the act of writing will show you where you need more authority. When you go back into research, you'll focus more sharply on what you really need.

Before writing each subsequent draft, work on something else for a while or take a break to put the brief out of your thoughts. Come back to it in a frame of mind that enables you to put yourself in the judge's position: If you were a skeptical judge, would you be persuaded?

Start practicing oral argument while you're writing the brief. It might seem illogical to spend time on oral argument when you're up against a closer deadline with the brief. But many lawyers discover that when they talk about a complicated subject, they say surprisingly interesting and perceptive things, and they understand the subject much more deeply. Many people learn not just by reading and listening, but also by talking and doing. The real reason for practicing oral argument early is to help you write a better brief.

Suppose you disregard this advice. You submit your final draft brief, rest for a few days, and then start developing an oral argument. As you practice, you come up with some terrific wording, and you wish you could put it in the brief—but it's too late.

Set up a schedule with a series of deadlines. Start from the date on which the brief is due, and figure out how many days it will take to have the final draft typed, proofread, and photocopied. Then set a deadline on which those tasks will begin and all rewriting must stop. Figure out how long it will take to turn a second or third draft into a final draft and so on, working your way backward in time to deadlines where each draft must be finished and, for the first draft, when each component must be done. Writing a brief is a big job, and writing it in the time available requires self-discipline.

Think of brief-writing as a collection of small tasks—rather than as one huge task. A huge task can be frightening. But a lot of small tasks can be organized and then done one by one. You haven't been given one big assignment. You've been given several smaller ones: a Question Presented, a Statement of Facts, and so on. You can write all these things separately—as separate wordprocessing files, if you prefer—and then stitch them together into a single document. Even the Argument can become two or more smaller jobs. If you have two points, writing each of them is a separate task. But be careful to coordinate all these smaller tasks, so that the eventual brief becomes coherent and internally consistent.

§31.3   Handling the Standard of Review and the Procedural Posture Below

On appeal the question isn't whether the appellant should have won in the trial court, but instead whether the relevant standard of review was violated in the particular ruling appealed from. For that reason, judges become annoyed with lawyers who write and speak as though there were no standards of review. In fact, the appellant's goal is to show that the standard of review has been violated, and the appellee's goal is to show that it has not.

How much error does it take to cause reversal? That depends on the appellate court and the procedural posture below. The appellate court matters because standards of review differ somewhat from one court to another. The procedural posture matters because different standards are applied to different rulings by the court below.

Many rulings of law — such as orders dismissing pleadings, summary judgments, directed verdicts, jury instructions, and judgments notwithstanding the verdict — are evaluated on appeal "de novo." For appeals from these rulings, the appellate court doesn't use a standard that defers in any way to the trial court. Instead, the appellate court measures error simply by asking itself whether it would have done what the trial court did. The appellate court can do that because all of these rulings present pure questions *of law*. They don't require the trial judge to determine facts or exercise discretion.

Most law school appellate advocacy assignments involve de novo standards of review. If that's true of your assignment, you probably will not have much difficulty arguing within the standard properly. A de novo standard is neutral, like a pane of clear glass through which light passes without distortion. The other standards are like filters and lenses that modify the image.

If the jurisdiction permits a judge's findings of fact to be challenged on appeal, the appellate court will apply a higher standard, one that grants a certain amount of deference to what the trial court has done. In federal appeals, for example, a judge's fact-finding will be reversed only if it's "clearly erroneous."[2]

And on an issue where the lower court has *discretion,* the result below will be reversed only for an "abuse of discretion," which, again, represents a degree of deference to the trial court. A trial court has a wide range of discretion on issues of equity and on issues concerning management of the progress of the litigation, such as rulings on discovery motions and on the conduct of the trial.

The diagram on the next page illustrates how standards of review work and how they are related to procedural tests in trial courts. (Read the diagram *from the bottom up.*)

The only way to find out which standard controls a given appellate issue is to research local law in the same manner that you would research rules governing the procedural posture in a trial court. Look for authority that tells you not only what the standard is, but also what it means and how it works. Where a court mentions the standard of review in a decision, it usually does so immediately after reciting the facts and immediately before beginning the legal analysis. This is an example of the type of language you'll find:

> A dismissal for failure to state a claim pursuant to Fed. R. Civ. P. 12 is a ruling on a question of law and as such is reviewed de novo. [Citation omitted.] Review is limited to the contents of the complaint.[3]

---

2. *See, e.g.,* Rule 52(a) of the Federal Rules of Civil Procedure.
3. *Kruso v. International Tel. & Tel. Corp.,* 872 F.2d 1416, 1421 (9th Cir. 1989).

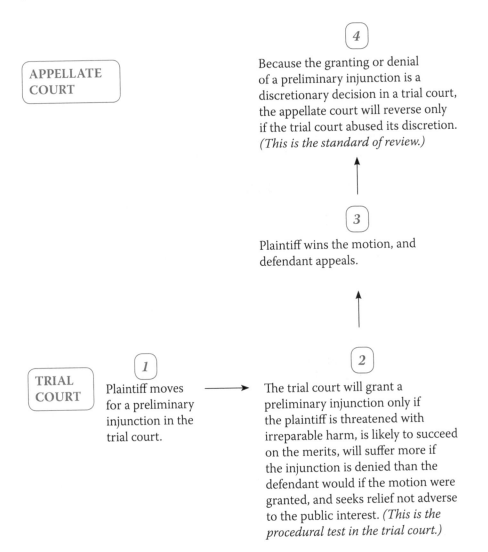

> APPELLATE
> COURT

4

Because the granting or denial
of a preliminary injunction is a
discretionary decision in a trial court,
the appellate court will reverse only
if the trial court abused its discretion.
(This is the standard of review.)

3

Plaintiff wins the motion, and
defendant appeals.

> TRIAL
> COURT

1

Plaintiff moves
for a preliminary
injunction in the
trial court.

2

The trial court will grant a
preliminary injunction only if
the plaintiff is threatened with
irreparable harm, is likely to succeed
on the merits, will suffer more if
the injunction is denied than the
defendant would if the motion were
granted, and seeks relief not adverse
to the public interest. *(This is the
procedural test in the trial court.)*

Here we learn what the standard is ("de novo"), and we learn a little — but certainly not everything — about how the standard operates ("Review is limited to the contents of the complaint"). Occasionally, a court will tell you much more about how the standard is used:

> "In reviewing the [National Labor Relations] Board's decision, we must scrutinize the entire record, 'including the evidence opposed to the Board's view from which conflicting inferences reasonably could be drawn.'" [Citation omitted.] Nevertheless, this court will defer to the Board's judgment and the Board's factual findings shall be conclusive if supported by substantial evidence on the record considered as a whole. [Citation omitted.] This "court may not substitute its judgment for that of the Board when the choice is 'between two fairly

conflicting views, even though the court would justifiably have made a different choice had the matter been before it *de novo.'*" [Citation omitted.] We shall also defer to the Board's inferences in areas where the Board is considered to have "specialized evidence and expertise." [Citation omitted.][4]

And the court might explain at the same time both the standard of review and the rules governing the procedural posture in the trial court:

> The grant or denial of a motion for preliminary injunction is a decision within the discretion of the trial court. [Citation omitted.] Appellate review . . . is very narrow. [Citation omitted.] Accordingly, a district court's decision will be reversed only where there is a clear abuse of discretion. [Citation omitted.] That discretion is guided by four requirements for preliminary injunctive relief: (1) a substantial likelihood that the movants will ultimately prevail on the merits; (2) that they will suffer irreparable injury if the injunction is not issued; (3) that the threatened injury to the movants outweighs the potential harm to the opposing party and (4) that the injunction, if issued, will not be adverse to the public interest. [Citation omitted.][5]

Occasionally, you'll come across an issue that's subject to a bifurcated or even (as in the example below) a trifurcated standard of review. Each portion of this test for laches has a different standard of review:

> Our standard of review on the laches issue has various components. We review factual findings such as length of delay and prejudice under the clearly erroneous standard; we review the district court's balancing of the equities for abuse of discretion; and our review of legal precepts applied by the district court in determining that the delay was excusable is plenary. [Citation omitted.][6]

How do you handle the standard of review in a brief? Do three things:

First, set out the relevant standard of review at or near the beginning of the Argument section of the brief (or, if you have more than one point, each point's standard of review can be set out shortly after the point heading).[7] While doing so, identify the procedural posture below and invoke the procedural test that governs it. And—if it can be done succinctly—tell the court how the standard was violated (if you are the appellant) or how it was not (if you are the appellee). For example, from an appellant's brief:

---

4. *NLRB v. Emsing's Supermarket, Inc.,* 872 F.2d 1279, 1283-84 (7th Cir. 1989).
5. *Haitian Refugee Center, Inc. v. Nelson,* 872 F.2d 1555, 1561-62 (11th Cir. 1989).
6. *Bermuda Express, N.V. v. M/V Litsa,* 872 F.2d 554, 557 (3d Cir. 1989).
7. This is required in federal appeals and in several states. For example, see Fed. R. App. P. 28(a)(9)(B) (The appellant's argument "must contain . . . for each issue a concise statement of the applicable standard of review (which may appear in the discussion of the issue or under a separate heading placed before the discussion of the issues)."). Rule 28(b) permits the appellee to omit this statement "unless the appellee is dissatisfied with the statement of the appellant."

> This is an appeal from a summary judgment, which is reviewed de novo in this court. [Citation omitted.] Summary judgment should occur only where there is no genuine issue as to any material fact and the movant is entitled to judgment as a matter of law. [Citation omitted.] In this case, the movant was not entitled to judgment as a matter of law.

This passage tells us that the standard is de novo, and that the appellant's theory of error is that the second element of the test for summary judgment wasn't satisfied. (The writer doesn't say that there was a genuine dispute as to a material fact; thus only one element of the summary judgment test is at issue.)

A good place to put this material is between a point heading and the first subheading. Cite to authority to prove the procedural rule that governed the trial court and the standard of review on appeal. Unless the law is unclear, a conclusory proof is usually sufficient because these rules are the type with which an appellate court would be routinely familiar. (Notice how this is handled in the Appendix G and H briefs.)

Second, argue through the standard of review. If, for example, you're appealing from a decision committed to a trial court's discretion, show throughout rule application (Chapter 11) that the trial court abused its discretion. If you are the appellee in such a case, show the opposite. It's not enough merely to state the standard of review at the beginning and then ignore it for the rest of the Argument. Instead, use it and corollary rules wherever they are relevant, weaving the substantive and procedural law together to show either error (if you seek reversal) or the absence of it (if you urge affirmance).

A de novo standard need not be referred to throughout the Argument unless the very neutrality of the de novo standard helps your case. Because the de novo standard grants no deference at all to the trial court, arguments can be based entirely on the substantive law once the court has been told that a de novo standard is in effect.

Third, throughout the brief (and in oral argument), describe the facts just as they were in the procedural posture in the trial court. (That's because the standard of review is geared to the procedural posture below.) If the appeal is from the dismissal of a complaint, for example, describe the facts as allegations ("the complaint alleges that the defendant struck the plaintiff"). Describe them as evidence ("Smith testified that the defendant struck the plaintiff") if the appeal is from a judgment resulting from a motion challenging the quality of evidence. But if the facts are undisputed, describe the facts as truth ("it is undisputed that the defendant struck the plaintiff").

If you are unsure of how to do any of these things, take a look at several opinions in which the court for which you are writing has used the same standard of review in appeals from the same procedural posture involved in your case. Chances are that you'll see them invoked near the beginning of the opinion and used at logically appropriate spots thereafter. Look for a definition of the standard, and try to learn its relationship to other procedural rules and get a feel for the court's expectations about how the standard should be used.

§31.4 Making Policy Arguments in an Appellate Brief

Policy matters in an appellate court for two reasons. First, when a court enforces a rule of law, it tries to do so in a way that accomplishes the policy behind the rule. In any court — trial or appellate — your odds of winning increase if you can show that the decision you want would achieve important public goals.

Second, a substantial part of an appellate court's work is clarifying ambiguous law and making new law. The higher up you go in the appellate system, the more that's true. When a court makes law in this way, it tries to do so consistently with policies that are already accepted in the law or should be.

When you appear before a court in a law-making case, judges naturally ask questions like this: What rule of law would a decision in your favor stand for (remembering that it would become binding precedent)? In what words would that rule be most accurately expressed? If the court does as you request, how would the law in the future treat facts that are similar to — but not exactly the same as — yours? What would be the practical effects in the courts, in the economy, and in society as a whole? Why is the rule you advocate better than the one your adversary urges?

In your brief, make policy arguments that would answer these questions persuasively. Here's how to do it:

1. Begin by identifying one or more public policies that a decision in your favor would further. Tell the court exactly which policy or policies you want the court to be guided by.
2. Then persuade the court that the policy or policies you've identified are valuable. Your adversary will urge competing policies. Show that yours are more important. But it's not enough just to say yours are worth more; prove it with argument.
3. Finally, show exactly how a decision in your favor will further the policy or policies you've identified. Don't assume that the court will understand how. Explain it specifically.

Policy arguments are much stronger if supported by authority. If the policy you urge has already been recognized by the courts in other cases, cite and explain those cases. If the legislature has adopted the policy in enacting statutes that aren't directly related to your case, cite those statutes and explain how they reflect the policy you're urging. If you lack legal authority, cite and explain nonlegal sources that show a genuine public need. For example, if you argue that the courts should adopt strict tort rules assigning liability for contamination with industrial chemicals, you can cite scientific studies showing the presence of PCB's and other toxic chemicals in the food supply.

When a court is being asked to clarify the interpretation of a statute, the court isn't free to attach to the statute any policy the judges like. Instead, the court must use the policy the legislature adopted when it enacted the statute. Sometimes that policy is expressed in the statute or the legislative history. If not, the court, with your assistance, must figure out what policy the legislature probably adopted.

32 Questions Presented

§32.1 Introduction

A Question Presented has several purposes. First, it defines the legal issue before the court. Second, it clarifies the relief the court is being asked to grant. And third, within limits, it persuades by framing the issue from your client's point of view. In some courts, the Questions Presented section of a brief is called a Statement of Issues. We say Question Presented in this chapter because it is the more commonly used term. Statement of Issues appears in the briefs in Appendices G and H because that is the term used in the court in which those briefs were filed. The two terms mean the same thing. A Question Presented is an appellate Issue. You should use the term acceptable in the court where your brief will be filed.

A Question Presented is made up of (1) an explicit or implicit reference to the controlling rule of law, (2) a precise legal question, and (3) a short list of the determinative facts that arguably affect the outcome:

> Has the manufacturer of an acoustical keyboard breached the implied warranty of fitness for a particular purpose where the purchaser was injured when the keyboard exploded the first time it was plugged in?

Here the controlling rule is the implied warranty of fitness for a particular purpose found in § 2-315 of the Uniform Commercial Code. The legal question is whether a keyboard manufacturer is liable. The critical fact is that the keyboard exploded the first time the purchaser plugged it in. All this adds up to the question "presented" by the situation.

The Question Presented above is persuasive as well as informative. The reader feels immediately curious about what happened as well as sympathy for the plaintiff. Why would a manufacturer *not* be liable in these circumstances?

Under § 2-315, if the manufacturer had reason to know of any particular purpose for which purchasers like the plaintiff buy its keyboards, and if the plaintiff relied on the manufacturer's skill or judgment, a court will hold that the manufacturer impliedly warrantied that the keyboard was fit for that purpose. What if the plaintiff is a musician who performs in front of live audiences with dramatic fire and water stage effects? What if the manufacturer had never heard of the plaintiff and had also never heard of anybody using one of its keyboards that way? The manufacturer's Question Presented might read something like this:

> Should this Court refuse to find an implied warranty of fitness for a particular purpose where the manufacturer did not know that the plaintiff musician intended to expose the keyboard to water as part of his stage performances?

Notice how this Question Presented is different even though it's in the same case. It contains the controlling law and legal question but a different and arguably more determinative fact. Reading these Questions together, it appears the case is likely to turn on what the manufacturer knew at the time of sale.

§32.2 Four Ways of Structuring a Question Presented

A Question Presented can be structured in four different ways. Each of them works better in some situations than in others.

Beginning with the verb (or part of the verb):   The following Questions Presented begin like the kind of question you're used to asking every day:

> Has the manufacturer of an acoustical keyboard breached the implied warranty of fitness for a particular purpose where the purchaser was injured when the keyboard exploded the first time it was plugged in?

> Should this Court refuse to imply a warranty of fitness for a particular purpose where the seller did not know that the plaintiff musician intended to expose the keyboard to water as part of his stage performances?

The question can begin with whatever verb is most appropriate to the issue:

> Does the First Amendment allow . . . ?

> Did the defendant newspaper give publicity to private facts . . . ?

Beginning with "Under": These Questions refer to the controlling rule before asking how it applies to the determinative facts:

> Under § 403 of the Traffic Code, is a driver guilty of failure to stop at a stop sign where the stop sign was hidden behind tree branches that the county highway department had failed to prune?

This structure works especially well with statutory issues. But it doesn't work well when the controlling rule of law is more widely known by its name ("the implied warranty of fitness for a particular purpose") than by its statutory section number ("§ 2-315"). Compare these:

> Under § 2-315 of the Maryland Commercial Code, is the manufacturer of an acoustical keyboard liable to a purchaser who was injured when the keyboard exploded the first time it was plugged in?

> Has the manufacturer of an acoustical keyboard breached the implied warranty of fitness for a particular purpose where the purchaser was injured when the keyboard exploded the first time it was plugged in?

Most judges know about the implied warranty of fitness for a particular purpose. But very few of them can remember its section number.

Beginning with "Whether": A Question Presented can begin with the word *Whether*, even though the result isn't a grammatically complete sentence:

> Whether the manufacturer of an acoustical keyboard breached the implied warranty of fitness for a particular purpose where the purchaser was injured when the keyboard exploded the first time it was plugged in?

This structure is used by many lawyers — and in some states by most lawyers. But it's often criticized. If the same word begins most of the Questions a judge reads, few of those Questions will seem memorable. *Whether*-type Questions, however, are widely used, and you should structure your Questions this way if preferred by your teacher or supervisor.

Reciting the determinative facts in complete sentences and then stating the issue, as a question, in a separate sentence: In some cases, the determinative facts are so complex that they can't be reduced to a short list. That tends to happen where a set of determinative facts raises several independent issues, of where the facts themselves are difficult to describe concisely. In such cases, lawyers sometimes use a different format, expressing the determinative facts in complete sentences and then posing the issue in a final sentence. Think of this as the multiple sentences format. For example:

This case involves the diversion of water from the Three Pines Wilderness Area. Plaintiff American Environmental Association was formed for the purpose of preserving wilderness areas like Three Pines. Some of its members who live nearby use Three Pines for weekend recreation while others visit it on annual camping trips. Like other visitors, they depend on a plentiful supply of water within the wilderness area. The issue on this appeal is whether the Association has standing to sue to enjoin the existing and threatened diversions.[1]

For comparison, here's the same issue expressed in a single sentence, using the beginning-with-the-verb format:

Does the American Environmental Association have standing to sue to enjoin existing and threatened diversions of water from the Three Pines Wilderness Area where the Association was formed for the purpose of preserving wilderness areas like Three Pines; some of its members who live nearby use Three Pines for weekend recreation while others visit it on annual camping trips; and, like other visitors, they depend on a plentiful supply of water within the wilderness area.

Which did you find easier to read?

Normally you should use one of the other formats. Use this one — the multiple-sentences format — only when the other formats produce a sentence so complicated that a reader has to read it two or three times to understand it.

§32.3   Writing an Effective Question Presented

First, write out the basic legal issue ("Is a manufacturer liable?" "Did police violate the Fourth Amendment?" "Does Ohio recognize a cause of action for . . .?" "Under § 403 of the Traffic Code, . . .?").

Second, make a list of the most determinative facts, omitting those that are merely explanatory or coincidental (see Chapter 10, §10.2). While writing and rewriting your motion memo or brief, you'll tinker with this list by adding or subtracting facts as you come to understand the issue better, and you'll gradually refine the list's wording as you learn the possibilities and limitations of each fact. But you can't begin to write a Question Presented without a list of determinative facts.

Third, choose a structure. Be prepared to change it later if it doesn't work out. Fill out the structure by combining the most determinative facts with the legal issue to form a single sentence.

Finally, review your Question Presented for effectiveness, using the criteria in the next section of this chapter. You might need to do this several times.

---

1. Girvan Peck, *Writing Persuasive Briefs* 102–03 (1984).

Given its complexity and conciseness, the Question Presented is often the last part of a document to reach its final form.

§32.4   How to Evaluate Your Questions Presented for Persuasiveness

To figure out whether you've written an effective Question Presented, ask yourself the following questions.

| 32-A | **Have you kept the Question concise?**   Trim the Question so that it contains as concise a summary of the law, the legal issue, and the determinative facts as possible. Your reader should be able to digest it quickly on the first read.

| 32-B | **Have you referred to or implied the controlling law and legal issue?**   The controlling law can be explicit or implicit, and the specificity required varies. For example, in a case involving the Fourth Amendment alone, it might be adequate to say, "Did the officers have reasonable, articulable suspicion to stop the suspect when . . . ?" But if the case involves a number of unrelated issues it might be necessary to say, "Did the officers have reasonable, articulable suspicion under the Fourth Amendment to the U.S. Constitution to stop the suspect when . . . ?"

| 32-C | **Have you listed the facts in a way the reader can easily understand?**   Facts that don't fit into the inquiry can be attached at the end of the Question in clauses that begin with "where" or "when." This example is from a different kind of acoustical keyboard case:

> Is the manufacturer of an acoustical keyboard absolved of liability under an implied warranty of fitness for a particular purpose where an ordinary consumer bought it in pieces from a street vendor and attempted to reassemble it himself even though the words "Do Not Open or Attempt to Repair This Product" were engraved on the outside?

The legal issue — the inquiry — is best placed near the beginning of a Question Presented because a list of determinative facts makes little sense until the reader knows the issue to which the facts relate. The following, for example, are not easy to understand:

> *Facts before inquiry:*   Where an ordinary consumer bought an acoustical keyboard in pieces from a street vendor and attempted to reassemble it himself even though the words "Do Not Open or Attempt to Repair This

Product" were engraved on the outside, is the manufacturer absolved of liability under an implied warranty of fitness for a particular purpose?

Facts and inquiry intermingled: Is the manufacturer of an acoustical keyboard, which was bought from a street vendor by an ordinary consumer who attempted to reassemble it himself even though the words "Do Not Open or Attempt to Repair This Product" were engraved on the outside, absolved of liability under an implied warranty of fitness for a particular purpose?

32-D   **Have you stated the Question from your point of view suggesting a positive answer?**   Stating the Question from your point of view means stating it in a way that favors your client in both a legal sense and an emotional sense. For example, a state prosecutor would want to admit incriminating evidence and convict the defendant, but the defendant would want to exclude illegally obtained evidence and be acquitted. Stating the question so that it elicits a "yes" answer helps you state it from your point of view and is less confusing to the reader.

At the beginning of this chapter, the two exploding keyboard Questions are completely different. But both ask a question to be answered in the affirmative:

Has the manufacturer of an acoustical keyboard breached . . . ?

Should this Court refuse to find . . . ?

Because judges are inclined to think you want a positive response to your Question, avoid drafting Questions where the answer you want is "no." That will only confuse your reader.

Avoid using double negatives:

Was the officer's conduct not unreasonable when . . . ?

Is a manufacturer not liable where it does not . . . ?

Double negatives are almost always confusing. They're very common in first drafts as you work with typical legal phrasing but can easily be removed to improve clarity and readability:

Was the officer's conduct reasonable when . . . ?

Is a manufacturer absolved of liability where it . . . ?

32-E   **Have you avoided begging the question?**   Don't ask a question in which the "facts" are really assumed conclusions of law. For example, under the Fourth Amendment to the U.S. Constitution, evidence is admissible in a criminal trial if the police seized it while stopping a defendant based on reasonable and articulable suspicion. The case law defines reasonable and articulable suspicion as reason to know the defendant was about to engage in criminal activity. This Question Presented begs the question:

> Did the officer have reasonable and articulable suspicion to stop the defendant when the officer had reason to believe the defendant was about to engage in criminal activity?

The answer to this Question *must* be yes, but that's because a reason to believe the defendant was about to engage in criminal activity is *always* reasonable and articulable suspicion. Thus, "the officer had reason to believe the defendant was about to engage in criminal activity" is a conclusion of law masquerading as a fact.

Remove the conclusion of law and replace it with real facts that suggest the reasonableness of the officer's suspicion. Let the facts speak for themselves:

> Did the officer have reasonable and articulable suspicion to stop the defendant when the defendant paced in front of a closed liquor store for 20 minutes, kept checking his cell phone, and kept one hand in his coat pocket at all times?

[32-F] **Have you presented the law in a balanced way?** When phrasing the legal question, you can state it from your point of view, but you can't distort the law. For example, several factors are used to determine whether a defendant was in custody when he was interrogated. The following Question doesn't present the issue before the court in a balanced way:

> Did the trial court err in excluding the defendant's confession on the ground that he was in custody when the defendant was repeatedly told he was free to leave the interrogation?

The writer has included the one fact most favorable to the prosecution in a way that suggests the only factor relevant to the custody determination is what the police told the defendant. But that's a distortion of the law. The Question below accurately conveys the complexity of the issue before the court:

> Did the trial court err in excluding the defendant's confession on the ground that he was in custody when the defendant was questioned for 30 minutes in a police interview room by a uniformed, unarmed officer but repeatedly told he was free to leave the interrogation?

Although some of these facts are unfavorable from the prosecutor's perspective, this is a more honest representation of the Question Presented. It also gives the prosecutor a chance to characterize the unfavorable facts and work them into the theory of the case.

32-G | **Have you included all determinative facts without exaggerating them?** Include all facts likely to be determinative, both favorable and unfavorable. Don't exaggerate or stretch the facts to your benefit. Does the following Question sound like an exaggeration of the facts?

> Is it in the best interest of a child to terminate her mother's parental rights when the mother barely knows her own daughter?

It may sound fair, but once you learn that the mother is in a rehabilitation hospital following a severe car accident and has been unable to communicate with her daughter for three months, it no longer seems accurate to say she "barely knows her."

32-H | **Do you sound strident or overly dramatic, risking your credibility?** Lawyers should be zealous advocates. But don't sound strident, use belligerent language, or write sarcastically. Any of these will work against you. In the case of the exploding keyboard and the performing musician:

> How could a manufacturer of an acoustical keyboard possibly be liable for such minimal injury to the plaintiff "musician," who can hardly expect to have been known to the manufacturer, where the manufacturer clearly had no idea that the plaintiff would expose the keyboard to water?

If the case were that one-sided, the plaintiff's lawyer would have settled it long ago. Adverbs like "possibly," "hardly," and "clearly" don't increase the persuasiveness of the Question. They tend to have the opposite effect. Describing the plaintiff's injury as "minimal" sounds disrespectful, and there's no need for the defendant to characterize the harm. Finally, using quotation marks to suggest the plaintiff isn't much of a musician is unprofessional. A simpler, less emotionally charged Question is far more effective.

32-I | **Have you referred to the parties in a clear way?** The least confusing references are generic ("a malpractice insurer," "a prisoner," "an employee," "a manufacturer," etc.).

Procedural designations such as "Appellant" and "Appellee" are often confusing (and several courts have rules that prohibit using them). The same is true of "plaintiff" and "defendant" unless the issue is really procedural or the Question itself makes clear what kind of plaintiff and what kind of defendant are involved. Although most uses of "plaintiff" and "defendant" are confusing, this isn't:

> Has a defendant been properly served when the summons was handed to him in a plain manila envelope?

A lawsuit begins when a defendant is served with a summons. This is a procedural issue, which you've probably studied in the course on Civil Procedure. What matters is the defendant's role *as a defendant.*

In a criminal case it's never confusing to refer to one party as the "defendant." The other party is always the prosecution, although different terms are used in different jurisdictions: "the State," "the People," or (in federal courts) "the government." A Question Presented might use one of those terms. Or if the issue is whether a prosecutor personally behaved properly, it might refer to the prosecutor: "the U.S. Attorney," for example.

Although a busy judge can be confused when the parties are referred to by name only, it may be tactically wise to try to personalize a party beset by some institutional opponent, if the context will make clear who is who.

Exercise
G.G. v. Gloucester County School Board

Appendices G and H contain briefs in *G.G. v. Gloucester County School Board,* filed in the U.S. Court of Appeals for the Fourth Circuit. Before doing this exercise, go to those appendices and read each brief's Statement of the Case.

The defendant School Board lost in the Fourth Circuit and filed a petition for certiorari in the U.S. Supreme Court. A petition for certiorari essentially asks for permission to appeal to the Supreme Court. About 7,000 to 8,000 certiorari petitions are filed each year, but the Court grants only about 80 of them.[2]

In this exercise are the Statements of Issues or Questions Presented from

1. the plaintiff G.G.'s Fourth Circuit brief (Appendix G),
2. the defendant School Board's Fourth Circuit brief (Appendix H),
3. the School Board's certiorari petition in the Supreme Court, and
4. G.G.'s brief in opposition to the certiorari petition in the Supreme Court.

(On this book's website are the full certiorari petition and the brief in opposition as well as other court filings and opinions in the case.)

The Fourth Circuit briefs use the term *Statement of Issues*. The Supreme Court submissions use the term *Questions Presented*. The two terms mean the same thing. Use the term required by or customary in the court where you will file your brief.

Evaluate the following Statements of Issues and the Questions Presented. For each one, what are its strengths and weaknesses?

1.   Plaintiff G.G.'s Fourth Circuit brief (Appendix G) —

---

2. These statistics are from the Supreme Court's website: https://www.supremecourt.gov/faq.aspx#faqgi9.

STATEMENT OF ISSUES

1. Should G. be granted a preliminary injunction to allow him to resume using the boys' restrooms during the pendency of the case?
2. Should the court's dismissal of the Title IX claim be reversed?

2.   Defendant School Board's Fourth Circuit brief (Appendix H) —

STATEMENT OF ISSUES

1. Whether the Fourteenth Amendment or Title IX requires the School Board to permit G.G., who was born and remains anatomically a female, to use the boys' restroom because G.G. identifies as a boy.
2. Should this Court affirm the District Court's denial of G.G.'s Motion for Preliminary Injunction?

3.   The School Board's certiorari petition in the Supreme Court —

(The Supreme Court appeal focused on a deference issue under *Auer v. Robbins,* 519 U.S. 452 (1997), which isn't included in the excerpts in Appendices G and H.)

QUESTIONS PRESENTED

Title IX prohibits discrimination "on the basis of sex," 20 U.S.C. § 1681(a), while its implementing regulation permits "separate toilet, locker rooms, and shower facilities on the basis of sex," if the facilities are "comparable" for students of both sexes, 34 C.F.R. § 106.33. In this case, a Department of Education official opined in an unpublished letter that Title IX's prohibition of "sex" discrimination "include[s] gender identity," and that a funding recipient providing sex-separated facilities under the regulation "must generally treat transgender students consistent with their gender identity." App. 128a, 100a. The Fourth Circuit afforded this letter "controlling" deference under the doctrine of *Auer v. Robbins,* 519 U.S. 452 (1997). On remand the district court entered a preliminary injunction requiring the petitioner school board to allow respondent — who was born a girl but identifies as a boy — to use the boys' restrooms at school.

The questions presented are:

1. Should this Court retain the *Auer* doctrine despite the objections of multiple Justices who have recently urged that it be reconsidered and overruled?
2. If *Auer* is retained, should deference extend to an unpublished agency letter that, among other things, does not carry the force of law and was adopted in the context of the very dispute in which deference is sought?
3. With or without deference to the agency, should the Department's specific interpretation of Title IX and 34 C.F.R. § 106.33 be given effect?

4. G.G.'s brief in opposition to the certiorari petition in the Supreme Court —

QUESTIONS PRESENTED

1. Whether, in the absence of any "special justification," this Court should depart from stare decisis and overturn long-standing principles of administrative law embodied in *Auer v. Robbins*, 519 U.S. 452 (1997), and similar precedent dating back to 1945?
2. Whether *Auer* deference applies to an agency's interpretation of its own regulation when (a) that interpretation is articulated in an opinion letter, a statement of interest and an amicus brief, and (b) the interpretation is not a post hoc justification to defend an agency decision under attack?
3. Whether a school board policy that categorically prohibits transgender students from using restrooms consistent with their gender identity, effectively excluding them from using the common restrooms used by other students, violates Title IX and its implementing regulations?

INTO THE
COURTROOM

33 Oral Argument

§33.1 Your Three Goals at Oral Argument

First, you want to engage the judges' attention by getting them *interested* in your case and *motivated* to rule in your favor. They'll hear many other arguments on the same day, and they'll read many other briefs in the week they read yours. They'll forget your theory of the appeal unless you touch their natural desire to do the right thing.

Second, you want to focus the judges' attention on *the few aspects of your case that are most determinative:* the one or two issues that are fundamental, the facts that are most prominent in your theory, the rule or rules for which a decision in your favor would become precedent, and the policy considerations that most compel the result for which you argue. Judges expect oral argument to help them find the heart of the dispute. That's because oral argument works best when it concentrates on the few large ideas that are most relevant, while details are best left to the briefs.

Third, you want *access to the court's thinking.* Ideally, you want to discover each doubt the judges have about your theory and every confusion they entertain about any part of your case—all so you can satisfy doubt and clear up confusion. And you want to learn which issues the judges think are most important: if those are profitable issues for you, you can concentrate on them, and if they're the wrong issues, you can try to persuade the court of that. The only way you can get access to the court's thinking is through the questions you're asked when the judges interrupt you. In fact, you go to court *for the express purpose of being interrupted* because the most effective thing you can do in oral argument is to persuade through your answers to the judges' questions. And when the judges interrupt, they usually aren't trying to debate with you. For the most part, they're telling you what troubles them and asking you to help them make the decision.

§33.2   Structure of an Oral Argument

The appellant typically begins by reminding the court of the nature of the case, the facts most essential to the appellant's theory, the procedural history, and the issue before the court. This is a reasonably effective opening:

Good morning, Your Honors. I'm Allison Korngold, representing Andrea Pafko, the appellant here and the defendant below. This is an appeal from a conviction for receiving stolen property.

> An alternate start — preferred in some courts — would be "May it please the court. I am . . . ."

At trial, the only evidence the State could produce involving Ms. Pafko was that she picked up a satchel that had been left in a street, next to a curb, and that she opened it, found $7,150, took it home, and still had it in her apartment the next day when two police officer knocked on her door, saying she had been seen carrying a satchel.

> The lawyer begins by telling the client's story. If the judges have read the briefs thoroughly and know the story, they might cut her off and start asking questions. But a compelling story, well told, can persuade, and the lawyer will tell this one unless she is interrupted with questions.

About an hour before Ms. Pafko found the satchel, a bank had been robbed a block away. Bank tellers testified that the robbers left with $7,150 in a satchel identical to the one Ms. Pafko found. They also testified that she was not one of the robbers.

The State produced no evidence that Ms. Pafko knew about the bank robbery or had any other reason to think the money had been stolen.

After the State rested, Ms. Pafko's trial lawyer moved to for a directed verdict of acquittal on the ground that the State had produced no evidence of one of the elements of the crime. If the state has no evidence of one of the elements, a trial court must grant that motion because a conviction would be based on jury speculation rather than proof beyond a reasonable doubt.

But the trial judge denied the motion, and Ms. Pafko was convicted.

An element of receiving stolen property is that, at the moment the defendant obtained the property, she must have known that it had been stolen or know of circumstances that would lead a reasonable person to believe that it must have been stolen.

Finding $7,150 in a satchel would not alone compel a reasonable person to believe that the money had been stolen. It was in the street leaning against the curb, where someone getting into a car could have dropped it. There was no evidence that Ms. Pafko had any reason to believe that that person wasn't the money's owner.

The case law . . . .

The story has ended, and the lawyer mentions one of the rules that she argues was violated by the trial court.

This is the trial court decision that the lawyer wants reversed.

Now the lawyer begins explaining the law and how it justifies reversal.

You don't need to sequence exactly as here. For example, it might be more effective in another case to state the procedural history or the issue, or both, before the facts. But the facts are what make this opening compelling, and they usually provide the energy in a compelling start. One of the leading appellate advocates of the twentieth century said that "in an appellate court the statement of the facts is not merely a part of the argument, it is more often than not the argument itself. A case well stated is a case far more than half argued."[1] Some courts, however, study the briefs so carefully before argument that they consider a fact recitation to be a waste of time, and in those courts lawyers are discouraged — either informally or through the courts' rules — from opening with the facts.

If you represent the appellee, your opening should be designed to show the court vividly how your theory differs from the appellant's:

---

1. John W. Davis, *The Argument of an Appeal*, 26 A.B.A. J. 895, 896 (1940).

If the court please, I'm Allan Kuusinen, for the State.

The evidence shows that the defendant found an amount of money so large that the person who lost it would have returned as fast as possible to retrieve it from the place where it was lost — unless that person was afraid to return. The true owner would have nothing to fear. But a person who stole the money might. Without speculating, a jury could have reasoned this way, which justified the trial court's denial of the defendant's motion for a directed verdict.

Except in the opening, an appellee's argument doesn't differ much structurally from an appellant's. Although some of what an appellee says grows out of notes taken while the appellant argues, most of an appellee's argument can be planned in advance. From the appellant's brief, the appellee knows before argument the theory the appellant will advance.

Unless the bench is "cold,"[2] the judges' questions may so occupy you that you'll be surprised to find that your time is about to or already has run out. Your time is finished when the chief or presiding judge, in a firm tone, says "Thank you." When your time has expired, conclude with a brief sentence in which you specify the relief you seek ("Therefore, the judgment below should be affirmed because . . ."). If you're in the midst of answering a question when your time runs out, ask for permission to finish the answer and, if permitted, finish quickly and concisely. If, on the other hand, the judges continue to ask you questions after your time expires, answer them fully. The court has impliedly enlarged your time. If you complete your argument before your time expires, conclude anyway, pause to see whether you'll be asked further questions, and, if not, sit down. Whatever the situation, you can signal your intent to finish by using an introductory phrase such as "In conclusion, . . ."

If the appellant has reserved one or two minutes for rebuttal,[3] the appellant can use that time, after the appellee's argument, in order to reply. A court considers its time wasted if an appellant uses rebuttal to reiterate arguments already made or to raise new arguments for the first time. Rebuttal should be used instead to correct significantly inaccurate or misleadingly incomplete statements made by the appellee, and preferably not more than one or two of those. If the appellee's misstatements are trivial, an appellant looks petty correcting them. If it turns out that there's no need for rebuttal, an appellant makes a confident impression by waiving it. A rebuttal ends with a sentence reminding the court of the relief sought.

---

2. A "hot" bench is one that erupts with questions. A "cold" bench is one that listens impassively.

3. The time reserved is subtracted from the time allowed for the appellant's main argument. You can reserve time by telling the court after you introduce yourself in the opening to your main argument.

§33.3   Questions from the Bench

Some questions are neutral requests for information about the record, the law, the procedural posture, or the theory of the appeal. Some are challenges, asking you how you would overcome an adverse policy or equity argument or a contrary interpretation of authority or the record. Some are expressed as concerns: the judge asks how a particular problem in the case can be resolved. Some questions are openly friendly, usually asking the lawyer to focus on an aspect of the case that the judge believes to be particularly persuasive. And some questions are neutral prompts, suggesting that whatever you're discussing at the time can be dispensed with in favor of more relevant material. Some questions are asked because the answer is crucial to the judge's thinking. Others grow out of the spontaneity of the moment, and the answer may have little or no impact on the decision.

When you hear a question, listen to it carefully, and don't be afraid to pause for a moment to think before answering. Never interrupt a question. Try to figure out the question's purpose and exactly what's troubling the judge. Then craft your answer to satisfy the skepticism or curiosity implied by the question. In the answer, don't say too little or too much. It's a mistake to give a one-sentence reply to a question that a judge plainly considers to be the crux of the case, but it is also a mistake to spend three minutes resolving a straightforward request for simple information.

Don't leap to big assumptions about a judge's predispositions from the questions the judge asks. A neutral judge might ask challenging questions just to see whether your theory will hold up. A friendly judge might ask challenging questions to cause you to argue matters that the judge believes might persuade others on the bench. And an adverse judge might ask friendly or neutral questions out of politeness and a sense of fairness.

In any event, answer the question on the spot. Don't promise to get back to it later at a place in your outline where you had already planned to discuss the subject. Other questions may prevent you from getting that far. And the answer will be most persuasive immediately after the question is asked. Even if a judge asks you to discuss an entire issue earlier than you had planned, do it and rearrange the order of your presentation to accommodate the judge's needs. Later, when you reach the spot where you had intended to discuss the issue, simply skip what you've already covered.[4]

In answering, state your conclusion first and your reasoning second. As you've seen in so many ways, the law-trained mind most easily understands

---

4. In many schools, students are assigned to coauthor briefs, usually in teams of two, and to split the oral argument. If your school follows this practice, you may be asked questions about material that your colleague intends to argue. Do not respond by saying that your colleague will answer the question. Judges resent that, and you should know enough of the other student's material to be able to give at least a summary answer. If you are arguing first, your colleague can, during her or his allotted time, elaborate on your summary.

discourse that lays out a conclusion before proving it. If you get wrapped up in a lot of preliminary material before you state a conclusion, the conclusion can be obscured or even lost.

Answer the question you are asked, not one you would rather have been asked. The only way you can persuade is by facing directly the problems raised by the question and by showing the judge why those problems should not prevent a decision in your favor. *In every fully litigated case, each side has points of weakness.* If your side of the case didn't have them, your adversary would have given up long ago. Where a judge has truly identified a point of weakness, face it and give a realistic counter-argument. Here are three examples:

> I agree, Your Honor, that in that hypothetical the police would have had probable cause, but the facts of the hypothetical are not the facts of this case. . . .

> Yes, *Soares* did so hold, but later rulings of this court have impliedly undermined *Soares* . . . .

> Certainly, the record does reflect two isolated events that might be construed as evidence of good faith by the defendant, but the record also includes many, many events, stretching over several years, that show exactly the opposite. . . .

Hedging and lack of candor harm your credibility. If you can project an aura of honesty and forthrightness, your arguments will be all the more persuasive.

During the answer, build a bridge to the rest of your argument. If the question causes you to make part of your planned argument out of order, you can return to your argument at a point that's logically related to the answer. If the answer covers material that you hadn't planned to speak about, use the answer to lead back to your planned argument. If you do this smoothly, it may be hard for a listener to tell when the answer has ended and you return to your planned presentation. Bridge-building helps you redirect the argument back to your theory of the appeal so you can show the court how your theory, as a coherent whole, satisfies each concern raised from the bench. It is, after all, the theory that you're selling.

You'll be better able to manage questions if you develop what one judge calls "controlled flexibility": "a relaxed resilience allowing one to respond to a judge's question, coupled with an internal gyro compass enabling one to return gracefully to a charted course."[5]

If you are asked a question to which you don't know the answer, the best thing to say is exactly that. Judges are skilled interrogators, and you'll quickly be found out if you try to fake your way through an answer. If you once knew the answer, you might feel a little better saying something like "I'm sorry, Your Honor, but I don't recall." Judges know that you're human, and, unless the

---

5. Frank Morey Coffin, *The Ways of a Judge* 131 (1980).

point you don't know is a big one, you gain credibility by admitting that you cannot answer.

If you think you understand the question but aren't certain, say that in your answer so the judge can help you out in case you have missed the gist of the question:

> If your Honor is asking about the possibility that the issue hasn't been preserved for review — and please correct me if I've misunderstood — trial counsel made a timely objection and moved for . . .

If you plainly don't understand the question, ask for clarification:

> I'm sorry, Your Honor; are you asking about whether the order appealed from is final?

This is one of the very few kinds of questions that *you* might ask during an oral argument.

§33.4 Delivery, Affect, and Style

The most effective way to present arguments is in a tone of what has been called "respectful intellectual equality":[6]

> [I]f the lawyer approaches a court with an appreciation so great that it amounts to awe, perhaps verging on fear, he will not be able effectively to stand up to the court's questioning. . . . It is just as important, however, not to talk down to a court, no matter how much the individual advocate may be more generously endowed with quick perception. . . . The only proper attitude is that of a respectful intellectual equality. The "respectful" part approximates the quantum and type of respect that a younger [person] should show when speaking to an older one. . . . It is not inconsistent with this element of respect, however, for the advocate to argue an appeal on the basis that it is a discussion among equals. . . . Counsel must stand up to the judges quite as he would stand up to the senior members of his own firm. If he permits himself to be overawed . . . , then he — and his case — are well on their way to being lost.[7]

Although the judges' power is their authority to decide your case, it's their *need* to decide the case that — paradoxically — causes them to look to you for intellectual leadership.

What works best in this situation isn't a speech, but a *conversation* in which you take the initiative, talking *with* the judges — not at them. It is a peculiar

---

6. Frederick Bernays Wiener, *Oral Advocacy,* 62 Harv. L. Rev. 56, 72-74 (1948).
7. *Id.*

species of conversation, limited by the formalities of the occasion and by a focus on the decision the bench must make, but it's a conversation nonetheless. If you do the following, you can create for yourself a persuasive presence that helps you to reach and engage the bench:

Look straight at the judges — preferably making eye contact — through-out the argument. Look at your notes only to remind yourself of the next subject for discussion, and even then get your eyes off your notes and back to the bench as quickly as possible. Whenever you look away from the judges, their attention can wander, partly tuning you out. And judges become annoyed with lawyers who read their arguments to the court.[8]

Stand up straight and don't distract the court with restless or anxious movement. Don't play with a pen, shuffle your papers around frequently, put your hands in your pockets, or sway forward and back. Limit your gestures to those that naturally punctuate your argument. A visually busy lawyer radiates nervousness, rather than the confidence needed to establish psychological leadership. Every lawyer — even the most experienced — is nervous before making an oral argument, but that anxiety tends to disappear once the lawyer becomes engaged in the conversation. For beginners, the moment of engagement — when you are so caught up in the work that you forget to be nervous — might not come for several minutes into the argument. But as you do more oral arguments, that moment will move closer and closer toward the opening, until eventually it coincides with the words "May it please the court" or "Good morning, Your Honors."

Speak loudly enough that the judges don't have to strain to hear you. If you're soft-spoken by nature, breathe in deeply before you begin and exhale while speaking your first words. Do this again whenever your voice falters. Make your lungs do the work, not your throat muscles. If you already have a powerful voice, don't get carried away. Nobody likes to listen to shouting.

Use the tone and volume of your voice to emphasize the more important things you say. A monotone becomes monotonous. Pause before or after your most important remarks. And speak slowly enough so the judges can understand you. The most common response to nervousness is to speak very quickly and garble your words. Instead, take deep breaths, and speak at a natural pace. Don't be afraid to pause and compose your thoughts. The judges won't mind a second or two of "dead air" while you do so.

Communicate tenacity and what one judge has called "disciplined earnestness": "a communicated sense of conviction that pushes a case to the limits of its strength but not beyond. One somehow brings together one's words and body language, facial expression and eye contact, to radiate a sense of conviction without making every point a life-and-death issue."[9]

---

8. *See* U.S. Sup. Ct. R. 28.1 ("Oral argument read from a prepared text is not favored") and Fed. R. App. P. 34(c) ("Counsel must not read at length from briefs, records, or authorities").

9. Coffin, *supra*, n. 5 at 132.

Unless asked, avoid multitudes of detail in discussing authority. Because oral argument works best when focused on the big ideas in the appeal, you're better off concentrating instead on rules of law, policy arguments, and broad descriptions of authority. Citations and the minutiae of authority are very hard to follow when delivered orally, and they ought to be in your brief anyway. If your case is built on a synthesis of authority, describe it generally ("the majority of jurisdictions," "the recent trend of cases in other states," "seven of the federal circuits," "this court has previously held"). But if there's controlling authority, that itself is a big idea and deserves attention, especially where you're asking a court to construe an unsettled statute or to overrule precedent. But even then, don't give the full citation. The name and sometimes the year of a case are enough. And if you must quote—as you might with a crucial statute or holding—limit yourself to the half-dozen or so essential words that the court must interpret.

Know your record thoroughly, use it to its full advantage, and don't discuss "facts" outside the record. Concentrate on the few facts that are most determinative, and mention along the way one or two facts that most bring the story to life. Some facts don't logically have legal significance, but they help the judges "see" the story and put the case into a realistic perspective.

§33.5 Formalities and Customs of the Courtroom

Dress not merely for business, but in conservative clothing that conveys the impression that you're a careful and reliable professional.

Stand at the lectern throughout your argument. Don't stroll out from behind it unless you must go to your materials in order to answer a question.

In court, lawyers don't speak to each other. They speak only to the bench and—when the bench gives permission—to witnesses and juries. But because there are no witnesses or juries in appellate courts, you'll speak only to the judges.

The dignity of the occasion will be demeaned if you speak in slang, in emotional rhetoric, or in terms that unnecessarily personalize the lawyers or judges. Even when discussing your adversary's arguments, refer to them as the party's, rather than as the lawyer's. There is a world of tonal difference between "The plaintiff mistakenly relies . . ." and "Mr. Maggione has mistakenly told you . . ." Similarly, don't speak to the bench in flattering language. Judges are satisfied with respect; they're offended by obsequiousness.

While your adversary argues, listen attentively and without facial expressions that could convey your opinion of what is transpiring. Make whatever notes you'll need to help you respond in your own argument (if you're the appellee) or in rebuttal (if you're the appellant). Don't interrupt your adversary's argument.

§33.6   Preparation for Oral Argument

Prepare two versions of the same presentation. One version should include the material that you *must* argue — in other words, the core of your case — and, when delivered without interruption, it should fill no more than 30 or 35 percent of the time you are allowed.

The other version is an expanded development of the first. It includes the first version, as well as supplemental material that makes the core of your case more persuasive, and, without interruption, it should fill about 80 or 90 percent of the available time. You'll know within the first three or four minutes of the argument whether the bench is hot or cold. If it's hot, you can deliver the core presentation and work the supplemental material into your answers. If the bench is cold, you can deliver the expanded argument.

There are many ways to prepare notes to use at the lectern. After you've argued several times, you'll figure out which type and style of notes work best for you. But the consensus of experienced advocates is that you're better off with the fewest notes because you'll need them only to remind yourself of the subjects you intend to cover and of a few key phrases that you intend to use. In fact, if you're well prepared, you'll know your case so well that a single page on a legal-size pad will often be sufficient. If, in preparing the argument, you come up with an excellent phrasing for a difficult concept, you might write down those few words to remind yourself to use them. Otherwise, your notes should be only a list of subjects to cover.

You can outline both versions of your argument on a single page divided by a vertical line. The core argument can be to the left of that line. To the right can be the ideas and facts that you would add to the core argument if the court asks few questions.

Some advocates take to the lectern notecards with synopses of the record and of the major relevant cases. You might or might not find such synopses helpful. If you already know your case thoroughly, the cards might only get in your way.

Take the record and both briefs to the lectern in case you are asked about their contents. Especially with the record, use tabs to mark for quick reference passages that the judges might want explained.

Plan your argument by weaving together policy, the facts, and the controlling rules of law into the seamless theory enunciated in your brief. Show how policy and the facts compel your conclusion, while the law can be used to justify it. If the standard of review and the procedural posture below place procedural burdens on you — requiring you to plead certain facts or produce evidence of them — be sure to show the court how you have carried those burdens. If the burdens rest on your adversary, show instead how your adversary failed to carry them.

Remember that you can't cover all the arguments you made in the brief. Focus on the most important material.

Make a list of every weakness in your case and every question that you would be tempted to ask if you were a judge — and prepare an answer to each of those questions. You're not just trying to win a case. You're helping judges make law. What rule will a decision in your favor stand for? It would become precedent. The judges will care deeply about policy concerns. If they do as you ask, how will the law in the future treat facts that are similar to — but not exactly the same as — yours? What would be the practical effects in the courts, in the economy, and in society as a whole? Why is the rule you advocate better than the one your adversary urges? Imagine hard questions that you might be asked. Then study your adversary's brief and the precedents that are contrary to your position.

Try also to predict which concessions you'll be asked to make. Figure out which concessions you cannot afford to make and which you'll have to make in order to protect the reasonableness of the rest of your case. If you think about this for the first time when you're actually asked to make the concession, a very large part of your case could easily disappear in a snap misjudgment.

Practice making your argument to a person who will ask you tough questions but who knows little about your theory of the appeal. If the person mooting you knows too much about your theory, the experience will be unrealistic.

Finally, check your research the day before you argue. In the time between submission of the brief and oral argument the law might have changed. Check to see whether controlling statutes have been amended or repealed, whether any of the key cases have been overruled, and whether any of the recent precedents has been reversed or affirmed. You need not check every citation in your brief, but you don't want to discover in the courtroom that some important texture of the law has changed.

§33.7 State v. Dobbs and Zachrisson: *An Oral Argument Dissected*

To help you understand how oral argument influences judicial decision-making, this chapter concludes with a dissection of the arguments in a real appeal,[10] comparing them to the decision subsequently made by the court to whom the arguments were addressed.

In the city where this case arose, Dobbs operated an illegal gambling business in one neighborhood, and Zachrisson ran a similar enterprise in another

---

10. The names of the parties, judges, and lawyers and the citations to local authority have all been changed. The wording of the local statutes has been altered slightly for clarity. To make the story easier to follow, many of the facts have been simplified, but not in ways that are relevant to the court's analysis. Some of the people described here are composites from a larger cast of characters in the original appeal.

area. Dobbs and Zachrisson were each indicted on 16 counts of bribery and one count of conspiracy to bribe. (They weren't indicted for illegal gambling, perhaps because the police lacked the evidence required by the gambling statute.) At trial, a police officer named Porfier testified that Zachrisson had given her money for not enforcing the law against him and Dobbs and for arresting their competitors instead. The prosecution also introduced tape recordings of conversations between Porfier and the defendants. Dobbs and Zachrisson testified in their own defense. A jury convicted on all 34 counts.

At trial, Zachrisson and Dobbs each asserted the defenses of entrapment and coercion, which are separately defined in the state's Criminal Code:

§ 32.   Defense of Entrapment

In a prosecution for any crime, it is an affirmative defense that the defendant engaged in the prohibited conduct because he was induced or encouraged to do so by a public servant, or by a person acting under a public servant's direction, where the public servant or the person acting under his direction acted for the purpose of obtaining evidence against the defendant for the purpose of a criminal prosecution, and where the methods used to obtain that evidence created a substantial risk that the crime would be committed by a person not otherwise disposed to commit it. Conduct that merely provides a defendant with an opportunity to commit a crime is not entrapment.

§ 963.   Bribery; Defense of Coercion

(a) In a prosecution for bribery, it is a defense that the defendant conferred a prohibited benefit on a public servant as a result of that public servant's coercion of the defendant.

(b) For the purposes of this section, a public servant coerces a defendant by instilling in the defendant a fear that if the defendant does not comply with the public servant's wishes, the public servant will cause physical injury to the defendant or another, cause damage to property of the defendant or another, cause criminal charges to be brought against the defendant or another, or otherwise abuse the public servant's power as an official of the government.

Porfier testified that initially she approached Zachrisson in an attempt to recruit him and perhaps others as informants. She suggested that Zachrisson set up a meeting with any other bookies that Zachrisson thought might be interested. Zachrisson suggested Dobbs. A meeting of the three of them was arranged, but Dobbs didn't show up. At this and other meetings, Porfier wore a "body wire" (a hidden microphone that transmits to a nearby tape recorder). Zachrisson told Porfier that he needed police protection from aggressive gamblers with mob connections who were moving into his territory. The jury heard a recording of Zachrisson telling Porfier that if she made it easier for him to make a profit, he could "send some money your way." Porfier told him that she would have to think it over, and that he should find out whether Dobbs wanted to make the same arrangement.

A week or so later, Zachrisson and Porfier met again. Porfier told Zachrisson that she would accept money from Zachrisson and Dobbs, that she wouldn't arrest them or their employees, and that she would arrest their competitors. Zachrisson told her that Dobbs was "interested." Zachrisson began making periodic payments to Porfier of $100 to $200 (all of which Porfier turned over to the police department). Zachrisson and Dobbs continued their operations without police interference, and some of their competitors were arrested.

A few months after this arrangement began, Zachrisson told Porfier that he and Dobbs — whom Porfier had still not yet met — wanted to expand their gambling enterprises and were willing to bring in Porfier as a silent partner. Zachrisson told Porfier that she would receive a percentage of the profits in exchange for police protection for Zachrisson and Dobbs. Porfier and Zachrisson met one more time, and that was the only meeting attended by Dobbs. Dobbs stated that he agreed with Zachrisson's goals, but Porfier did not start receiving a share of the profits until a few weeks later.

Zachrisson testified that he paid Porfier because he was afraid that he would be arrested if he did not, and he presented evidence that during the time these payments were being made he had complained to others that Porfier was "shaking me down." Dobbs testified that Porfier had threatened to put him out of business if he did not agree to pay her off.

Both defendants moved for directed verdicts of acquittal on the grounds of coercion and entrapment. The trial court denied the motions. On appeal to the state's supreme court, both defendants argued in their briefs that their convictions should be reversed because the motions should have been granted.

Dobbs asserted two additional grounds for reversal. First, he argued that the trial court committed reversible error in instructing the jury that if they convicted him of conspiracy, they could also convict him of bribery because of the acts of a co-conspirator (Zachrisson).

Second, Dobbs argued that his rights to a speedy trial had been violated. Delay in coming to trial might arise from prosecutorial tardiness, from tardiness on the defense side of the case, from court congestion, or from some combination of these sources. When a defendant moves to dismiss an indictment for lack of a speedy trial, the trial court tries to determine the sources of delay. Delay due to defense tardiness is ignored as "excludable time." Otherwise, defendants would profit from procrastination by their own lawyers. Delay caused by prosecutorial tardiness is "chargeable time" because prosecutors are expected to take the initiative in moving cases to trial. You'll see in a few moments whether this state treats court congestion delay as excludable or chargeable time.

Reproduced below is a condensation of the transcript of the oral arguments in the state supreme court. Immediately after the transcript is a synopsis of the court's opinion. When you compare the oral arguments to the court's decision, try to understand the cause-and-effect relationship: how do the arguments seem to have influenced what the court did?

THE CHIEF JUDGE: Mr. Womack?

WOMACK [for Zachrisson]: May it please the court. I'll argue the issues of coercion and entrapment. My brief sets out the statutory definition of coercion in a bribery case. The evidence at trial was that Zachrisson, after he had made one or two payments, went to a friend of his and complained about the police. The friend then went to a judge in a neighboring county and reported that Zachrisson was being "shaken down" by the police, that over a period of months the police had been intimidating Zachrisson and asking him for money in exchange for favors. You can't read the summary of the meetings here and not be convinced that the police were the principal participants, instigators and initiators of all the activity that led up to the money changing hands. It's a question of law as to whether this was voluntary.

JUDGE BECENTI: The police denied it, didn't they?

WOMACK: Yes.

JUDGE BECENTI: Doesn't that make it a question of fact, to be resolved by a jury?

WOMACK: No. Entrapment can be decided on the undisputed, undeniable facts here.

JUDGE BECENTI: As a matter of law?

WOMACK: As a matter of law. Porfier has known the defendants for approximately six years, knew that they were small-time gamblers, knew that they were involved with after-hours bars, having dealings with them for over a year and a half. Those are misdemeanors, but bribery is a felony. The testimony was that everybody knew the defendants were gamblers. Yet the police spent all that time, seeing them on a regular basis and never arrested them for any gambling offenses.

JUDGE BECENTI: They investigated organized crime and gambling, didn't they — an ongoing thing?

What do you think of this opening? Does it suggest immediately that what happened in the trial court should make us uncomfortable? How would you have improved it?

WOMACK: If they were investigating organized crime, what came of it? Why did it take them almost two years to get the defendants for bribery?

JUDGE STEIN: Doesn't that argument cut both ways because if it took that long the coercion wasn't very effective?

WOMACK: I disagree. Porfier exacted promises of a hundred dollars a week from these defendants. Porfier manufactured a crime. She got very little money from Zachrisson and then pressured him to introduce her to Dobbs. And that in itself was improper conduct.

JUDGE BECENTI: You'd have to argue that that's entrapment as a matter of law, wouldn't you? The facts were decided against you in the trial court, and we're bound by that.

WOMACK: Yes, I would argue that it was entrapment as a matter of law and that coercion was proved. Porfier engaged in improper conduct because she decided that she wanted to get the defendants for a higher crime than gambling. And in this way Zachrisson's reluctance to commit the crime was overcome by persistence. I believe in this case that's obvious. Zachrisson resisted making payments, and the payments did not begin until long after the demands had started. Profier just kept going because she wasn't satisfied with arresting the defendants on petty gambling charges.

JUDGE STEIN: Is there anything wrong about that, as long as it doesn't amount to entrapment? If something is going on, is there any reason why police can't wait be- fore arresting until they accumulate more evidence?

WOMACK: No, Your Honor, if it's indeed going on, but in this case it wasn't going on when Porfier first got involved. I see my time is up. Thank you.

Generally, rhetorical questions do not persuade. It is more effective to lay out each step of the argument.

Do you find this theory persuasive? If you don't, is that because the theory is faulty or because it isn't being adequately supported by the facts and law at the lawyer's disposal?

Has the lawyer persuaded you? Why or why not?

THE CHIEF JUDGE: Ms. Underwood?

UNDERWOOD [for Dobbs]: Your Honors, Johnny Dobbs met with this police officer only once, and that was after the officer demanded that Dobbs be there. He came only after she made five separate demands that he meet with her. Dobbs met with the officer on one occasion and never saw her again. There was no evidence in this trial that he had anything else to do with Officer Porfier. And at that one meeting, he said only one thing of any substance. When the officer suggested that she should arrest some competing gamblers to shake them down, Dobbs said, "Do we really have to arrest people? I don't want that to happen." He disagreed with the plan proposed. And when somebody said, "Johnny, you're not saying much," he replied, "You don't learn anything by talking." These are not words of joining a conspiracy. These are not words of attempting to bribe anyone. And if this is the only evidence in the case, he cannot be considered to have joined a conspiracy. He certainly didn't do it through his own words. The law is clear and settled that the words of somebody else cannot bind a defendant to a conspiracy. There was no evidence that he ever committed any other act in this whole scheme. On this kind of record, the jury should not have been instructed that they could convict Dobbs of bribery.

In fact, Porfier tried five times to get Dobbs to meet with her. And when he finally did meet with her — and this leads into the issues of coercion and entrapment — the first thing she said was "I can put you out of business; I can go into your neighborhood tomorrow and arrest your people and close you down." These words are coercive as a matter of law. And it is also entrapment as a matter of law because the police officer forced the meeting where she made these coercive statements. Here, the police officer created the crime of bribery . . .

Notice how this lawyer starts off with her best facts to undermine the bench's confidence that whatever happened in the trial court was probably not unjust. (Remember that appellants have the burden of demonstrating error and that appellate courts are affirmance-prone). This presentation paints a vivid picture with a few, very carefully selected facts. As you read the synopsis of the state supreme court's decision, try to figure out what effect that picture had on the bench. (The synopsis is printed at the end of this transcript.)

This transition is smooth but also clearly announced so that the bench can follow the lawyer's organization.

JUDGE ORTIZ [interrupting]: You haven't mentioned your speedy trial issue, which you argue in your brief. You still press it?

UNDERWOOD: Yes, absolutely, every point in the brief. In the trial court we tried to demonstrate — and the court wouldn't permit us — that other cases that had been indicted after Dobbs were tried before him, even though those other defendants were not in jail.

JUDGE ORTIZ: You consistently answered ready?

UNDERWOOD: Every time.

JUDGE ORTIZ: There was an 18-month delay?

UNDERWOOD: Yes, Your Honor.

JUDGE ORTIZ: The only excuse given in the trial court was calendar congestion?

UNDERWOOD: Yes.

JUDGE ORTIZ: And you sought no continuances or adjournments during this period?

UNDERWOOD: Not one.

JUDGE ORTIZ: When you made your motion for speedy trial relief, you claimed both a constitutional violation and a violation of our speedy trial statute?

UNDERWOOD: Yes, both issues raised below . . .

JUDGE BECENTI [interrupting]: Were there extensive plea bargaining negotiations?

UNDERWOOD: Not one minute of it, Your Honor.

JUDGE STEIN: Has there been any showing of prejudice?

UNDERWOOD: Yes, in the human sense, but not in the sense that we couldn't find any evidence.

JUDGE BECENTI: Any lost witnesses, anything like that?

UNDERWOOD: No.

JUDGE STEIN: Were the defendants in jail during this time or were they out on bail?

UNDERWOOD: No, Dobbs was not in jail.

Notice how the lawyer picks up the questions and uses it as a springboard for argument.

Are Judge Ortiz's questions hostile? Or does he seem to be helping the lawyer make clear that the delay was not caused by the defense and that the question has been properly preserved for appellate review?

This exchange seems to have sparked the interest of Judges Becenti and Stein. What do you think Judge Ortiz was trying to accomplish?

JUDGE STEIN: Have you read our opinion in *Weatherby*?

UNDERWOOD: Yes, Your Honor, I know . . .

JUDGE STEIN [interrupting]: That must not have disappointed you.

UNDERWOOD: Well, . . .

JUDGE ORTIZ [interrupting]: You say this was 18 months?

UNDERWOOD: Yes.

JUDGE ORTIZ: *Weatherby* was 18 and a half months.

UNDERWOOD: Yes, I know, Your Honor.

JUDGE ORTIZ: And Weatherby is now at home.

UNDERWOOD: If the court please, I chose to concentrate today on the other grounds for reversal because I know Your Honors were aware of that, and I feel that that was an argument I didn't need to press any further. I think I've taken all my time. Thank you very much.

THE CHIEF JUDGE: Mr. Lysander?

LYSANDER [for the State]: May it please the court . . .

JUDGE STEIN [interrupting]: What about *Weatherby*, Mr. Lysander, isn't that dispositive of the speedy trial issue?

LYSANDER: Your Honor, in this case, the speedy trial motion was made orally and not in writing. It was made on the eve of trial and without any prior notice to the prosecution. *Weatherby* is distinguishable because there the issue was raised in the trial court in a way that permitted the prosecution to find out the reason for every delay and to put that reason in the trial court record. That didn't happen here.

JUDGE STEIN: In this appeal, did the prosecution oppose the motion in the trial court on the ground that it needed an opportunity to prove that each delay was justified?

LYSANDER: I'm not sure, Your Honor.

JUDGE STEIN: Perhaps the motion should have been made in writing and with prior

Weatherby seems at least superficially to favor Dobbs. If Judges Stein and Ortiz had to make a decision on this issue right now, how do you think they would rule? Why do you think so? As you later read the argument for the State and the synopsis of the court's decision, remember the prediction you made here.

Judge Stein has gotten *very* interested in the speedy trial aspect of the case.

Do you think this lawyer was prepared to answer questions on the speedy trial issue?

notice to the prosecution, but if it were not and if the prosecution didn't object to that, I would think that your procedural objection would have been waived.

LYSANDER: Your Honor, this was a pre-*Bachman* case. Before your holding in *State v. Bachman,* both the prosecution and defense were presenting their arguments in trial courts under somewhat lax procedural standards. However, . . .

JUDGE STEIN [interrupting]: But the defendant shouldn't be prejudiced then by that fact, if there were relaxed standards.

LYSANDER: That's correct, Your Honor, but I'm simply saying that the prosecution would be prejudiced in that we were never given the opportunity to have a hearing to develop a complete factual record for the reasons for each delay.

JUDGE STEIN: But wasn't the only excuse advanced trial court congestion?

LYSANDER: The prosecution answered ready for trial for the first time only three months after the indictment, and there was difficulty getting a free courtroom on that date.

JUDGE STEIN: And we held in *Weatherby* that courtroom congestion is no excuse.

LYSANDER: But you also held in *Greenfield* that the trial court's inability to schedule a trial was an excuse. And there has never been an allegation of prejudice to Dobbs because of the delay, and Dobbs was the only defendant to raise this issue in the trial court.

JUDGE ORTIZ: But the question is now before us, and it was raised below — although you say it was raised orally instead of on papers —

LYSANDER: That's correct.

JUDGE ORTIZ: The only excuse the prosecution offered is calendar congestion, is that correct?

LYSANDER: That is the only excuse I am aware of, but we never had an opportunity for

Read coldly in a transcript, this answer might seem flippant. But if it is spoken in the proper tone of voice it becomes exactly the "respectful intellectual quality" that persuades. We can never know how much the court was influenced by this answer (or by the prosecution's brief), but compare the answer to the court's decision on this issue.

Has this lawyer had any effect at all on Judges Ortiz and Stein? When you read the synopsis of the court's decision, notice how they vote.

a hearing, so I don't know what would have developed had there been a hearing.

JUDGE ORTIZ: At the time the motion was made, there was no excuse given other than that?

LYSANDER: No, but as a practical matter, when a motion like that is made on the eve of trial all of a sudden — just before a three-and-a-half-week trial that everybody has been preparing for — on the eve of trial when the defendant suddenly claims his speedy trial rights have been violated, the prosecutor would have to do an investigation in order to be able to account for each and every continuance that happened in the past.

JUDGE STEIN: Was there any request by the prosecutor for additional time to answer the motion — so the prosecutor could develop the record that you're now suggesting could have been developed?

LYSANDER: I don't believe that there was, Your Honor, but if there had been, that would have defeated the ends of getting the trial completed as soon as possible. [pauses] Concerning the question of whether the defendants were entrapped by the police. . . .

(The remainder of the State's argument is omitted here.)

STATE v. DOBBS AND ZACHRISSON

BECENTI, J.

Dobbs's bribery convictions are reversed. His conspiracy conviction is affirmed. All of Zachrisson's convictions are affirmed.

Dobbs's bribery convictions are reversed because the trial court erroneously instructed the jury that they could convict him of bribery for the payments made by Zachrisson. There was no evidence that Dobbs actually made any bribe payments. Guilt of a substantive offense like bribery may not be predicated solely on a defendant's participation in an underlying conspiracy.

A conspirator is not necessarily an accessory to a crime committed in furtherance of the conspiracy. Under section 129 of the Criminal Code a person is criminally responsible, as an accessory, for the act of another if the person "solicits, requests, commands, importunes, or intentionally aids" the other person to engage in that offense. Conspicuously absent from the statute is any reference to one who conspires to commit an offense. That omission cannot be supplied by construction. It may be true that in some instances a conspirator's conduct will suffice to establish liability as an accessory, but the concepts are different. To permit mere guilt of conspiracy to establish the defendant's guilt of the substantive crime without any evidence of further action on the part of the defendant would be to expand the basis of accessory liability beyond the legislative design.

But we reject Dobbs's further claim that his statutory and constitutional rights to a speedy trial were violated by the delay between his indictment and his trial. Dobbs does not claim to have been prejudiced by the delay in coming to trial. He was not incarcerated, and he does not assert that any of his witnesses disappeared or suffered a fading of memory. *State v. Weatherby* is therefore distinguishable from this appeal. Moreover, when Dobbs moved in the trial court to dismiss for lack of a speedy trial, court congestion was assigned as the reason for the delay, and the prosecution was ready for trial within three months of the indictment. Thus, Dobbs is not entitled to dismissal pursuant to our speedy trial statute, which requires that the prosecution be ready on time but places no corresponding obligation on the trial court. See *State v. Greenfield*.

Finally, both defendants urge that the prosecution failed to disprove the bribery defense of coercion beyond a reasonable doubt and that the evidence establishes the affirmative defense of entrapment as a matter of law. The record does not support these contentions. The defendants' motions were correctly denied, and the issues were properly submitted to the jury.

The record before us presents a conflict between the prosecution's version of events and that of the defendants. The defendants asserted that the police officers induced their participation in the bribery scheme and employed coercive tactics to ensure compliance. Although the record does reveal some evidence of conduct that might be construed as harassment, there is also evidence of mutual cooperation. Hence, resolution of the issues was a purely factual matter within the province of the jury.

[There were no dissents.]

APPENDICES

Appendix
Statute Analysis
Exercises

This appendix includes two exercises.

Exercise A
Plagiarism and the Board of Bar Examiners

Hardy and Tisdale were enrolled in a law school course in which students write and submit papers. They were given identical assignments. Tisdale wrote a draft of the first half of his paper before Hardy did, and Hardy asked to see it. That was forbidden by the course rules. Tisdale showed Hardy what he had written anyway and sent him a copy of the wordprocessing file as an email attachment.

Hardy downloaded the attachment and changed as many of the words as he could. When he was finished, the first half of the two papers had approximately the same organization, although about 80 percent of the words were different — similar, but different.

Tisdale and Hardy then got into an argument insulting each other's taste in music, one of them saying unkind things about Coldplay and the other saying unkind things about Foo Fighters. They stopped speaking to each other. Tisdale wrote the rest of his paper and didn't show it to Hardy. Hardy researched to find what he would need for the second half of his paper. On the due date, they submitted their papers.

But a paper derived from another can never really be purged of all noticeable traces of the original. The teacher instantly recognized the similarity between the first half of Hardy's paper and the first half of Tisdale's.

In the second half of Hardy's paper, the teacher also noticed phrases that didn't "sound like" him. The teacher had a vague memory of having seen those phrases previously somewhere else. To design assignments and to keep up in their field, teachers read cases, articles, and books constantly. The teacher logged onto LEXIS and then onto WESTLAW, typing in the suspect phrases from Hardy's paper and searching for all the sources in which they appeared. In this way, a teacher can easily check a student's paper for plagiarism. The teacher found a number of instances where Hardy had copied passages word for word from sources he did not cite and without quote marks around the copied words.

When confronted with all this, Hardy claimed that by changing most of the words in Tisdale's draft he had not misrepresented someone else's work as his own, and that the plagiarism in the second half of his paper was not deliberate. He said that while researching he must have copied into his notes the phrases in question and then forgot that they came from the sources he had read. When writing the paper, he assumed that the words in his notes were his own. The teacher rejected that explanation and gave Hardy a failing grade for the course. The law school suspended him for a year.

Tisdale was also punished, but it's Hardy who poses the issue in this Exercise.

Hardy tried to transfer to another law school. But law schools do not consider transfer applications from students who are in trouble for academic dishonesty. After a year, Hardy returned to the law school that had suspended him. Last spring, he graduated. He has applied for admission to the Wisconsin bar.

In every state, an applicant for admission to the bar must prove to the bar examiners that she or he has the type of character needed to practice law. The applicant must fill out a detailed character questionnaire and submit supporting documents, including an affidavit from the applicant's law school. A false, misleading, or incomplete answer on the questionnaire is itself grounds for denying the application for admission. Every state's questionnaire asks, among other things, whether the applicant has ever been accused of academic dishonesty, and the law school's affidavit must answer the same question.

On his questionnaire, Hardy described what he had done and what the school had done. And in its affidavit, the law school reported — as it must — the same thing.

After admission to the bar, a lawyer can be professionally disciplined if the lawyer commits misconduct in violation of the state's code governing lawyers' ethics. In most states, one agency reviews the character of bar applicants, and a different agency investigates complaints of unethical conduct by lawyers. Admission to the bar and discipline of already-admitted attorneys are two separate processes, although the two have the same goal of protecting the public from unethical lawyers.

As a practical matter, a failing grade in a course can seriously damage a student's chances of finding a good job. Character trouble with the bar examiners or suspension from law school would make a student extremely unattractive to employers. For an admitted attorney, the same is true of professional discipline, even if the discipline falls short of disbarment or suspension.

Provisions governing admission to the bar are usually found in a state's court rules as well as in the bar examiners' own rules. A state's ethics code, too, is often found in the state's court rules. All these rules resemble statutes and are interpreted the same way statutes are.

Your research has found the following: two Wisconsin Supreme Court Rules governing admission to the bar; three Wisconsin Board of Bar Examiners Rules; a Wisconsin case, *In re Radtke*, interpreting one of the Bar Examiners' Rules; and three cases from other states, each interpreting another state's statute or court rule.

Will Hardy be admitted to the Wisconsin bar?

Wisconsin Supreme Court Rules

SCR 22.46. Character and fitness investigations of bar admission applicants

(1) . . .

(2) [T]he applicant shall make a full and fair disclosure of all facts and circumstances pertaining to questions involving the applicant's character and fitness. Failure to provide information or misrepresentation in a disclosure constitutes grounds for denial of admission.

SCR 40.06. Requirement as to character and fitness to practice law

(1) An applicant for bar admission shall establish good moral character and fitness to practice law. The purpose of this requirement is to limit admission to those applicants found to have the qualities of character and fitness needed to assure to a reasonable degree of certainty the integrity and the competence of services performed for clients and the maintenance of high standards in the administration of justice.

. . .

(3) An applicant shall establish to the satisfaction of the board that the applicant satisfies the requirement set forth in sub. (1). The board shall certify to the supreme court the character and fitness of qualifying applicants. The board shall decline to certify the character and fitness of an applicant who knowingly makes a materially false statement of material fact or who fails to disclose a fact necessary to correct a misapprehension known by the applicant to have arisen in connection with his or her application.

. . .

(5) The dean of a law school in this state shall have a continuing duty to report to the board any information reflecting adversely upon the character and fitness to practice law of an applicant for bar admission under SCR 40.03.

Rules of the Wisconsin Board of Bar Examiners

BA 6.02 Relevant conduct or condition.

The revelation or discovery of any of the following should be treated as cause for further inquiry before the Board decides whether the applicant possesses the character and fitness to practice law:

. . .

(b) academic misconduct

. . .

(d) acts involving dishonesty or misrepresentation

. . .

BA 6.03 Use of information.

The Board will determine whether the present character and fitness of an applicant qualifies the applicant for admission. In making this determination through the processes described above, the following factors should be considered in assigning weight and significance to prior conduct:

(a) the applicant's age at the time of the conduct
(b) the recency of the conduct
(c) the reliability of the information concerning the conduct
(d) the seriousness of the conduct
(e) the mitigating or aggravating circumstances
(f) the evidence of rehabilitation
(g) the applicant's candor in the admissions process
(h) the materiality of any omissions or misrepresentations
(i) the number of incidents revealing deficiencies

IN RE RADTKE v. BOARD OF BAR EXAMINERS
601 N.W.2d 642 (Wis. 1999)

Per Curiam.

We review . . . the decision of the Board of Bar Examiners (Board) declining to certify that Terry George Radtke satisfied the character and fitness requirement for admission to the Wisconsin bar. . . .

[T]he Board properly concluded . . . that Mr. Radtke failed to meet his burden . . . to establish the requisite moral character and fitness to practice law. . . . Prior to his graduation from Marquette University School of Law in May 1998, Mr. Radtke was a lecturer in the Department of History at University of Wisconsin-Milwaukee (UWM) from August 1984 to May 1991. [I]n the fall of 1990 he had prepared a paper and submitted a version of it for publication to a number of journals, including the Business History Review. He explained that the paper . . . "did not include several key cites to secondary sources in the bibliography and paraphrased several sources that were not quoted." He stated that he "simply forgot to include the necessary footnotes in the paper" and asserted that the allegation that he had engaged in "professional plagiarism" arose from a letter the editors of Business History Review sent to the UWM History Department chair about the missing citations. . . .

. . . In respect to the alleged plagiarism, Mr. Radtke asserted that he had not provided source citations to materials quoted in his paper and to various facts . . . , most of which he had taken from secondary articles. He acknowledged that he should have mentioned those articles as sources.

. . . Mr. Radtke's descriptions of his paper were at variance with the evidence. . . . Mr. Radtke deliberately had copied a substantial portion — more than half — of his article from other people's work, presented it as his own, and lied to the Board.

[margin note: misrepresentation of situation per the evidence]

. . . Mr. Radtke minimized his conduct by characterizing what he did as "paraphras[ing] several sources that were not quoted" and having "simply forgot[ten] to include the necessary footnotes" and "several key cites to secondary sources in the bibliography." The argument that if he had intended to plagiarize, he would not have set forth text from scholarly journals verbatim, thereby running the risk of detection by any person knowledgeable in the field, is disingenuous. . . .

Mr. Radtke has failed to establish that any of the Board's findings is clearly erroneous. Each of the foregoing findings of fact is adequately supported by the credible evidence and the reasonable inferences that can be drawn from it. . . .

Mr. Radtke's final argument . . . asserted that the Board erred in concluding that his unprofessional conduct and incomplete and untruthful disclosures were relevant to his character and fitness because it failed to take into consideration each of the nine factors listed in BA 6.03. We find no merit to that argument. First, Mr. Radtke incorrectly stated that the Board considered only two factors — the seriousness of his conduct and his candor in the admission process. In fact, the Board also explicitly considered the lack of evidence of his rehabilitation and the materiality of his omissions in the admission process. Second, we rejected the same argument in Saganski v. Board of Bar Examiners, 595 N.W.2d 631 (Wis. 1999), holding that it is sufficient that the Board consider those BA 6.03 factors that are applicable to the conduct of the applicant.

[margin note: failed to take into consideration relevant factors in 6.03]

[W]e affirm the Board's determination declining to certify Mr. Radtke's character and fitness for bar admission. [In considering] the effect Mr. Radtke's conduct in the plagiarism incident and in the bar admission application process has on his eligibility to reapply for bar admission . . . , we take into account Mr. Radtke's professional record during the eight years following the plagiarism incident. Mr. Radtke . . . admitted his mistake in the submission of his article for publication and took full responsibility for it, subsequently published the article with proper footnotes, published a book, completed his doctoral thesis and obtained his doctorate, and earned a law degree. He did all of that without any allegation of questionable conduct.

While Mr. Radtke's recent characterizations of the plagiarism incident and the impact it had on his professional employment cause great concern . . . , we determine that Mr. Radtke should be permitted to reapply for bar admission. [A] one-year period is the appropriate time for him to wait before reapplying.

[margin note: can ultimately reapply]

IN RE ZBIEGIEN
433 N.W.2d 871 (Minn. 1988)

Per Curiam.

[The petitioner has graduated from law school and has applied for admission to the bar of this state.]

draft paper –
plagiarized

[In a law school seminar in products liability, the petitioner submitted a draft paper that] was plagiarized in large part from the works of other authors. Nearly all of the first 12 pages were taken verbatim or nearly verbatim from a number of law review articles without proper citation in the endnotes. In addition, some endnotes were taken from other sources in such a way as to give the appearance that they were petitioner's own work. Several other portions of the paper were paraphrased or had words or phrases omitted or substituted for the originals as they appeared in various published sources. Again, no proper citation was given. . . . [The petitioner received] a course grade of "F". . . . *failed course*

[The petitioner] admitted the extensive plagiarism . . . both in the form of direct quotes not properly indented and footnoted and paraphrased passages not appropriately credited to the original sources. [He said that his computer printer had not been printing properly, and he did not proofread the paper as it came out of the printer because at the time his wife was disabled from an auto accident, and his teenage son had ran away from home.] . . .

The [State Board of Law Examiners, however,] found that . . . petitioner plagiarized a substantial amount of text and footnotes taken verbatim, or nearly verbatim, from various published sources without proper identification [and] that the alleged computer problems did not explain away the plagiarism. . . .

Petitioner appeals from that determination. . . .

Rule II.A of the Minnesota Rules of the Supreme Court for Admission to the Bar provides that an applicant must establish good character and fitness to the satisfaction of the Board.

"Good character" is defined as "traits that are relevant to and have a rational connection with the present fitness or capacity of an applicant to practice law." Definition 4, Minn. R. Admis. Bar (1986). . . .

Plagiarism, the adoption of the work of others as one's own, does involve an element of deceit, which reflects on an individual's honesty. . . . The petitioner clearly plagiarized large sections of his paper. [Plagiarism] is an affront to honest scholars everywhere and to other members of [a law school] class whose legitimate pursuits would be weighed against this appropriated material. Petitioner was guilty of this act. . . .

punishment enough – won't repeat behavior

It is the view of this court that [this] petitioner's conduct, wrongful though it was, does not demonstrate such lack of character that he must be barred from the practice of law. He has been punished [already in practical terms because the Board's investigation has delayed his admission to the bar] for over a year. [In dealing with law school officials and when testifying before the Board, the petitioner was filled with genuine remorse and shame.] We . . . believe that this conduct will not be repeated. We hold that, under the facts and circumstances of this case petitioner will not be barred from the practice of law. . . .

already punished + review won't repeat behavior

KᴇʟʟᴇY, J [dissenting].   DISSENT

   . . . When this court admits an applicant to the practice of law, it certifies to the public that . . . it knows of no reason why the applicant-admittee does not possess the character which the profession demands of all admitted attorneys in this state. We judge an applicant's character by the standard that it must reflect those traits of integrity, honesty and trustworthiness necessary for a lawyer to possess when he or she represents clients, when dealing with professional peers, and when appearing before the courts. Yet, in this case, notwithstanding that we know that this petitioner has . . . recently engaged in outright dishonesty by plagiarizing and claiming as his own the intellectual works of others with no attempt at appropriate attribution of source, the majority would conclude, even as it condemns the petitioner's conduct, that he has been "punished" enough by the delay in his admission. . . .

   [D]enial of admission . . . has not as its purpose punishment but rather protection of the public and the integrity of the legal system. . . .

   Even though I would deny the petition, I would not foreclose forever, petitioner's admission to the Bar. I would, however, require that he prove that after a reasonable period of time had elapsed he then . . . demonstrates that from the experience he has learned to conduct his affairs in a manner that this court can, with confidence, certify to the public that his character does reflect traits of integrity and trustworthiness.

IN RE LAMBERIS

443 N.E.2d 549 (Ill. 1982)

Sɪᴍᴏɴ, J.

   [The respondent is a lawyer admitted to the bar of this state.]

   In writing a thesis which he submitted to [a law school] in satisfaction of a requirement for a [post-J.D.] master's degree in law, the respondent [while a member of the bar] "knowingly plagiarized" . . . [i]n preparing pages 13 through 59 of his 93-page thesis [by using two books' words] substantially verbatim and without crediting the source. . . .

   The purpose for which respondent used the appropriated material . . . displays a lack of honesty which cannot go undisciplined, especially because honesty is so fundamental to the functioning of the legal profession. . . .

   [Under] DR 1-102(A)(4) of the [Illinois Code of Professional Responsibility] "[a] lawyer shall not . . . engage in conduct involving dishonesty, fraud, deceit, or misrepresentation." . . .

   Having decided that the respondent's conduct warrants some discipline, we must decide whether to impose disbarment, suspension or censure. The Hearing Board recommended censure; the Review Board recommended suspension for six months; and the Administator argues here for disbarment. . . .

[I]n the 10 years since respondent entered private practice, no client has ever complained about his conduct, professional or otherwise. . . .

[Although] the respondent's conduct undermined the honor system that is maintained in all institutions of learning[, the law school involved] has already . . . expelled [him], an act which will also undoubtedly ensure that the respondent will be hereafter excluded from the academic world.

In view of the respondent's apparently unblemished record in the practice of law and the disciplinary sanctions which have already been imposed by [the law school], we choose censure as the most appropriate discipline for the respondent.

previous recognized taken into account

IN RE WIDDISON
539 N.W.2d 671 (S.D. 1995)

GILBERTSON, J.

[The applicant has graduated from law school and applied for admission to the bar of this state.]

[During his] second year of law school, he wrote and submitted a casenote for law review publication [which] included . . . material from secondary sources which he had failed to cite. . . . The faculty advisor . . . assigned [the applicant] a failing grade in the law review course. . . .

student

[After the applicant took the final exam in the course on Worker's Compensation, the professor discovered two students' examination answers] were strikingly similar. . . . [T]he professor assigned a failing grade to each examination[, one of which was the applicant's].

& incident

[The applicant] has the burden of proving by clear and convincing evidence his qualifications for admission to practice law in this state. . . . One of those qualifications is that he "be a person of good moral character." SDCL 6-16-2. SDCL 16-16-2.1 defines "good moral character" as including, but not limited to, "qualities of honesty, candor, trustworthiness, diligence, reliability, observance of fiduciary and financial responsibility, and respect for the rights of others and for the judicial process." That statute also provides that "*[a]ny* fact reflecting a deficiency of good moral character may constitute a basis for denial of admission." SDCL 16-16-2.1 (emphasis added). Good moral character is a prerequisite to practice law in every state. . . .

"The state bears a special responsibility for maintaining standards among members of the licensed professions" such as attorneys at law. [Citations omitted.] . . . The same zeal to protect the public from the unfit within the bar must also be applied to the unfit who would seek to enter the bar. . . .

[The applicant] has not met his burden of proving good moral character. [We affirm the order denying his application for admission to the bar], with leave to reapply at a future date provided [the applicant] is able to rectify his character deficits and show he has gained an understanding of, and the ability to put into practice, the qualities of honesty, candor, and responsibility required [of lawyers].

Exercise B
The Ironwood Tract

Fourteen years ago, Palo Verde Development Corporation purchased a deed to an Arizona parcel known as the Ironwood tract. The tract is unimproved terrain. It has never been fenced, and nobody has ever constructed a building or anything else on it. It is one mile from a paved road and 65 miles from downtown Phoenix.

Today, the nearest residential development is Verde River Estates, nine miles from the tract, toward Phoenix along the same road. From the date of the purchase until this past September, no employee of Palo Verde had set foot on the tract.

Palo Verde built Verde River Estates during the last two years. The company had planned to build next on the Ironwood tract. When the last Verde River Estates units were sold in September, the company sent a surveying team to the Ironwood tract, but they were chased off the land by Homer Chesbro, whose Black Canyon Ranch adjoins the Ironwood tract.

Chesbro bought the Ranch eleven years ago from a person who told him that he was buying both the Ranch and the tract. Although the metes and bounds description in Chesbro's deed does not include the tract, that together with most of the rest of the deed is in language that only lawyers can understand.

For the past eleven years, Chesbro and his employees have grazed cattle on the Ironwood tract two or three times a month throughout the year. The land cannot support more grazing, and the soil will not support farming or other intensive agriculture, although luxury housing could be built on it.

Chesbro had no idea that Palo Verde had a deed to the property. And Palo Verde didn't know that Chesbro was using the tract or that he thought his deed included it.

If Chesbro claims that he acquired title by adverse possession, will Palo Verde succeed in an action to eject him and quiet its own title? Your research has uncovered three statutes and five cases.

ARIZONA REVISED STATUTES

§ 12-521. Definitions

A. In this article, unless the context otherwise requires:

1. "Adverse possession" means an actual and visible appropriation of the land, commenced and continued under a claim of right inconsistent with and hostile to the claim of another.

2. "Peaceable possession" means possession which is continuous, and not interrupted by an adverse action to recover the estate. . . .

§ 12-526. Real Property in Adverse Possession and Use by Possessor; Ten-Year Limitation . . .

A. A person who has a cause of action for recovery of any lands, tenements or hereditaments from a person having peaceable and adverse possession thereof, cultivating, using and enjoying such property, shall commence an action therefor within ten years after the cause of action accrues, and not afterward. . . .

§ 12-527. Effect of Limitation on Title

When an action for recovery of real property is barred by any provision of this article, the person who pleads and is entitled to the bar shall be held to have full title precluding all claims.

[These sections are descended from provisions in the Arizona Civil Code of 1901. The Arizona Supreme Court has held that what is now § 12-527 provides a cause of action through which a person who occupies land through adverse possession can obtain title to it after the requisite number of years have passed. *Work v. United Globe Mines*, 100 P. 813 (Ariz. 1909), *aff'd*, 231 U.S. 595 (1914). Because the Arizona statutes reproduced above were modelled after Texas statutes, the *Work* court relied on a Texas case, *Moody v. Holcomb*, which interpreted those Texas statutes. *Moody* was decided before 1901. Compare *Work* to the first two cases below, *Arizona Superior Mining Co. v. Anderson* and *State v. McDonald*. Added together, these three cases tell you how the Arizona courts will react to the other out-of-state cases in this exercise.]

ARIZONA SUPERIOR MINING CO. v. ANDERSON
262 P. 489 (Ariz. 1927)

[The parties disagree over whether this case should be tried in Pima County or Maricopa County. The relevant Arizona venue statute is ambiguous.]

Counsel . . . have directed our attention to decisions [interpreting similar statutes in other states, but we are free to disregard precedent from states where] the language of the statute . . . is different from the language of our statute. [The situation is different where the other state's statute is the one from which our statute is drawn. In adopting our statute] from another state, we took it with the construction theretofore placed upon it [by the courts of that state].

STATE v. MCDONALD
352 P.2d 343 (Ariz. 1960)

[The issue is whether the plaintiff can be made to pay the fees and expenses of the defendant's expert witnesses. The governing Arizona statute, A.R.S. § 12-1128, is ambiguous.]

A.R.S. § 12-1128 was adopted from California [in 1901. After that date, two California cases interpreted the original California statute to mean] the usual costs attending trial allowed by statute. [Citations omitted.] . . .

Although we are not bound to follow the interpretation [afterward] placed on a statute by [the] state from which our statute [had earlier been] adopted, it is persuasive. [Citation omitted.] . . .

ADAMS v. LAMICQ
221 P.2d 1037 (Utah 1950)

This action was commenced by the appellant to quiet title to an eighty acre tract of land in Duchesne County, Utah. . . .

[T]he respondents claimed title to the land . . . by virtue of seven years' adverse possession[, during which they used the land as a winter range for sheep].

The . . . tract in question consisted of unbroken and unimproved brush lands suitable only for grazing. . . . The property was [not inclosed by a fence. T]he respondents during the winter grazed all of the eighty acres . . . , entering thereon in November and remaining until April, at which time they moved their sheep onto higher grazing lands in Colorado for the summer and early autumn. The respondents did not leave anyone upon or in charge of the eighty acres during the summer months while they were away. . . .

. . . Sec. 104-2-9, Utah Code Annotated 1943, provides: "For the purpose of constituting an adverse possession . . . , land is deemed to have been possessed and occupied in the following cases: . . . (3) Where, although not inclosed, it has been used for the supply of fuel, or of fencing timber for the purposes of husbandry, or for pasturage, or for the ordinary use of the occupant." (Italics added.)

In *Kellogg v. Huffman*, 137 Cal. App. 278, 30 P.2d 593, it was held under Sec. 323, subd. 3, Cal. Code Civ. Proc., which is identical to Section 104-2-9, subd. 3, quoted above, that pasturing during the entire grazing season of each year during which feed is available, if done to the exclusion of others, is a sufficient use and occupation of land, which is reasonably fit for grazing purposes only, to constitute the occupation and possession necessary to establish title by adverse possession. . . .

Thus we conclude that the respondents . . . had continuously claimed, occupied, and used [the property] for at least seven years prior to the commencement of this action. . . .

KELLOGG v. HUFFMAN
30 P.2d 593 (Cal. Ct. App. 1934)

This is an action to quiet title to 160 acres of land in the Kettleman Hills in Fresno county. . . . This property was rough and arid and was situated in what was, until about 1929, a sparsely settled country used only for grazing purposes. . . .

The appropriate portion of section 323 of the Code of Civil Procedure reads as follows: " . . . For the purpose of constituting an adverse possession . . . land is deemed to have been possessed and occupied in the following cases: . . . (3) Where, although not inclosed, it has been used for the supply of fuel, or of fencing-timber for the purposes of husbandry, or for pasturage, or for the ordinary use of the occupant."

... To establish adverse possession it is only necessary that land be put to such use as can reasonably be made thereof, and such a use is sufficiently continuous if, during the required time, it be so used at all times when it can be used for the purpose to which it is adapted. [Citations omitted.] It is well settled in this state that pasturing during the entire grazing season of each year during which feed is available, if done to the exclusion of others, is a sufficient use and occupation of land, which is reasonably fit only for pasturage purposes, to constitute the occupation and possession necessary to establish a title by adverse possession. [Citations omitted.] ... "... It is sufficient that the use is in accordance with the usual course of husbandry in the locality." [Citation omitted.]

[There was ample evidence of adverse possession through use of the land for grazing purposes.]

DE LAS FUENTES v. MACDONELL
20 S.W. 43 (Tex. 1892)

This was an action on trespass to try title. ...

Appellants ... complain that the court erred in sustaining the defendant's plea of the statute of limitations of five years. ... The [land] was never inclosed [by fences]. It is fit only for grazing purposes. There have never been any houses upon it. No part of it has ever had any inclosures upon it, except small pens, made of posts and brush, for the purpose of penning sheep. These were renewed every year. ... The land was used for "grazing and lambing purposes." How many sheep were kept upon it does not appear. One witness states that in 1871 there were 13,000 sheep upon the land. ... Cattle belonging to others were permitted to graze upon the land. ...

There have been several cases decided in this court in which the effort has been made to show an adverse possession of land by merely grazing cattle and horses upon it, but it has uniformly been held that the possession was not sufficient to meet the requirements of the statute. [Citations omitted.]

[T]he mere occupancy of land by grazing live stock upon it, without substantial inclosures or other permanent improvements, is not sufficient to support a plea of limitation under our statutes. Uninclosed land, in this state, has ever been treated as commons for grazing purposes; and hence the mere holding of live stock upon it has not been deemed such exclusive occupancy as to constitute adverse possession. ... There must be "an actual occupation of such nature and notoriety as the owner may be presumed to know that there is a possession of the land" [citation omitted]; "otherwise, a man may be disseised without his knowledge, and the statute of limitations run against him, while he has no ground to believe that his seizure has been interrupted" [citation omitted].

We think the testimony insufficient to show adverse possession. ...

Appendix
Precedent Analysis
Exercise

Emil Risberg's Diary

Returning from an expedition across the Arctic ice cap in the nineteenth century, Emil Risberg and his companions became stranded at the northern tip of Greenland. After several weeks they all died of scurvy and exposure. A few years later, their hut was found, their bodies were buried at sea, and their possessions were returned to their families. Emil Risberg's widow received, among other things, his diary.

Risberg had measured the group's geographic position every day during the expedition, and he recorded those measurements, as well as a mass of other detail, in his diary. His measurements showed that he and the group he led had travelled farther north than anyone else had gone at the time. The diary brought Risberg much posthumous fame, and it wasn't until early in the twentieth century that any explorer got closer to the north pole. The diary was passed on in Risberg's family through inheritance. Four years ago, when the diary became controversial, it was owned by Risberg's great-granddaughter, Olga Risberg.

Controversy began when a researcher named Sloan announced that Risberg had faked his measurements and that he could not possibly have gotten as far north as the diary showed. Sloan supported his argument with a large amount of scientific evidence involving things like the ocean currents that shift the ice pack and the distances that can be travelled in a day over ice. Olga Risberg took this very badly.

Within a month or two, she went to the officers of the New York Geographical Society, whom she had never met before. She gave them the diary, together with a letter that contained the following sentence:

> I donate my great-grandfather's diary to the Society because I believe the Society is best situated to evaluate the measurements recorded in it and to establish once and for all that Emil Risberg went where he claimed to have gone.

No officer of the Society signed a contract obligating it to do the study in exchange for the gift. The Society had not asked Olga Risberg to make a gift of the diary, and no one at the Society said anything to her about conducting a study or about her motivation for the gift. At the time, the diary had an appraised value of $15,000.

Olga is an architect living in a suburb of Minneapolis. The total value of her home, car, and savings greatly exceeded (and still greatly exceeds) $15,000.

The Society did nothing to evaluate the diary. Two years ago, Olga demanded that the Society either resolve the controversy or return the diary to her. The Society replied in a letter that, among other things, stated the following:

> When you donated the diary to the Society, you expressed some hope that it would be evaluated. But the Society made no promise — orally or in writing — to study the controversy surrounding the diary. If and when our board of directors chooses to go ahead with a study, we will do so, but you made a gift, which we accepted without conditions.

Sloan has just died. In his papers are notes showing that he had faked his own measurements, that he had started the controversy to build his reputation, and that all along he had believed that Risberg's diary was accurate. Olga has been besieged with offers to buy the diary from people who were unaware that she had donated it to the Society. All of the offers are well into six figures.

Olga Risberg is your client. She wants the Society either to complete an objective and thorough study very soon or to reconvey title to the diary back to her so that she can either sell it or have somebody else do the study. She will be satisfied with either, and she is willing to sue.

You have concluded that the gift cannot be set aside on the grounds of fraud. You are now exploring whether Olga Risberg will be able to persuade a court to impose a constructive trust on the Society's title to the diary. You have learned from *Sharp v. Kosmalski* that the elements of a constructive trust are "(1) a confidential or fiduciary relation, (2) a promise, (3) a transfer in reliance thereon and (4) unjust enrichment."

All four elements are disputed because the Society concedes none of them. But for this exercise, we'll focus on the first element alone — whether the relationship between Olga Risberg and the Society was "confidential or fiduciary."

Of all the cases you found while researching, the three in Parts 1, 2, and 3 below are most closely on point.

Part 1

Read *Sharp v. Kosmalski* below. On the question of what a "confidential or fiduciary relationship" means, what rule or rules does *Sharp* stand for? What policy or policies does it stand for?

SHARP v. KOSMALSKI
351 N.E.2d 721 (N.Y. 1976)

GABRIELLI, J.

Upon the death of his wife of 32 years, plaintiff, a 56-year-old dairy farmer whose education did not go beyond the eighth grade, developed a very close relationship with defendant, a school teacher and a woman 16 years his junior.... Plaintiff came to depend upon defendant's companionship and, eventually, declared his love for her, proposing marriage to her. Notwithstanding her refusal of his proposal of marriage, defendant continued her association with plaintiff and permitted him to shower her with many gifts, fanning his hope that he could induce defendant to alter her decision concerning his marriage proposal. Defendant was given access to plaintiff's bank account, from which ... she withdrew substantial amounts of money. Eventually, plaintiff ... executed a deed naming her a joint owner of his farm.... [N]umerous alterations ... were made to plaintiff's farmhouse in alleged furtherance of "domestic plans" made by plaintiff and defendant.

In September, 1971, while the renovations were still in progress, plaintiff transferred his remaining joint interest to defendant.... In February, 1973, ... defendant ordered plaintiff to move out of his home and vacate the farm. Defendant took possession of the home, the farm and all the equipment thereon, leaving plaintiff with assets of $300.

Generally, a constructive trust may be imposed "[w]hen property has been acquired in such circumstances that the holder of the legal title may not in good conscience retain the beneficial interest" [citations omitted]. In the development of the doctrine of constructive trust as a remedy available to courts of equity, the following four requirements were posited: (1) a confidential or fiduciary relation, (2) a promise, (3) a transfer in reliance thereon and (4) unjust enrichment [citations omitted].

... The record in this case clearly indicates that a relationship of trust and confidence did exist between the parties and, hence, the defendant must be charged with an obligation not to abuse the trust and confidence placed in her by the plaintiff....

... Even without an express promise ... courts of equity have imposed a constructive trust upon property transferred in reliance upon a confidential relationship. In such a situation, a promise may be implied or even inferred from the very transaction itself. As Judge Cardozo so eloquently observed: "Though a promise in words was lacking, the whole transaction, it might be found, was 'instinct with an obligation' imperfectly expressed (Wood v. Duff-Gordon, 222 N.Y. 88, 91)" (Sinclair v. Purdy, 235 N.Y. 245, 254 ...)....

... Indeed, in the case before us, it is inconceivable that plaintiff would convey all of his interest in property which was not only his abode but the very means of his livelihood without at least tacit consent upon the part of the defendant that she would permit him to continue to live on and operate the farm. . . .

The salutary purpose of the constructive trust remedy is to prevent unjust enrichment. . . . A person may be deemed to be unjustly enriched if he (or she) has received a benefit, the retention of which would be unjust. . . . This case seems to present the classic example of a situation where equity should [impose a constructive trust in response to] a transaction pregnant with opportunity for abuse and unfairness. . . .

Part 2

Read *Sinclair v. Purdy*, below. On the question of what a "confidential or fiduciary relationship" means, what rule or rules does *Sinclair* stand for? What policy or policies does it stand for?

SINCLAIR v. PURDY
139 N.E. 255 (N.Y. 1923)

CARDOZO, J.

... Elijah F. Purdy [owned a half] interest in real estate in the city of New York. . . . Elijah was a clerk of what was then known as the Fifth District Court. His ownership of real estate subjected him to constant importunities to go bail for those in trouble. The desire to escape these importunities led him to execute a deed conveying his undivided half interest to his sister Elvira[, who already owned the other half]. . . . The relation between [brother and sister] was one of harmony and affection, and so continued till the end. . . . There is evidence of repeated declarations by Elvira that, though the [whole] title was in her name, a half interest was his. . . . Elijah died at the age of 80 in 1914. [A niece, who would have inherited from Elijah, brought this suit to establish a trust in favor of Elijah — and thus in favor of the niece — over the property deeded to Elvira.]

... The sister's deposition shows that her brother disclosed his plan to her before the making of a deed. . . . It was an expedient adopted to save him the bother of going upon bonds. She does not remember that she made any promise in return. He trusted, as she puts it, to her sense of honor. A little later she learned that the title was in her name.

We think a confidential relation was the procuring cause of the conveyance. The grantor could not disclose the trust upon the face of the deed. If he had done so, he would have defeated the purpose of the transfer, which required that title, to outward appearance, be vested in another. He found, as he thought, in the bond of kinship a protection as potent as any that could be assured to him by covenants of title. . . . "The absence of a formal writing grew out of that very confidence and trust, and was occasioned by it." [Citation omitted.]

In such conditions, the rule in this state is settled that equity will grant relief. [Citations omitted.] . . .

. . . Here was a man transferring to his sister the only property he had in the world. . . . He was doing this, as she admits, in reliance upon her honor. Even if we were to accept her statement that there was no distinct promise to hold it for his benefit, the exaction of such a promise, in view of the relation, might well have seemed to be superfluous. . . . Though a promise in words was lacking, the whole transaction, it might be found, was "instinct with an obligation" imperfectly expressed (Wood v. Duff-Gordon, 222 N.Y. 88, 91). It was to be interpreted, not literally or irrespective of its setting, but sensibly and broadly with all its human implications. . . .

Part 3

Read *Tebin v. Moldock* below (two opinions). The first opinion is from an intermediate appellate court. The second is from the state's highest court. On the question of what a "confidential or fiduciary relationship" means, what rule or rules does the case stand for? What policy or policies does it stand for?

TEBIN v. MOLDOCK
241 N.Y.S.2d 629 (App. Div. 1963)

BREITEL, J.P.

. . . Plaintiffs are the son, sister and two brothers of a New York decedent, all of whom are residents of Poland. Defendant is decedent's niece, and a native-born American. Decedent emigrated to the United States from Poland in 1913. She died in 1956, a widow, leaving only plaintiff son as a surviving descendant. The action was to impose a constructive trust, in favor of plaintiffs, of certain funds deposited in savings institutions, and a multiple dwelling. The assets had once belonged to decedent but she, in the last five years of her life, had transferred them to defendant niece. . . .

[We hold that] a constructive trust [must] be imposed on the . . . assets of decedent in the hands of defendant niece. While the evidence does not establish fraud or undue influence, it does inescapably establish that the assets were transferred on certain promises to hold for the benefit of the son, which promises were made in a confidential relationship. These promises were relied upon, and for their breach equity is bound to provide appropriate relief.

Hermina Tebin, the decedent, was born in Poland in 1882. She married there, but later separated from her husband, left her two sons with her parents, and emigrated to the United States in 1913. One son died in 1920 without issue. The other, who was born in 1904, is the first-named plaintiff in this action.

Since coming to this country decedent lived in New York, earned her livelihood as a midwife, acquired the lower east side multiple dwelling in which she lived, and accumulated cash funds in the amount of about $19,000. During this period of over 40 years, she saw her son in Poland once when she travelled there in 1928, and stayed for some two months. She maintained an intermittent correspondence with him throughout and until the end of her life. . . .

In 1920, decedent brought her sister Aniela to the United States. . . . Defendant niece is Aniela's daughter, whom decedent knew as a growing child, befriended and assisted as a young woman training for an educational career, and who, in decedent's later years, handled her moneys and affairs when illness and age closed in.

[Decedent's health began to deteriorate in 1947. In 1951, she gave bank accounts and a deed to the multiple dwelling to the niece, who signed an] agreement [providing] that decedent should retain the use, free, of her apartment, and receive for her life the net income from the property less a management fee to the niece. The [agreement] recited that the niece was the sole and entire owner of the property.

In August 1951 decedent made a will in which the niece was named as the sole beneficiary of her estate. It contained the following clause:

> Third: I have given certain oral instructions to my said niece, with respect to my son Kazimierz Tebin, and having full faith and confidence in her honesty and integrity, I feel certain that she will carry out my instructions. Nonetheless, in the event that she fails to carry out my instructions, it shall be a matter for her own conscience and not otherwise.

As decedent's end approached, the niece handled more and more of the aunt's affairs, faithfully, and paid all her expenses of living, hospitalization and medical services, out of the funds theretofore transferred to the niece. After the aunt's death, the niece from the same sources paid the funeral expenses. . . .

Presently, the niece holds the real property and about $14,000 of roundly $19,000 transferred to her.

Plaintiffs assert that the niece and her mother frightened decedent with the representation that if any assets were ever received by the son, he being in a Communist country, the assets would be taken from him and that Stalin would kill him. . . .

Plaintiffs also claim that the assets were transferred to the niece on her promise that she would hold them for decedent's son and advance funds as he needed and could profitably use them.

The niece and her mother assert that the relation between the decedent and her son was not a close one, the decedent often complained of the greediness of the son and his persistent and exclusive interest in receiving remittances and gifts. Moreover, it is asserted that the niece was to send moneys to the son only in her exclusive discretion and judgment, and never in excess of $25 in any one month. . . .

In July, 1952 decedent came to Mr. Solon, a lawyer, and retained him to recover her property. . . . Decedent had told Mr. Solon the Stalin story and that she had transferred the assets to the niece to provide her lifetime needs and take care of her son. While there were some ensuing conversations about bringing a lawsuit nothing further was done to prosecute the matter. . . .

The niece testified that decedent told her:

> that she was an older woman, that she wanted someone . . . who would look after her needs while she was alive [and] that all during her lifetime [her son] had always written to her and asked her to help, and that since she was giving me everything she had, she thought that he probably would, after her death, seek me out and ask me for help, and she asked me to see that he never got his hands on any lump sum of money. That is why she was giving it to me. But she knew that if he would write to me and ask me for help, and if I felt that he needed it, that I would help him. . . .

In August, 1952 decedent wrote to her son in Poland:

> I was very sick with my heart [because] Aniela and her daughter Janina scared me by telling me that if I leave my estate to you Stalin will take it away from you after I die and that . . . you may be shot to death. So I gave all to Janka — $14,000 and a house and now they are trying to commit me to an insane asylum so they could keep everything for themselves. I will try to have you come here and take it all back because they stole it from me by fraud and they bribed the lawyer.
>
> Keep this letter so that you could appear as a witness if necessary. . . .

It is evident . . . that a secret agreement had been effected between aunt and niece for the benefit of the aunt during her lifetime, and the son. . . .

[A constructive trust will be imposed where] the one who entrusted property did so because of certain understandings, and the one to whom the assets are given acquiesced even in silence (e.g., Sinclair v. Purdy, 235 N.Y. 245, 253-254 . . .). . . .

In dealing with the problem of a secret trust or the breach of a confidential relationship the ordinary rules imposed by the Statute of Frauds . . . are not applicable. Equity in this area has always reached beyond the facade of formal documents, absolute transfers, and even limiting statutes on the law side. . . .

Accordingly, the judgment . . . should [provide] for a constructive trust in [the son's] favor. . . .

TEBIN v. MOLDOCK
200 N.E.2d 216 (N.Y. 1964)

PER CURIAM.

[On appeal, the] judgment should be modified to limit the scope of the constructive trust imposed on defendant Janina Moldock to an obligation to pay $25 a month for the benefit of Kazimierz Tebin. . . .

[W]e conclude the record supports a finding that defendant, occupying a relationship of confidence and trust with decedent, undertook to devote a small part of the property given to her for the benefit of plaintiff. On the basis of defendant's own testimony this would approximate $25 a month. No such breach of confidence or of fiduciary obligation, either before or after decedent's death, has been established as would warrant forfeiture by defendant of the major interest in decedent's property which it was clearly decedent's intent that defendant should have.

Part 4

Is there a way of synthesizing some or all of these cases so that they stand for a unified view of the law? Don't feel bound to your previous answers about the rules and policies that each case stands for. When you think about the three together, you might — or might not — see a bigger picture.

Part 5

Compare Olga Risberg's facts to those in each case in this Exercise. Are they analogous? Distinguishable?

Part 6

Based on your answers to Parts 1 through 5, how do you think a court would rule on the issue of whether Olga Risberg and the Society had a "confidential or fiduciary relationship"? This is your tentative prediction.

Part 7

Will the tentative prediction you made in Part 7 seem reasonable, just, and realistic to a judge on a human level?

Part 8

Based on your answers to Parts 1 through 7, how will the court resolve the issue of whether Olga Risberg and the Society had a "confidential or fiduciary relationship"? This is your final prediction.

Appendix
Sample Office
Memorandum

This appendix contains an office memorandum of the type described in Chapter 16.

To: Theresa Wycoff

From: Christine Chopin

Date: March 1, 2017

Client: Eli Goslin

Re: constructive trust

ISSUE

Will a constructive trust in favor of Eli Goslin be imposed on the title to his home and only asset, where (1) he deeded the home over to his nephew after the nephew promised to make the remaining three years of payments to prevent foreclosure, (2) Goslin made no statement at the time that would reveal his reasons for giving the deed, and (3) the nephew has since then threatened to throw Goslin out of the home?

BRIEF ANSWER

A New York court will probably impose a constructive trust in Goslin's favor on the nephew's title to the house. Goslin is able to prove each of the four elements of the New York test for a constructive trust: (1) a confidential or fiduciary relationship between Goslin and his nephew; (2) a promise, implied by the nephew's actions, to hold title while allowing and helping Goslin to live in the house; (3) Goslin's transfer of title to the nephew in reliance on that promise; and (4) unjust enrichment by the nephew if the promise is broken. New York courts have uniformly held these elements to be satisfied where—as happened here—a person in a vulnerable situation deeds the bulk of her or his assets to someone like a trusted relative who pays either nothing or a fraction of the property's fair value.

FACTS

Eli Goslin, the client, is a 74-year-old arthritic widower who has been retired for 12 years and whose only income is from Social Security. His sons are both in the military and are frequently stationed for long periods overseas. His daughter lives in Singapore.

Until last year, he also had income from an investment, but when that business went bankrupt, he became unable to meet the mortgage payments on his house. The house was Goslin's only asset. He has lived there for 24 years, and when these events occurred, the mortgage had only three more years to run. He has no other place to live.

After Goslin found that he could no longer pay, the mortgage, Herbert Skeffington, a nephew, offered to make the remaining $11,500 in payments as they became due. Within a few days afterward, Goslin, without stating his purpose to anyone, gave a deed to the property to Skeffington and got

-1-

the bank to agree to transfer the mortgage to him. At the time, the house was worth approximately $95,000 and was unencumbered except for the mortgage that Skeffington had offered to pay. Aside from the promise to make mortgage payments, Skeffington gave no value connected to the deed.

Goslin has told us that he made the deed for the following reason: "At the time, it seemed like the right thing to do. He was going to pay the mortgage, and after a certain point—maybe after I'm gone—the place would become his. I didn't think it would end up like this." Skeffington had not asked for a deed, and Goslin arranged for the deed before telling the nephew about it. Goslin knew at the time that Skeffington would not need a deed to make the mortgage payments. The bank would have been willing to accept Skeffington's check if it were accompanied by Goslin's payment stub, or, alternatively, Skeffington could simply have given the money to Goslin, who could in turn have paid the bank.

As far as Goslin knows, Skeffington has made the payments as they have become due.

At the time of the deed, neither party said anything about changing the living arrangements in the house. Goslin continued to live alone there until a few weeks ago, when Skeffington's rental apartment was burned out and he moved, along with his wife and two children, into the house. Goslin neither agreed to nor protested this. A few days later, Skeffington ordered Goslin to move out, which Goslin has refused to do. Since then Skeffington has, at the top of his voice, frequently repeated the demand. While yelling at Goslin, Skeffington has twice, with the heels of his palms, suddenly shoved Goslin in the chest and sent him staggering. Skeffington has threatened to strike Goslin again and to pack up Goslin's belongings and leave them and Goslin on the sidewalk. Skeffington takes the position that his family has no other place to go, and that the house is the only thing he owns.

Skeffington is 36 years old, and throughout Skeffington's life he and Goslin have seen each other at least monthly at family get-togethers, including each other's weddings. Seventeen years ago, Goslin contributed $3,200 to Skeffington's college tuition. The two of them have never discussed whether this was to be treated as a gift or a loan, and Goslin does not recall which he intended or even whether he had an intent at the time. He says that he considered both the tuition money and his nephew's offer to pay the mortgage to be "the sort of thing people in a family do for each other." In any event, except for the mortgage payments, the nephew has never given Goslin money directly or indirectly, and he has not announced an intention to compensate Goslin for the tuition money.

DISCUSSION

Goslin will probably be able to get a constructive trust imposed on his nephew's title to the house.

Under New York law, a constructive trust will be imposed where the record shows "(1) a confidential or fiduciary relation, (2) a promise, (3) a transfer in reliance thereon, and (4) unjust enrichment." *McGrath v. Hilding*, 363

-2-

Headings here show where each element is discussed. Under the first heading, the first sentence states the first element's subconclusion and the second sentence states its supporting rule.

N.E.2d 328, 330 (N.Y. 1977); *Beason v. Kleine*, 947 N.Y.S.2d 275, 277 (App. Div. 2012). These elements are flexible, however, and New York courts will impose a constructive trust even if not all of the elements are established. *Simonds v. Simonds*, 380 N.E.2d 189, 193-94 (N.Y. 1978); *Rowe v. Kingston*, 942 N.Y.S.2d 161, 163 (App. Div. 2012).

Confidential or Fiduciary Relationship

Goslin's relationship with his nephew satisfies the first element. A confidential or fiduciary relation exists where one person is willing to entrust important matters to a second person. *Sharp v. Kosmalski*, 351 N.E.2d 721, 723 (N.Y. 1976); *In re Estate of Falise*, 863 N.Y.S.2d 854, 860 (App. Div. 2008). Family relations are routinely held to be confidential, including those between aunts or uncles and nieces or nephews. *See, e.g., Rowe*, 942 N.Y.S.2d at 163 (finding a confidential relation between the plaintiff and his aunt and uncle where they lived together in plaintiff's home); *Falise*, 863 N.Y.S.2d at 860 (finding a confidential relation between the decedent and his nephew where they "maintained a father and son relationship").

A substantiating proof of the rule. synthesizing three holdings, *Sharp*, *Falise*, and *Rowe*.

Although Goslin and Skeffington had not lived together prior to the deed, as in *Rowe*, or behaved as father and son, as in *Falise*, their relationship should qualify as confidential. Goslin and his nephew have seen each other at least monthly at family get-togethers since the nephew was a boy, they attended each other's weddings, and Goslin contributed to the nephew's college tuition.

A counter-analysis, smoothly introduced. It would have been awkward to begin "Skeffington's lawyer might argue . . ."

Implied Promise by the Transferee

The sub-conclusion for the second element.

A court will probably find a promise by the nephew to permit Goslin to continue to live in his home. All that is required is a promise, and it need not be written. The Statute of Frauds, which generally requires that contracts for land transfers be in writing, will not prevent a constructive trust. *Sharp*, 351 N.E.2d at 723-24; *Pattison v. Pattison*, 92 N.E.2d 890, 894 (N.Y. 1950); *Tebin v. Moldock*, 241 N.Y.S.2d 629, 638 (App. Div. 1963) ("Equity in this area has always reached beyond the facade of formal documents, absolute transfers, and even limiting statutes on the law side").

The supporting rule, synthesized from three cases. Because it's at least a little surprising, it needs an extended explanation and proof. Some corollary rules explain the meaning of "All that is required is a promise." (The first corollary rule tells you that the promise need not be written.)

The promise need not be express if it "may be implied or inferred from the very transaction itself." *Sharp*, 351 N.E.2d at 723. In *Sharp*, a 56-year-old farmer conveyed his farm to a 40-year-old woman who had declined his offer of marriage but lived with and accepted gifts from him. After the transfer, the woman ordered the farmer off the property. Although the record contained no evidence of an express promise, the Court of Appeals held that a promise could be inferred from the parties' behavior because it was "inconceivable that plaintiff would convey all of his interest in property which was not only his abode but the very means of his livelihood without at least tacit consent upon the part of the defendant that she would

-3-

permit him to continue to live on and operate the farm." *Id.* at 724; *see also Falise*, 863 N.Y.S.2d at 860-61 (finding a nephew's implicit promise to pay money from bank accounts titled in his name to his uncle's children); *Johnson v. Lih*, 628 N.Y.S.2d 458, 459 (App. Div. 1995) (finding a nephew's implicit promise to deed his uncle's property not only to himself but his sister too).

Like the farmer in *Sharp*, Goslin owned nothing of substance other than his home. At the time of the transfer, he had already been retired for nine years, and his only income was from Social Security. Thus, as in *Sharp*, it is inconceivable that Goslin would have transferred his property to Skeffington without the understanding that he would permit Goslin to continue to live there.

Skeffington could claim the transfer was an outright gift, but New York courts have been reluctant to accept such claims under suspect circumstances. *See Sharp*, 351 N.E.2d at 724; *Sinclair v. Purdy*, 139 N.E. 255, 258 (N.Y. 1923). In *Sinclair,* a brother, who was employed as a court clerk and continually being asked to pledge his property for other people's bail, deeded it over to his sister, receiving nothing in return. The Court of Appeals held that the circumstances implied a promise that the sister would hold her brother's share for his benefit, and Judge Cardozo wrote:

> Here was a man transferring to his sister the only property he had in the world. . . . Even if we were to accept her statement that there was no distinct promise to hold it for his benefit, the exaction of such a promise, in view of the relation, might well have seemed to be superfluous.

Sinclair, 139 N.E. at 258. Here, too, a distinct promise would have been superfluous given the nature of Goslin and Skeffington's relationship and Goslin's financial circumstances. Skeffington offered to pay the mortgage because Goslin could no longer afford it. Goslin has no other place to live, and the house is his only asset. It would make no sense for him to give it away without an implied promise that he could continue to live there.

Nor can Skeffington's promise to make the mortgage payments be considered payment for the title in lieu of a promise to permit Goslin to stay in his home. Skeffington offered to make the payments before Goslin deeded him the property, and if Skeffington took clear title at that time, the mortgage payments would benefit him, not Goslin. Moreover, the amount remaining on the mortgage was far below the market value of the home and would not have been adequate compensation for it.

Of all the facts here, the most troubling is that Goslin was not required to deed the home to Skeffington in order to accept his nephew's offer to pay the mortgage. Skeffington could have made the payments for Goslin without owning the home. Presumably, Goslin gave Skeffington the deed

-4-

Margin notes:

Rule application begins. This element is the heart of Goslin's controversy, and the reader needs an extended explanation of why the rule will be applied this way. The rule application centers on analogies to *Sharp* and *Sinclair*. Notice how the reader is given the holding and enough of the facts to understand the comparison.

These paragraphs include counter-analyses.

to motivate Skeffington to pay the mortgage while Goslin continued to live there, honoring his relationship with his nephew. It seemed "the sort of thing people in a family do for each other." This is a case where equity will likely step in to accomplish "that which should have been done." *Simonds*, 380 N.E.2d at 193.

Transfer in Reliance on the Promise

Goslin should be able to meet the requirements of the third element. The transfer to Skeffington is not in dispute, and even though Goslin deeded the property to his nephew without his knowledge, that will not prevent the imposition of a constructive trust. *See Falise*, 863 N.Y.S.2d at 861 (imposing a constructive trust based on an uncle's transfer of title to bank accounts to his nephew without the nephew's knowledge).

Unjust Enrichment

Goslin should also be able to establish the fourth element. Unjust enrichment occurs where "property has been acquired in such circumstances that the holder of the legal title may not in good conscience retain the beneficial interest." *Sharp*, 351 N.E.2d at 723 (quotations omitted); *see Falise*, 863 N.Y.S.2d at 859. In *Falise*, the decedent titled two bank accounts containing roughly $500,000 in his nephew's name and, in a note opened after his death, asked his nephew to distribute the money equally among the decedent's children. In turn, the nephew claimed the money belonged solely to him. Even though the nephew had helped care for his uncle, the court held he would be unjustly enriched by keeping the money. *Falise*, 863 N.Y.S.2d at 860-62.

Similarly, Skeffington helped care for his uncle by making mortgage payments, but he would be unjustly enriched by acquiring a home worth $95,000 in exchange for $11,500 in remaining mortgage payments. A court will probably find that Skeffington has tried to convert his assumption of a family responsibility into a windfall. Skeffington's offer to pay the remaining mortgage could be seen by both parties as reciprocation for Goslin's help in putting the nephew through college, although that finding is not necessary for a ruling in Goslin's favor.

CONCLUSION

Goslin can likely demonstrate all the elements of a constructive trust. He had a relationship of trust and confidence with his nephew, and they have maintained a lifelong friendship. Under these circumstances, a court is likely to find that Skeffington "promised" to permit Goslin to live in the home in exchange for the deed to the property, and Goslin acted accordingly. Given Goslin's dire finances, it makes no sense to assume he gave the

Margin notes:

The nephew must concede part of this element, and the rest is proved through the explanations of the first two elements.

The sub-conclusion for the final element.

An analogy to *Falise*.

property to Skeffington outright. Finally, Skeffington would be unjustly enriched because he would have clear title to a $95,000 asset in exchange for $11,500 in mortgage payments. The only way to rectify this situation is to impose a trust.

Appendix
Sample Email
Memo

This appendix contains an email memo of the type explained in Chapter 17.

From: Matthew Donohoe <MDonohoe@lms.law.com>

To: Cheryl Lopez <CMLopez@lmslaw.com>

Date: Thurs, Aug 4, 2016 at 1:44 PM

Subject: Alisha Singh/Hostile Work Environment Claim

Hi, Cheryl.

As you requested, here is the summary of my research on the Singh case so you can update the client when you meet with her tomorrow. I think that she has a viable Title VII sexual harassment claim against her employer, NRG Designs, under a hostile work environment theory.

The facts she presents satisfy the five factors established in *Andrews v. City of Philadelphia*, 895 F.2d 1469, 1482 (3d Cir. 1990), which is still cited as the controlling case. Following is a brief summary of the factors and how Singh satisfies them:

- **The employee suffered intentional discrimination because of the employee's sex.** Sexually explicit conduct and pornographic materials in the workplace satisfy this requirement. *Koschoff v. Henderson*, 109 F.Supp.2d 332, 347 (E.D. Pa. 2000) (citing *Andrews*, 895 F.2d at 1482 n.3). The pornographic emails sent to all employees and the coworkers teasing Singh for being uptight satisfy this requirement.
- **The discrimination was pervasive and regular.** Because the conduct Singh describes occurred at regular intervals over an extended period of time, it should satisfy this factor despite the fact that no one incident was severe. See *Spain v. Gallegos*, 26 F.3d 439 (3d Cir. 1994).
- **The discrimination detrimentally affected the plaintiff.** Singh can show that she is detrimentally affected based on her perception of the workplace as hostile and abusive. See *Spain*, 26 F.3d at 449. Her account is corroborated by her requests to be removed from the email list and complaints to an upper-level supervisor about the conduct.
- **The discrimination would detrimentally affect a reasonable person of the same sex in that position.** The ongoing nature of the harassment and the fact that it has affected her relationships with her coworkers, as reflected in her performance evaluation should meet the requirement that a reasonable person would be detrimentally affected. In addition, Singh might be able to show that her promotion denial stemmed directly from her reaction to the emails and teasing. This would provide concrete evidence of objective harm. *Spain*, 26 F.3d at 450.
- **The existence of respondeat superior liability.** NRG is liable for the actions of Singh's supervisor as well as those of her coworkers. NRG is liable for her supervisor's actions because his conduct caused a tangible employment action (the promotion denial). See *Durham Life Ins. V.*

Evans, 166 F.3d 139, 152 (3d Cir. 1999). NRG is liable for her coworkers' actions because management had been aware of the problem for eighteen months and has failed to address the allegations promptly and adequately.

I have attached the key cases, and I am in the process of drafting a longer memorandum of law with supporting authority, which I will get to you by next week as we agreed, but I hope this gives you enough information for your meeting.

Take care,

Matt

Matthew Donohoe, Esq.
Lopez, Moritz and Smith LLP
MDonohoe@lms.law.com
(555) 740-4531

This e-mail message and any attached files are confidential and are intended solely for the use of the addressee(s) named above. This communication may contain material protected by attorney-client, work product, or other privileges. If you have received this confidential communication in error, please notify the sender immediately by reply e-mail message and permanently delete the original message.

Appendix
Sample Client
Advice Letter

This appendix contains a client advice letter of the type described in Chapter 19.

The client is Ada Warren of Lincoln Notch, Vermont. She is in her late fifties. When the Lincoln Creamery fell on hard times a few years ago, she lost her job as office manager and lived thereafter on savings. When her cousin Virgil died last year, she inherited his farm near Grafton, which she sold to a Boston developer for a half million dollars. She then booked a cruise on the Pride of Seaside, a six-cabin sailing yacht.

The degree of formality in a client letter will differ according to the client's expectations. A corporate client expects formality. An individual client might not. Contractions, for example, are appropriate in a letter to Ms. Warren. They probably are not appropriate in a letter from your law firm to General Electric's general counsel.

Huber & Stanislaw
Attorneys at Law
6 Front Street
Seaside, ME 01203
(603) 555-1111

March 14, 2017

Ada Warren
22 Green Mountain Road
Lincoln Notch, VT 05862

Dear Ms. Warren:

As I promised when we met last week, I've researched your rights against Seaside Cruises and the state Marine Police. I believe that you probably would win a lawsuit against Seaside but lose a suit against the police. In the second half of this letter, I'll explain why.

After you and I spoke last week, I examined the police logs and talked to some of the passengers. I was able to get some information (though not much) from the police officers and the captain of the Pride of Seaside. My advice later in this letter is based on my understanding of the facts, which are described in the next few paragraphs. If I've gotten any of the facts wrong, please tell me so that I can determine whether the law would treat the situation differently.

Facts

You boarded the Pride of Seaside at 8:30 in the evening. The boat left the dock at 9:00 p.m., and you went below at about 9:30 and were asleep by about 10:15. You had felt ill earlier in the evening and had wanted to rest. At 10:40 p.m., the boat was boarded by Officers Magrane and Kroyer of the State Marine Police, who suspected that a sailor had marijuana hidden behind his bunk. They found what they were looking for, arrested the sailor, and ordered the captain to sail to the Marine Police dock. There, the boat was impounded and the sailor was taken away by the police. The other passengers and the rest of the crew were awakened by the ruckus and came on deck, where they were told by Officer Kroyer that they would have to leave the boat. Officer Magrane drove the passengers (except you) in a police van to a hotel, where they slept.

Neither the crew nor the police searched the boat to make sure no one else was aboard. The police officers didn't ask for a list of passengers. The crew didn't offer a passenger list to the police or compare the passengers on deck with the boat's passenger manifest. The police say they thought it was the crew's responsibility to get everyone off the boat. The captain says that he thought the police were doing that.

You slept soundly through the night. At 12:15 a.m., Officer Kroyer sealed the boat. He locked every outer door and hatch, removed the gangway, locked it in a shed, and went home. As a result, you wouldn't have been able to get to the deck because all the doors and hatches were locked from the outside, and even if you had been able to get to the deck, you wouldn't have been able to leave the boat.

-1-

No one else was at the dock until Officer Tedescu arrived at about 6:30 a.m. Tedescu found a note from Kroyer that the boat had been impounded but not yet been searched except for the sailor's bunk. He rolled out the gangway, walked on board, and at 6:45 unlocked the door to the passageway outside your cabin. You awoke at about 7:00 a.m., opened your cabin door, and found Officer Tedescu standing in the passageway. Officer Tedescu explained what had happened, and you suddenly felt light-headed and fell to the floor of the passageway. In his written report, Officer Tedescu used the word "fainted" to describe this. You revived in a moment or two, and he drove you to a hospital, where an emergency room physician decided that you needed no treatment.

You were shocked at the indignity of learning that you had spent the night locked up in a police boat yard rather than cruising at sea as you thought you had been. For you, this was the same as being locked up in a jail cell over-night. Both are shameful, treating you like a criminal. Except for collapsing or fainting, you didn't suffer physically from these events. Seaside Cruises has refused to refund the $3,500 that you paid for this two-week cruise. They have not provided any passenger with a refund.

Possible Lawsuits

When we met last week, you said that you aren't sure that legal action would be worth the effort, but that you feel taken advantage of and wanted to know what your rights are. I'll explain what I think would happen if you were to sue Seaside Cruises and the Marine Police.

Seaside Cruises: The law considers Seaside to be a common carrier. Airlines, railroads, and bus companies are also common carriers. Common carriers owe a very high degree of care to their passengers, including the duty to rescue a passenger from harm. Based on the facts we have at this point, I think you would probably win on this claim. Seaside's employees should have made sure you were off the boat before it was locked up or at least have told the police that you were aboard.

> Common carriers are explained in a nontechnical way so the client will understand.

But it's harder to predict how much money a jury would award on this claim. It might be small on the ground that you were unaware at the time that you were locked into the boat. Or it might be larger if the jury can appreciate the depth of the indignity.

On the other hand, Seaside Cruises does owe you a refund of $3,500. You paid for a service (a cruise) that Seaside did not provide. The law is clear that they aren't entitled to keep the money, even though the cruise was prevented by police seizure of their boat.

You can bring both claims against Seaside—for the refund and for failing to get you off the boat—in a single lawsuit.

The Marine Police: If you were to sue the state for false imprisonment, I believe that you wouldn't succeed. In this state, a false imprisonment claim can succeed only if the person confined knew of the confinement while it was occurring or was harmed by it. The law defines "harm" in this sense as eco-nomic loss or physical injury.

> Here the prediction is negative.

You did suffer an economic loss (the $3,500 that Seaside has not refunded), but not because you were locked in the boat. If the police had driven you to a hotel, Seaside still would have refused to refund the money.

-2-

Because you learned of your confinement only after Officer Tedescu had unlocked the boat, the only way of succeeding in a suit against the police would be to show that the confinement caused you physical injury. The only physical injury is your collapse when Officer Tedescu told you that you had been confined. But a jury could conclude that you collapsed because you were still ill from the night before.

Moreover, in a case called *Osborne v. Floyd*, our state supreme court recently decided that the physical injury must be caused by the confinement itself. It isn't enough for the harm to be caused by knowledge of the confinement. In *Osborne*, a man was comatose and unaware he had been locked into a cellar. His medical condition didn't deteriorate before rescuers broke down the door. But after he regained consciousness and learned what had happened, he experienced nightmares. The court held that the nightmares weren't sufficient, and an injury would have to be physical for him to recover. I think the courts would treat your collapsing onto the floor the same way, especially because the emergency room physician decided that you needed no medical treatment. I wish this weren't so, but unfortunately, it is.

Let's talk further in a few days. If, after thinking this over, you're interested in suing Seaside Cruises, I can explain what a lawsuit would cost so you can decide whether to go ahead. It might be possible to reduce the expense of suing if other passengers join with you and sue to get the refunds they're entitled to. Please call my office when you feel ready.

Sincerely,

Gary Stanislaw

The analogy can help the client accept the bad news.

A useful thing to say with bad news.

-3-

Appendix Sample Motion Memorandum

This appendix contains a motion memorandum of the type described in Chapter 25. A preschool has sued a commercial painter for negligence. This is the preschool's memo in support of its motion for summary judgment.

For the preschool, winning this motion is in many ways harder than it looks. First, no reported case has determined whether a painter is liable on facts like these.

Second, what this painter did is not unusual. If the law fills this gap as the preschool would like, a lot of behavior previously deemed blameless would suddenly become tortious. Maybe that should happen, but judges will think long and hard before doing it.

Third, as a plaintiff the preschool must in this motion persuade the court that the defendant is completely defenseless: that he has no affirmative defenses and does not have enough evidence to create a triable issue on any of the elements that the preschool must prove. That is hard to do, and this is perhaps the hardest kind of summary judgment for a movant to win.

Finally, courts hesitate in general to grant summary judgments to negligence plaintiffs, preferring that juries decide whether flexible tests like negligence have been satisfied. Courts much more readily grant summary judgments to negligence defendants.

The memo has done its job if — as a judge — you would want strongly to grant summary judgment to the preschool despite all the obstacles described above. The writer must both motivate you to do that and help you justify the decision. Where are motivating arguments implied in the Statement of Facts (see Chapter 7)? Which parts of the Argument express motivating arguments, and which express justifying arguments (see §24.3)?

SUPERIOR COURT OF CONNECTICUT
JUDICIAL DISTRICT OF NEW LONDON

TULTA PRESCHOOL, INC.,

                                        Plaintiff

          -against-   No. CV17-8956

MICHAEL D. RAUCHER, dba
RAUCHER PAINTING CONTRACTORS

                                        Defendant

MEMORANDUM IN SUPPORT OF
PLAINTIFF'S MOTION FOR
PARTIAL SUMMARY JUDGMENT

Petra Diaz, Esq.
Attorney for Plaintiff
94 Front Street
Coff's Harbor, CT 14218
(203) 555-1111

CONTENTS

Tulta's burden of proof is reflected in the subheadings. The procedural test for summary judgment requires that Tulta prove that there's no genuine dispute of material fact (subheading A) and that Tulta is entitled to judgment as a matter of law, in this instance on the four elements of negligence (sub-headings B through E). For how to organize this way, see §13.2 in Chapter 13.

PRELIMINARY STATEMENT

The plaintiff, Tulta Preschool, Inc., teaches children from two to five years of age in Coff's Harbor, Connecticut. The defendant, Michael D. Raucher, is a commercial painter doing business as Raucher Painting Contractors.

Raucher contaminated Tulta Preschool's building and grounds by power-sanding toxic lead-based paint off the exterior of an adjacent building. Lead paint dust and chips are dangerous, especially to small children. Tulta Preschool was forced to close and could not reopen until its building and land had been cleaned according to government regulations at a cost of $34,550. Tulta also had to refund $17,992 in tuition for the period when it was closed, and its reputation and value as a business have been injured severely.

In this motion, Tulta Preschool seeks partial summary judgment determining that Raucher is liable to Tulta. If the motion is granted, the only issue for trial would be the size of the damages award.

STATEMENT OF FACTS

Lead is a poison. If it gets into a child's body, it can cause permanent brain and neurological damage, leading to learning disabilities, behavioral problems, or reduced IQ. (Aff. Leonard Crosetti, M.D., at ¶3 (Feb. 23, 2013).) Lead can also impair a child's ability to process vitamin D and to make red blood cells, and it can irreversibly damage the kidney (*Id.* ¶5). The most common source of lead poisoning is microscopic lead paint dust that cannot be detected through visual inspection (*Id.* ¶2). If the floor inside a building or the soil outside is contaminated with lead dust, young children can literally eat lead because they frequently and unexpectedly put their hands and other things in their mouths while playing (*Id.* ¶3). If a young child sees a paint chip, that chip might also end up in the child's mouth and be sucked on or swallowed whole (*Id.*).

Within 135 feet of a neighboring preschool, Raucher power-sanded toxic lead paint off every inch of the wood exterior of an antique store at 32 Seabank Road, including all the siding and trim and an intricate wood porch. (Dep. Michael Raucher at 18:11-18:23 (Nov. 18, 2012).) He did nothing to prevent paint chips and dust from flying onto Tulta Preschool's grounds (*Id.* at 19), and, helped by the wind, they did exactly that. (Aff. Jane Greenburg at ¶9 (Feb. 24, 2013).)

Mr. Raucher and Lead Paint

The store was built in 1901. (Aff. Petra Diaz at ¶8 (Feb. 27, 2013).) At that time and until the 1950's, most exterior paint contained substantial amounts of lead, and some paint was as much as 50% lead (Greenburg Aff. at ¶6). Lead paint might be found in or on any building built before 1978, when the sale of lead paint was prohibited, but it is most frequently found in those built before the 1950's (*Id.*). Raucher admits that he knew the store's approximate age from its building style and details (Raucher Dep. at 6:2-6:16).

Sanding prepares a worn paint surface to be repainted (Raucher Dep. at 11:2-12:25). Raucher believed at the time he began to sand that much of the building had probably never been stripped of the paint it had accumulated over

-1-

This is the opening paragraph described in §27.2, question 27-D. It's intended to motivate the judge from the very first sentence.

the years, and that he would in many places be removing all the paint that had ever been applied to the store, right down to the original coat from 1901 (*Id.* at 12).

Before beginning to sand, Raucher could have had some paint chips tested for lead at a local lab for $45 per chip (Greenburg Aff. at ¶26). For $250 to $400, he could have hired a technician to examine virtually all the store's outside surfaces for lead with a hand-held x-ray gun (*Id.*). For as little as $15, he could have bought in any hardware or paint store a limited testing kit that would have given him some confirmation of the presence of lead (*Id.*).

Raucher did none of these things. And he did nothing to encourage the store owner to test for lead before Raucher began work (Raucher Dep. at 86:16). In fact, he has never tested any paint for lead or encouraged any customer to do so (*Id.* at 87:19). He believes that no painter he knows has ever done any of these things (*Id.* at 89-4).

There are well understood methods of safely removing or encapsulating lead paint. It can be wet-sanded by hand, which is time-consuming but spreads little dust and paint chips (Greenburg Aff. at ¶8). Or the paint can be stripped following abatement procedures with a work area shrouded in impermeable plastic barriers, which is expensive but, when done properly, leaves no dust or chips behind (*Id.* at ¶7). Or the paint can be enclosed inside something new, like aluminum siding, which also leaves no dust or chips but can diminish the architectural character of an old building (*Id.*).

Raucher has not learned how to do any of this, and he believes that no painter of his acquaintance has either (Raucher Dep. at 67). But he has seen newspaper stories and television commentary about the dangers of lead paint, and he knows that lead paint can no longer legally be sold because it is considered dangerous (*Id.* at 42:6, 52:9).

Raucher believes that concerns about lead are "all exaggerated" because "I've been painting and sanding all my life, and there's nothing wrong with me or with any of the other painters in Coff's Harbor" (*Id.* at 67:18-67:22). At his deposition, he elaborated as follows:

Q: Why do you keep on power-sanding old paint, after what you've read in the newspaper and seen on TV?

A: People aren't going to pay for all this expensive stuff, and most painters aren't going to learn how to do it. People expect to pay three or four thousand dollars maximum to repaint a house, and painters expect to do the job the way they've always done it, with power-sanders and tarps—and not wearing white hazardous materials suits and trapping every last chip in plastic sheets to be taken away to hazardous waste dumps and all the other crazy things you're talking about. I'm a painter. My job is to sand and paint. That's what painters do.

Id. at 68:19-69:14

A Preschool Contaminated with Lead

Raucher power-sanded the building at 32 Seabank Road during a school vacation week. (Aff. Sharon Williams at ¶4 (Feb. 20, 2013).) No one was at Tulta Preschool at the time (*Id.*). When some Tulta teachers arrived the following

Monday, they noticed "a film of blue dust over most things on that side of the school, plus scattered bunches of blue chips" (*Id.* at ¶10). They also noticed that every inch of the exterior of 32 Seabank Road had been stripped of paint down to the bare wood (*Id.* at ¶11).

The teachers stopped all the arriving children in the parking lot and immediately sent them home (*Id.* at ¶13). Many parents were forced to leave their jobs and come home to care for their children (*Id.* at ¶14). Some parents missed more than a week of work (*Id.* at ¶15).

Environmental Assessments, Inc. tested Tulta Preschool's soil, walkways, and various interior surfaces (Greenburg Aff. at ¶12). Dust had entered the building through air-conditioning vents and had been spread inside by a ventilation fan (*Id.* at ¶19). Most of the interior and exterior surfaces tested by Environmental Assessments contained lead dust in amounts exceeding the guidelines promulgated for soil by the U.S. Environmental Protection Agency (EPA) and for interior floors by the U.S. Department of Housing and Urban Development (HUD) (*Id.* at ¶23).

To restore Tulta Preschool to a safe condition, an abatement company had to clean up visible dust and chips, scrub with a deleading solution most hard surfaces outside and many inside, remove and replace the top layer of soil wherever grass was not already growing (such as under swings), and build a solid fence between the two properties so that additional dust and chips would not later blow onto Tulta Preschool's grounds (Williams Aff. at ¶28). Everything removed by the abatement company, including soil, had to be taken to a toxic waste dump (Greenburg Aff. at ¶19).

The cost of testing and abatement totalled $34,550 (*Id.* at ¶31). Tulta Preschool also had to refund tuition for the period when it was closed, totalling $17,992 (*Id.* at ¶33). Applications for the following year were fewer than normal, and Tulta Preschool has acquired a reputation as "the place where that lead paint thing happened" (*Id.* at ¶36).

Lead poisoning symptoms develop so gradually and sporadically that parents and others frequently do not recognize them as symptoms and instead assume that "that is just the way this child is" (Crosetti Aff. at ¶14). According to Dr. Leonard Crosetti, a lead-specialist pediatrician ready to testify in this case, harm to the quality of life for a lead-poisoned child can last a lifetime. (*Id.* ¶11). Annexed to Dr. Crosetti's affidavit are 14 articles from medical journals showing that Dr. Crosetti's observations reflect medical research on this question.

ARGUMENT

Tulta Preschool Should Be Granted a Partial Summary Judgment Determining That Mr. Raucher Negligently Caused Tulta Preschool's Injuries.

"[L]ead is the number one environmental poison for children," the New York state legislature determined when amending its Lead Poisoning Prevention Act. "Environmental exposure to even low levels of lead increases a child's risk of developing permanent learning disabilities, reduced concentration and attentiveness, and behavior problems. These problems may persist and

This is the opening paragraph described in §24.3, question 24-D, which explains why the Chapter 11 paradigm is being varied here.

-3-

406

adversely affect the child's chances for success in school and life. Higher levels of lead can cause mental retardation, kidney disease, liver damage and even death." N.Y. Laws 1992, ch. 485, § 1 (1993).

In New York City, there was a public uproar when city workers sandblasted toxic lead paint off a bridge above a residential neighborhood. The mayor appointed a task force to choose a different method of paint removal, but even that was enjoined because the people affected—those who lived in the shadow of the bridge—had not been given sufficient opportunity to be heard. *Williamsburg Around the Bridge Block Ass'n v. Giuliani*, 644 N.Y.S.2d 252 (1st Dep't 1996).

If Coff's Harbor were to have a seaside village's equivalent of the Williamsburg Bridge fiasco, it would be what Raucher did to the building adjacent to Tulta Preschool. The evidence of that is so overwhelming that Tulta Preschool should be granted summary judgment on the question of liability, leaving for trial only the computation of damages.

> Here begins an umbrella paradigm (§13.2). Motivating arguments were made above—in the first and second paragraphs of the Argument. See §24.3, question 24-B.

Summary judgment "shall be rendered if . . . there is no genuine issue as to any material fact and . . . the moving party is entitled to judgment as a matter of law." *Appleton v. Board of Educ.*, 757 A.2d 1059, 1062 (Conn. 2000) (quoting Practice Book 384). Raucher has pleaded no affirmative defenses. All the issues in this motion therefore concern Tulta Preschool's claim of negligence. The elements of negligence "are well established: duty; breach of that duty; causation; and actual injury." *RK Constructors, Inc. v. Fusco Corp.*, 650 A.2d 153, 155 (Conn. 1994). Although no reported case in any state has determined whether a painter commits negligence on facts like these, there is ample reason to hold Raucher liable.

A. Raucher has no evidence contradicting Tulta's evidence on the elements of negligence, and therefore no material fact regarding liability is genuinely in dispute.

> Subheading A states the writer's conclusion on whether there's a genuine dispute of material fact. See the note in the margin next to the subheadings in the memo's table of contents. Under subheading A here, the first paragraph states the rules governing genuine disputes of material fact. These rules are so well known that the cites alone can prove them.
>
> The remaining paragraphs under subheading A apply the rules to the facts. The last two paragraphs are counter-arguments, which are more extensive

The party resisting summary judgment "must provide an evidentiary foundation to demonstrate the existence of a genuine issue of material fact." *Appleton*, 757 A.2d at 1062. It is not enough for the resisting party to claim that its version of a fact is true. The resisting party must demonstrate that there is a genuine issue by submitting admissible evidence that could be believed by a reasonable fact-finder. *Miles v. Foley*, 752 A.2d 503, 506 (Conn. 2000).

Raucher admits to power-sanding the building at 32 Seabank Road. He has no evidence that Environmental Assessment's testing was inaccurate. He does not deny that Tulta Preschool's property was abated, or that the school was closed during the period of the abatement, or that Tulta refunded tuition for that period.

Raucher does contend that lead paint is not really dangerous because "I've been painting and sanding all my life, and there's nothing wrong with me or with any of the other painters in Coff's Harbor" (Raucher Dep. at 67:18-67:22). This is a lay opinion, not evidence admissible at trial, and it does not create a genuine issue. "Only evidence that would be admissible at trial may be used to support or oppose a motion for summary judgment." *Home Insurance Co. v. Aetna Life & Casualty Co.* 663 A.2d 1001, 1008 (Conn. 1995). Mr. Raucher is not a physician and is not qualified

than usual because
Tulta must show that
Raucher has no real
evidence.

to determine whether he or anybody else has been lead-poisoned or whether lead is medically dangerous to small children, which is the crux of this case.

Even if he were so qualified, his opinion could not be accepted by a rational jury. The scientific evidence unanimously contradicts it (Crosetti Aff. at 2-19 and attached exhibits). And although lead is far more dangerous to children than to adults, courts have recognized, at least since *Dandurand v. Hydrox Co.*, 222 Ill. App. 267, 278 (1921), that painters themselves are in danger of lead poisoning. The children of painters are also in danger because lead dust can attach itself to work clothing and from there be distributed around a painter's home and family car. *Weaver v. Royal Ins. Co.*, 674 A.2d 975 (N.H. 1996).

The paradigm con-
clusion (Chapter 11.)
can be expressed in a
heading.

B.   Raucher should be held to the duty of care of a skilled lead paint abator working in the vicinity of children.

Notice how two cases
below are synthesized
to support the duty
formulation specified
in the subheading.
This is paradigmed
proof of the first ele-
ment of negligence.

If a general contractor—the kind that builds and remodels houses—contracts to dig a well, the contractor will be held to "that degree of care which a skilled well driller of ordinary prudence would have exercised under the same or similar conditions." *Sasso v. Ayotte*, 235 A.2d 636, 637 (Conn. 1967). In *Sasso*, the general contractor dug a well in such a way that overflow from a septic tank came through the house's fresh water taps. The general contractor made mistakes that a skilled well driller would not have made, and the general contractor was held liable.

A skilled remover of toxic lead paint is a lead abatement contractor, who must follow abatement procedures recognized by HUD including isolating the work area in plastic shrouds to contain the paint being removed. If a painter undertakes to strip toxic lead paint, the painter should be held to the standard of care that an abator would in the same circumstances. If the painter causes injury that a skilled abator would have prevented, the painter should be liable.

But the standard to which Raucher should be held is even higher than that. Children often do not recognize danger, and they can do unanticipated things very suddenly. "One is required to exercise greater care where the presence of children is reasonably to be expected." *Scorpion v. American-Republican, Inc.*, 37 A.2d 802, 804 (Conn. 1944). The *Scorpion* defendant was a newspaper company that left its editions bound in wire on sidewalks, where "newsboys" unbound and delivered them. An eight-year-old child injured her eye on wire left as litter on a residential sidewalk, and the newspaper was held liable because it should have known that children use residential sidewalks, and that many children would not realize that they could hurt themselves while handling the wire.

Implicit analogies.

A counter-argument.

When Raucher claims that he only did what painters have always done and what other painters would do with the same building, he misconstrues the standard of care by which his conduct should be judged. He did more than remove paint, which is something that painters do and know how to do. He removed toxic lead paint, which requires special skills and knowledge if it is to be done safely.

Enactments are used
to support a policy
argument.

Our statutes are evidence of the gravity of this situation. The owner of "any dwelling" where a child six years or younger lives "shall abate, remediate, or manage" paint, plaster, or anything else that contains toxic levels of lead. Conn. Gen. Stats. § 19a111c (2012). And local health directors in this state are authorized to relocate families from their homes when anyone in the family has

-5-

a lead blood level above a point specified by statute. Conn. Gen. Stats. § 19a-111 (2012).

C. *Raucher breached the duty of care.*

Sasso and *Scorpion* establish the duty that Raucher breached.

Using relatively inexpensive testing methods, Raucher could have determined that the exterior paint on the building at 32 Seabank Road was toxic. Lead paint dust and chips would not have contaminated Tulta Preschool if Raucher had wet sanded by hand, abated according to HUD procedures, or encapsulated the paint. Although the job would have become much more expensive, Raucher could have learned how to do any of these things himself, or he could have hired a qualified abatement company to do one of them as a subcontractor. But instead he power-sanded lead paint and contaminated Tulta Preschool, which had to be closed until, at great expense, it could be deleaded.

Like the general contractor who dug a well in *Sasso*, Raucher created an environmental hazard by ignoring what specialists know how to do. The general contractor was held liable, and so should Raucher. And like the newspaper company that left wire on the sidewalk in *Scorpion*, Raucher left substances particularly dangerous to children in places where children could find them without understanding their danger. In his case, the endangered were 130 children who have not yet reached the age of kindergarten. The newspaper was held liable, and so should Raucher.

It is not a defense to say that Raucher was not working on Tulta's property and is therefore not responsible for what happened there. When a person in control of land projects a dangerous situation onto neighboring property, that person is liable for the resulting damages. *Spagnolo v. Lanza*, 147 A. 594 (Conn. 1929). No case holds that this kind of liability is imposed only on landowners. As Raucher's own conduct demonstrates, anybody in control of land, even if only for a few days to paint a building, has the capacity to create an environmental disaster on adjoining property.

A counter-argument.

D. *Tulta Preschool has suffered harms remediable by negligence damages.*

The conclusion is stated in the heading.

This state has always recognized that negligence injuries include loss of income, such as wages. *Bach v. Giordano*, 128 A.2d 323, 324 (Conn. 1956). Damage to property is also considered a negligence injury. *Whitman Hotel Corp. v. Elliott & Watrous Eng'g Co.*, 79 A.2d 591, 595 (Conn. 1951). In *Whitman Hotel* a construction company conducted blasting operations near the plaintiff's hotel, and vibration from the blasting cracked pipes in the hotel, leading to water damage.

The rule together with rule proof and explanation.

Tulta Preschool suffered both kinds of injury. It had to refund $17,992 in tuition for the period when it was closed for abatement to remove lead paint dust. (Greenburg Aff. at ¶ 33). And the abatement itself cost $34,550 (*Id.*). When Raucher power-sanded lead paint next to Tulta's property, he caused the same type of injury that the construction company did with blasting operations in *Whitman Hotel*.

Rule Application.

-6-

409

> *E.   Raucher's breach proximately caused harm to*
> *Tulta Preschool.*

The injury and proximate cause arguments are less complicated than the earlier elements, and the arguments here is shortened. The big issue in this motion is whether Raucher owed a duty to Tulta.

The element of proximate causation is satisfied if "the defendant's conduct is a substantial factor in bringing about the plaintiff's injuries" through "an unbroken sequence of events" with a "causal connection . . . based upon more than conjecture and surmise." *Paige v. St. Andrew's Roman Catholic Church Corp.*, 734 A.2d 85, 91 (Conn. 1999).

An example of conjecture and surmise is *Coste v. Riverside Motors, Inc.*, 585 A.2d 1263 (Conn. App. 1991), where a plaintiff employee asked his employer, the defendant, for permission to leave work early because a storm was covering roads with snow. The employer refused, and when the employee drove home later, after finishing work, he collided with another car on a slippery road. The court held that it would be conjecture to determine whether the accident occurred because the plaintiff drove later rather than earlier or "whether the accident would have occurred had the road been better sanded or plowed, or had the plaintiff taken another route home, or had he driven a different make and model car, or had he been a better driver." *Id.* at 1266.

No other possible causes exist in this case, however. Raucher power-sanded lead paint on the exterior of a building right next to Tulta Preschool. Lead paint dust was found immediately afterward on the school's playground, exterior wall, and inside the preschool's building, brought in through the ventilation system. There is no evidence of any other paint sanding occurring anywhere else nearby, and there is no evidence that the lead paint dust could have had any other source.

CONCLUSION

This is the overall conclusion. See Chapter 25.

Tulta Preschool should be granted partial summary judgment determining that Raucher is liable in negligence. Raucher owed a duty of reasonable care to Tulta to avoid contaminating Tulta's property with lead paint dust and chips and to avoid creating a risk of lead poisoning in the vicinity of his work site. There is abundant evidence that he breached that duty, at great expense to Tulta and to Tulta's reputation, and that only the coincidence that he powersanded during a school vacation week prevented him from immediately injuring the health of 130 children as well. There is no evidence, admissible at trial, to the contrary, and therefore no rational jury can return a verdict against the preschool on the question of liability.

Respectfully Submitted,

Petra Diaz, Esq.

Petra Diaz, Esq.
Attorney for Plaintiffs
94 Front Street
Coff's Harbor, CT 14218
(203) 555-1111

Appendix
Excerpts from Appellant's Fourth Circuit Brief in *G.G. v. Gloucester County School Bd.*

This appendix includes excerpts from the Appellant's brief in the U.S. Court of Appeals for the Fourth Circuit. Appendix H includes excerpts from the appellee's brief in the same case. On this book's website are the complete briefs, which are about twice the size of the ones in these appendices and address a number of issues not in these appendices. Also on the website are the parties' later submissions in the U.S. Supreme Court and the Supreme Court's rulings.

The appellant is a young transgender man. At the time of the lawsuit, he was a high school student. The Gloucester County School Board had forbidden him to use the boys' restroom in his school. In the litigation documents, he is identified by his initials for privacy reasons.

G.G. argued that the School Board had discriminated against him in violation of Title IX of the Education Amendments of 1972 as well as the Equal Protection Clause in the Fourteenth Amendment to the U.S. Constitution. In the District Court he moved for a preliminary injunction that would require his high school to allow him to use the boys' restroom. The District Court denied the motion and dismissed his Title IX claim.[1]

---

1. *G.G. ex rel. Grimm v. Gloucester County School Bd.*, 132 F. Supp. 3d 736 (E.D. Va. 2015).

G.G. appealed to the Fourth Circuit. This appendix includes excerpts from his brief as appellant. The Fourth Circuit reversed,[2] and the School petitioned the U.S. Supreme Court for a writ of certiorari.

These briefs are governed by Rules 28(a) and 28(b) of the Federal Rules of Appellate Procedure:

Rule 28. Briefs

(a) **Appellant's Brief.** The appellant's brief must contain, under appropriate headings and in the order indicated:

(1) a corporate disclosure statement if required by Rule 26.1;

(2) a table of contents . . . ;

(3) a table of authorities . . . ;

(4) a jurisdictional statement . . . ;

(5) a statement of the issues presented for review;

(6) a concise statement of the case setting out the facts relevant to the issues submitted for review, describing the relevant procedural history, and identifying the rulings presented for review, with appropriate references to the record . . . ;

(7) a summary of the argument, which must contain a succinct, clear, and accurate statement of the arguments made in the body of the brief, and which must not merely repeat the argument headings;

(8) the argument, which must contain:

(A) appellant's contentions and the reasons for them, with citations to the authorities and parts of the record on which the appellant relies; and

(B) for each issue, a concise statement of the applicable standard of review (which may appear in the discussion of the issue or under a separate heading placed before the discussion of the issues);

(9) a short conclusion stating the precise relief sought; and

(10) the certificate of compliance, if required by Rule 32(a)(7).

(b) **Appellee's Brief.** The appellee's brief must conform to the requirements of Rule 28(a)(1)–(8) and (10), except that none of the following need appear unless the appellee is dissatisfied with the appellant's statement:

(1) the jurisdictional statement;

(2) the statement of the issues;

(3) the statement of the case; and

(4) the statement of the standard of review.

---

2. *G.G. ex rel. Grimm v. Gloucester County School Bd.*, 822 F.3d 709 (4th Cir. 2016).

To make these appendices more helpful to students, the briefs have been edited to reduce their size. Among other things, the appellant's jurisdictional statement and both parties' corporate disclosures have been omitted. Also omitted are certificates of compliance and service, the appellant's request for oral argument, and issues concerning the District Court's exclusion of various evidence, the appellant's request for reassignment to another District Court judge, and deference to administrative agencies' interpretation of their own regulations under Auer v. Robbins, 519 U.S. 452 (1997). To adjust for these omissions, some point headings are renumbered in the appendices, and some subheadings are relettered. To streamline the briefs for students, the Statements of the Case, Summary of Argument, and Argument have been shortened. In addition, the following are omitted: footnotes, citations not necessary to the argument, and some attorney details. A few typographical and grammatical incongruities have been resolved, and citations have been conformed to the Bluebook (20th ed.), sometimes by substituting a complete cite for a short-form one. In a very few instances, a word, such as the conjunction "and," has been inserted as a consequence of a deletion. To preserve readability, deletions have not been marked with ellipses or brackets.

No. 15-2056

UNITED STATES COURT OF APPEALS
FOR THE FOURTH CIRCUIT

G.G., by his next friend and mother, **DEIRDRE GRIMM**

Plaintiff-Appellant,

v.

GLOUCESTER COUNTY SCHOOL BOARD

Defendant-Appellee.

On Appeal from the United States District Court
for the Eastern District of Virginia
Newport News Division

BRIEF OF PLAINTIFF-APPELLANT

AMERICAN CIVIL LIBERTIES UNION
OF VIRGINIA FOUNDATION, INC.,
Rebecca K. Glenberg
Gail Deady
Richmond, Virginia

AMERICAN CIVIL LIBERTIES UNION
FOUNDATION
Joshua A. Block
Leslie Cooper
New York, New York

Counsel for Plaintiff-Appellant

TABLE OF CONTENTS

Notice that the two briefs don't tackle the Title IX and Equal Protection arguments in the same sequence. The School Board's brief in App. H addresses Equal Protection first and then Title IX.

-i-

TABLE OF AUTHORITIES

Cases

INTRODUCTION

This is a preliminary statement as described in Ch. 30 (§30.1). Here it's called an Introduction. It tells the court in a nutshell what the appeal is all about. While doing that, lawyers also introduce the court to their theory of the appeal (Ch. 31, §31.1).

Plaintiff G.G. is a 16-year-old transgender boy who has just begun his junior year at Gloucester High School. He is a boy and lives accordingly in all aspects of his life, but the sex assigned to him at birth was female. In accordance with the standards of care for treating Gender Dysphoria, he is undergoing hormone therapy; he has legally changed his name; and his state identification card identifies him as male. In every other context outside school, he uses the boys' restrooms, just like any other boy would.

During his sophomore year, with the permission of school administrators, G. used the boys' restrooms at school for seven weeks without incident. After some parents complained, however, the Gloucester County School Board (the "Board") passed a new policy that singles out transgender students for different treatment than all other students. The policy prohibits G. from using the same restrooms as other boys and relegates him to single-stall, unisex restrooms that no other student is required to use.

G. alleges that the Board's policy of excluding transgender students from the restrooms used by all other students violates his rights under Title IX and the Fourteenth Amendment by stigmatizing transgender students, depriving them of physical access to school resources, jeopardizing their health, and impairing their ability to participate equally in the educational benefits and opportunities of school. G. seeks a preliminary injunction to stop the ongoing irreparable harm he experiences each day he is subject to the Board's policy.

STATEMENT OF ISSUES

See the exercise at the end of Ch. 32 (Questions Presented).

1. Should G. be granted a preliminary injunction to allow him to resume using the boys' restrooms during the pendency of the case?

2. Should the court's dismissal of the Title IX claim be reversed?

STATEMENT OF CASE

Gender Dysphoria

This brief explains the story in much detail. Partly that's to help the court grasp medical and other facts that aren't widely understood. And partly it's to give the court a feeling for how the plaintiff has experienced the situation. A judge's work isn't limited to logical reasoning.

"Gender identity" is a well-established medical concept, referring to one's sense of oneself as belonging to a particular gender. J.A. 36. All human beings have a gender identity. *Id.* It is an innate and immutable aspect of personality that is firmly established by age four, although individuals vary in the age at which they come to understand and express their gender identity. *Id.* Typically, people who are designated female at birth based on their external anatomy identify as girls or women, and people who are designated male at birth identify as boys or men. *Id.* For transgender individuals, however, the sense of one's self—one's gender identity—differs from the sex assigned to them at birth. *Id.*

The medical diagnosis for that feeling of incongruence is Gender Dysphoria, a serious medical condition codified in the *Diagnostic and Statistical Manual of Mental Disorders* (DSM-V) (American Psychiatric

-1-

Association 2013) and *International Classification of Diseases-10* (World Health Organization 2010). The criteria for diagnosing Gender Dysphoria are set forth in the DSM-V (302.85). J.A 37. Untreated Gender Dysphoria can result in significant clinical distress, debilitating depression, and suicidal thoughts and acts. *Id.* The World Professional Association for Transgender Health has established international *Standards of Care for treating people with Gender Dysphoria* (the "WPATH Standards"). J.A. 37. Leading medical and mental health organizations, including the American Medical Association, the Endocrine Society, and the American Psychological Association, have endorsed the WPATH Standards as the authoritative standards of care. *Id.*

Under the WPATH Standards, treatment for Gender Dysphoria is designed to help transgender individuals live congruently with their gender identity and eliminate clinically significant distress. J.A. 38. Attempting to change a person's gender identity to match the person's sex assigned at birth is ineffective and harmful to the patient. *Id.* "It is important to note that gender nonconformity is not in itself a mental disorder. The critical element of gender dysphoria is the presence of clinically significant distress associated with the condition." Am. Psychiatric Ass'n, *Gender Dysphoria Fact Sheet* 1 (2013).

Under the WPATH Standards, social role transition—living one's life fully in accordance with one's gender identity—is a critical component of treatment for Gender Dysphoria. J.A. 38. For a transgender male, that typically includes dressing and grooming as a male, adopting a male name, and presenting oneself to the community as a boy or man. *Id.* The social transition takes place at home, at work or school, and in the broader community. *Id.* If any aspect of social role transition is impeded, it undermines a person's entire transition. *Id.* Negating a person's gender identity poses serious health risks, including depression, post-traumatic stress disorder, hypertension, and self-harm. J.A. 40.

G.'s Gender Dysphoria

At a very young age, G. was aware that he did not feel like a girl. J.A. 28. By approximately age twelve, G. acknowledged his male gender identity to himself and to close friends. J.A. 29. By ninth grade, most of G.'s friends knew his gender identity, and they treated him as male when socializing away from home and school. *Id.*

G.'s untreated Gender Dysphoria, and the stress of concealing his gender identity from his family, caused him to experience severe depression and anxiety. *Id.* G.'s mental distress was so severe that he could not attend school in 2014 during the spring semester of his freshman year. *Id.* Instead, he took classes through a home-bound program that follows the public high school curriculum. *Id.*

In April 2014, G. told his parents that he is transgender. *Id.* At his request, he began seeing a psychologist with experience working with transgender youth. *Id.* G.'s psychologist diagnosed G. with Gender Dysphoria and, consistent with the WPATH Standards, recommended that he begin living in accordance with his male gender identity in all aspects of his life. *Id.* G.'s psychologist also provided G. with a "Treatment Documentation Letter" confirming he was receiving treatment for Gender Dysphoria and, as part of that treatment, should be treated as a boy in all respects, including with respect

It includes empathy, which is why motivating arguments are essential.

Motivating arguments are usually introduced in a Statement of the Case, where they are implied by the way the story is told rather than expressly stated. They are expressly stated in the Argument. In Ch. 24, see question 24-B (motivating arguments). In Ch. 27, see question 27-A (implying motivating arguments in the Statement of the Case).

Never *express* motivating arguments in a Statement of the Case. Imply them by the way you tell the story. Express them in the Argument section of the brief.

to his use of the restroom. *Id.* G. uses the boys' restrooms in public venues such as restaurants, libraries, and shopping centers. J.A. 30.

In July 2014, G. successfully petitioned the Circuit Court of Gloucester County to change his legal name to G. J.A. 29. G. now uses that name for all purposes, and his friends and family refer to him using male pronouns. *Id.*

Also consistent with the WPATH Standards, G.'s psychologist recommended that he see an endocrinologist to begin hormone treatment. *Id.* G. has received hormone treatment since late December 2014. J.A. 30. Among other therapeutic benefits, the hormone treatment has deepened G.'s voice, increased his growth of facial hair, and given him a more masculine appearance. *Id.*

In June 2015, the Virginia Department of Motor Vehicles approved G.'s request for the sex designation "M" for male to appear on his driver's license or identification card. J.A. 60.

School Response

In August 2014, before beginning his sophomore year, G. and his mother informed officials at Gloucester High School that G. is a transgender boy and that he had legally changed his name to G. J.A. 30. G. and his mother also met with the school principal and guidance counselor to explain that G. is a transgender boy and that, consistent with his medically supervised treatment, he would be attending school as a male student. *Id.*

G. initially agreed to use a separate restroom in the nurse's office because he was unsure how other students would react to his transition. *Id.* When the 2014–15 school year began, however, G. was pleased to discover that his teachers and the vast majority of his peers respected the fact that he is a boy and treated him accordingly. J.A. 30–31. G. found the separate restroom stigmatizing and inconvenient, so he asked the principal permission to use the boys' restrooms. J.A. 31. On or about October 20, 2014, the principal agreed that G. could use the boys' restrooms. *Id.* For approximately the next seven weeks, G. used the boys' restrooms without incident. *Id.*

Nevertheless, some adults in the community were angered when they learned that a transgender boy was attending the school and using the boys' restroom. J.A. 57–58. Those adults contacted members of the Board to demand that the transgender student be barred from using the boys' restrooms. *Id.*

Shortly before the Board's meeting on November 11, 2014, Board member Hooks added the following policy for discussion on the agenda:

> Whereas the GCPS recognizes that some students question their gender identities, and
> Whereas the GCPS encourages such students to seek support, advice, and guidance from parents, professionals and other trusted adults, and
> Whereas the GCPS seeks to provide a safe learning environment for all students and to protect the privacy of all students, therefore
> It shall be the practice of the GCPS to provide male and female restroom and locker room facilities in its schools, and the use of said facilities shall be limited to the corresponding biological genders, and

-3-

420

students with gender identity issues shall be provided an alternative appropriate private facility.

Gloucester County School Board Minutes, Nov. 11, 2014 ("Nov. 11 Minutes") at 4.

G. and his parents attended the meeting to speak against the policy. J.A. 31. Doing so required G. to identify himself to the entire community, including local press covering the meeting, as the student whose restroom use was at issue. *Id.* "All I want to do is be a normal child and use the restroom in peace," G. said. *See* Gloucester County School Board Video Tr., Nov. 11, 2014 ("Nov. 11 Video Tr."). "I did not ask to be this way, and it's one of the most difficult things anyone can face." *Id.* 26:14. "This could be your child . . . . I'm just a human. I'm just a boy." *Id.* 27:02.

Most speakers at the meeting urged the Board to prohibit G. from using the restrooms that other boys use. *See* Nov. 11 Minutes at 3. Speakers voiced many stereotypes and misperceptions about transgender people and expressed fears that equal treatment for transgender students would lead to dire consequences. Some speakers pointedly referred to G. as a "young lady" to negate his gender identity. Nov. 11 Video Tr. 14:55; 18:07; 20:36; 1:06:48. One speaker claimed that permitting transgender students to use the same restrooms as others would lead to teenage pregnancies and sexually transmitted infections. *Id.* 34:40. Another cited the Bible and complained about "morality creep." *Id.* 53:35. And another said G.'s use of the boys' restrooms would lead to boys wearing dresses to school and demanding to use the girls' restroom for improper purposes. *Id.* 20:55.

The Board deferred voting on the policy until its meeting on December 9, 2014. *See* Nov. 11 Minutes at 4.

At the Board's December 9, 2014, meeting, most speakers again opposed permitting transgender students to use the same restrooms as other students. *See* Gloucester County School Board Minutes, Dec. 9, 2014 ("Dec. 9 Minutes") at 3. Several speakers threatened to vote Board members out of office if they did not require transgender students to use separate restrooms. Gloucester County School Board Video Tr., Dec. 9, 2014, ("Dec. 9 Video Tr.") 42:34; 50:53; 59:34; 1:17:56. Some speakers said allowing transgender boys to use the boys' restroom would make the restrooms "coed." *Id.* 39:23; 41:11. Speakers again referred to G. as a "girl" or "young lady." *Id.* 38:00; 1:17:40. One speaker who described herself as a "former lesbian" said "we have forgotten than God created a man and a woman" and complained that prayers have been removed from schools. *Id.* 1:19:48. Another called G. a "freak" and compared him to a person who thinks he is a dog and wants to urinate on fire hydrants. *Id.* 1:22:55; 1:23:19.

The Board voted 6–1 to pass the policy prohibiting transgender students from using the same restrooms as other students. Dec. 9 Minutes at 4.

Aftermath

The public, community-wide debate about which restrooms he should use has been humiliating for G., who feels that he has been turned into "a public

-4-

spectacle" in front of the entire community "like a walking freak show." J.A. 31.

The day after the Board adopted the new policy, the principal told G. he could no longer use the same restrooms as other boys. J.A. 32. G. must now use separate, private facilities instead of using the same restrooms as other students. The Board has asserted that G. may use the girls' restroom, but that is not a realistic possibility for G. or other boys who are transgender. Even before G. transitioned, other students objected to his presence in the girls' restroom because they perceived him to be a boy. *Id.*

G. refuses to use the separate, single-stall restrooms because they are even more stigmatizing and isolating than the restroom in the nurse's office. *Id.* No other students actually use these restrooms, and only one of the restrooms is located anywhere near the restrooms used by everybody else. *Id.* Adding to the stigma, everyone knows the restrooms were installed specifically for G. so that other boys would not have to share the same restroom with him. *Id.* The separate restrooms physically and symbolically mark G. as "other," isolate G. from the rest of his peers, and brand him as unfit to share the same restrooms as other students. *Id.* Every time G. has to use the restrooms at school, other students are visibly reminded that the school considers him to be different than other students, making him feel alienated and humiliated. J.A. 32–33.

To escape such stigma and humiliation, G. tries to avoid using the restroom entirely while at school, and, if that is not possible, he uses the nurse's restroom. J.A. 32. Using the nurse's restroom still makes him feel embarrassed and humiliated, which increases his dysphoria, anxiety, and distress. J.A. 32–33. G. feels embarrassed that everyone who sees him enter the nurse's office knows he is there because he has been prohibited from using the same boys' restrooms that the other boys use. J.A. 33. To avoid using the restroom, G. limits the amount of liquids he drinks and tries to "hold it" when he needs to urinate during the school day. J.A. 32–33. As a result, G. has repeatedly developed painful urinary tract infections and has felt distracted and uncomfortable in class. *Id.*

Dr. Randi Ettner—a psychologist and nationally recognized expert in the treatment of Gender Dysphoria in children and adolescents—recently conducted an independent clinical assessment of G. and concluded that "excluding G.G. from the communal restroom used by other boys and effectively banishing him to separate single-stall restroom facilities is currently causing emotional distress to an extremely vulnerable youth and placing G. at risk for accruing lifelong psychological harm." J.A. 41. Dr. Ettner determined that G. has Gender Dysphoria and that medically necessary treatment for G. includes testosterone therapy and social transition in all aspects of his life—including the use of the boys' restrooms. J.A. 42.

Dr. Ettner explained that ages 15–16 are particularly vulnerable years for teenagers, when nothing is more important than fitting in with one's peers. J.A. 39–40. That vulnerability is even greater for transgender teenagers who, because of Gender Dysphoria, already feel different and must take additional steps to fit in with their peers. J.A. 40. As a result of those challenges, transgender students are at far greater risk for severe health consequences—including suicide—than other students, and more than 50 percent of transgender youth will have attempted suicide at least once by age

By this point, are you able to see things through G.G.'s eyes—how he has experienced all these events?

-5-

422

20. *Id*. Stigma also causes many transgender youth to experience academic difficulties and to drop out of school. J.A. 41. Transgender students' stress and victimization at school are associated with a greater risk for post-traumatic stress disorder, depression, life dissatisfaction, anxiety, and suicidality in adulthood. *Id*.

Dr. Ettner concluded that the stigma G. experiences every time he needs to use the restroom "is a devastating blow to G. and places him at extreme risk for immediate and long-term psychological harm." J.A. 42.

Procedural History

G. originally filed the Complaint and Motion for Preliminary Injunction on June 11, 2015, the day after the end of the 2014–15 school year, with the goal of obtaining a preliminary injunction before September 10, 2015, the first day of the 2015–16 school year. J.A. 25.

On September 4, 2015 — a few days before school began — the court denied G.'s Motion for Preliminary Injunction. J.A. 137.

SUMMARY OF ARGUMENT

This case is not about whether schools may provide separate restrooms for male and female students. It is about how to provide transgender students with equal, non-discriminatory access to those existing restrooms, as Title IX and the Fourteenth Amendment require. A preliminary injunction is necessary to stop the ongoing irreparable harm the Board has inflicted on G. by preventing him from using the same restrooms as other students and relegating him to separate, single-stall facilities.

G. has established a likelihood of success on his Title IX claim. Title IX's prohibition on discrimination "on the basis of sex" protects transgender students from discrimination based on their transgender status or gender nonconformity. Discrimination against transgender people is necessarily discrimination based on sex because it is impossible to treat people differently based on their transgender status without taking their sex into account. Requiring transgender students to use separate restrooms from other students violates Title IX by stigmatizing transgender students, depriving them of physical access to school resources, jeopardizing their health, and impairing their ability to participate equally in the educational benefits and opportunities of school.

G. has also established a likelihood of success on his Equal Protection claim. For the same reasons that excluding G. from using the same restrooms as other students violates Title IX, it also discriminates based on gender and requires heightened scrutiny under the Fourteenth Amendment. The Board has not carried its burden under heightened scrutiny to show that forcing G. to use separate restrooms substantially advances an interest in privacy or any other important governmental interest.

Because G. is likely to prevail on the merits, the remaining preliminary injunction factors necessarily weigh in his favor.

-6-

The wrap-up in a Statement of the Case takes the reader to the procedural event — the lower court's ruling — that has been appealed.

As you read the Summary of Argument and the Argument itself below, identify every place where the brief makes a policy argument.

See Ch. 31, §31.3 (standards of review).

This is the four-element test G.G. must satisfy. See Ch. 28 (procedural postures). The brief is organized around these elements. Because G.G. must satisfy all of them, the Argument includes several paradigmed proofs. For how to organize in this situation, see Ch. 13 (combining separate paradigm proofs).

In persuasive writing, the paradigm is modified to emphasize motivating arguments. See question 24-D in Ch. 24.

This paragraph identifies a gap in the law and lays a foundation for filling the gap in later paragraphs. In Ch. 7, see §7.5 on gap-filling.

ARGUMENT

I. Preliminary Injunction Standard.

This Court "evaluate[s] the court's decision to deny a preliminary injunction for an abuse of discretion, reviewing the court's factual findings for clear error and its legal conclusions de novo. A court abuses its discretion when it misapprehends or misapplies the applicable law." *League of Women Voters v. North Carolina*, 769 F.3d 224, 235 (4th Cir. 2014) (internal quotation marks omitted; alterations incorporated).

To obtain a preliminary injunction, "[p]laintiffs must demonstrate that (1) they are likely to succeed on the merits; (2) they will likely suffer irreparable harm absent an injunction; (3) the balance of hardships weighs in their favor; and (4) the injunction is in the public interest." *Id.* at 236. "While plaintiffs seeking preliminary injunctions must demonstrate that they are likely to succeed on the merits, they need not show a certainty of success." *Id.* at 247 (internal quotation marks omitted).

II. G. Has Established a Likelihood of Success on His Title IX Claim.

A. Excluding Transgender Students from Using the Same Restrooms as Other Students Discriminates Against G. on the Basis of Sex.

G. is a boy and lives accordingly in all aspects of his life. He is undergoing hormone therapy; he has legally changed his name; and his state identification card identifies him as male. In every other context outside school, he uses the boys' restrooms, just like any other boy would. At school, however, the Board has singled him out for different treatment than everyone else. Most non-transgender boys would feel humiliated if they were publicly labeled as different and forced to use a separate restroom from all the other boys. G. feels that way too.

By singling out G. for different and unequal treatment because he is transgender, the Board has discriminated against him based on sex, in violation of Title IX. This Court has not addressed whether discrimination against transgender individuals constitutes discrimination based on sex. *See Lewis v. High Point Reg'l Health Sys.*, 79 F. Supp. 3d 588, 589 (E.D.N.C. 2015). Within this Circuit, however, two district courts have already held that discrimination against transgender people is sex discrimination, *see id.* at 589–90; *Finkle v. Howard Cty.*, 12 F. Supp. 3d 780, 788 (D. Md. 2014), and another two have issued rulings where the defendant conceded that Title VII applied, *see Muir v. Applied Integrated Tech., Inc.*, No. 13-0808, 2013 WL 6200178, at *10 (D. Md. Nov. 26, 2013); *Hart v. Lew*, 973 F. Supp. 2d 561, 581 (D. Md. 2013).

Discrimination based on transgender status is discrimination based on sex under Title IX and other federal civil rights statutes because an individual's "transgender status is necessarily part of his 'sex' or 'gender' identity." *Rumble v. Fairview Health Servs.*, No. 14-CV-2037 SRN/FLN, 2015 WL 1197415, at *2 (D. Minn. Mar. 16, 2015). By definition, transgender individuals are people whose gender identity is not congruent with the sex assigned to them at birth. Accordingly, when an official "discriminates against someone because the person is transgender," the official necessarily "has engaged in disparate treatment related to the sex of the victim." *Mia Macy*, EEOC DOC 0120120821, 2012 WL 1435995, at *7 (Apr. 20, 2012) (internal quotation marks omitted). Just as it is impossible to discriminate against a person for being a religious convert without discriminating based on religion, it is impossible to treat people differently based on their transgender status without treating them differently based on sex.

In addition, discrimination based on a person's transgender status also inherently involves impermissible discrimination based on a person's gender nonconformity. Under Title IX and other federal civil rights statutes, discrimination "on the basis of sex" includes discrimination for "failing to act and appear according to expectations defined by gender." *Glenn v. Brumby*, 663 F.3d 1312, 1316 (11th Cir. 2011). For example, in *Price Waterhouse v. Hopkins*, 490 U.S. 228 (1989), the Supreme Court ruled that an employer discriminated on the basis of "sex" when it denied promotion to an employee based, in part, on her failure to conform to stereotypes about how women should behave. The employee was advised that if she wanted to advance in her career she should be less "macho" and learn to "walk more femininely, talk more femininely, dress more femininely, wear make-up, have her hair styled, and wear jewelry." *Id.* at 235. *Price Waterhouse* thus "eviscerated" the reasoning of some lower court decisions that attempted to narrow Title VII by drawing a distinction between discrimination based on sex and discrimination based on gendered behavior. *Smith*, 378 F.3d at 573.

Under *Price Waterhouse*, it does not matter whether a plaintiff is perceived "to be an insufficiently masculine man, an insufficiently feminine woman, or an inherently gender-nonconforming transsexual." *Schroer v. Billington,* 577 F. Supp. 2d 293, 305 (D.D.C. 2008). Transgender individuals are people who not conform to the general assumption that a person's gender identity will correspond to the sex assigned to that person at birth. Thus, "it would seem that any discrimination against transsexuals (as transsexuals)—individuals who, by definition, do not conform to gender stereotypes—is . . . discrimination on the basis of sex as interpreted by *Price Waterhouse*." *Finkle*, 12 F. Supp. 3d at 788; *see Rumble*, 2015 WL 1197415, at *2 ("Because the term 'transgender' describes people whose gender expression differs from their assigned sex at birth, discrimination based on an individual's transgender status constitutes discrimination based on gender stereotyping."). There is inherently "a congruence between discriminating against transgender and transsexual individuals and discrimination on the basis of gender-based behavioral norms." *Glenn*, 663 F.3d at 1316.

The *Price Waterhouse* line of cases confirms what is already evident from the text of Title IX. "[I]ntentional discrimination against a transgender individual because that person is transgender is, by definition, discrimination based on sex." *Macy*, 2012 WL 1435995, at *11 (internal quotation marks omitted; alterations incorporated). By treating G. differently than every other boy because of the sex assigned to him at birth, the Board is treating him differently based on "sex" under Title IX.

-8-

In statutes prohibiting sex discrimination, what did Congress mean by the word "sex"? This is a classic statutory interpretation problem, like the *McBoyle* case in Ch. 8 (working with statutes). Both this brief and the one in App. H use some of the statutory interpretation tools explained in Ch. 8.

Both briefs discuss *Glenn v. Brumby* and *Price Waterhouse v. Hopkins*. Use the App. H brief's Table of Authorities to find that brief's discussion of these two cases. How do the two briefs differ in the way they handle them?

On the Title IX issue, the rule proof part of the paradigm (Ch. 11) was mostly in subpoint A above. Rule application starts here in subpoint B.

B. Excluding G. from Using the Same Restrooms as Other Students Deprives Him of Equal Access to Educational Opportunity.

At the most basic level, Title IX protects students from "physical deprivation of access to school resources" based on gender. *Davis ex rel. LaShonda D. v. Monroe Cnty. Bd. of Educ.*, 526 U.S. 629, 650 (1999). The Board has physically deprived G. and other transgender students of equal access to school resources by excluding them from the same restrooms used by everyone else. *See Lusardi v. McHugh*, EEOC DOC 0120133395, 2015 WL 1607756, at *8 (Apr. 1, 2015) (excluding transgender woman from restrooms used by other women deprived her of a basic term and condition of employment); *Kastl v. Maricopa Cty. Cmty. Coll. Dist.*, No. CIV.02-1531PHX-SRB, 2004 WL 2008954, at *2 (D. Ariz. June 3, 2004) ("[N]either a woman with male genitalia nor a man with stereotypically female anatomy, such as breasts, may be deprived of a benefit or privilege of employment by reason of that nonconforming trait. Application of this rule may not be avoided merely because restroom availability is the benefit at issue."); *cf. Snyder ex rel. R.P. v. Frankfort-Elberta Area Sch. Dist.*, No. 1:05-CV-824, 2006 WL 3613673, at *1 (W.D. Mich. Dec. 11, 2006) (requiring black elementary school student to use separate restroom in response to harassment from other students deprived her of "equal access to restroom facilities" in violation of the Equal Education Opportunity Act).

Singling out G. for different treatment than all the other boys also interferes with his medically necessary treatment for Gender Dysphoria. As Dr. Ettner explained, when authority figures deny transgender students access to the restroom consistent with their gender identity, they shame those students—negating the legitimacy of their identity and posing health risks, including depression, post-traumatic stress disorder, and self-harm. J.A. 41. The harm caused to transgender students' physical and psychological wellbeing necessarily interferes with their ability to thrive at school. For example, the depression and anxiety G. previously experienced as a result of concealing his gender identity at school and from his parents was so great that G. could not attend school during the spring of his freshman year. J.A. 29.

Excluding G. from the same restrooms used by all other students further denies G. equal educational opportunity by publicly shaming him and physically isolating him from the rest of his peers. The policy is an official school decree marking G. and other transgender students as unequal based on other students' supposed disapproval or discomfort with them. It sends a message to G. and the entire school community that G. is not a "real" boy and should not be treated as such. The intention and effect of the transgender policy were crystallized in the words of one of its supporters: "[W]e have a thousand students versus one freak." Dec. 9 Video Tr. 1:22:53.

This stigma has real consequences for G. and other transgender students. Transgender students are at far greater risk for severe health consequences—including suicide—than the rest of the student population, and more than 50 percent of transgender youth will have had at least one suicide attempt by age 20. J.A. 40. The stress and victimization transgender students experience at school is associated with a greater risk for post-traumatic stress disorder, depression, anxiety, and suicidality in adulthood. J.A. 41.

III.   G. Has Established a Likelihood of Success on His Equal Protection Claim.

For the same reasons that excluding G. from using the same restrooms as other students discriminates based on sex under Title IX, it also triggers heightened scrutiny under the Equal Protection Clause. *Glenn*, 663 F.3d at 1318–19. "[A]ll gender-based classifications today warrant heightened scrutiny." *United States v. Virginia,* 518 U.S. 515, 555 (1996) (internal quotation marks omitted). Heightened scrutiny applies even when discrimination is based on physical or anatomical differences. *Tuan Anh Nguyen v. INS*, 533 U.S. 53, 60 (2001). And it applies whether the asserted justification for discrimination is benign or invidious. *Miss. Univ. for Women v. Hogan*, 458 U.S. 718, 724 (1982). The "analysis and level of scrutiny applied to determine the validity of the classification do not vary simply because the objective appears acceptable." *Id.* at 724 n.9.

The Board cannot carry its burden of proof under this heightened-scrutiny standard. Just six days before adopting the new policy excluding transgender students from the same restrooms as their peers, the Board identified alternatives to protect the privacy of all students, such as "adding or expanding partitions between urinals in male restrooms," "adding privacy strips to the doors of stalls in all restrooms," and "[d]esignat[ing] single-stall, unisex restrooms." Dec. 3 Press Release 2. Such gender-neutral alternatives demonstrate that excluding transgender students from the same restrooms used by everyone else is not substantially related to the asserted interest in privacy. *See Wengler v. Druggists Mut. Ins. Co.,* 446 U.S. 142, 151 (1980) (invalidating sex-based classification where sex-neutral approach would serve the needs of both classes); *Orr v. Orr*, 440 U.S. 268, 281 (1979) (same).

Despite these additional privacy measures, the district court stated that excluding transgender students from the same restrooms as other students would vindicate non-transgender students' constitutional right to bodily privacy. J.A. 160–62. In support, the court cited precedent regarding prisoner's privacy rights related to the involuntary exposure of genitals to members of the opposite sex. *Id.* Excluding G. from the boys' restroom, however, has no relationship to preventing exposure to nudity — especially in light of the additional privacy measures the Board has already implemented. According to the court, even with no exposure to nudity, the Board's privacy concerns also encompass students' purported objections to "[t]he mere presence" of a transgender person "in the restroom." J.A. 162. But such concerns, even if sincerely held, have nothing to do with the constitutional right to bodily privacy invoked by the court.

While privacy interests may justify separate but truly equal and non-stigmatizing restroom facilities for boys and girls, they cannot justify policies that stigmatize one group of students as inherently unfit to use the same restrooms as everyone else. Some students may (or may not) be uncomfortable with "[t]he mere presence" of a transgender person "in the restroom." J.A. 162. But discomfort with transgender people is not a legitimate basis for imposing unequal or stigmatizing treatment.

Ultimately, if other students are not comfortable using a restroom with a transgender person present, they have the option — like any other student — to

Likelihood of success on the merits is the first element of the preliminary injunction test.

G.G. pleaded two claims. Point II addressed his Title IX claim. Here Point III addresses his Equal Protection claim. If the court believes that he is likely to succeed in proving either claim in the trial court, he has satisfied the first element.

-10-

427

use one of the new single-stall unisex facilities the Board has installed. But the Board cannot place the burden on transgender students to use separate restroom facilities to address other students' discomfort with their "mere presence."

IV. G. Has Satisfied the Remaining Preliminary Injunction Factors.

A. *An Injunction Is Necessary to Prevent Irreparable Harm to G.*

Because G. is likely to succeed on the merits, he has also established irreparable harm. "[T]he deprivation of constitutional rights unquestionably constitutes irreparable injury." *Melendres v. Arpaio*, 695 F.3d 990, 1002 (9th Cir. 2012) (internal quotation marks omitted). The violation of G.'s rights under Title IX also constitutes irreparable harm that cannot be compensated by monetary damages.

In this case, moreover, G. faces irreparable harm with serious medical consequences. The expert declaration by Dr. Ettner was more than sufficient to corroborate G.'s testimony about the psychological distress he experiences as a result of being singled out for different treatment than every other boy at Gloucester High School and forced to use separate single-stall restroom facilities. Excluding G. from the same restrooms as other students increases G.'s risk of depression, anxiety, and self-harm. J.A. 33, 40. It impairs his ability to perform well academically. J.A. 33, 41. It subjects him to physical pain associated with avoiding the restroom. J.A. 32–33. And, at a time of life when fitting in with peers is all-important, it publicly labels him as different from every other student in his school. J.A. 39–40. These harms are irreparable.

B. *The Balance of Hardships Weighs in Favor of an Injunction.*

The balance of hardships weighs strongly in favor of a preliminary injunction. As explained earlier, allowing G. to resume using the boys' restrooms will not affect privacy interests related to nudity. Any student with privacy concerns based on G.'s "mere presence" in the restroom has the option of using the new single-stall restrooms instead. J.A. 162. The Board cannot credibly argue that using separate single-stall restrooms would be too burdensome for other students but is not a hardship for G.

The court distorted its analysis of the balance of harms by drawing a false equivalence between the burden imposed on G. from being relegated to using a separate restroom and the burden that would be imposed on students who choose to use a separate restroom in order to avoid the "mere presence" of G. The court stated, "It does not occur to G. that other students may experience feelings of exclusion when they can no longer use the restrooms they were accustomed to using because they feel that G.'s presence in the male restroom violates their privacy." J.A. 162. There is simply no equivalence on this record between the burden placed on a student who chooses to use a separate restroom

-11-

Point IV addresses the other elements of the preliminary injunction test.

Subpoint A argues that G.G. has satisfied the second element (threatened with irreparable harm).

Subpoint B argues that G.G. has satisfied the third element (balance of hardships favors an injunction).

in order to avoid G. and the stigma and isolation caused by singling out G. and forcing him to use separate restrooms that no other student is required to use.

C. An Injunction Is in the Public Interest.

An injunction in favor of G. is in the public interest. It is always in the public interest to "uphold[] constitutional rights." *Centro Tepeyac v. Montgomery Cty.*, 722 F.3d 184, 191 (4th Cir. 2013) (en banc) (internal quotation marks omitted). Similarly, the "public interest is certainly served by promoting compliance with Title IX." *Doe*, 888 F. Supp. 2d at 778; *accord Cohen v. Brown Univ.*, 991 F.2d 888, 906 (1st Cir. 1993) ("[T]he overriding public interest l[ies] in the firm enforcement of Title IX.").

> Subpoint C argues that G.G. has satisfied the last element (public interest).

CONCLUSION

For the foregoing reasons, the denial of Plaintiff's motion for preliminary injunction should be reversed, and the dismissal of the Title IX claim should be reversed.

Respectfully submitted,

American Civil Liberties Union of Virginia Foundation, Inc.	American Civil Liberties Union Foundation
_____/s/_____	Joshua A. Block
Rebecca K. Glenberg	Leslie Cooper
Gail Deady	New York, New York
Richmond, Virginia	

Counsel for Plaintiff-Appellant

Dated: October 21, 2015

Appendix H

Excerpts from Appellee's Fourth Circuit Brief in *G.G. v. Gloucester County School Bd.*

This appendix includes excerpts from the appellee's brief. Excerpts from the appellant's brief are in Appendix G.

The introductory note at the beginning of Appendix G explains the lawsuit, the appeal, Rule 28 of the Federal Rules of Appellate Procedure, and the material that is omitted or edited in these Appendices.

On this book's website are the complete, unedited briefs, which are about twice the size of the ones in Appendices G and H. Also on the website are the parties' submissions in the U.S. Supreme Court and the Supreme Court's rulings.

No. 15-2056

UNITED STATES COURT OF APPEALS
FOR THE FOURTH CIRCUIT

G.G., by his next friend and mother, **DEIRDRE GRIMM**

Plaintiff-Appellant,

v.

GLOUCESTER COUNTY SCHOOL BOARD

Defendant-Appellee.

On Appeal from the United States District Court

for the Eastern District of Virginia

Newport News Division

BRIEF OF DEFENDANT-APPELLEE

David P. Corrigan
Jeremy D. Capps
M. Scott Fisher, Jr.
Harman, Claytor, Corrigan & Wellman
Richmond, Virginia

Counsel for Appellee

TABLE OF CONTENTS

Notice that the two briefs don't tackle the Equal Protection and Title IX arguments in the same sequence. G.G.'s brief in App. G addresses Title IX first and then Equal Protection.

TABLE OF AUTHORITIES

Cases

Constitutional Provisions

Statutes

Other Authorities

INTRODUCTION

This is a preliminary statement as described in Ch. 30 (§30.1). In this court, it's called an Introduction. It tells the court in a nutshell what the appeal is all about. While doing that, lawyers also introduce the court to their theory of the appeal (Ch. 31, §31.1).

The fundamental issue in this appeal is whether the Fourteenth Amendment or Title IX require the Gloucester County School Board to permit a student, who was born and remains anatomically a female, to use the boys' restroom, because the student now identifies as a boy. Appellant ("G.G.") was born a girl and is biologically a female. G.G. has female anatomy. G.G. enrolled in Gloucester High School as a girl and started ninth grade as a girl. At the beginning of G.G.'s sophomore year, school officials were informed that G.G. was transgender and now identified as a boy. G.G., however, is still biologically and anatomically a female. There is no allegation, medical evidence, or medical testimony that G.G. is a boy or has male chromosomes.

The restrooms and locker rooms in Gloucester County schools are separated based on the students' biological sex. The school has boys' restroom and locker room facilities and girls' restroom and locker room facilities. After informing the school that G.G. identified as a boy, G.G. voluntarily chose not to use the boys' restroom. G.G. instead used a separate restroom in the nurse's office. In late October of 2014, G.G. asked to use the boys' restroom. On October 20, 2014, school personnel at the high school allowed G.G. to use the boys' restroom.

Taking the safety and privacy of all students into consideration, the School Board on December 9, 2014, adopted a restroom and locker room resolution. In implementing this resolution ("policy"), the School Board maintained the practice of providing separate restrooms and locker rooms based on students' biological and anatomical sex. The School Board also provided three unisex, single-stall restrooms for any student, including G.G., to use for greater privacy. G.G., however, refuses to use either the girls' restrooms or the single-stall restrooms.

STATEMENT OF ISSUES

See the exercise at the end of Ch. 32 (Questions Presented).

1. Whether the Fourteenth Amendment or Title IX requires the School Board to permit G.G., who was born and remains anatomically a female, to use the boys' restroom because G.G. identifies as a boy.

2. Should this Court affirm the District Court's denial of G.G.'s Motion for Preliminary Injunction?

STATEMENT OF THE CASE

The Statement of the Case is shorter in this brief than in the appellant's brief in App. G. That's because the School Board's story is less complex than G.G.'s story. As you read this Statement of the Case, list the most important facts

G.G. is a 16 year old high school student in Gloucester County, Virginia. J.A, 9, ¶1, J.A, 11, ¶9. G.G. is biologically a female. G.G. was born a girl and has female genitalia. J.A, 28, J.A, 33, ¶31. G.G. enrolled in high school as a girl. J.A, 29; J.A, 12, ¶20; J.A, 57. At the beginning of G.G.'s sophomore year, school officials were informed that G.G. was transgender and identified as a boy. G.G., however, is still biologically and anatomically a female. J.A, 33; J.A, 38–39.

When school officials were informed that G.G. was transgender, school officials immediately expressed support. J.A, 9, ¶2; J.A, 14, ¶28. School officials agreed to refer to G.G. using his new name and by using

-1-

436

male pronouns. J.A, 14, ¶28. School officials changed G.G.'s name in the school records. At G.G.'s request, school officials have permitted G.G. to continue with the home-bound program for the school's physical education requirements. J.A, 14, ¶29.

After informing the school that G.G. identified as a boy, G.G. voluntarily chose not to use the boys' restroom and instead used a separate restroom in the nurse's office. J.A, 9–10, ¶3; J.A, 15, ¶30. In October of 2014, G.G. asked to use the boys' restroom. School personnel at the high school complied with that request on October 20, 2014.

After receiving numerous complaints from parents and students, the School Board on November 11, 2014, considered the difficult issues associated with a transgender student seeking to use the restroom that does not correspond with the student's anatomical sex. J.A, 57–58. During the discussion, several citizens expressed concerns to the School Board. J.A, 15-17, ¶¶34–38. The School Board also considered G.G.'s concerns. J.A, 16–17, ¶38; J.A, 31, ¶21.

Taking the safety and privacy of all students into consideration, on December 9, 2014, the School Board adopted a restroom and locker room resolution that provided:

> Whereas the GCPS recognizes that some students question their gender identities, and
> Whereas the GCPS encourages such students to seek support, advice, and guidance from parents, professionals and other trusted adults, and
> Whereas the GCPS seeks to provide a safe learning environment for all students and to protect the privacy of all students, therefore
> It shall be the practice of the GCPS to provide male and female restroom and locker room facilities in its schools, and the use of said facilities shall be limited to the corresponding biological genders, and students with gender identity issues shall be provided an alternative appropriate private facility.

J.A, 18, ¶43.

In implementing the resolution, the School Board maintained its existing practice of providing separate restrooms and locker rooms based on a student's biological sex. The School Board also provided three unisex, single-stall restrooms for any student to use. J.A, 17, ¶41; J.A, 19, ¶47; J.A, 57–58. Under the policy, G.G. is not permitted to use the boys' restrooms. J.A, 18, ¶45. Based on G.G.'s biological sex, G.G. is permitted to use the girls' restroom. G.G. chooses not to do so. J.A, 18–19, ¶46; J.A, 57–58. G.G. is permitted to use the unisex, single-stall restrooms, but also refuses to use those restrooms. J.A, 19, ¶48; J.A, 58.

G.G. filed a Complaint and Motion for Preliminary Injunction against the School Board on June 11, 2015, alleging that the School Board's policy violates the Equal Protection Clause of the Fourteenth Amendment and Title IX.

From the bench, the Court granted the School Board's Motion to Dismiss G.G.'s Title IX claim in Count II of the Complaint. *J.A, 116.*

-2-

---

from the School Board's point of view. As you read the rest of the brief, look for places where those facts are woven into legal arguments.

The wrap-up in a Statement of the Case takes the reader to the procedural event — the lower court's ruling — that has been appealed.

As you read the
Summary of
Argument and the
Argument itself
below, identify
every place where
the brief makes a
policy argument.

SUMMARY OF ARGUMENT

The School Board's policy of separating students in restroom and locker
room use based on the students' biological and anatomical sex does not
violate the Equal Protection Clause or Title IX. Moreover, by providing three
single-stall restrooms for any student to use, G.G. is being treated the same
as all students at Gloucester High School. Transgender status is not a suspect
classification under the Equal Protection Clause, and G.G. does not ask this
Court to recognize it as a suspect classification. In fact, G.G. is not asking that
transgender status alone be treated as a separate classification. Transgender
status is also not a class protected by Title IX.

G.G.'s attempt to state a cause of action under the Equal Protection Clause
and Title IX by construing the phrase "based on sex" to include gender identity
is not persuasive. *Price Waterhouse v. Hopkins*, 490 U.S. 228 (1989) does
not support G.G.'s assertion that by virtue of transgender status alone, the
School Board's policy violates the Equal Protection Clause and Title IX. The
School Board's policy is not grounded in the false assertion that G.G. does
not conform to the stereotypes, behaviors or mannerisms expected of G.G.'s
biological sex or gender identity. Instead, it is grounded in the biological and
anatomical differences between boys and girls.

No court has held that a transgender student has the constitutional right,
or the right under Title IX, to use a restroom that is inconsistent with that
student's biological sex in a school setting. In fact, the only United States
District Court to have considered the issue held that a University did not
violate the Equal Protection Clause or Title IX by maintaining a policy of
sex segregated bathrooms and locker rooms or by requiring the transgender
plaintiff to use the bathroom and locker room that correlated with his
biological sex. *Johnston v. Univ. of Pittsburgh*, 97 F. Supp. 3d 657 (W.D. Pa.
2015). The same result is dictated here.

ARGUMENT

I.   Standard of Review on Appeal.

See Ch. 31, §31.3
(standards of
review).

Compare this with
the standard of
review discussion
in G.G.'s brief in
App. G. As the
plaintiff below
and the appellant
on appeal, G.G.
must satisfy these
procedural tests.
The School Board's
brief stresses the

The denial of a preliminary injunction is an immediately appealable
interlocutory order. 28 U.S.C. § 92(a)(1). This Court evaluates a district
court's decision to deny a preliminary injunction under an abuse of discretion
standard. *Aggarao v. MOL Ship Mgmt. Co.*, 675 F.3d 355, 366 (4th Cir.
2012). Pursuant to this standard, the Court reviews the District Court's factual
findings for clear error and reviews its legal conclusions de novo. *Pashby v.
Delia*, 709 F.3d 307, 319 (4th Cir. 2013). Because preliminary injunctions are
"extraordinary remed[ies] involving the exercise of very far-reaching power,"
this Court should be particularly "exacting" in its use of the abuse of discretion
standard when it reviews an order granting or denying a preliminary injunction.
Pashby, 709 F.3d at 319.

A preliminary injunction is "an extraordinary remedy involving the exercise
of a very far-reaching power, which is to be applied 'only in [the] limited
circumstances' which clearly demand it." *Direx Israel, Ltd. v. Breakthrough*

-3-

438

Med. Corp., 952 F.2d 802, 811 (4th Cir. 1992) (quoting *Instant Air Freight Co. v. C.F. Air Freight, Inc.*, 882 F.2d 797, 800 (3d Cir. 1989)). It is "never awarded as of right." *Winter v. Natural Resources Defense Council, Inc.*, 555 U.S. 7, 24 (2008). Instead, a preliminary injunction is a "drastic remedy not to be granted unless the movant clearly establishes the burden of persuasion as to the four requisites." *American Civil Liberties Union of Florida, Inc. v. Miami-Dade County School Bd.*, 557 F.3d 1177, 1198 (11th Cir. 2009) (citations omitted).

In deciding whether to grant a preliminary injunction, G.G. must demonstrate that (1) G.G. is likely to succeed on the merits, (2) G.G. is likely to suffer irreparable harm, (3) the balance of hardships tips in G.G.'s favor, and (4) the injunction is in the public interest. *Winter*, 555 U.S. at 20. A preliminary injunction must be denied if G.G. does not satisfy every factor of this test. *Pashby*, 709 F.3d at 320–21.

barriers G.G. must overcome.

The brief is organized around the four-element preliminary injunction test. See Ch. 28 (procedural postures). The School Board argues that G.G. can't satisfy these elements.

II.   G.G. is not likely to succeed on the merits, because the School Board has not violated the Equal Protection Clause.

The District Court did not abuse its discretion in denying G.G. a preliminary injunction, because G.G. is not likely to succeed on the merits of the Complaint. The Equal Protection Clause of the Fourteenth Amendment provides that "[n]o State shall . . . deny to any person within its jurisdiction the equal protection of the laws." U.S. Const. Amend. XIV, § 1. The equal protection requirement "does not take from the States all power of classification," *Personnel Adm'r of Massachusetts v. Feeney*, 442 U.S. 256, 271 (1979), but "keeps governmental decision makers from treating differently persons who are in all relevant respects alike." *Nordlinger v. Hahn*, 505 U.S. 1, 10 (1992).

Thus, "[t]he [Equal Protection] Clause requires that similarly-situated individuals be treated alike." *Giarratano v. Johnson*, 521 F.3d 298, 302 (4th Cir. 2008). In order to make out a claim under the Equal Protection Clause, a plaintiff must demonstrate (1) that he has been treated differently from others similarly situated and (2) that the unequal treatment was the result of intentional discrimination. *Morrison v. Garraghty*, 239 F.3d 648, 652 (4th Cir. 2001). G.G. was not denied equal protection of the law on the basis of sex.

Because more than one element is involved, this brief's Argument includes several paradigmed proofs. For how to organize in this situation, see Ch. 13 (combining separate paradigm proofs).

A.   All students are treated the same.

The School Board's policy does not discriminate against any class of students. Instead, the policy was developed to treat all students and situations the same. To respect the safety and privacy of all students, the School Board has had a long-standing practice of limiting the use of restroom and locker room facilities to the corresponding biological sex of the students. The School Board also provides three single-stall bathrooms for any student to use regardless of his or her biological sex. Under the School Board's restroom policy, G.G. is being treated like every other student in the Gloucester Schools. All students have two choices. Every student can use a restroom associated with their anatomical sex, whether they are boys or girls. If students choose not to use the restroom associated with their anatomical sex, the students can use a

Notice how this brief and G.G.'s brief, in App. G, interpret the same facts very differently.

-4-

private, single-stall restroom. No student is permitted to use the restroom of the opposite sex. As a result, all students, including female to male transgender and male to female transgender students, are treated the same.

B.   There is no evidence of intentional discrimination.

G.G. cannot demonstrate, under the allegations in the Complaint or in the evidence presented on the Motion for Preliminary Injunction, that there was intentional discrimination. The School Board did not develop the restroom and locker room policy in an attempt to stigmatize, embarrass or otherwise reject G.G. Indeed, when school officials were informed that G.G. was transgender, school officials immediately expressed support. J.A, 9, ¶2, J.A, 14, ¶28. School officials changed G.G.'s name in the official school records, refer to G.G. using his new name, and refer to G.G. using male pronouns. J.A, 14, ¶27. G.G. has not alleged that school officials have in any way harassed or discriminated against G.G. in his educational opportunities or engaged in any form of discriminatory treatment with respect to G.G.'s transgender identification. *Nofsinger v. Virginia Commonwealth Univ.*, 523 F. App'x 204, 206 (4th Cir. 2013) (failed to establish that any differential treatment was the result of discrimination.)

C.   G.G.'s transgender status does not create a suspect class or evidence of discrimination under the Equal Protection Clause.

The United States Supreme Court and this Court have not recognized transgender status as a suspect classification under the Equal Protection Clause. In fact, no Circuit Court has recognized transgender status, alone, as a suspect classification under the Equal Protection Clause. To the contrary, Courts have rejected the notion that transgender status, or other classifications of sex, is a suspect classification. *See, e.g., Etsitty v. Utah Transit Authority*, 502 F.3d 1215, 1222 (10th Cir. 2007) (holding that transsexuals are not a protected class under Title VII); *Wrightson v. Pizza Hut of Am., Inc.*, 99 F.3d 138, 143 (4th Cir. 1996) (Title VII does not afford a cause of action for discrimination based upon sexual orientation); *Williamson v. A.G. Edwards & Sons, Inc.*, 876 F.2d 69, 70 (8th Cir. 1989) ("Title VII does not prohibit discrimination against homosexuals").

G.G. asserts on brief that G.G. is a boy. (Appellant Br., p. 20). The Complaint and evidence on the preliminary injunction, however, establish that G.G. was born a girl and remains anatomically and biologically a girl. G.G. has female genitalia. G.G. enrolled in high school as a girl. G.G. has been diagnosed with Gender Dysphoria by a psychologist, and now identifies as a boy. The Complaint does not allege, however, that G.G. is a boy anatomically. Medical evidence was not introduced at the preliminary injunction hearing to establish that G.G. is a boy. Accordingly, the Complaint and evidence show that G.G. is biologically and anatomically a girl.

This point is not made to be insensitive to G.G.'s diagnosis of Gender Dysphoria. Instead, it is made to show that G.G. is not being treated differently from any other similarly situated students. The School Board's policy provides at its most basic level that if a student is anatomically a female, the student can use the girls' restrooms or a single-stall restroom, but the student cannot use a restroom designated for anatomical males. The reverse is true with anatomical males. Accordingly, because G.G. does not seek to create a new classification for transgender status, the Equal Protection claim cannot survive under the facts of this Complaint.

Ignoring this underlying flaw in the case, G.G. attempts to redefine the meaning of sex. G.G. contends that "sex" does not mean biologically male or female. Instead, G.G. tries to obtain protected status under the Equal Protection Clause by arguing that sex encompasses gender "nonconformity." Appellant Br., p. 38. This argument implicitly attempts to create a classification based on transgender status, despite G.G.'s steadfast refusal to assert this very claim. This position is evident in G.G.'s assertion that "discrimination based on a person's transgender status also inherently involves impermissible discrimination based on the person's gender nonconformity." (Appellant Br., pp. 22–23). That assertion misinterprets *Price Waterhouse v. Hopkins*, 490 U.S. 228 (1989), is not supported by the cases cited by G.G., and would create a new sex classification not currently protected under the Constitution.

Price Waterhouse holds that discrimination based on behavior that is inconsistent with a sex stereotype is prohibited. A policy based on anatomy, however, is not "sex stereotyping" under *Price Waterhouse*. In *Price Waterhouse*, the Supreme Court considered a Title VII claim based on allegations that a female employee at Price Waterhouse was denied partnership, because she was considered "macho" and "overcompensated for being a woman." 490 U.S. at 235. The female employee had been advised to "walk more femininely, talk more femininely, dress more femininely, wear make-up, have her hair styled, and wear jewelry." *Id*. The Court found that such comments were indicative of gender stereotyping, which Title VII prohibited as sex discrimination. Accordingly, the Court found that "an employer who acts on the basis of a belief that a woman cannot be aggressive or that she must not be" has acted on the basis of sex. *Id*. at 251.

The use of *Price Waterhouse* and subsequent employment cases to support a transgender stereotype theory in the school restroom context is not analogous. In the employment context, as in *Price Waterhouse*, employees allege that they are discriminated against because the employer believes the employee is not behaving in accordance with the employee's biological sex. Nevertheless, G.G. suggests that the federal cases he cites stand for the proposition that transgender status alone can support a discrimination claim based on gender non-conformity. See, *e.g.*, Appellant Br., pp. 22–23. Contrary to that suggestion, those cases do not stand for the proposition that transgender status supports an Equal Protection Claim.

For example, in *Glenn v. Brumby*, 663 F.3d 1312 (11th Cir. 2011), the plaintiff was a male and intended to take steps to transition to a female, including wearing women's clothing to work. The plaintiff's supervisor told the plaintiff that his appearance was not "appropriate." The supervisor found the plaintiff's appearance "unnatural" and "unsettling." *Id*. The court in *Glenn* concluded that the transgender plaintiff's discrimination claim arose from the failure to act according to socially prescribed gender roles. That is, the plaintiff's claim could proceed because of evidence of sex stereotyping—acts

Both briefs discuss *Price Waterhouse v. Hopkins* and *Glenn v. Brumby*. Use the App. G brief's Table of Authorities to find that brief's discussion of these two cases. How do the two briefs differ in the way they handle them?

-6-

441

"which presume that men and women's appearance and behavior will be determined by *their sex . . .*" *Id.* at 1317, 1320 (emphasis added) ("All persons, whether transgender or not, are protected from discrimination on the basis of gender stereotype."). Thus, the plaintiff was seeking protection on the basis of his biological sex—male.

Similarly, *Smith v. City of Salem*, 378 F.3d 566 (6th Cir. 2004), is a classic sex stereotyping case where the Sixth Circuit concluded that the plaintiff had stated a cause of action by alleging that the defendant's discrimination was motivated by his appearance and mannerisms, and the defendant's belief that this behavior was "inappropriate for his perceived sex." The same is true with *Barnes v. City of Cincinnati*, 401 F.3d 729, 738 (6th Cir. 2005), where the plaintiff was a male to female transsexual. The plaintiff alleged discrimination based upon his mannerisms and the way he behaved. There, supervisors told the plaintiff he was not sufficiently masculine, and numerous supervisors and peers criticized him for lacking a quality known as command presence." Thus, the sexual stereotyping claim was again grounded in plaintiff's biological sex. *Id. See also Rosa v. Park West Bank & Trust Co.*, 214 F.3d 213, 215 (1st Cir. 2000) (reasonable to infer from the Complaint that the plaintiff was told to go home and change because the supervisor thought that the plaintiff's attire did not accord with his male gender.) In sum, sex stereotyping cases are all grounded in allegations that the transgender plaintiffs were discriminated against because their behaviors, mannerisms or appearance did not correspond to notions attributable to their biological sex.

Here, G.G.'s behavior, mannerisms and appearance are not at issue. In fact, G.G. does not seek constitutional protection based on biological and anatomical sex. Instead, G.G. asks the Court to provide protection based on gender identity. Yet the Complaint and evidence show that while G.G. now identifies as a boy, G.G. was born biologically and anatomically female, enrolled in school as a female, and remains biologically and anatomically female. The Complaint and evidence submitted during the hearing on the motion for a preliminary injunction do not show that the School Board acted on an impermissible stereotype associated with G.G. being a girl or, for that matter, a boy.

The School Board acted based on the admitted and legitimate biological and anatomical differences between boys and girls. Accordingly, it is apparent that G.G. is seeking protection based on transgender status alone, not stereotypes about biological sex, and there has been no unlawful discrimination under the Equal Protection Clause based on G.G.'s sex. The District Court's Order denying the Motion for Preliminary Injunction should be affirmed.

D. There is a substantial interest for the restroom policy.

Even if G.G. could assert an Equal Protection claim, the School Board's policy does not violate the Equal Protection Clause. Only one United States District Court has considered whether a public school can prohibit a transgender student from using a bathroom or locker room that is not associated with that student's biological sex.

In *Johnston v. Univ. of Pittsburgh*, 97 F. Supp. 3d 657 (W.D. Pa. 2015), the plaintiff was born a biological female. The plaintiff entered college as a female, but later identified as a male. The plaintiff was diagnosed with Gender Identity Disorder, legally changed his name, and began living as a male. The plaintiff used the men's restrooms and locker rooms on campus. The plaintiff, however, remained anatomically a female.

Thereafter, the plaintiff was told that he could not use the men's restrooms or locker rooms. When the plaintiff refused to comply with this policy, he was expelled from the University. The plaintiff filed suit against the University alleging that the school's policy violated the Equal Protection Clause of the Fourteenth Amendment and Title IX. In short, *Johnston* is nearly "on all fours" with this case, except that it arose in a university instead of a high school setting, and the plaintiff in *Johnston* was expelled whereas G.G. is simply offered an alternative restroom. The District Court, in a detailed analysis and opinion, rejected these claims.

Johnston held that transgender status is not a suspect classification, and that providing separate restroom and locker room facilities for college students based on their biological sex did not violate the Equal Protection Clause. As the Court noted, this holding is consistent with the holdings of numerous other courts that have considered allegations of discrimination by transgender individuals, whether under the Fourteenth Amendment or Title VII. *See Frontiero v. Richardson*, 411 U.S. 677 (1973); *Etsitty v. Utah Transit Auth.*, 502 F.3d at 1221–22; *Ulane v. Eastern Airlines, Inc.*, 742 F.2d 1081, 1084 (7th Cir. 1984); *Sommers v. Budget Mktg., Inc.*, 667 F.2d 748, 750 (8th Cir. 1982).

The same result should be reached here. Not only is the School Board's policy rationally related to protecting students' safety and privacy rights, but it is substantially related to this important governmental interest. G.G. frames the question as "whether an important interest in privacy is substantially furthered by the new policy regulating the restroom use of transgender students." (Appellant Br., p. 39). That ignores, however, the underlying basis for the policy's existence.

The policy was implemented to ensure that the safety and privacy rights of all students, both boys and girls, are respected and protected. In doing so, the School Board focused on those privacy rights by providing three single-stall restrooms that any student can use for increased privacy. Thus, contrary to G.G.'s suggestion, the question is whether the School Board's policy of providing separate bathrooms based on anatomical sex, along with providing single-stall restrooms for all students, serves the governmental interest in protecting all students' safety and privacy.

The answer is yes. This case is not an employment case involving adults. It is a case that involves the public education of children, kindergarten through twelfth grade. In fact, the School Board's interests here are much more compelling than in *Johnston*, because the School Board is responsible for the care and education of minor children, from kindergarten through twelfth grade, not adults in college as in *Johnston*. There is no question that the School Board has a substantial interest in protecting the safety and privacy of minor children while they are in school.

As *Johnston* noted, the issue presents "two important but competing interests." G.G.'s interest is performing "life's most basic and routine

-8-

functions" in the school restroom in an environment consistent with G.G.'s gender identity. On the other hand, the School Board has an interest in "providing its students with a safe and comfortable environment for performing these same life functions consistent with society's long-held tradition of performing such functions in sex-segregated spaces based on biological or birth sex." *Johnston*, 97 F. Supp. 3d at 668. In analyzing these issues, *Johnston* held that segregating "bathroom and locker room facilities on the basis of birth sex is substantially related to a sufficiently important governmental interest." *Id*. at 669. That conclusion is a correct statement of the law and should be followed in this case.

This Circuit has recognized a right to bodily privacy. *Lee v. Downs*, 641 F.2d 1117, 1119 (4th Cir. 1981) ("Most people, however, have a special sense of privacy in their genitals, and involuntary exposure of them in the presence of people of the other sex may be especially demeaning and humiliating.") Parents have an interest in the safety of their children, and children have a strong privacy interest of their own. *United States v. Virginia*, 518 U.S. 515, 551 (1996) (recognizing that admitting women to VMI would undoubtedly require alterations necessary to afford members of each sex privacy from the other sex); *Doe v. Luzerne Cty.*, 660 F.3d 169, 177 (3d Cir. 2011) (recognizing right of privacy from involuntary exposure of body particularly while in the presence of members of the opposite sex); *Beard v. Whitmore Lake Sch. Dist.*, 402 F.3d 598, 604 (6th Cir. 2005) ("Students of course have a significant privacy interest in their unclothed bodies.").

The School Board has a responsibility to its students to ensure their privacy while engaging in personal bathroom functions, disrobing, dressing, and showering outside of the presence of members of the opposite sex. This is particularly true in an environment where children are still developing, both emotionally and physically. *See, e.g.*, *Burns v. Gagnon*, 727 S.E.2d 634, 643 (Va. 2012) (school administrators have a responsibility "to supervise and ensure that students could have an education in an atmosphere conducive to learning, free of disruption, and threat to person.").

As *Johnston* recognized, the context of this dispute is important. Here, the School Board is balancing the needs, interests and rights of children in kindergarten through twelfth grade. The right to privacy for students strongly supports maintaining sex-segregated bathrooms and locker rooms.

The School Board is not unsympathetic to G.G.'s recent identification as a boy, but G.G.'s identification does not alter the biological and anatomical differences between G.G. and other male students, nor does it erase the biological and anatomical differences between a male student who identifies as a female and other female students. G.G. cannot reconcile these facts with the position that the School Board does not have a legitimate interest in protecting other students' privacy.

The School Board has taken both G.G.'s interests and the interests of its other students into consideration and developed a policy that attempts to accommodate the best interests of all of its students. In doing so, the School Board bolstered these privacy rights by providing single-stall restrooms for any student to use. Accordingly, there is not only a rational basis, but a substantially related basis for the School Board's policy requiring students to

-9-

use the restroom and locker room associated with their biological sex, or to use a single-stall restroom of their choice.

III.   G.G. is not likely to succeed on the merits because the School Board's policy does not violate Title IX.

The School Board's policy does not violate Title IX. Title IX prohibits discrimination "on the basis of sex" in educational programs. 20 U.S.C. § 1681(a).

As discussed in detail under the Equal Protection argument, courts have not permitted discrimination claims to proceed based upon transgender status alone. Instead, all of the cases have been premised on some form of discrimination based on the plaintiff's behaviors, mannerisms or appearance, and those plaintiffs have sought protection on the basis of their biological sex. *Johnston* addressed this precise issue as well, and held that being transgender itself is not a protected characteristic under Title IX. As the Court noted, the exclusion of gender identity from the language of Title IX is not an issue for the court to remedy, but one within the province of Congress to identify the classifications which are statutorily prohibited. *Id.* at 75–77.

This is consistent with the plain language of the statute and the legislative history of Title IX. Title IX was enacted in order to open up educational opportunities for girls and women in education and to address discrimination toward women. *See, e.g.*, 117 Cong. Rec. 30,155–30,158 (August 5, 1971); 117 Cong. Rec. 39,248–39,261 (November 4, 1971); *Johnston*, 97 F. Supp. 3d at 677. The legislative history, statutory language and implementing regulations do not refer to gender identity or transgender individuals in the enforcement scheme.

IV.   G.G. cannot satisfy the remaining factors justifying the imposition of a preliminary injunction.

A.   *The balance of hardships does not tip in G.G.'s favor, and G.G. is not likely to suffer irreparable harm.*

The District Court did not abuse its discretion in finding that G.G. did not submit sufficient evidence to establish that the balance of hardships weigh in his favor. J.A, 154. As discussed under the Equal Protection claim, the School Board is charged with the responsibility to care and protect minor children while they are in school. *Linnon v. Commonwealth*, 752 S.E.2d 822, 826 (Va. 2014). Those children have a right to privacy protected by the Constitution. *Lee*, 641 F.2d at 1119. That right, as explained above, is of paramount concern for the School Board, and outweighs the interests of G.G. This is particularly true where G.G. seeks to impose an injunction on the School Board before the difficult issues associated with G.G.'s claims are litigated, before the

Likelihood of success on the merits is the first element of the preliminary injunction test. G.G. pleaded two claims. Point II addressed his Equal Protection claim. Here Point III addresses his Title IX claim. The School Board is arguing that in the trial court G.G. will probably lose on *both* claims and therefore has no likelihood of success on the merits.

Point IV addresses the other elements of the preliminary injunction test.

Subpoint A argues that G.G. hasn't satisfied the second element (threatened with irreparable harm) and the third element (balance of hardships).

Court has considered whether G.G. even has a viable legal claim, and in direct contradiction to the holding of the only Federal Court to have actually considered the issues raised in G.G.'s Complaint.

As the District Court correctly recognized, the School Board's strong interest in protecting student privacy outweighs the claims of hardship by G.G. Moreover, the School Board, and school officials, have recognized and accepted G.G. as a transgender individual. They are supporting G.G., have changed his official school records, refer to G.G. with male pronouns, and are allowing him to participate in his school educational opportunities as a transgender male. The School Board has also provided three single-stall bathrooms for G.G. and any other student to use. G.G. can also use the bathroom in the nurse's office. G.G. has voluntarily chosen not to use the locker room at the high school. This evidence discounts the notion that G.G. will suffer irreparable harm if a preliminary injunction is not granted. The competing hardship is to the remaining students in the school system. Their safety and privacy interests will go unprotected if an injunction is entered until the issue is resolved on the merits.

G.G.'s assertions concerning the Court's consideration of Dr. Ettner's declaration and G.G.'s declaration miss the point. Dr. Ettner saw G.G. on one occasion. In the declaration, Dr. Ettner devotes only three paragraphs to G.G. specifically. J.A, 41–42. Those three paragraphs do not divulge any particular facts related to G.G. While Dr. Ettner opines that G.G. is suffering emotional distress, Dr. Ettner does not offer an opinion differentiating between the distress that G.G. may suffer by not using the boy's bathroom during the course of this ligation and the distress that he has apparently been living with since age 12. J.A, 29. Similarly, while G.G. asserts that his feelings of dysphoria, anxiety and distress increase when he uses the restroom at school, because he is reminded that everyone knows he is transgender, G.G. did not present evidence that those feelings would be lessened by using the boy's restroom. As the District Court rightly pointed out, there was no evidence presented from G.G.'s treating psychologist, nor was there any medical evidence presented in support of the preliminary injunction.

While G.G. disagrees with aspects of the District Court's opinion, a close review of that opinion shows that the District Court did consider in detail the evidence presented on the motion for a preliminary injunction. That opinion discredits the assertion that there was "clear error" in the Court's factual findings. In sum, G.G. did not present sufficient evidence to carry the burden required to impose a preliminary injunction on the School Board under the circumstances of this case.

B.   An injunction is not in the public interest.

Subpoint B argues that G.G. hasn't satisfied the last element (public interest).

An injunction is not in the public interest, because the School Board's policy does not violate the Equal Protection Clause or Title IX, and the School Board is not discriminating against G.G. by maintaining separate sex-segregated bathrooms. As the District Court candidly pointed out, there are significant concerns with the precedent that would be set if the Court granted the Motion for Preliminary Injunction without full consideration of the case on the merits.

-11-

CONCLUSION

For the reasons stated above, this Court should affirm the District Court's Order denying G.G.'s Motion for Preliminary Injunction. This Court should further affirm the District Court's Order granting the School Board's Motion to Dismiss the Title IX claim. Finally, this Court should direct the District Court to enter an Order granting the School Board's Motion to Dismiss the Equal Protection claim on remand.

Gloucester County School Board

By Counsel

/s/ David P. Corrigan
David P. Corrigan
Jeremy D. Capps
M. Scott Fisher, Jr
Attorney for Gloucester County
School Board
Harman, Claytor, Corrigan & Wellman
Richmond, Virginia

Dated: November 23, 2015

-12-

Index

Index